BATTLIN'
BASTARDS
AND
PIGBOATS

BATTLIN'
BASTARDS
AND
PIGBOATS

*The POW and submarine
interface during WWII*

Robert K. Harmuth

To order additional copies of this book, contact:
Xlibris Corporation
1-888-7-XLIBRIS
www.Xlibris.com
Orders@Xlibris.com

CONTENTS

AUTHOR'S NOTE

EARLY IN 1995, I was introduced to two men who came within a whisper of giving their last breath for America. This is their story along with the huge impact on the Allied POWs captured by the Japanese by the American submarine. It is a history of World War II in the Pacific, a narrative of the men who defended the Philippines and survived the Bataan Death March, and the skills of the Submarine Force that played such a huge role in bringing Japan to her knees.

My special thanks to Mansfield Young of the 194th Tank Battalion and Manny Eneriz of the 31st All American Infantry Regiment who fill the main roles of this book. Without their steadfast assistance and memory retention, the book would have been impossible. Appreciation must also be given to the Defenders of Bataan and Corregidor who were all helpful and heroes to the man. In 1995, the world celebrated the Fiftieth Anniversary of the end of WWII and the internet was literally clogged with useful information from WWII veterans. I'm grateful to Hubert Smart, BMCS, USN, Ret for technical and computer support. Many books have been written before and since. Thanks to all the authors and writers that preceded this writing which provided excellent background and thought. And finally, thanks to all the men who proudly wore the dolphins of the U.S. Submarine Force during WWII.

There are a number of conclusions reached in this book which may be novel individually, in their entirety, or repetitive of thoughts past. Among the points I hope to leave with you are:

America truly did abandon the defenders of the Pacific at the outset of WWII and prior. The men who were to defend American and Allied holdings fought gallantly and did, in the end, achieve a victory of sorts in slowing the Japanese war machine. A more definitive victory may well have been achieved, such as stopping the Japanese, if General MacArthur had followed policy refined over a decade of Japanese aggression in the Pacific.

The Submarine Force, despite being hampered by inferior torpedoes, leadership, and tactics at the beginning of the war, almost single handedly dealt the Japanese merchant marine and Navy a death blow that left Japan without resources. When combined with the courageous action of the men in their shiny flying machines, Japan was doomed. No intent is desired to belittle the roles played by every man of every service.

The rapidity and thoroughness of the Submarine Force and aviation just barely saved the day before Japan could deploy its own nuclear weapons, jet aircraft, and biological/chemical weapons. They sunk vital nuclear and jet supplies while forcing Japanese nuclear research to Korea causing a three month delay.

The use of the atomic bomb by the United States was a necessity and saved hundreds of thousands, if not millions, of lives on both sides of the war. Politics and the need to halt communist expansion permitted the rapid rebuilding of Japan without due punishment and reparations for the inhumane and barbaric behavior to conquered countries and in particular, to the Prisoner of War.

And not least of all, God was on our side as was uncannily obvious at turning points in the war such as the Battles at Midway and the Coral Sea. For the POWs, God, in whatever shape or form, often was the difference between survival and death. There is a saying that "there are no atheists in foxholes." The same was true in POW camps and on board hell ships.

Unfortunately, lessons learned in WWII and following wars and conflicts are not remembered today. Not the least of these unremembered lessons is "Be Prepared." Maybe the Boy Scouts will save the next day.

CHAPTER ONE

THE GATHERING STORM CLOUDS OF WAR

WAR CAME AS no particular surprise; but the devious and uncivilized attack did. War with Japan was expected but the attack on Pearl Harbor caught the American People by surprise. America was not ready for war; not in Pearl Harbor nor in the Philippines; not on Wake Island nor Midway, Guam, the Aleutians; not in Singapore, Shanghai, Hong Kong nor elsewhere in the Pacific. It was 7 December 1941 in Pearl Harbor and 8 December in Manila on the opposite side of the International Dateline and America was determined to deny war was imminent.

Prior to the war, many of the world's diplomatic codes were compromised permitting countries to read each other's message traffic. Japanese messages were intercepted and decoded by the U.S. Army, Navy and Washington, D.C. clearly pointing toward war at any moment. This was particularly true of message traffic between Germany and Japan.[2] In the months just prior to war, the Japanese made every effort to become self-sufficient "annexing" oil and ore rich areas of the Southern Pacific. They placed 100,000 troops in Formosa and Hainan and agreed with the French Vichy Government to place 40,000 men in Indo-China. They built up bases in Camranh Bay and the Mandate Islands for submarines, improved bases and airstrips in Formosa, Spratley, Saipan, and Mandates, and placed oil storage facilities in Itu Abo, Lord North, and the Tobi Islands.[3]

As early as 1923, Japanese writings, plans and strategy in the Pacific included the occupation of Guam and the Philippines with little or no intent to keep it secret. They made plans for the conquest of the Pacific, including the eastern Pacific, well in advance of 1941. There was one key secret; Admiral Yamamoto's plan for Hawaii. It avoided an invasion of the islands following an attack on Pearl Harbor due to high estimates of supplies needed to sustain the invasion.[4]

In 1934, Major General Frank Parker, Commander of the Philippines, reported Japanese immigrants increasing at an alarming rate. They were observed mapping harbors and coastlines. They appeared to be ordinary citizens in a labyrinth of jobs in cities.[5] The Japanese continued to build a war machine, unopposed by the world powers except by verbal condemnation. Most of Japan's industry was devoted to war. The Western and Free World feared the rise of communism while Japan preyed on their fear and invaded Asia on the pretense of halting communism.[6]

The Japanese road to Pearl Harbor and the Philippines began in 1931 with the invasion of Manchuria and China in 1937. Chiang Kai-shek came to power and fought both the Japanese and communism. In China, the Japanese developed an attitude of cruelty with no respect for an enemy, particularly a vanquished or surrendered foe.[7] The military became the political power and coined a motto for Japan to follow, "Hokko Ichiu" – bring the eight corners of the world under the one roof of Japan. As Japan penetrated deeper into China, the horror of their actions increased and cruelty became a source of entertainment for the Japanese troops. On 11 December 1937, the war moved a step closer near Nanking when Japanese bombed three Standard Oil steamships and sank the *USS PANAY*, a gun ship. Japan apologized and the world appeared pacified.[8]

General MacArthur received little funding and equipment for the Philippines in 1938 and President Quezon lost patience with the United States. He traveled to Tokyo and talked to the Japanese leadership. Upon his return, he requested earlier independence for the Philippines than 1946. America refused despite Quezon's argument the modest American buildup accomplished little more than to antagonize Japan. Defenses failed to improve and the standing Philippine army dwindled to 350,000 men. MacArthur sent Dwight Eisenhower to Washington to request support but he failed.[9] The opposite occurred in Japan in 1939 when the National General Mobilization Bill activated all people and resources under the direct control of the government and that was the military.[10] Japan opened two new fronts and China came closer to war with the Soviet Union over disputed land along the Soviet-Manchurian border. Vice Premier of Defense Tojo, an advocate for war, was confronted by Premier Kanoye and reassigned as Inspector General in December 1938, which temporarily defused world fear. By this time, Japan had 1.6 million men committed in China, continued victorious, and added Hainan to its conquest list.[11]

In response to Japanese threats, the United States terminated its Treaty of Commerce with Japan, including cessation of oil exports to Japan. Secretary of State Hull backed Japan into a corner and many considered the treaty cessation as an ultimatum. Meanwhile, most of the world attention worried about Europe where Germany conquered one country after another. The time was perfect for Japan to grab Indochina and the Dutch East Indies with all their resources.[12] Then Japan signed a Tripartite Pact with Germany and Italy and the lines of war were drawn.

Great Britain and the United States developed a war plan called Rainbow Five that called for the defense of Europe prior to any Pacific Ocean involvement. The major problem was the archaic Asiatic Fleet that was expected to stop a Japanese invasion of the Philippine Islands. War Plan Orange-2 (WPO) was developed to defend the Philippines which called for a delaying action throughout the islands with final resistance and halt of the Japanese in Bataan. WPO excluded submarines from direct operations with the Asiatic Fleet and relegated the boats to serve as advance long-range scouts for the fleet.[13] MacArthur, however, intended on beating any invasion force on the beaches[14] which placed WPO dead in the water.[15] MacArthur was assured amphibious invasions were ineffective following the Battle for Gallipoli in WWI.[16]

Late in 1939, Admiral Stark ordered Submarine Division 14 to the Asiatic Fleet in Manila with the P-boats *PORPOISE, PIKE, SHARK, TARPON, PERCH, PICKERAL,* and *PERMIT.* The Asiatic Fleet was first formed in December 1922 primarily to protect American interests in China and along the Yangtze River.[17] With the S-boats already assigned to the Philippines, the thirteen submarines were the most lethal arm of the Asiatic Fleet. A year later, Submarine Division 17's six S-boats and eleven new fleet boats with the tender *CANOPUS* moved to Manila.[18] Naval strategists had moved the S-boat submarines to the Asiatic Fleet in the 1920's and 1930's which was called China Station. By the end of 1940, war with Japan was so imminent, the U.S. Navy removed 2,000 dependents from their Asiatic Stations and the Asiatic Fleet began extensive training in January 1941 that lasted through October. Unfortunately, the U.S. Army and MacArthur did not follow the Navy's lead for readiness. In May, Admiral Hart learned he would not receive the promised additional surface ships for his Asiatic Fleet but did receive 23 new fleet submarines.[19] Submarine Division 15 joined the Asiatic Fleet while Pearl Harbor and San Diego was left shorthanded. The Asiatic Fleet had 29 submarines and three submarine tenders but the combined U.S. Pacific and Asiatic Fleet was still overwhelmed by the Japanese Fleets: 10 carriers to 3, 10 battleships to 8, 35 cruisers to 24, and 111 destroyers to 80. The Japanese also had at least 60 submarines.[20]

In Washington, a long range-planning meeting took place on the first Saturday of 1941. It was a meeting of four men at the Carnegie Institute. The United States was to bring the world into the nuclear age.[21]

In the United States, there was considerable patriotism toward Japan from Japanese-Americans. In Hawaii, only 8% of Japanese born renounced their citizenship and Hawaiian born Japanese (Issei) followed the invasion of China with pride. Supportive newspaper articles, meetings, and rallies were some of the ways the

Issei firmed their allegiance to Japan. As war drew closer, millions of yen from Japanese-Americans in America purchased Japanese War Bonds. Women sewed clothing and bags for their Japanese brethren in China and some traveled to China to provide "comfort" to the Japanese soldier. Books were written depicting a Japanese invasion of Hawaii.[22] In California, Japanese-American fishermen shuttled supplies to Japanese submarines patrolling the West Coast.[23] The adverse activities would manifest itself in interning Japanese-Americans after the attack on Pearl Harbor.

Japan took Indochina following faltering oil supplies in July 1941 and the Vichy French moved their navy to Saigon, DaNang and Camranh Bay. The British expected to supplement Singapore with a modern fleet including the new carrier *INDOMITABLE* but it went aground enroute so only the *PRINCE OF WALES* and *REPULSE* arrived. The U.S. Fourth Marines were recalled from China to Manila on the *SS PRESIDENT HARRISON* but the ship was captured before leaving China. The first Americans were prisoners of Japan.[24]

Although he argued against a war with America, Admiral Yamamoto became the Commander of the Japanese Combined Fleet. He recognized the only chance to win the war was to destroy the American Fleet which meant a surprise attack against Pearl Harbor. Ambassador Grew heard of the plan and reported it to the Chief of Naval Operations (CNO), Admiral Stark. He in turn told Admiral Kimmel in Pearl but added he felt the entire idea appeared absurd. Meanwhile, Tojo worked his way back into grace and rewrote the moral code for the military including guidance about the treatment of prisoners of war (POW) and gave a pep talk for the "banzai charge." A POW was to be considered a dishonorable person, death was mandatory and the atrocities in China became a military policy.[25]

When the United States broke the Japanese code system again in mid-1941, as Britain had done with Germany, the direction of Japan's foreign policy became clear. The Pacific Fleet was placed on alert as the fleet awaited an attack. In the Philippines, aircraft

99-HARM

scouted the South China Sea and returned with reports of Japanese troop transports massing. General MacArthur certainly should have been aware of an impending war.

Japan began the war with over six million tons of merchant shipping and added another four plus million during the war. By the end of the war, 2,117 Japanese navy and merchant ships had been sunk with little more than wood hull vessels remaining. Fifty-five percent of the sinking was at the hands of American submarines that were also involved in a multitude of operations supporting the war effort. Fifty-two submarines were lost and one in every five Submariners remain on eternal patrol.[26]

On 18 November 1941, Admiral Nagumo, Commander of the Pearl Harbor Strike Force, departed Japan for the Kurile Islands where the fleet assembled. The force departed the Kuriles on 26 November and on 2 December, Yamamoto sent his infamous prearranged signal, "Climb Mount Niitake."[27]

Navy ship locations were classified yet Japan had a current status of ships in Pearl Harbor thanks to sympathetic Japanese-Americans on Oahu. Location of units at sea were mostly unknown although the *TEIA MARU* visited Hawaii often as a recognized passenger liner. She reported vessel locations and scoped out the route for Admiral Nagumo well ahead of the Japanese fleet departure from the Kuriles.[28] U.S. merchant ships already traveled south of the usual trade and great circle routes to avoid a possible Japanese threat to the Hawaiian Islands. Washington promised MacArthur many things that he translated into boisterous statements to his army about defeating the "Japs" on the beaches. Instead of storing supplies in Bataan according to WPO, he stockpiled in advance bases. If his defenses failed, Luzon was lost.[29]

On 1 November and again on 1 December 1941, Japan changed naval radio calls and codes. It was an indicator something was at hand but not one fleet air unit was included in the code. On 27 November, Roosevelt sent MacArthur the following cable:

"NEGOTIATIONS WITH THE JAPANESE APPEAR TO BE TERMINATED TO ALL PRACTICAL PURPOSES WITH ONLY THE BAREST POSSIBILITIES THAT THE JAPANESE GOVERNMENT MIGHT COME BACK AND OFFER TO CONTINUE PERIOD JAPANESE FUTURE ACTION UNPREDICTABLE BUT HOSTILE ACTION POSSIBLE AT ANY MOMENT PERIOD IF HOSTILITIES CANNOT REPEAT NOT BE AVOIDED THE UNITED STATES DESIRES THAT JAPAN COMMIT THE FIRST OVERT ACT PERIOD THIS POLICY SHOULD NOT REPEAT NOT BE CONSTRUED AS RESTRICTING YOU TO A COURSE OF ACTION THAT MIGHT JEOPARDIZE YOUR DEFENSE PERIOD"

MacArthur thought the message ambiguous but failed to ask for clarification.[30]

Admiral Kimmel asked Naval Intelligence, Commander Rochefort, for their best estimate of Japanese fleet dispositions during the last week in November. A large special task force had been formed and associated with naval air units. He expected an attack on Southeast Asia and the Netherlands East Indies within a week or two. Corregidor's intelligence unit concurred with his findings. The CNO sent a message on 27 November to Pearl and Manila, "THIS DISPATCH IS A WAR WARNING . . . " He went on to warn of an attack by Japan on the Philippine Islands within days as well as other attacks on Thailand, the Kra Isthmus or Borneo. The Asiatic Fleet was ordered to carry out appropriate portions of War Plan Rainbow Five. MacArthur was appraised of the naval warning but took little or no action to prepare for the inevitable so close at hand.

The CNO was correct in assessing Japan's war strategy which included destroying the American East Asian Fleet, Clark Air Field and Cavite Naval Shipyard on Luzon. The plan called for General Homma to capture the Philippines in fifty days. Meanwhile, a slow buildup continued in the Philippines as MacArthur laid out plans to stop, at all costs, any Japanese landing on the beaches.[31] He ordered security at airfields doubled and 24-hour a day air patrols but he remained convinced Japan would not strike until well into 1942.[32] Corregidor reported Japanese fleet movements and submarines southbound through the South China Sea and Singapore reported Japanese battleships and cruisers just south of Indochina. Reconnaissance aircraft spotted a large convoy anchored in Camranh Bay and the *USS ISABEL* was ordered to shadow the convoy. But, no one knew the whereabouts of the Japanese aircraft carriers.

The Japanese really didn't care if anyone knew where their fleet units were – what could anyone do about it? They didn't worry about Southeast Asia but they did worry about the detection of Kido Butai or the strike force headed for Pearl Harbor including the carriers *AKAGI, KAGA, HIRYO, SORYU, SHOKKA* and *ZUIKAKI*. On 30 November at position 42N 170W, the strike force received orders to attack Pearl.[33] Two hours following the strike on Pearl, Singapore awakened to the sound of exploding bombs. The lights of the city were on, providing a beacon to the Japanese pilots. Sixty-three people were killed and 133 injured without a single Japanese loss. It was another perfect surprise.

A signalman on *USS SCULPIN* read a flashing light from the tower at Cavite just before midnight on 8 December: "JAPAN HAS ATTACKED PEARL HARBOR X GOVERN YOURSELF ACCORDINGLY." The submarines were underway immediately along with a small force of the Asiatic Fleet and headed for Corregidor. Under the command of Captain John Wilkes, experienced crews who had been training extensively for months manned 29 submarines. On that day, five new fleet boats and four S-boats were already deploying to predesignated patrol areas with complete loads of warshot torpedoes. Unknown at the time, many of the torpedoes were anything but reliable. Three days later on 10 December, the only major overhaul facility west of Hawaii was lost at Cavite as well as the submarine *USS SEADRAGON* and the auxiliary vessel *USS BITTERN.*[34]

Intelligence reports indicated a massive buildup of enemy aircraft on Formosa. General Bereton, Chief of Staff of the Far East Air Force (FEAF), repeatedly asked MacArthur to go on the offensive and bomb the Japanese. He received permission to prepare but to wait for orders prior to the actual attack. MacArthur was under orders not to precipitate the war but he already had news from Pearl. Admiral Bulkely suggests that Quezon requested MacArthur refrain from going on the offensive first so Japan would be compassionate if they conquered the Philippines. Catching the Japanese air armada on the ground on Formosa would have had a great negative impact on Japan's air strikes on Luzon. The Japanese Naval Air Force had assembled 108 new Zeroes plus reserve aircraft for a total of 250 fighters; 81 G4M Betty medium bombers; 36 older G3M Nell medium bombers; 15 reconnaissance aircraft and 27 transports. The 5th Air Division had another 72 fighters, 27 medium bombers, 54 light bombers plus a multitude of auxiliary aircraft. Only 175 fighter aircraft were in the Philippines, many of which were ancient and slow. Japan flew reconnaissance aircraft over the Philippines from 2 through 5 December, many of which were detected. Their photographs of Clark and Iba Fields showed 32 B-17s and 74 smaller aircraft. PBYs flew over Formosa and the seas surrounding the Philippines and noted some of the build up. Nevertheless, MacArthur refused to believe an invasion of Luzon was imminent and consequently was ill prepared.[35]

The majority of the Filipinos were not aware of the attack on Pearl. It was the Feast of the Immaculate Conception and hundreds of barrios were beginning fiestas in honor of the holy day. In Manila, things were different. The people read about the attack at Pearl in the morning newspaper and the news broadcasts on KMZH radio. MacArthur received a Trans-Pacific telephone call at 0340 local time informing him of the attack. He also had the major intelligence center against Japan in his command with deciphering equipment including the top secret Purple message traffic.[36]

Warning reports were received from Nielson Field outside Manila of bombers heading toward Lingayen Gulf. Messages at 0930 on 8 December indicated Baguio and Tuguegarao were bombed and at 1000 Bereton's aircraft were airborne for Formosa.[37] At 1030 Allied ground forces were positioned within four hours of their war defensive positions.[38] By 1200, most aircraft on Luzon were airborne expecting an attack at any time. At 1225, 27 new Betty aircraft followed by 27 Nells with Zeroes above flew over Fort Sotenberg. Most of the Asiatic Fleet departed to the south leaving the Philippines to themselves and the American submarines.[39]

Speaker of the House of Representatives Sam Rayburn rapped his gavel and growled, "the President of the United States." It was 12:28 on 8 December 1941 in Washington, DC. "Yesterday, December 7, 1941 – a date which will live in infamy . . . I ask that the Congress declare that since the unprovoked and dastardly attack by Japan on Sunday, December 7th, 1941, a state of war has existed between the United States and the Japanese Empire." His words were met with a thunderous roar of approval. Japan had committed a fatal error.

Four days following Pearl Harbor, Adolph Hitler declared war on the United States followed a few hours later by Benito Mussolini. President Roosevelt, advised by General Eisenhower, decided American global policy would be to defeat Germany first and leave the Philippines abandoned. The policy meant 23,000 American and 98,000 Filipino military personnel on Luzon were expendable. Roosevelt broadcast on short wave radio and the Voice of Freedom, "The resources of the United States have been dedicated by their people to the utter and complete defeat of the Japanese warlords. I give to the people of the Philippines my solemn pledge that their freedom will be redeemed and their independence established and protected. The entire resources, in men and material, of the United States stand behind that pledge . . . The United States Navy is following an intensive and well-planned campaign which will result in positive assistance to the defense of the Philip-

ROBERT K. HARMUTH

pine Islands." It was a political statement to temporarily pacify the Filipinos.

Earlier that day, Guam was invaded and on 11 December, Wake Island was also invaded. Two days later, the last Indian, Scottish and Canadian troop was removed from the China mainland. They were moved across the bay to Hong Kong although they knew their future was doomed.

99-HARM

CHAPTER TWO

ROAD TO THE BATTLE FOR BATAAN

ON THE FERTILE plains of the San Joaquin Valley and along the shores of Northern California, two lads grew up and became the closest of friends. With parents of strong stock and humble means, the boys graduated from high school and eagerly looked forward to the future. Unfortunately, the rumblings of a war in Europe and a threatening situation in the Pacific blocked their view of a rosy and prosperous future. They discussed the future with their parents and realized it likely would include being drafted into the military so one decided to enlist and get his duty to country behind him. The boys grew up in the small town of Mountain View, California within a block of each other on Washington Street.

Manny Eneriz was the son of a trash collector and was raised in a devote Roman Catholic family. He was an ambitious young man with a strong desire to succeed in life. He worked hard as a youth helping his father and decided to become a meat cutter or butcher. Learning from friends of his father, by 1940 he became skilled at his new trade and picked up the nickname "Butch," named for his occupation.

His closest friend, Salvadore, was the son of a goat rancher who had aspirations similar to Manny. Beside their common future outlook and close friendship, Salvadore had a very good-looking sister who caught Manny's eye. Unlike Manny, Salvadore decided to remain home and help his father with the goats rather than enlist in the Army.

Manny visited his recruiter when he was 19 and enlisted in the U.S. Army for a term of four years; one year of training, two years overseas, and one year stateside. His initial days in the army were a bit unusual. He reported for duty in San Francisco and was taken to Angel Island in San Francisco Bay near Alcatraz. He and other recruits remained on the island until they boarded the ship, *SS WASHINGTON*. The ship departed for the Philippines via Pearl Harbor where they received a few hours of liberty to see the sights. Japanese sympathizers were busy worldwide in a comprehensive and widespread covert intelligence [40] network. Americans enroute to the Philippines and other Western pacific duty stations were queried skillfully in Hawaii where most American troops had a stopover.[41]

The *WASHINGTON* joined a few other naval ships and departed for Manila in the Philippines. On the 29th day of the voyage, they made land fall on a few islands guarding the Philippine Island Group. It was a beautiful sunset in the San Bernadino Straits as the sun settled in the west above the volcano, Mount Mayon. The following morning, the ship entered Manila Bay, passed close aboard to Corregidor, and berthed at the soon to be infamous Pier #7. It was a typical trip for the American soldier traveling to the Philippines for duty. The weather was good and the seas calm – a nice way for Manny to begin his overseas Army duty. There was a steady stream of vessels carrying Americans and equipment, usually in groups of two or more transports accompanied by a naval armed escort. Many of the troop transports were former passenger liners such as from the President Lines.[42]

The new recruits climbed down the accommodation ladder and mustered on the pier. Then they marched off the pier, dodging cargo and forklifts, into Manila and to the barracks where they were to receive basic or boot training. The port was a hub of activity as a number of ships were in, discharging supplies and equipment. Manny selected the Philippines over Panama and Hawaii since he was conversant in Spanish. Following basic training, he reported for duty with the 31st Infantry Regiment, an all American unit.[43] The 31st was rich in history that earned a nickname of "American Foreign Legion`1``" since they had never been stationed in the United States. They also were called "American Polar Bears" after serving duty in Vladivostok during WWI.[44]

Manny was assigned a tent and bunk then reported to his sergeant. "What kinda work ya want to do Private Eneriz?" "I'd sure like to be a meat cutter, sir." "Enough of the 'sir' crap Eneriz. I'm a sergeant. We don't need no meat cutters right now." "Okay Sarge, how about being a cook?" "Don't need annoder of those either." "Well, what is available?" "You can be a rifleman or a machine gunner. Take your pick." "But I want to be in food preparation Sarge." "Pick up your Enfield son and ask da cook if you can make your own supper. That's as close as it gets. Savvy?" "Aye aye Sarge, I got it," Manny muttered dejectedly. "See me in six months and I'll see if we need a cook then."

Manny was issued a bulky bag that contained a multitude of items deemed necessary for the American fighting man in the Philippines. Among the items were a gas mask and a light and cool pith helmet which he later surrendered for the fondly called WWI "metal beanie," a level-brim steel helmet. It had a multitude of uses; a cooking pot, a wash basin, a pillow at night, and least of all, protection for the head.

On Luzon, MacArthur had two tank battalions, the 192nd and 194th. Actually, D-Company of the 192nd was transferred to the 194th so each battalion was composed of three companies. Both tank battalions were mixes of National Guard units from across America; notably Illinois, Ohio, Kentucky, Wisconsin, Minnesota, and California. Each battalion was equipped with fifty-four M-3 light tanks known as General Stuart tanks. The tank weighed roughly 13-tons, stood 7-feet high and was equipped with a 37mm canon and a number of .30 caliber machine guns. Each tank carried a crew of four men; the tank commander, the gunner, driver and assistant driver. The tanks were archaic, uncomfortable, and ill equipped to communicate within the tank and with other tanks.

They were, however, powerful and thick skinned so most of the tankers liked the vehicle.[45]

Mansfield Young joined the National Guard in Salinas, California in 1939 and later became a member of C-Company in the 194th Tank Battalion. He grew up in Ventura and Meiners Oaks in California after spending his youth in Wyoming and Utah. The American economy was poor including the great depression. Joining the military seemed the appropriate move for Mansfield so he joined the National Guard in October 1939 and was inducted into the Army in February 1941. He received his basic camp training at Fort Lewis in Tacoma, Washington and was a member of the 144th Field Artillery in February 1941. He was a member of a 155 Rifle Squad or the Long Toms as a Private. He was "shanghaied" to the 194th Tank Battalion just before the battalion deployed. Mansfield felt the reason he was transferred was his performance as the unit bugler. Harry James he was not.[46] He was a dedicated young man and the Army provided him opportunities and travel away from home but he faced the definite possibility of being in the middle of a big war. The muscles in his 5-foot 8-inch lean frame flexed in anticipation of the unknown. He certainly wasn't frightened of the Japanese, just a bit scared of the unknown.

Just before 2100 on 8 September 1941, Mansfield climbed up the long gangway aboard the SS PRESIDENT COOLIDGE with the rest of the battalion. Shortly thereafter, COOLIDGE cast off her lines and was underway for Honolulu, accompanied by a cruiser and fleet tanker that carried PT-boats. They stopped in Honolulu for about ten hours to refuel and replenish on the 13th. He was lucky and managed liberty for a few hours; long enough to see Waikiki and Hotel Street. Underway that evening, COOLIDGE rendezvoused with the cruiser USS ASTORIA as an escort to the Philippines.[47]

Mansfield and the 194th arrived in Manila on 26 September. Most of the men came from National Guard units in California and carried all new equipment. The Stuart tanks were supported by the 17th Ordnance Company who later supported the self-propelled 75mm guns, which were organized into the Provisional Self-Propelled Artillery Group. The *HMCS SAN JOSE* was scheduled to arrive in Manila on 16 December with 60 Bren gun carriers and 75 GM trucks for the 194th. They carried other equipment designated for Hong Kong and Singapore but arrived in the Western Pacific too late to help.[48]

The 194th disembarked *COOLIDGE* mid-afternoon along with the 200th California and the 17th Ordnance Company. Mansfield was assigned as the radio operator and assistant driver in one of the tanks. The equipment was offloaded the following morning. The first obstacle the tankers faced was obtaining fuel, an aviation gasoline, for the tanks. MacArthur's "well prepared" quartermasters would not provide the fuel since it was time for their daily siesta that took priority over operational needs. The 194th's supply officer sought help from the Navy Base at Cavite and fuel was arranged immediately. The sailors delivered to the soldiers.[49]

The M3 Stuart tank was an iteration of the M2A4 manufactured by American Car and Foundry Company with improvements and thicker skin as a result of experience in Europe. It reached speeds of 36 mph for a range of about 70 miles. The engine compartment was in the rear and the drive shaft ran through the driving compartment between the drivers. The turret held the canon and was occupied by the tank commander and gunner who stood and turned with the turret.[50]

A police escort led the 194th out of Manila that evening. The long column moved slowly and carefully on the 60-mile trip to Fort Stotsenburg. The trip was precarious since the tankers had not driven the Stuarts before and it was dark. They drove all night and Mansfield was kept busy advising the tank commander of curves and obstacles in the road. He and the driver took turns driving, reminding themselves constantly to stay on the left side of the road. They arrived at the fort early in the morning only to find no arrangements were made for their arrival. The tankers were exhausted and a few men hysterical from claustrophobia. The confinement in the tank didn't bother Mansfield but his muscles ached and his butt was sore as hell. There were no cushions on the metal seats.[51]

Like Manny, Mansfield was assigned a structure resembling a tent with wooden floors and sides with a canvas top. It was the rainy season and the tent was anything but watertight. The men constantly dried cloths and material while fighting mildew. The rain and humid environment increased maintenance on the seventeen tanks assigned C-Company of the 194th,a responsibility for Mansfield. The next couple months were a time of frustration and shortage. The battalion received no fuel for training, no ammunition to fire the 37mm guns and the tankers never trained with infantry. The guns had yet to be fired, in fact, cosmoline removal from the gun barrels was one of Mansfield's first chores. Spare parts for the tanks and guns were shipped on the SS YAKA that arrived in mid-October but the marine terminal and army supply system never moved the supplies out of the port area.

General King ordered the 194th to plan and participate in the defensive scheme at Clark Air Base that adjoined Fort Stotsenberg. The Commanding Officer at Clark, Colonel Maitland, was sufficiently astute to order reconnaissance flights to search for the Japanese. These flights actually detected Japanese beach markers for the invasion at Lingayen Gulf but the warnings went unheeded.[52] Top priority in the Manila area remained concentrated on uniform regulations. A specific target for the Military Police (MP) was the working soldier's soft brimmed hat called the "sloppy joe." Mansfield incurred the wrath of the MPs for the hat and narrowly avoided the stockade but was rescued by one of his officers.[53]

Mansfield drove his battalion commander to Manila on 20 November to meet the SS PRESIDENT SCOTT at Pier #7. The 192nd Tank Battalion, under command of Colonel Weaver, arrived on the ship. Weaver took command of both battalions as the tank group commander. The 194th then received the 192nd's D Company so both battalions were at equal strength of three companies.

General MacArthur organized a comprehensive spy organization after taking command. One of his men infiltrated a Japanese spy ring called Legionairos del Trapajo who announced the Japanese were about to invade Luzon. The Japanese spies were still shouting "bansai" when MacArthur's man reported his findings to USAFFE. No one is sure what happened to the report but reportedly MacArthur received the it.[54]

Preparedness and training of allied forces in the Philippines, even in the few months prior to 7 December 1941, reflects anything but credit and glory on MacArthur. Ordnance personnel followed WPO and pre-positioned huge stocks of ammunition in Bataan although some feel the chore was incomplete. The Quartermaster Corps sat on its haunches and accomplished little in stockpiling food and stores. Even after the invasion, with huge supplies of food in Rizal Stadium in Manila and other areas of Luzon, the quartermasters moved insignificant quantities.[55] On 8 December, there was a total of 3,000 tons of canned meat and fish and an inadequate supply of rice available to the defenders. This broke down to rations for 100,000 men for only 30 days. Within the month, all troops were placed on half rations of about 2,000 calories per day that was later drastically cut.[56]

War with Japan was expected momentarily by most commands except MacArthur despite confirmations by numerous decoded messages and actual fleet/aircraft sightings. The Submarine Base at Pearl Harbor printed pre-dated postcards in July 1941. The cards were to be used by submariners to inform relatives and friends outside of Hawaii they were still alive and a brief status report. Submarine Forces Pacific (SubPac) also prepared for war and shifted to war patrol training and exercise mode in the summer of 1941.[57] Admiral Stark sent two warnings to Admirals Kimmel and Hart on 24 November. The question remains why the remainder of military in the Pacific, including MacArthur, was not vigorously preparing for the inevitable war.[58]

Manny and Mansfield were pleasantly surprised when they arrived in the Philippines. Local Philippine civilians could be hired inexpensively. A resident live-in cost a penny or two a day. They did most of the non-military chores such as laundry, cleaning and cooking. But military advancement was slow with a soldier rated corporal after four years service.[59] However, food, alcohol, dancing and Filipina prostitution was so abundant, a private could enjoy the good life.

In late fall, the "Manila Times" reported Japanese aircraft over Luzon for the second time in a week. At night, Manny and many infantrymen was stationed atop high places like buildings, church steeples and trees. They were lookouts for Japanese parachutists.[60] The army went on alert when in early December, reports were received from all over Luzon about unidentified or confirmed Japanese aircraft overhead. On 6 December at Nichols Field south of Manila, Colonel George, a senior aviator, announced the Japanese had over 3,000 aircraft on Formosa and reconn flights were detected daily. The 21st Pursuit Squadron realized war was at hand yet the entire squadron was trained in P-35 fighter aircraft and all their craft were new P-40s that no one had flown. The aircraft were still being removed from crates and the .50 caliber machine guns were plugged in cosmolene.[61] On 8 December when the Japanese arrived in force, they were installing gun sights in the new aircraft.[62]

The communications center for Manila was the Pan Am Building at Nichols Field. Nichols and Nielson Fields were only a few miles apart in the southern Manila suburbs and the home bases for P-40s, P-35s, and P-26s flown by the 17th Pursuit squadron. The 21st and 34th Pursuit Squadrons were stationed at Nichols.

7 December 1941 was another hot and sultry day. The temperatures and humidity reached the normal nineties and the day concluded with a typical brilliant sunset. During the dry season, temperatures reached the nineties and cooled to the eighties at night. Occasional thundershowers caressed the landscape during the days with such vigor one felt they could swim into the sky. The fragrance of jasmine, orchids, bougainvillea, acacia and hibiscus drifted across the countryside. A peaceful Philippines was, indeed, a special God's creation.

Liberty activity for the soldiers and sailors in Manila was usually conducted under the slow rotating fans in the nightclubs and bars. Dewey Boulevard and adjoining streets were sites for many entertainment establishments such as the Silver Dollar Saloon, Poodle Dog Bar, Alcazar Club, Laura Guerrite's Little Club, Madame Savory's French Restaurant, Myakos Japanese Restaurant and the Santa Ana Cabaret. The Bayview Hotel, with its wonderful view from atop the building, was a favorite for many. In Cavite, some of the more popular recreational stops were the Dreamland, Mopey Joe's, Legaspi Landing Restaurant and the Metropolitan Club. A favorite Japanese nightclub was the Nishikawa Hotel which eventually turned out to be a contact point for the Japanese underground.[63]

Another big attraction for the American on liberty in Manila was the Jai Alai games. Americans loved athletic events regardless of sport. A favorite bunkroom for soldiers was the Miyako Hotel. Soldier or sailor, the Americans enjoyed dancing and it was difficult to top the Santa Ana Ballroom. The favorite dates for a night were the Russian women who the men believed were free of venereal disease. Singing, closely representing noise, floated out of the favorite Fiesta Room as the newly arrived air crews of the 27th Bombardment Group enjoyed themselves as they partook of the local San Miguel beer. The party continued into the early hours of 8 December when a telephone ring was barely audible above the din of giggling girls and drunken talk. "No shit! Those dirty sons of bitches!" The word had arrived from Pearl Harbor.

The Philippines Islands were placed on alert and Army Air Corps flew some search and intercept flights out of Clark Air Base. Clark and the other air bases prepared for a Japanese attack but years of neglect in readiness couldn't be rectified overnight. At Clark, preparations included rolling gasoline barrels off the tarmacs and airstrips while the 194th took up defensive positions in the woods between airstrips.[64]

Iba Airfield continued to detect unidentified aircraft approaching Luzon from the South China Sea. Iba, located west of Clark, had the only functioning radar on the Philippine Islands. The air incursions were later interpreted as familiarization runs and intelligence patrols by the Japanese to test the defenses of Luzon. MacArthur went on the radio and to newspapers to disclaim any threats or rumors of alerts in the Philippines to prevent panic on the islands. Mansfield and fellow tankers were ordered on half alert with half the men on duty at any given time. On 6 December, he was ordered to draw and distribute ammunition for B-Company. Mansfield struggled with the boxes and belts of ammunition, then commenced loading his tank. A dismaying fact came to light as he loaded the 37mm ammunition into the holding racks. The only rounds received were armor piercing which was useless against infantry, aircraft and artillery. There was no other 37mm ammo in the Philippines. They had yet to fire a round and what they had was useless. Recuperating oil, needed to fire the 37mm canon was not available until eight hours after the Japanese attack on Clark. So much for the preparation phase in the defense against the Japanese by the tank battalion.[65]

The state of air defenses in the Philippines was equally unprepared. The Signal Corps successfully decoded the infamous "East Winds will blow favorably on 8 December" on 7 December but not one aircraft scrambled. The old aircraft were archaic and tired while the new planes had not been flown and test fired. Few bomber crews had high altitude experience and the airstrips were short or too soft to handle the B-17 bombers at most fields. Although there were seven radar installations on the islands, only the set at Iba worked.[66] MacArthur relied on lookouts that had not been taught aircraft recognition. Radio communications between military bases was virtually not existent and the ammunition supply for aircraft was so low, most pilots had yet to fire a round. MacArthur counted on the Far East Asiatic Fleet to stop any Japanese threat of invasion – at least the Navy was in some resemblance of alert.[67] The Asiatic Fleet was underway, submarines poised for war patrols, and Admiral Hart issued the orders, "SUBMARINES AND AIRCRAFT

WILL WAGE UNRESTRICTED WARFARE." The *USS CANO-PUS* moved to Cavite.[68]

Residents awakened to air warnings from the Air Warning Room at Nielson Field reporting the first wave of Japanese bombers inbound. The B-17s at Clark scrambled to be airborne followed by P-40s from Clark and Nichols to intercept the bombers over Lingayen Gulf.[69]

Contact reports were heard from numerous directions, reporting a wide variety of targets. People panicked so most civilians on military bases were sent home. The confusion wasn't confined to just the Philippines as Formosa went to alert at a report of incoming American aircraft. The Japanese strikes on Iba and Clark passed their own bombers inbound for Formosa after attacks on Bagio and Tuguegarao. General Bereton's air raid on Formosa never deployed.

The B-17s from Clark circled Mount Arayat awhile then were given permission to return to Clark at 1100. The bombers landed followed by P-40s to refuel and crew lunch. Quiet and calmness returned to the field. Meanwhile, the radar at Iba was busy all night and early morning sending interceptors up on numerous reports. Fighter pilots rested in their cockpits until they were alerted by radar and coast watchers a large formation was inbound from the west.[70] Sirens sounded in Manila and the fighters took off to intercept but Clark remained quiet and complacent.[71]

Mansfield nodded off inside the tank under some trees at Clark when the word was received at 0900 that Japanese aircraft were sighted over Lingayen Gulf. As fighter aircraft rose to meet the Japanese, the huge flight of bombers turned east and bombed Camp John Hay near Bagio. The camp was not strategically important but a resting-place for military personnel. A few hours later, the "all clear" signal sounded but the 194th remained on alert. Thirty-five minutes the Japanese arrived.[72]

Mansfield stood atop his tank in a hedgerow of trees dividing the two main landing strips at Clark. The ammo belts were laid out for the machine guns and each weapon on the tanks had been cleaned and oiled. He had done everything humanly possible to be ready and patiently awaited the chow wagon, which had not been by for over a day. "Ain't we ever goin ta get some chow around here?" the gunner on the next tank mumbled. "Know what you mean. My belly button's tickling my back bone already," answered Mansfield. "What da ya say we go out in town tonight and rustle up some vitals," suggested the gunner. "Sounds good to me but right now I think we oughta just go over to Charlie Corn's PX to . . . " "Zeros nine o'clock and high!" shouted Sergeant Gillis.[73]

Just before noon, the air warning officer at Nielson sent a warning via teletype to Clark. The teletype reached no one so they tried the radio but no one answered. Finally, a junior officer at Clark answered the telephone and promised to get the word about the air raid to the base commander. Meanwhile, Bereton completed his plan for a raid on Formosa including B-17s from Mindanao who were to rendezvous at Clark that evening. Shortly after noon, every fighter on Luzon was airborne except at Clark where the junior officer had yet to make his report. The Philippines Islands were confronted with communication failures and an American air raid plan that never happened. If the attack had taken place, the invasion results may have been drastically altered.

About 1230, there was no air coverage for all the aircraft sitting on the ground at Clark while twenty miles away, over Tarlac, 27 Bettys flew toward Clark. A magnificent "V" formation passed over Fort Stotsenberg and the Japanese pilots looked down on the pretty white buildings, rows of mango trees and acacia, and the brilliant green polo field. A moment later they stared in disbelief at the neat rows of B-17s and P-40 aircraft on the ground.[74] There are various reports as to the disposition of American aircraft on the ground at Clark. One report states only half the bombers were parked on the field.[75] Colonel Berry was there and reports only five B-17s under repair with archaic B-18s and O-10s on the ground at Clark. The older aircraft were mistaken as B-17s.[76] Most accounts record all the B-17s were on the ground at the time of the attack. Incredibly, MacArthur ordered all aircraft at Clark to remain on the ground.[77] What possible reason precipitated such an order?

Mansfield heard reports of enemy aircraft and looked skyward for the intruders. A quick glance to the north and he saw the sun glitter off the wings of a huge number of planes with red balls. He glanced back to the runway and saw the rows of fighters and bombers, wing tip to wing tip. "My God, they're sitting there like fish in a bucket!" It was ten hours following Pearl Harbor when he heard the scream of dropping bombs. Luzon was hit as was Guam, Wake, Midway, Singapore, Shanghai and others. The attack on Wake Island was observed from the submarines *TAMBOR* and *TRITON* who watched helplessly.[78]

Following the bombers came Zeros to mop up anything remaining. "Lead'em a little more Young. Keep the line of fire out ahead of the sonsa bitches," hollered Sgt Gillis, the tank commander. "I am, damn it," Mansfield screamed back. "Well, lead'em more! God damn Californian couldn't hit a coon in his lap," muttered Gillis. Just then, the Zero started trailing smoke. "Eye like a hawk Young baby, you nailed his ass." Mansfield kept firing his .30 caliber machine gun and quietly said, "I'm not sure it was me Sarge."

Some tankers from the 192nd were angered by the attack for a strange reason. They had been on liberty in Sapangbato the night prior and drank too much. They ate "ballot's," which are aged duck eggs only days from hatching. Bernard Shaw became violently ill watching the egg consumption and left. His friends set him up for breakfast the next morning. He was to be served ballots vice hard-boiled eggs. As Shaw headed for a table with a tray of food and eggs, "Air attack! Air attack! Everyone to their battle stations."[79]

Japanese aircraft surrounded Clark. Sergeant Knox of the 192nd immediately dropped into the turret and shut the hatch. He quickly realized he could no good there so climbed back up and manned a machine gun while yelling for more ammo. Never having been a duck hunter, he didn't lead the planes either but blazed away at dozens of them. All the gunners were taught how to lead aircraft the next morning.[80]

Clark was in utter chaos with command, leadership, discipline and order virtually non-existent. Officers, enlisted, and civilians ran in different directions in varying states of hysteria and panic. Lack of training and drills was obvious.[81] One of the few men who kept it together was LCOL Rosy O'Donnell who was a B-17 pilot without a plane. He rounded up a bunch of his fellow pilots and motored to Manila. They found an old banana boat and talked the skipper into taking them to Mindanao where the remaining B-17s were located.[82]

The Japanese had excellent intelligence reports and were not fooled by fake aircraft decoys sitting around the field. Glenn Berry ventured a few quick glances out of his bunker to see complete disaster. All the P-40s, B-17s, B-18s, and O-10s were ablaze or blown up. He watched in horror as an aircrew dashed for cover in the trees only to be caught by strafing Zeros. The hangars were on fire or knocked down and fuel tanks burned furiously giving off huge bellowing black clouds of smoke. The ground shook from exploding bombs and munitions at the burning ammo shelter.[83] Eighteen bombers, fifty-three P-40s, three P-35s, and thirty miscellaneous aircraft were lost.[84]

Glenn Berry was a lieutenant in the 14th Bomber Squadron. As soon as the air raid was over, he was ordered to clear the runways and take care of the dead and wounded. He formed working parties and started cleaning up the field. The gruesome tasks included the removal of the five-man crew in a B-18 and gun crews who had taken direct hits. Many pilots valiantly attempted to get airborne but in vain. Wounded inundated the hospital.[85] The question remains why Berry was directed to accomplish these tasks. Was there no plan to handle the expected eventuality?

Manny wasn't surprised by the sneak attack. The 31st had been on alert since early on 5 December. The 31st Infantry Regiment or 31st Infantry (US) was one of three regiments in the 10,400 man Philippine 31st Division. The other two regiments were the 45th and the 57th Infantry, led by American officers and Filipino enlisted called the Philippine Scouts. The Scouts were equipped as well as their American counterparts and fought as well or better than any military outfit in the Philippines.

The 31st was badly undermanned in August especially for officers and non-commissioned officers though a large increment of additions arrived on 27 October on the *USS GRANT*. The manning level was 1,400 men or 50%. More than half the men were draftees rather than trained infantrymen. Like Manny, most of the men received their basic training in the States then were sent to the Philippines for their first duty station.[86]

The ground shook again during the predawn morning on 9 December when Nichols Field came under attack. The skies glowed brightly as aircraft exploded and fuel supplies transformed from liquid to gas. The Pan Am Building was leveled with all the communications equipment. The last major airfield on Luzon was gone for all practical purposes. The Americans and Filipinos were to fight the remaining battles without air support. The stress from the bombing caused most nurses to miss their menstrual cycles but by then, the men's minds had turned to guns not women.[87]

Manny's barracks was inside the ancient Spanish Walled City inside Manila called Intramuros. About 0300, the men were awakened by a loud series of explosions. He climbed to the top of the 12-foot thick wall and looked out over Manila. The port area and Cavite was covered in brilliant flashes and the glow of fires. The men were called to quarters for muster then assigned tasks preparatory to fighting. Manny filled machine gun ammo belts and drew his battle gear. A few hours later, the work momentarily stopped as the men listened to President Roosevelt's speech to Congress. At first light, Manny and K-Company were trucked to Nichols Field to defend the perimeter of the airfield. The men dug foxholes and awaited the arrival of the Japanese. At noon, lunch was served and a number of the P-40s landed for chow. Fifteen minutes later, an incoming flight of Japanese was reported and Manny ran for his foxhole.[88]

He barely made it into the foxhole before the first bombs and bullets beat the ground nearby. Manny managed to sneak a few peeks out of his foxhole only to be greeted by another wave of Zeros, the Mitsubishi Type "O" fighters. One headed straight for him and appeared only a few feet off the ground. Only the tip of his tin pot showed above the ground as he watched the Zero turn slightly as he flew overhead, the pilot grinned ear to ear. The pilot saw Manny and threw him a wave and laughed. Later in the day, the trigger-happy soldiers shot down one of the few remaining American planes by mistake. In just one major strike, the Japanese wiped out the air bases at Clark, Nichols, Neilson, Iba, Vigan, Rosales, La Union, and San Fernando.[89]

With the airfields destroyed, the Japanese concentrated their attention on the Far East Asiatic Fleet and the naval facilities at Cavite Naval Yard in Manila Bay. Cavite was only six miles from Nichols. The following day the bombers returned to finish off Nichols and attack Cavite. The air raid at Nichols was swift and the few remaining assets were destroyed. The bombers turned and hit Cavite for two tortuous hours. Zeros completed the destruction after the bombers were finished, leaving the port shrouded in heavy smoke and flames. Exploding ordnance rocked the port for hours after the raid including over 200 torpedoes for submarines and the PT boats. Two submarines were hit, one sunk and the other severely damaged. Four of the remaining gunboats were to experience a short life; *USS PENQUIN* was sunk in 1937 with the *MINDANOA, OAHU,* and *LUZON* sunk between December 1941 and May 1942.[90]

From start to finish, it took the Japanese less than 24-hours to gain complete control of the air and seas. All that remained to defend Luzon was a hungry army and submarines at sea. On 12 December, the Japanese struck the 194th camp area with bombs filled with spikes, rivets, and junk. Mansfield ran for his tank and manned the machine gun. Colonel Miller, the battalion commander, was in the shower when the Japanese attacked. He ran outside with his .45 pistol and blazed away at the attacking aircraft. As he emptied his clip, the men chuckled at their leader audibly as he fought off Goliath with a pistol; and he did it stark ass naked.[91]

Luzon was invaded at five points within the first two weeks of hostilities and MacArthur didn't stop one. MacArthur positioned five of his seven divisions on Luzon in the north and two in the south. In the north, the 11th and 21st Divisions were in the Lingayen Gulf area, the 91st at Aparri to Cabanatuan, the 71st was in reserve at Camp O'Donnell, and the 31st Infantry Regiment covered the area west of the Zambales and Subic Bay. In the south, the 41st and 51st divisions covered Batangas and Tayabas.[92] Mingled in the Filipino Divisions were "Quezon Boys" who were similar to American ROTC cadets. There was two other Regular Philippine Divisions. The 1st Regular Division was the peacetime army unit maintained by the government. Additionally, the 2nd Philippine Constabulary Division was formed after all forces retreated to Bataan from remnants of other units.

The first landing took place at first light at Basco on Batan Island north of Luzon almost coincident with the attack at Pearl Harbor. Two days later, 10 December, the Japanese landed at Vigan and Aparri. The main invasion took place on 22 December at Lingayen Gulf utilizing the 14th Army under the command of General Homma. Two battleships, four heavy cruisers, a light cruiser, two seaplane carriers plus numerous destroyers protected an invasion fleet of 80 transports. The task force was detected and reported by American submarines. The *STINGRAY, S-38, S-40, SALMON, PERMIT, PORPOISE,* and *SAURY* rushed to Lingayen Gulf to meet the invasion. Unfortunately, the shallow waters of the gulf and faulty torpedoes prevented the submarines from halting the invasion.[93]

Luzon looked like a dark green belt with a brilliant white beach from the decks of the invasion fleet. Even the sea was green like jade. The mountains to the south were a dark shadow of purple above the green plain and the sky was a clear and deep blue. It was almost too pretty to start a war. A couple American aircraft attacked the invasion convoy but were soon driven away.[94] MacArthur was forewarned of the landings but was fooled again as to location. He set up defenses near the mouth of the Agno River but the Japanese landed 40 miles away and were opposed only by bad weather. The seasoned Japanese force advanced quickly through Luzon from the north and the east as MacArthur withdrew slowly toward the Bataan Peninsula. Unknown to any of the Allies, while MacArthur failed to stockpile Bataan before the war, the Japanese stockpiled their own supplies in caves and tunnels of the peninsula.[95]

The Lingayen Gulf is protected by shallow water and reefs while the gulf itself is shallow. Only the submarine *S-38* was small enough to get in to attack the invasion force while the remaining submarines kept a lookout for Japanese destroyers. *S-38* fired four torpedoes at four heavily laden troop transports and missed all four. After being depth charged, she got free from the soft mud bottom and attacked again. Setting the torpedoes shallower, and sunk the *HAYO MARU. S-38* took another beating and finally escaped the gulf on Christmas Day.[96] The other submarines in the area fired at Japanese vessels but were frustrated by unreliable torpedo detonator devices and depth settings.[97] It would be two years before the torpedo problems were resolved.

Seventy-three GATO Class Fleet Boat submarines were manufactured in Groton, Portsmouth, Mare Island, and Manitowac, Wisconsin with *USS DRUM* already on patrol. They carried a full electronics package of radar and sonar which was upgraded as the war progressed. *DORADO* and *HERING* were the only two boats of the class not to operate in the Pacific. Of the 73 boats of the class, 10 were lost with a loss of 1,450 submariners.[98] The Japanese submarines suffered much more. Midget submarines at Pearl failed miserably, as did their full size counterparts. *GUDGEON* was vectored to intercept three Japanese submarines returning from patrols off the United States West Coast. The Japanese were talking actively on the radio when *GUDGEON* permanently silenced the I-173.[99]

The 4th Marine Regiment returned from Shanghai in the *SS PRESIDENT MADISON* and *SS PRESIDENT HARRISON* in December 1941. They settled into the Olangapo Naval Station at Subic Bay and were assigned defense by the Naval Amphibious Patrol Squadron of PBY aircraft. The Marines camped in the hull of the decommissioned cruiser, *USS ROCHESTER* and successfully fought off Japanese air strikes on 12 December from the decks of the old cruiser. The old ship had to be scuttled the next day after the invasions of Luzon and with the approach of the Japanese to Olongapo.[100]

Corregidor was also attacked on 10 December by Japanese aircraft. The Japanese bombers flew over Corregidor at an altitude of 12,000 feet. No targets were hit except by the gunners on the rock. Out of the sortie of dozens of aircraft, only three bombers escaped the 3-inch anti-aircraft fire of the defenders. Corregidor was never again attacked by low flying bombers.[101]

Allied troops had long departed Bagio when the Japanese arrived at the convent. A Japanese officer arrived just in time to prevent mass rape of the nuns but he permitted the destruction of the convent. A priest was almost killed by beating and the chapel ruined. It was a harbinger of things to come.[102]

MacArthur made another unexplainable decision and declared Manila an "open city" on Christmas day without consulting or advising any of his commanders[103] while Davao in southern Mindanao was invaded by 5,000 Japanese troops.[104] Manila billowed with black, acrid smoke as supplies and fuel was burned. The Pasig River was filled with black burning oil as it ran through Manila from reserve oil tanks dumped by the Allies. Everywhere, the city was alive with gangs and looters with armloads of stolen goods.[105]

There was little fuel at Corregidor and not much at Mariveles while Manila scuttled her fuel supply. Submariners salvaged only 300,000 gallons of diesel oil in barges which was little for their needs. There were hundreds of submariners on Corregidor and Mariveles left behind from shops, tenders and the sunken *SEALION.*

SEAWOLF and *SWORDFISH* removed 250 men in-groups of 25 then left the Philippines, ashamed they had failed to stop the Japanese.[106]

Following the destruction of most American aircraft on Luzon, the remaining bombers flew south to the relative safety of Mindanao and the fighters operated out of three dirt airstrips on the southern end of the Bataan Peninsula. By 4 January 1942, only ten fighters remained in service. As the Japanese moved artillery forward toward the front, a couple thousand Allied aircraft, ground, sailors, marines, and support personnel were divided into battalion sizes to help fight on the land.

CHAPTER THREE

THE BATTLE CONTINUES INTO BATAAN

THE U.S. NAVY departed the Philippines on 10 December 1941 but left behind a ragtag number of units that was formed into the Bataan Navy. It included five PT-boats, two Q-boats, three minesweepers, three river gunboats, the submarine tender *USS CANOPUS (AS-9)*, and two yachts. *CANOPUS* eventually berthed at Mariveles and provided invaluable support to all Allied Forces. A Naval Battalion was formed under the command of Commander Bridget from 120 marines and 480 sailors who were remnants of crews left behind. The sailors dyed their white uniforms with coffee to make them less visible but the resultant color was akin to baby poop yellow. Other than the marines, few sailors knew much about hand held weapons. Submarines assigned to the Asiatic Fleet deployed immediately and submarine war patrols commenced from Pearl Harbor. *USS GUDGEON* departed on 11 December, *USS POLLACH* on the 13th followed closely by *USS PLUNGER.*[107]

In the interim between the beginning of the war and the liberation of all POWs, there existed a continuing theme, the American submarine. It began with the submarine tender *CANOPUS* who was assigned to Submarine Squadron 20 (SubRon 20). She fought courageously in support of the Philippines, Navy, Army, Coast Guard units, and all Allied personnel during the early days of the war until the fall of Bataan. She symbolized the heroic defense of Luzon by Allied forces. Built from a passenger liner purchased from Grace Lines in 1921, she was converted to a tender or mother ship for older "pigboats." She was a floating home and repair facility for submarines and fondly called "the old lady" by everyone she encountered. She had been on "China Station" since 1925 in Cavite Navy Yard.

The crew of *CANOPUS* watched in horror on 8 December at the sneak attacks by Japan. She was lightly armed with four 3-inch antiaircraft guns and a multitude of .50 and .30 caliber machine guns. When Admiral Hart received word of the attack on Pearl, his fleet was already deployed except for a few submarines and they were on a high readiness alert. Captain Sackett, skipper of *CANOPUS*, moved her alongside a pier with only a few feet of water under her keel. If she were sunk, *CANOPUS* could still operate as a tender with her decks above water. Spares and torpedoes were barged to Corregidor and the ship skillfully camouflaged by her crew.

Civilians and contractor personnel were placed under Navy command and Navy Civil Engineering Officers led a work force to strengthen storage areas and air raid shelters. The work should have been accomplished long before. Air-raid sirens wailed on 10 December as a formation of 63 Bettys closed on Cavite and the Naval Yard.[108]

The Japanese obliterated the Naval Base at Cavite, the only Allied repair facility in the Far East. Bombers inflicted light damage at Sangley Point Air Station but Cavite no longer existed. Admiral Rockwell ordered a complete evacuation of the area while he and CDR Jim Wilson, the Public Works Officer, watched a final wave of destruction from across the bay at Canacoa.[109] The submarine *USS SEA LION* was sunk and *USS SEADRAGON* severely damaged. The following days were hectic with attempted repairs and reorganization of personnel. People remained hidden in shelters during the day and came out at night. The night hours weren't safe as Japanese sympathetic Philippine fifth-column organizations known as "Saks" raised hell. The Saks remained active for the duration of the war and were vital in providing intelligence to the Japanese during the initial Battle for Luzon.

Repair work was conducted on board *CANOPUS* or at Sangley. Patients were moved from the Naval Hospital at Canacao to Sternberg Army Hospital in Manila. LT Cecil Espy, CEC, USN reestablished a transportation system and motor pool. Epsy became a POW later and died in a prison of war camp.[110] Subsequent air raids devastated Sangley Point, killing many marines in their barracks and nurses in their quarters. Sangley was evacuated on Christmas day following a mass burial of Americans and Filipinos. CDR Dorsey and LT Champlin found some navigation charts and triangulated a radio transmitter at Sangley Point operated by Japanese who were spotting for the bombers. Demolition of the fuel dock was delayed when the *USS PEARY* came in unexpectedly for bunkers. She got underway in the midst of another air raid and managed the 25-mile trip to Corregidor. Local officers aided her through the minefields and returned in a small boat. *PEARY* was sunk later fighting near Australia.[111]

Some of the CEC officers went to Corregidor to assist restoring utilities that took a pounding from the bombings. The air raids seemed to be continuous at times with Fort Drum and Fort Hughes hit as well. As the Allied troops slowly moved into Bataan, severe bombing on the peninsula was observed from Corregidor. General Parker's Southern Force headquarters was in Batangas south of Manila and General Wainwright's Northern Force headquarters was in Fort Stotsenburg near Clark[112]

Mansfield raced for his tank with bullets kicking up dirt around him. It was 12 December and the Japanese attacked Clark again. The aircraft came in low from the northeast vice the usual westerly direction. The 194th manned their weapons in a hurry and blazed away at the attackers but the aircraft were difficult to see from the tank positions among the trees. The planes were so low, some bombs didn't have time to arm prior to striking the ground but those that did explode scattered nails and rivets. They were anti-personnel bombs.[113]

That evening, the 194th Tank Battalion was ordered to proceed immediately for the Calumpit Bridge to the south. They departed in a downpour of rain and soon it was dark. Visibility was difficult and the entire crew kept an eye out for traffic and animals. The strain on eyes and mind was exhausting so Mansfield made coffee a few times using the heat from the transmission in his helmet to heat the coffee. Unfortunately, coffee has a bad habit of running through kidneys in a hurry with the constant vibration and jolting of the tank. The handy helmet was used again – but not the same one used for making coffee. The entire tank crew stared into the darkness through their armored slots and wiped rain from their eyes. A few tanks and other vehicles ran off the road and some missed the turn in San Fernando but the vehicles were easily pulled back on the road. None of the tankers had been on the road before. Little did they know they would travel the route a couple more times under more severe conditions. The battalion arrived at the rendezvous completely exhausted about 0600 the following morning. The area was near the bridge in an wide open area, completely devoid of any cover.[114]

Most of the non-rated men were assigned duties on both tanks and half-tracks. Although mentally and physically drained, Mansfield immediately serviced the half-tracks. Rain continued to fall as he looked at his surroundings that provided little comfort. Rice paddies surrounded the bridge. As he finished changing the oil and was cleaning up, the battalion received orders to report to the South Luzon Force. The reconnaissance team and half-tracks were to depart immediately and scope out a new bivouac area for the battalion as a new defensive position. While the North Force headed for Lingayen Gulf, the South Group headed for anticipated Japanese landing sites at Batangas and Natsugbu. Mansfield was assigned as a machine gunner in the back of a half-track when not in a tank so he crawled up and made himself as comfortable as possible. It was better than walking. His relative comfort was short lived as he hung on for dear life as the half-track bounced and lurched down the road. Eventually, they found an ideal spot north of Muntinlupa amidst a grove of huge mango trees, not far from both anticipated Japanese landing sites. The remainder of the battalion made the trip the following day in the tanks and support vehicles.[115]

The following week and a half were spent conducting reconnaissance missions in the area. The 194th had never been in the area. The majority of the reconn runs were conducted in jeeps that gave Mansfield some time to rest and relax. Not far from Muntinlupa and south of Manila was the infamous Bilibid Prison which had been built by the Spanish and currently held numerous Filipino, Japanese, and German prisoners.

The quiet life ended abruptly with reports the Japanese landed at Legaspi in southern Luzon, far from the position of the 194th. Not a single Allied military unit was near Legaspi and the Japanese landing was virtually unopposed. Smaller groups of Japanese also landed at Aparri and Vigan in northern Luzon but in mass at Santo Tomas in the Lingayen Gulf on 20 December. The Battle for Luzon was underway in earnest despite Manila newspaper articles to the contrary stating the Japanese were run off the island.

Colonel Miller was called to Fort Santiago, U.S. Armed Forces Far East (USAFFE) Headquarters, in Manila on 22 December. During the meeting, it was decided the 194th would move back to the north to provide withdrawal support for the North Force. As the Allies retreated to the south, they passed through the 194th's new position that protected their rear. It was a precarious assignment, especially without infantry. C-Company was left behind to support the retreat of the South Force to the north. On 24 December, the 194th received orders to proceed north to Carmen on the Agno River. Mansfield watched the other two companies depart with some anxiety in his heart. Later in the day, A-Company was attacked by Japanese aircraft near San Jose but suffered no casualties or damage. The 194th moved up Highway #3 through Cabanatuan enroute the front.[116]

Down south, Mansfield and his half-track escorted General Jones on a reconn patrol when they ran into a Japanese ambush.

Mansfield and crew returned fire with a vengeance, killing the entire ambush unit while receiving no casualties themselves. Unfortunately, the half-track was totaled by enemy gunfire. Mansfield jumped out of the vehicle and checked the Japanese to insure they were dead, then himself to make sure he was still in one piece. They removed all the guns from the half-track and trudged by foot back down the trail to the camp.

Fellow tankers in the 192nd were ordered into battle to the north by General Wainwright. Since they didn't know the strength nor disposition of the Japanese, a tank platoon was ordered to investigate a reported Japanese troop movement only to run directly into a tank trap on the same road. The lead tank received a direct hit and the other four in the column were to unabler to turn around nor return fire. A Japanese 47mm anti-tank gun shredded the platoon.

The 194th was sent to reconnoiter the Banbam River area and set up a holding line. They became heavily engaged with the enemy along the Agno River. Near Carmen, the tankers appreciated just how useless armor piercing ammunition was against artillery and infantry. Despite the shortcoming, the 194th slaughtered over 500 Japanese on the battlefield with machine guns. They managed to hold the line along the southern bank of the Agno River from Carmen to Highway #13.[117]

A large share of the Philippine Army abandoned the battlefield leaving the tankers alone except for the Philippine Scouts and the 31st Infantry Regiment. (the 31st Infantry Regiment, an all American unit will be referred to as the 31st) As the battle line shifted back and forth, Manny kept busy digging one foxhole after another. Unknown at the time, the 194th stood alone on the eastern flank as General Weaver recalled the 192nd.

On the 25th, the Japanese installed a 240mm canon on Batangas that was effectively used against Corregidor. It not only inflicted damage but also demoralized the defenders. When the rock was bombed, the defenders knew it would soon end but the gun never ceased firing. Shells and bombs seemed to rain on Corregidor without end.[118]

General Homma experienced little resistance from the 71st Philippine Division which was poorly trained and equipped. Most of the men received no instruction on how to use their WWI Enfield rifles. The Philippine 11th Division did no better and the Japanese easily broke away from the beaches at Lingayen Gulf. As the Japanese raced south toward Manila, they landed another force at Lamon Bay just 60 miles south of Manila. MacArthur was caught between two armies and hightailed it for Bataan. As evacuees from Manila arrived at Hospital #1 in Limay, MacArthur ordered his family and staff to board the *SS DON ESTERBAN* for transportation to Corregidor. Then, it was Christmas Day.

On Christmas Eve, Japanese bombers struck Manila but *CANOPUS* remained unscathed. On Christmas Day, *CANOPUS* moved to safer waters inside the confines of Mariveles Bay at the southern tip of the Bataan Peninsula. Captain Sackett moved her into a small cove and camouflaged the ship which fooled the Japanese for a few days. The wisdom of declaring Manila an Open City so quickly and without consultation with the Navy is questionable. The move stranded 3,000 American and Allied citizens plus the Manila residents to face the Japanese Army alone.[119]

On 29 December, Japanese bombers found *CANOPUS* and damaged her. Brave and competent damage control parties saved her. Sackett then placed a large list on the ship, painted large holes on her decks, lit smoke pots to imitate fires, and moved her guns ashore. Then *CANOPUS* was open for business again as the men worked nights and slept days. The last submarine departed in January so her entire effort was in direct support of the fight for Bataan. Small craft sailors received invaluable assistance and every passing soldier found at least one night of respite for their starving bodies including a clean bed and full meal.

Mansfield celebrated Christmas with a decent hot meal that was most welcome for his hungry body and attended church services provided by one of the Army Chaplains. It was a beautiful day and for a few fleeting moments, he forgot the terror at hand. To the north, the rest of the 194th enjoyed a similar day near Gerona. Some of the men enjoyed the opportunity to attend mass in a nearby church while the Japanese celebrated with almost continuous air strikes against the defender's positions.[120]

Bataan was selected as the place to delay the Japanese in WPO three years earlier due to the close proximity to Manila and the very rugged terrain. The peninsula is 35 miles long and 20 miles wide at its northernmost extremity. The peninsula forms the western side of Manila Bay while its western shore is on the South China Sea. A few miles south is the Island of Corregidor. The southern end of the Zambales Mountain Range runs down the middle of the peninsula with the area dominated by the volcanoes Mount Natib to the north and Mount Bataan to the south, both exceeding 4,000 feet in height. The foothills of the Zambales fall off abruptly into the sea on the west. To the east is a swampy marshland with cultivated lowlands. Most of the peninsula is covered in dense jungles or rain forests and the coastline is rocky with numerous cliffs thereby reducing the likelihood of a seaward invasion. The valley between the two mountains is relatively flat with the 2,000 foot high Mount Samat overlooking the valley used primarily for agriculture. The peninsula is a very rocky and hostile environment with rock and stone often covered by dense woods and near impenetrable jungle. The land festered with disease and ugly life forms while being a treasure for an entomologist. A single road ran down the east and the west sides of the peninsula and linked together near Mariveles Harbor. A narrow cobblestone road ran across, east to west, about 15 miles north of Mariveles. Only one road entered the peninsula from San Fernando. A natural weakness of moving into Bataan was the steep slopes of Mount Natib that prevented coordination between the Allies on either side of the mountain. To the south, there was no escape as the peninsula ended in the sea.[121]

Fifty million bushels of rice was to be stored at all times at a rice depot in Cabanatuan. It was a part of WPO that required

99-HARM

900,000 pounds of rice to supply 10,000 Americans for six months in Bataan. Another 1,080,000 pounds was supposed to be stored for the Philippine Scouts and 9,000,000 for the Philippine Army. 10,980,000 pounds of rice were mandated to be on hand. The National Agriculture and Rice Corporation was founded years earlier for that explicit purpose. Not one grain of that rice was moved to Bataan even though it was on hand. Mismanagement and indecision with supplies was as cruel to the Allies as was the Japanese offensive.[122]

In another battle for supplies, a ship convoy was sent to the Philippines by the War Department before the attack at Pearl Harbor but was diverted from Manila to the Fiji Islands due to the Japanese invasion. The convoy was scheduled to arrive near Christmas and carried 4,600 men, an artillery brigade with twenty 75mm guns, eighteen P-40 fighters and fifty-two A-24 attack bombers. How the Allies could have used the support and supplies.[123]

Glen Berry at Clark was given yet another task. He was directed to organize the withdrawal of all military personnel from Clark to Bataan. The withdrawal took a few days as the motorized convoy moved slowly south. Berry did accomplish the task and received the Bronze Star for his achievement.[124]

On Bataan, MacArthur divided the army into two corps. He utilized the physical geography of Bataan as the dividing points by using Mounts Natib and Silanganan, then drawing a line north and south down the center of the peninsula. The first line of defense was an east-west line beginning near Matatang. South of this line was the Main Line of Defense or MLR with a reserve line further south. The east half of the peninsula was called II Corps commanded by General Parker who had 25,000 troops along a 15,000-yard line beginning near Abucay.[125]

II Corps defended the relatively flat area. Heavily wooded in some areas and near the coastline where there were numerous swamps, fishponds, and rice paddies. The line was protected on the east by the lowlands and west by Mount Natib. The defenders built numerous gun emplacements and foxholes but failed to con-

ROBERT K. HARMUTH

sider the Japanese might traverse the steep slopes of Natib. On the coast and straddling the east road was the fresh 57th Philippine Scout Infantry with the Philippine 41st in the center and the 51st to the west. These troops were backed by the 41st Field Artillery Regiment with sixteen 75mm guns and eight 2.95 howitzers. The 51st had eight 75mm guns on wood trailers. II Corps was inexperienced and ill equipped. In reserve was the 21st Division which lost 600 men a few nights earlier. The 11th was also there but had been badly mauled earlier and took up positions east and south of the 21st.[126]

General Wainwright commanded I Corps that defended the west half of the peninsula and was organized on 7 January. I Corps was comprised of 22,500 men and was primarily the same troops he had in North Force; the 26th Cavalry, 1st Regular Division, 31st Philippine Division, the 91st Division, and the beaten up 71st. I Corps defended a line about four miles long from the west coast to Mount Silanganan. The heart of I Corps was the Scout 26th which had fought valiantly south from Lingayen Gulf. The western units were battle experienced but short of equipment and ammunition.

On 31 December, Admiral Nimitz became Commander, Pacific Fleet and shifted his flag to the submarine *USS GRAYLING* since all major ships in Pearl had been destroyed. The admiral was a submariner and enjoyed the fact his submarines were his first line of defense.[127] Little did he know his submarines would accomplish so much to end the war yet would have to fight for the slightest of recognition at war's end.[128]

By 5 January 1942, all the Allied troops had made their way into Bataan through the bottleneck at Layac Junction. Bridges across the Pamanga River at Calumpit and the Cuolo River at Layac Junction were blown thereby forming another impasse between the Allies and the Japanese.

Manny had yet to see a shot fired in anger except during the air raids. The entire 31st had missed major encounters with the Japanese but that changed drastically on 28 December. The regiment was ordered forward to prepare a defensive position, a line if you will, between Dilalupihan and Layac Junction. The 'Main Line of Resistance" (MLR) was ten or eleven miles to the south of the 31st's position. By 5 January 1942, the 31st was in position and received orders to "shoot anything that moves in front of you."[129]

As Manny squatted in his foxhole, his mind drifted back to Mountain View and the wide-open spaces around Salinas. The cool breezes and sunny skies were anything like Bataan. The place crawled with insects. If it wasn't the bugs and mosquitoes, the snakes and spiders kept them company. He looked around and felt like an extra in a Tarzan film. The creeper ferns, rattan vines, and kava brush tied the area like a knot a Boy Scout couldn't untie. He had pushed through marshes and swamps with pools the size of football fields and fought with the bottom as the rotten smelly bogs grabbed at his boots. The top of the water was covered with algae and rotting flotsam while the mosquitoes rose from the marsh surface as dark clouds of discomfort.

Manny wondered what would happen next as he sat on the bottom of his foxhole with a vegetation canopy for a roof. At the moment, 5-6 January, the majority of the 31st were situated in the middle of an artillery dual with rounds constantly flying overhead in both directions. It certainly would have been nice to have someone to talk to during this period of terror of the unknown. Most of the men rid themselves of most of their unnecessary gear and equipment that weighed heavily on them when they moved. Some of the men were ill as they sat in the filth of their foxhole. They were in a tangled jungle not far from Olangapo on Subic Bay.

The following morning, action began early with artillery fire from the 75mm guns of the 23rd Field Artillery. Their first salvo was on target and the next order was, "fire for effect." Morale sky-rocketed as American rounds found their target salvo after salvo – until about 1000. Then the Japanese returned fire with their heavier 105mm and 155mm howitzers. Japanese spotter aircraft directed the artillery and American fire faltered. The Filipino 88th Artillery Battery commenced firing in support of the 23rd but only succeeded in adding targets for the Japanese spotters. The 88th lost three of four 75mm guns and half their men within a few minutes.[130] A large thicket of bamboo caught fire near the 23rd's positions and quickly destroyed the immobile weapons. The Japanese slowly silenced the American artillery, then concentrated on the infantry.[131] It was not a good day.

Manny hugged the bottom of his foxhole and wished he had dug it deeper as incoming artillery rounds pounded closer to the 31st's positions. The ground heaved and rolled with every explosion and by 1500, the Filipino Artillery Battery was quiet. Lookouts reported Japanese armor activity over the next ridge followed by infantry. Small arms started, sounding akin to a parade of snare drums. In the air, a number of Japanese Val dive-bombers dropped bombs and strafed their position but the jungle canopy hid the location of the 31st. Fortunately, no one was injured nor killed in the first attacks in K-Company although some other companies and the 31st Regiment Medics had a few injuries and deaths.[132].

As Japanese artillery fell accurately along the 31st's lines, many foxholes were dug deeper. The men were scared but held their positions. Around 1400, the Japanese probed the 31st's lines with a few patrols across the Culo River. The probe successfully located a weakness between the 31st and the 72nd Infantry Regiment. A couple patrols moved forward between the two units but B-Company of the 31st quickly filled the gap and fought furiously. As the small arms fight waged, C-Company moved over in support of B-Company. The 3rd Battalion, Manny's battalion, was located just behind the defensive line as a reserve unit. I-Company and L-Company were called up to support the battle while Manny and K-Company were held in reserve. The Japanese were quickly repelled.[133]

Manny was grateful and said a prayer of thanks until, "K-Company, move out!" Under the cover of darkness, K-Company moved up to the battle line. The stillness of the night was broken by sounds emanating from every direction. He jumped at the rustle of every leaf and scream of any number of little critters in the jungle. He sweat profusely and it wasn't warm. The company reached the B-Company position and jumped into their foxholes and Manny relaxed a bit within the confines of the hole. He dozed off in a restless sleep when he heard, "Sarge, there's some crazy looking green lights below about three hundred yards out." Manny peered out of his foxhole and stared into the blackness in front of him. He saw weird green lights that seemed to dance about. Captain Talbot shouted out, "I've got them. They're Japs down there in the sugar cane and using green flashlights for some reason. Stand by to open fire men! Bring those machine guns up here on the ridge." Manny flipped off the safety of his M-1 and rolled a bead of sweat across his sights. He was ready. "Commence firing!" ordered Talbot. The entire length of the K-Company line erupted with a roar as the ridge flickered with the flash of gunfire. Two lines of tracers led down the slope from the .30 caliber machine guns and into the cane field. The green lights jumped about for a few seconds then went out. The sounds of screams filled the air from wounded and dying Japanese, then . . . "Cease fire!"

The roar of gunfire fell to a few scattered shots, then silence. K-Company jumped out of their foxholes and cheered wildly. They cheered in victory and in relief. Manny sat down on the edge of his hole, sighed, smiled, and looked at his shaking hands. They won their first encounter – and his pants were still clean and dry.

The joy of victory was short lived as the Japanese launched a massive attack early the following morning. The Allies were forced to retreat and did so successfully under cover fire. The Japanese were so successful the Allies narrowly avoided being cut off with the loss of the east road. A couple untested company commanders were relieved for their inability to cope with the fighting. It was the first trial under fire for most of the officers and men.[134] The order to withdraw was received about 2200 and the 26th Cavalry moved out first. The remainder of the defensive line moved out at 0100 to the east down Route #7 to Highway #101 which is the main north-south road along Manila Bay. This left the Philippine 71st and 72nd to hold until the other units were clear. By dawn on

7 January, Manny and the 31st were safely behind the MLR. Needless to say, they were happy to get out of their holes but not pleased about retreating before the Japanese.

Unknown to the Japanese was the Allied retreat into Bataan was part of the WPO plan. The holding action in Bataan completely fooled the Japanese into thinking the task of conquering Luzon was a cakewalk. The Americans and Filipinos rapidly and passively retreated, giving little resistance to the advancing Japanese army. The Japanese War Plan schedule required taking Luzon by 15 January 1942. Three weeks after landing on Luzon, the Japanese felt confident the battle was virtually over and moved up plans for the invasion of the Dutch East Indies by a month. Field Marshall Terauchi in Saigon pulled out the elite Japanese 14th Army's 48th Division and 5th Air Group for the invasion of Java. All that remained on Luzon was the 16th Army Division, 65th Brigade, the 7th Tank Regiment, and a new air unit with less than 70 aircraft. The 65th Brigade of 6,600 draftees replaced the 15,000 man battle tested 48th Division.

With the departure of the 48th, Japan readied to move into Bataan with the 9th Regiment of the 16th and the 65th Brigade. Japanese intelligence reports indicated Allied manpower at under 25,000 men when actually the count was over 100,000 men. General Masaharu Homma split his forces in two; one group headed south on the east road while the other traveled cross-country to the naval base at Olangapo.

The 192nd tankers were in the Lingayen Gulf area when the Japanese landed and were ordered to retreat back to Bataan. Twenty-four of their light tanks fought a delaying action in Baliuag at the bridge. They lost one tank when the bridge was blown prematurely. The crew was rescued and the guns saved then the tankers continued south.[135] Nine more tanks of the 192nd didn't make it to Bataan. Meanwhile, the 194th was conducting similar operations.[136]

Pieces and parts of units straggled into the Bataan Peninsula causing a nightmare in reorganization. Ten days prior to the first battle, only 14 of 28 combat regiments designated to defend Bataan were actually in the peninsula. Manila fell on 29 December after which the Japanese Imperial Air Force turned its entire attention on the southern tip of Bataan and Corregidor where they felt the Allies had withdrawn. In reality, the remnants of all the units were in Bataan frantically building defensive positions further north on the peninsula. Some of the last straggling units had less than a day's rest prior to the opening battles for Bataan.

The 194th moved out from their encounters along the Agno River and moved south, covering the general withdrawal into Bataan. The MLR was strengthened near Tarlac and on 28 December, the South Force withdrew toward Calumpit where the 194th was to defend the bridge while the remainder of the South Force crossed enroute Bataan via San Fernando. Mansfield and C-Company rejoiced on the 29th as they rejoined the rest of the battalion. [137]

The medical corps scrambled to set up medical facilities for the ever-increasing number of casualties. The main hospital in Manila overflowed so the corpsmen and medics set up field hospitals in schools and churches. Medics stationed at Fort McKinley moved to Estado Mayor along the Pasig River. From there, they trucked beds and equipment from the old wooden barracks to the field hospitals. On the 18th, the field hospitals overflowed so the medics moved in the new Jai Alai Building. The playing field was filled with bunks and equipment. No sooner was the field set up and all medical personnel were ordered out of the city because MacArthur declared Manila an open city. [138] MacArthur's order caught the medics unprepared as well as the Navy and most Army units.

Frantically, medics and corpsmen gathered as much equipment and medicine as possible and headed into the Bataan Peninsula. The convoys of wounded and equipment stopped at Camp Limay where a medical facility was again set up. The hospital utilized the old Philippine Army barracks and was designated as Hospital #1.[139] Hospital #2 was an open-air hospital under the trees. Each bunk had a foxhole or trench dug alongside so during an air raid, the patient just rolled out of his bed and into the hole. Near the end, Japanese camped all around the hospital knowing they were safe from the prowling guns of Corregidor which wouldn't endanger fellow Americans.[140]

Only a month passed before Hospital #1 heard the sounds of war to the north. The Allies continued their slow retreat to the south as the front slowly closed on the hospital. The hospital was moved again, this time to the tip of Bataan in full view of Corregidor. The move had to be done at night to escape ever-present Japanese aircraft. The path was tortuous in the mountain area named Little Bagio reminiscent of the recreational area at Bagio. A narrow road from Mariveles was the only means to reach the area. The hospital remained safe until April when Japanese aircraft found and bombed the facility. Despite huge red crosses, the buildings and tents were bombed with serious injuries and many deaths.[141]

As the 194th moved slowly southward, they were ordered to turn around and face the onslaught south of Manila and outside of Piis. LT Needham decided to conduct a reconnaissance to check on Japanese strength even though reports indicated nothing but small arms weapons in the area. His tank traveled less than a few hundred yards when it was struck in the turret by a hidden anti-tank gun. The Salinas, California Tank Battalion lost its first member to the war.[142]

Mansfield and crew eventually solved the problem of remaining uneaten by mosquitoes at night. They couldn't remain in the tanks at night without horrible cramps in the morning so they slept on the ground alongside the tank. The men found mosquito netting that slipped over the head and kept their hands in their pockets while sleeping.[143]

New Year's Eve was not a night for celebrating for any Allied unit. Mansfield was in a Manila suburb when one of the 194th tanks collided with the statue of Jose' Rizal. The tankers worked all night to repair the damage but by dawn, the tank remained inoperable. As they continued struggling with the tank, a Filipino shouted, "Hey Joe, you better take off. The Japs are right behind me!" Quickly, the men stripped the tank and threw everything useable in a half-track then broke a hole in the engine block. They had to move fast to catch up with the rest of 194th. The only guide they had through the countryside was an old Sonoco Motor Oil map.[144] At the same time, the 192nd was south of San Fernando watching the city go up in smoke.

As both tank battalions acted as rearguards, they joined near the Calumpit bridge just before the Army Engineers blew it up. For some reason, the bridge blew before the last 17 tanks of the 194th crossed the river. A detachment of the 200th Coastal Artillery joined the tankers at the bridge prior to the daily Japanese air raid. The 200th put up a fierce wall of anti-aircraft fire that drove the aircraft off and climbing for altitude and safety above the fire but not before three of the aircraft buried themselves into the surrounding terrain.[145] The tank crews removed the guns and left the tanks blocking the road. Unbeknownst to the tankers, there was a ford in the river less than a block away. One of the 192nd's half-tracks was the last vehicle to safely cross the bridge as it headed south.

Mansfield's company received orders on 3 January 1942 to return to the front line near Guagua. One of the tanks broke down and required assistance. The tank was found and repairs begun while the Scouts opened fire with self-propelled 75mm canons at the Japanese several miles away. It was a harrowing experience for Mansfield and they supported the Scouts with machine gun fire. Repairs were effected and the company rewarded by local Filipinos bearing fresh chicken. Suddenly, the ground shook with Japanese incoming artillery, raising the roofs on the local's homes, called nipas.

That evening, the 194th lookouts spotted a large group of Japanese close by. The tankers were alerted and opened up with the machine guns and Thompson sub machine guns, driving the enemy away. At dawn, the men looked at Guagua and saw nothing but ruins and the smoldering remainds of a church. The battalion set off to the south and was overtaken by a long column of Filipino troops in brightly colored buses known as Pambuscos. "Hey Joe, whatcha goin to do?" The tankers felt it was the only sentence the Filipinos knew. "Get your asses back in the buses and bail out of here before the Nips decide to use you for target practice!" "But Joe, those aren't my orders," replied a sergeant. A little persuasion got them back in the buses but the last bus was too slow. A Zero screamed out the sky and blew the bus completely off the road killing or maiming the passengers.[146]

It was a day for unusual activities and the next incident happened minutes later with the 192nd. Bill Hauser and his half-track was ordered north toward Lubao to check out the area. As they traveled up the road, they came upon a vicious crossfire between two Filipino units shooting at each other from opposite sides of the road. Neither side recognized the other. Hauser had to pass through them and he would return fire if they fired upon him. He slowly crept down the road and both sides ceased fire until he passed. When he was clear, the gunfire recommenced.

Much to the surprise of Generals Wainwright and Sutherland, the Quartermaster Corps reported on 24 December there was 20,000 more men than anticipated on the peninsula. Immediately, the men went from three meals a day to two rice meals, which was reduced further in late January. If the men were fed three meals a day, the chow would have run out in 30 days. Thus was formulated the infamous "Bataan Ration." The ration wasn't close to a half ration and consisted of:

3.7 ounces of rice

1.8 ounces of sugar

1.2 ounces of canned milk

2.44 ounces of canned fish, salmon or sardines, tomatoes when available, 10 men per can[147]

Since 10 December, the quartermasters moved 35 train loads of supplies from the fronts to depots at Tarlac and Guagua in the north and Los Banos below Manila in the south. The problem was to get the supplies into Bataan. Barges were used in Manila but in the north, food, gasoline, ammunition, and other supplies were destroyed for there was no means to move them. Yet, the Allies failed to utilize thousands of empty vehicles moving into Bataan from the north. Huge quantities of rice weren't moved since the Commonwealth Government forbade rice and sugar from leaving the province. In Tarlac, Japanese owned wholesalers refused to sell the quartermasters clothing, canned beef, and fish. USAFFE Headquarters did not permit the Americans to confiscate supplies. It was another example of Japanese civilian support inside an Allied nation.[148]

On 30 December, outside the Malinta Tunnel on Corregidor, a bizarre ceremony was staged. It was the second inaugural of Manuel Quezon as President of the Philippines. On New Year's Day, the inter-island steamer *MAYON* lifted 600 men of the 19th Bombardment Group from Mariveles Harbor and took them to the DelMonte Plantation on Mindanao to rebuild the airstrip. The ship also laid an underwater telephone cable for communications between Bataan and Corregidor.

The stores and businesses in Manila were boarded up and quiet but the streets were a madhouse of activity as thousands of citizens moved back into the "open city" after hiding for a week or more in the countryside. General Homma was near the city gates when he halted his men. Every man was made to shower and put on a clean uniform for entering Manila. He wanted his army to enter the city and parade, not pillage. Huge clouds of smoke continued to rise from the city from burning supplies and anything useful to the Japanese. Although the senior general in Luzon was ultimately held responsible for atrocities caused by his subordinates, most accounts paint General Homma as an honorable man.

A few American submarines were diverted in January from war patrols to move badly needed supplies to the defenders. The primary effort was 3-inch anti-aircraft rounds and machine gun ammunition to Corregidor. The Japanese established a functional naval blockade around Corregidor and the Bataan Peninsula that most surface ships could not penetrate. It was effective against the submarines due to serious torpedo malfunction. In December, January, and February only eleven Japanese ships were confirmed sunk after American submarines fired 223 torpedoes. The following months were tough on the Asiatic Fleet submarines. *S-36* ran aground and was scuttled in Makasar Strait; *SHARK* was sunk off Mendanao with the loss of all hands; *PERCH* was depth charged and scuttled with all hands taken prisoners of war, and *PIGEON* was sunk off Corregidor.[149]

MacArthur set areas and lines of resistance on 2 January along the two roads leading into Bataan with the Filipino 11th and 21st Infantry Divisions. The 26th Cavalry and both tank battalions supported them. The South Force was already in Bataan and Wainwright's North Force moved south conducting holding maneuvers. They dug in between the Zambales Mountains to the west and the swamps of Pamoangan to the east. However, Homma sent the major portion of the 14th toward Manila expecting it to be the point of most resistance. The Filipinos stopped the Japanese the first night at a small barrio called Pio. But they were pushed back by heavy artillery and overwhelming numbers the following day. A highlight of the encounter was the 21st's artillery that broke attack after Japanese attack with their antiquated 75mm guns at almost point-blank range with no infantry support. During the night of 4 January, the 21st retreated under cover of darkness to their next point of resistance on the south side of the Germain River.[150]

During the night of 2 January, the Filipino Army retreated to San Fernando with the 194th covering their rear. The remaining South Force and 192nd also passed through San Fernando and crossed the bridge leading to Betis. Mansfield rode on his tank and observed the abandoned city. It was a ghost town and silent except for an occasional hand grenade from the Fifth Column. Betis had been a quaint little barrio amidst a background of forests and renowned for furniture construction and woodcarving. The main dirt road through the town was lined with fascinating little wood shops filled with busy craftsmen. Both North and South

Forces headed south to a new defensive line. Mansfield 's group was assigned outpost duty on the road south of Betis. In the morning of 3 January, Mansfield's platoon heard and sighted the lead tanks of the Japanese 7th Tank Regiment. He called in a report to the 194th headquarters. His platoon exchanged fire for a few hours with the superior Japanese numbers but luckily none of the American tanks were hit. At least Mansfield fired armor-piercing shells at armor. Then they moved south to join the rest of the 194th in Guagua.[151]

While the 21st was busy with the Japanese, the 11th had yet to face a major battle having been kept busy with reconn duties. The 11th met the foe on 3 January at the Guagua-Porac Road. Mansfield and C-Company provided tank support to the 11th until the Japanese massed in such strength, their artillery forced C-Company to fall back. Mansfield was knocked around inside the tank as exploding rounds narrowly missed. Shrapnel banged off the tank's thick skin and small arms fire rattled the tank alongside his head. He greeted the withdrawal with relief and a thank you prayer. The tankers remained on the road and as they moved slowly south, they encountered small groups and units of the enemy which they dispatched easily. It would have been easier if they had the correct ammunition. The 37mm guns got hot and the tanks filled with acrid smoke from the breech but Mansfield and his colleagues loved it. They were having a turkey shoot at the expense of the Japanese infantry. The 11th fought from their foxholes as the tanks backed down the road and exacted a heavy toll of the enemy.[152]

About 1300 on 5 January, the Japanese 7th supported by 150mm howitzers broke through the Allied lines near Guagua. The tankers came under fire again and Mansfield ducked and jumped as rounds landed nearby. A-Company of the 192nd from Janesville, Wisconsin caught the majority of the rounds when they attempted a counterattack near Guagua. Late in the afternoon, the tanks moved back toward Lubao where they were confronted by a Japanese infantry battalion. The tankers shredded the battalion but Lubao was in ruins. As the tanks departed the area, they came

ROBERT K. HARMUTH

under heavy artillery and mortar attack that backed them down the road toward Santa Cruz.[153]

The 194th finally cleared the shelling and hunkered down in a line along the road and the Gumain River. Their tanks, half-tracks, and Bren gun carriers dug in along a line perpendicular to the road while squads of men dug in on the flanks and forward outposts. At dusk, aircraft bombed the positions, injuring a few men.

A full moon lighted the area when the Japanese attacked the tankers across a flat turnip field. The 194th barked and bit in response, mowing down Japanese infantry by the dozens with machine guns and the 75mm canon on the half-tracks. Some of the Japanese wore white T-shirts that made perfect targets in the bright moon light. It was another slaughter; this time it was the Minnesota B-Company along with Mansfield and the California C-Company that drew the majority of Japanese blood. "You don't have to lead'em Mansfield baby. Pour it to 'em!" shouted one of his tank mates inside the tank. His Sarge put him on a .30 caliber machine gun on the turret. Mansfield swung the gun toward the yelling Japanese and sent streams of yellow fire up and down the charging horde. His teeth clenched and jaw muscles working, he watched the tracers spit out as he fired short bursts. The empty brass shell casings clanged off the turret and ground while the driver fired his machine gun from inside the tank. In minutes, there were no Japanese troops left standing and the screams of terror were reduced to groans of agony from the wounded. The battle was over. The 11th and 194th, both of whom had been fighting since 2 January, were pulled back in the evening of the 5th for some rest. "Amen to that" mumbled Mansfield. On the other side of the battlefield, the Japanese units that fought the 194th and the 11th were so badly mauled, they were pulled out and replaced by the Formosa 1st Infantry.[154]

Across the north of the peninsula was Highway #7 that leads eastward from Olangapo to Dinalupihan. There it meets Highway #110 that runs from north to the southern tip of Bataan ending near the port city of Mariveles. South of the road intersection was the barrio of Layac where the Culo River crosses Highway #110.

The bridge over the river became a key site in the temporary defensive line for the Allies to hold while the real Abucay-Mauban Defense Line was established. This was a major defensive effort by the 31st and they held the line through March and into the first few days of April 1942.[155]

A strange sight greeted the locals on 5 January along Highway #110. For as far as the eye could see was a continuous column of American and Filipino troops covered in dirt and grime, thoroughly exhausted as they marched and stumbled southward. Some of the men wore denim and others olive drab and khaki. Mingled in the column were Army nurses. Among the marchers moved vehicles of every size, shape, and description including some odd looking pieces of equipment that were artillery pieces made obsolete prior to the conclusion of WWI. Near the rear of the column appeared the new General Stuart tanks serving rear guard action. The 192nd and 194th significantly contributed to the success of the Allied withdrawal into Bataan. The tankers protected the rear throughout the withdrawal and stymied the Japanese a number of times in direct head-on confrontations. The successes were a result of the battalion commanders' planning since Wainwright rarely utilized the tanks in his strategies.

Men were separated from their units in the melee but knew they had to move south into Bataan. Some divisions marched and counter marched in absolute confusion. Meanwhile, MacArthur reported to Washington, the withdrawal was a well-greased and organized operation. It was a dream in his mind.[156] The long column wandered through villages and barrios, past old huts, farm animals, and hungry dogs. Men occasionally stopped at the smell of cooking or glanced with a yearning look at a chicken in a yard. It was an exhausted and hungry lot that moved down the east road, most dragging their weapons and bedrolls behind them. Many carried bandoleers of ammunition and a rifle with a well-worn .45 holster on one hip and a canteen on the other. They struggled into Bataan, a peninsula with insufficient farmland to "raise breakfast for a platoon."[157]

The next move was to funnel the 11th and 21st Divisions across the large steel span Culo River Bridge ahead of the advancing Japanese. On 5 and 6 January, the North Force passed through Layac and crossed the bridge to the south. A delaying action was carried out by 2,500 men of the 71st, 26th Philippine Scout Cavalry, and Manny with the 31st Regiment. The bridge was blown and the Allies faced yet another challenge. The Main Line of Defense was being constructed and organized at Abucay but the Japanese had to be delayed south of Layac and along the Culo River long enough to complete the defense line. Wainwright formed a covering force then turned over the organization to General Parker, Commander Bataan Defense Force.[158]

The Culo River runs roughly east to west at the delaying line with the 71st Infantry on the right as they faced north. The eastern flank was marsh and rice patties, then the east coastline of the peninsula. Next to them was the 72nd Infantry that was badly mauled two weeks earlier at Sison. Both regiments were poorly trained and their equipment even worse. The 31st moved up from the south the evening of 4 January and took up positions in the center of the covering line just west or left of the 71st. Manny and the 31st was about to see action for the first time as a complete regiment but they lost many key men to the Filipino units requiring leadership. New personnel filled many 31st's key billets. The 31st rode in the back of trucks all the way from Cabcaben. Manny climbed out of the truck, stiff and sore, and readied himself for the fight. He was grateful to start the fighting rather than remain in the truck longer. Their weapons were barely adequate so the area was searched for additional guns such as riot guns to use against Japanese snipers. Snipers often hid in treetops and the riot guns sprayed the foliage with lead shot.[159]

The 26th Cavalry arrived the night of the 5th, greatly reduced in numbers and settled in to the west of the 31st and in the foothills of the Zamabales Mountains. The 71st's artillery positioned behind the 31st. The 71st only had eight guns. The tankers backed up the center of the line. Again, communications were not complete and no unit could talk with the tankers. There was little protection for the men except some small trees and underbrush.[160]

Mansfield and C-Company tanks rolled into position and prepared for the attack. As the radioman for the tanks, he remained glued to the radio but never received an order. The men sat at the ready in and on their tanks, listening to the battle and awaiting orders that never arrived. During the holding and rear guard action from Lingayen Gulf to the present position, the 194th lost 24 tanks.[161]

Meanwhile, Manny was doing what he did best; digging a foxhole but at least the ground near the river was soft. As he scooped the last few handfuls of dirt out of his hole, "Okay men, pick up your gear and get back into the trucks! We're moving back to Layac." "Damn, and it was such a nice hole too," mumbled Manny as he climbed back into the back of the truck. The 31st rumbled back to Layac and took up new positions directly in the center of the line. "Okay, let's get those foxholes dug, asap!" The ground was harder and Manny scrapped and dug frantically with his tiny shovel.

As the sun rose at 0722 on the 6th and despite the previous rough day, Manny was wide-awake. K-Company was pulled back near the 192nd tankers and held in reserve. Nothing moved as far as they eye could see and lookouts were posted in forward and camouflaged positions. Taking advantage of the quiet, most of the men tried to get some well-deserved sleep until about 1000 when the American 155mm opened fire without response from the Japanese.

Shortly thereafter, lead Japanese units were sighted approaching the defensive line down the road to Layac. Silently, General Selleck awaited the Japanese to come into range. At 1030, he gave the artillery "guns free." The artillery immediately took the road under fire and the first few rounds landed squarely on target whereupon the artillery shifted to rapid fire. They walked artillery rounds up and down the road, then directed fire to follow the fleeing Japanese into the fields. The Philippine Scout artillery was magnificent and caught the leading Japanese artillery unprepared. Eventually, Japanese artillery returned fire and their accuracy was devastating. Despite the heroic actions of Selleck and the Scouts, the Filipinos sagged, then gave way to the artillery barrage while Japanese aircraft again acted as spotters.

Manny listened to the artillery rounds landing ahead of him around the B Company and C-Company positions. About 1600, Japanese patrols found a gap between the 72nd and the 31st and attacked right into B-Company. The men fought well for awhile but then panicked. The fight moved to C-Company that was left alone without B-Company on their right flank. K-Company was called in from reserve status to plug the hole left by B-Company. Manny raced forward, running at a crouch and ducking at the sounds of passing shells and exploding artillery. He found a foxhole and dove into its safety. K-Company fought bravely and fiercely. Manny's right arm ached from the recoil of his rifle and constantly moving the bolt action. Within the first few rounds he fired, he stopped shaking and deliberately fired round after round at the advancing enemy. Order was restored and the Japanese driven back. K-Company was returned to the reserve position while the hole was plugged by I-Company and L-Company.[162]

I-Company caught hell from Japanese artillery that zeroed in on their position. K-Company was called up again to support I-Company and the Filipinos to their right. Manny felt he was walking into the "Valley of Death." The Japanese artillery altered the landscape around the Allied positions as Manny and K-Company moved forward again. Enemy fire was heavier than before and he ran a few steps then embraced the earth awaiting another short lull. K-Company advanced to the right of I-Company's position and the defenses were restored. The battle quieted for a few minutes, giving K-Company the opportunity to shift left into foxholes originally dug by B-Company. As the men crawled into the safety of the holes, the Japanese commenced firing again with greater severity.

Manny barely had time to brush the dirt off when the bullets flew over his new burrow. He thanked God for the foxhole and commenced deepening it. Periodically, he peered over the berm at the enemy and sought a target, then emptied his clip on the enemy. Suddenly, white flares erupted all around their position. They were signals from Japanese infiltrators that they had successfully passed through the Allied lines. "My God, how does one fight an enemy that's all around you," asked Manny to no one in particular. The incoming artillery rounds bombarded their positions. Manny no longer jumped and flinched at each explosion for he learned how to judge the closeness of the impact by the shrill scream of the incoming round. They weren't aware of it at the time but they faced General Homma's infamous 14th Division. At 2200, orders were passed down the line to withdraw with K-Company remaining to cover the rest of the battalion. It is said by some that the term "Battlin' Bastards" was coined during this encounter.[163]

K-Company moved forward to the edge of a rice paddy and set up their machine guns on the south berm. The entire company assumed the prone position along the berm with their weapons at the ready and waited, hearts in their throats. The wait was brief. About midnight they heard the rustling of equipment and splashing feet moving across the rice paddy. The company commander ordered, "Turn on the lights!" The paddy was illuminated by six spotlights, catching the Japanese infantrymen by surprise. "Commence Firing!" The Japanese had nowhere to seek refuge as K-Company opened fire with .50 and .30 caliber machine guns and small arms. Boot camp training rang in Manny's ears, "pick your target, follow it and slowly squeeze." The enemy dropped in large numbers but eventually returned fire at the searchlights. "Keep firing at them men. Give it too 'em!" The one-sided battle continued for only ten minutes but it seemed like seconds. Manny and his company poured lead into the paddy until no more return fire was heard. The quiet was awesome with only the sound of moans and groans of wounded forward of K-Company's position.[164]

Manny awakened with a start following a sound sleep of a few hours. It was sunrise and he looked out of his foxhole to the night's battle scene in front of him. He stared in disbelief at a mound of dead humanity. "God, how awful," he mumbled in anguish as he observed the aftermath of the battle. A number of Japanese trucks emerged at the north end of the rice paddy flying a white flag. They returned to the field to pick up the dead. Manny shuttered involuntarily a few times as he watched the dead bodies picked up and thrown into the back of a truck like sacks of potatoes. A dead soldier was worth little to the Japanese.

The withdrawal went well and covering units moved south, breaking contact with the enemy. But breaking contact was a blessing for the Japanese since the Allies didn't know the enemy's location while the Japanese tracked the Allies by air reconnaissance. The Japanese bombarded Hermosa, leveled the little town, and moved in from the northwest as the 31st moved directly south on 8 January and arrived on the Abucay-Hacienda Line on the 9th.

At 1500 on the 9th, General Nara attacked under a barrage of artillery with flags flying and bugles blaring. The general expected to see the Filipinos flee but they stood their ground and returned a withering cross fire of artillery. The Japanese were halted so Nara called in an air attack against the Scout artillery but the attack was ineffective. The Scouts camouflaged their pieces well and spotter aircraft saw only bamboo, mango groves, cane fields, and coconut palms. But the artillery couldn't stop the Japanese by itself and eventually, the enemy was on the move again. The artillery did keep the Japanese off the roads which slowed the advance, bogging down tanks and trucks in the wet rice fields. Nara received reports from the aircraft of huge masses of vehicles on the roads moving south, indicative of an Allied retreat.[165]

The 57th placed Scouts in the field in advance of their positions who observed the Japanese stockpile supplies around Hermosa and advance on the village of Orani. This prompted Allied artillery to open fire on 10 January which left Hermosa burning and killing many of the enemy. Again, the artillery slowed the advance but soon the Japanese reached the Main Line of Resistance (MLR). There, the Japanese advance came to a halt.

Thus began a series of days for Manny and the 31ˢᵗ of fighting one day, retiring to rest and regroup, only to go forward and fight again. Manny and Mansfield found themselves on the same battlefield in the engagement near Layac Junction where the 31ˢᵗ and 194ᵗʰ fought side by side. On days the 31ˢᵗ wasn't fighting, they received replacements from broken or scattered units. They even received a few men from a chemical warfare group. In the rear area of the 31ˢᵗ's position, the medical personnel desperately worked on the injured and dying. Many days, while his company rested, Manny forfeited his time to scour the area for food. He did this often which gave him the opportunity to cut meat and cook. He was given a truck to find meat for the dinner table – and he was usually successful.

On 10 January, the New York Times reported, "The anticipated assault by heavily reinforced Japanese forces on United States and Philippine units on Bataan was unleashed with tremendous force yesterday. The terrain on which the enemy action was begun is hilly, and densely wooded. The American-Filipino Forces, although inferior in numbers of men, tanks, and planes, (the Allies) had previously (positioned provisions) in anticipation of just such a Japanese attack." It was a bit optimistic.

On the 11ᵗʰ, Admiral Hart asked to be relieved, possibly due to the lack of support for the Far East Asiatic Fleet. It was thought by many, he wanted to return to the States to campaign for support for the Allies in the Pacific.[166]

Submarines provided some supply relief but the volume of cargo was necessarily minimal. *SEADRAGON* provided more substantial support by sinking the *TAMAGAWA MARU* near Lingayen Gulf that was loaded with troops and supplies. She then put into Corregidor on 4 February and retrieved two tons of submarine spare parts, 23 torpedoes, and 25 personnel including many members of the Cast Unit.[167] *SARGO* delivered .30 caliber ammunition in early February to soldiers still fighting on Mindanao. *SWORDFISH* went to Corregidor on 19 February and loaded torpedoes and removed Philippine President Quezon and party.

SEAWOLF also visited Corregidor on 27 January and delivered .50 caliber ammo and 3-inch antiaircraft shells while back-loading torpedoes and 25 passengers including 16 pilots.[168]

The roads to and in Bataan were overwhelmed with people and troops with equipment. The road from San Fernando to Orion was so heavy with dust, it formed columns or spoors in the sky seen for miles. The thin asphalt layer of surfaced roads crumbled under the weight of the traffic. Japanese bombers flew missions daily into the Philippines but did not strafe nor bomb the roads used by the military and refugees for some unknown reason. A consensus believed the Japanese saved the roads for their own use in the near future when they would assault Corregidor.

The real test in the defense of Bataan began along the Abucay-Hacienda Line. On the night of 11 January, the Japanese quietly moved forward through a tall sugar cane field along the Calaguiman River near Mabatang. The advance was detected by the Scouts and the 24th Artillery opened a barrage that rained on the cane field precipitating a Banzai attack. The Scout artillery and small arms butchered the Japanese but they continued to charge. The Japanese formed bridges across the barbed wire perimeter by the sheer mass of their own bodies, then continued forward into the Scouts foxhole positions. The battle continued with hand-to-hand fighting. The Scouts had a major problem, however. They were running out of ammunition, as were the artillery groups. Fortunately, the Japanese charge failed.

On the 12th, the Japanese generated another attack across the cane field but it died before it got a good start as the Scouts and the 41st held their ground. A second attack commenced almost immediately. This time the enemy crossed an Allied mine field successfully by driving carabao ahead of them. The Allied line bent, buckled a bit, then held.

The Japanese 141st Infantry stood at the ready across from the center of II Corp's 41st led by General Lim. Lim's division was untested but was eager for battle. On the 8th, the Japanese started the advance with heavy infantry probes, artillery, and air strikes.

The 41st fought well on the first day but began to give ground on the 9th. The battle continued for days but by the 14th of January the division faltered and lost all their outposts. Wainwright came to the rescue and sent in the 31st Philippine Division from I Corps who arrived on the 15th only to see the Japanese 141st drive a wedge between the 41st and 51st.

MacArthur made one of his infamous speeches intended to boost morale by making promises, "Help is on the way from the United States, thousands of troops and hundreds of planes are being dispatched. The exact time of arrival of the reinforcements is unknown as they will have to fight their way through Japanese attempts against them. It is imperative that our troops hold until these reinforcements arrive. No further retreat is possible. We have more troops on Bataan than the Japanese have thrown against us; our supplies are ample; a determined defense will defeat the enemy's attack . . . " In reality, food was scarce, ammunition short, and no reinforcements showed up. In MacArthur's defense, Washington did make him a number of promises not kept.

Addition of the Filipino 31st was of little help and the situation became desperate so USAFFE[169] Headquarters committed the two remaining regiments of Scouts; the 45th and American 31st Regiment. With the reinforcements, Parker counterattacked on the morning of 16 January. Initially, the Filipinos did well but they advanced beyond their flanks and support. They were trapped by the Japanese 9th Infantry and fled wildly leaving a gapping hole in the Abucay Line. By the day's end, the 51st no longer existed.[170] A War Department communiqué that day stated, "Ground fighting continues all along the front line. Enemy shock troops with special training are attempting aggressive infiltration. Attack planes and dive bombers are being used incessantly by the Japanese against our front line troops."

The 41st fought valiantly on the 17th and managed to regain most of the territory lost but it was a bloody battle. On the 18th, most of the day was spent tending to the wounded and dead on both sides. The Japanese moved up tanks and artillery to support their position while on the Allied side of the line, food supplies were critically short.

Manny returned to the 3rd Battalion camp near Balanga on the 17th with a freshly killed carabao, intending to butcher the carcass as a supper treat for the men. The entire 31st was preparing to move up to the 51st position along the east road across from Mount Samat. "No time to cook tonight Manny! Get your gear. We're moving out in ten minutes. He reported to K-Company to draw extra bandoleers of M-1 ammunition, grabbed a handful of rice, threw his gear together and fell in with the rest of the company. By that time, everyone had thrown away their gas masks and used the case to carry other gear.

At 2000, the men filled their canteens, moved into the assembly area, mustered and climbed aboard buses for a ride to the front. They arrived on the line about 0300 and found a hot breakfast waiting for them. It was a very unusual treat. Manny settled down and enjoyed his breakfast, a meal he didn't have to help prepare was indeed a treat. As the men finished the breakfast, a messenger arrived with news the 51st had broke, the 41st held and the 31st was to counterattack back to the original MLR.

The men walked the remaining distance with G-Company in the lead and K-Company covering the rear. Following the 31st were the antitank company, engineers, and self propelled artillery of the 194th with Mansfield and company. They marched 13 miles, most of it uphill, and when the sun came up, the steel helmets became head clamps of unbearable weight. The extra ammunition weighed heavily on the men and their path was dust and dirt that they continually ate and inhaled. The leggings were another source of irritation but like the helmets, they had to wear keep them. Japanese aircraft buzzed them continually but were dropping their bombs on Corregidor. After only a few ten-minute breaks, they reached their positions just prior to sunset. The 43rd Infantry was pleased to see the 31st since they had taken 450 casualties that day. Fatigued and hungry, they settled in around the Abucay Hacienda and watched the last spotter planes fly off to the north as

darkness fell. Stragglers from the front rushed their positions screaming in terror the enemy was approaching.

The men settled into their positions for the night and were
advised to get some sleep for no one knew what to expect the next
day. "Hey, Manny, what ya think we'll be doin manana? "Hell
Bob, how the hell would I know. Just so I don't have to cook.
Damn, you know, I wanted to cook when I joined this outfit."
"Hey, we love it when you cook Manny. We always seem to get
something special when you cook. Course a glass of water is special
these days." "Well, at least if I'm cooking, we're not fighting,"
Manny mumbled back. They tried to sleep but the unknown had
them too worried.

The battalion commanders had a meeting and it was decided
to counterattack at 0800 the following morning. By the time the
company commanders had the word, it was time to awaken the
regiment and move forward. The 1st and 2nd battalions advanced
and Manny with the 3rd Battalion remained in reserve. Allied artillery commenced firing and the Japanese returned fire while the
31st slowly moved forward. It was neither the time nor the place
for a comfortable stroll. The men ducked and jumped for cover
from incoming artillery rounds but made it to the line on time.[171]

The 45th made it on time despite tortuous events with their
supply vehicles that constantly mired in the soft ground. The Scouts
were great warriors, many the descendants of Chief Lapu of Abu
on the Island of Cebu. They received orders on 16 January to meet
the 31st for the attack on the 17th. Unfortunately, the Scouts had
no time to reconnoiter before the key battle. A victory by the Allies would reestablish the MLR and cause the Japanese to regroup.
A loss meant leaving a gaping hole in the line the Japanese could
penetrate.

The mighty 31st attacked at precisely 0815 and the fight was
furious. The 31st slowly gained ground until portions of the 1st
battalion was pinned down by enemy fire. Before anyone could
come to their aid, the men in B-Company found they were lying
in a huge nest of ferocious Filipino red fire ants. The men flew off

the ground and continued the advance. Spotter aircraft kept Japanese bombers appraised of the battle and the 31st came under attack repeatedly from the air. As the battle waged, the two battalions were slowly split leaving a gap in the line.

K-Company was called forward to fill the gap and Manny found himself dodging enemy bullets again. The company crawled through a wild area of ragged terrain and tangled woods with only a few small clearings. The countryside was cracked with a labyrinth of ravines and gullies which made keeping track of everyone difficult. They were to fill the gap between B-Company and G-Company. The men of K-Company took turns hacking through the tangled vegetation and soon it was dark. They dared not use flashlights so they advanced utilizing only the flash of gunfire. Manny was grateful he still wore his leggings in the mess that grabbed at his leg at every step. They arrived in the gap about 0300.[172] Then it was shovel and hole digging time. Unbeknownst to the men along the line, the Japanese were busy using the darkness to infiltrate the lines. They used fire crackers and small arms fire from behind the line to confuse the picture. Reportedly, the Japanese also had a paper bullet which exploded after coming to rest giving the illusion rounds were being fired from the bullet point of rest which added to the confusion.

The battle came to a stalemate on 18 January so the 45th and 31st tried again on the 19th. The Army Air Corps still had four P-40s which they used to support the effort and the Allies moved forward a short distance to the banks of the Balantay River only to be stopped again. The Allies tried again on the 20th and 21st only to be countered on each effort. The Japanese went on the attack ten times between the 21st and the 24th directly at the 31st but the Americans stood tall and repelled the charges. The Japanese got close to the 31st's position a couple times which almost ended in hand-too-hand combat. A couple of foxholes over from Manny, they found a Japanese shoe on the lip of the foxhole – with the foot in the shoe.

The attacks and counterattacks inflicted high casualties on some units and wore down both sides physically and mentally. The Japanese 9th Infantry managed to move south along the side of Mount Natib and did an end-around on the MLR. They were spotted near Guitol and the only Allied forces to meet the threat was the battered and beaten Filipino 57th and 31st. Exhausted, they moved west to meet the danger. The Japanese 141st Infantry moved westward and launched an attack on 22 January against the weakened Allied flank. Japanese aircraft and artillery pummeled the area and the Scouts were forced to slide back to a point south of the Hacienda to cover the 31st's withdrawal. Even the spotter aircraft dropped bombs made of captured Allied artillery rounds with fins.[173]

On 23 January, several air strikes tore into the middle of the 31st positions and the remains of the 51st crumbled. The Japanese were in an advantageous position but by the end of the month the offensive ground to a halt. Over 7,000 Japanese were killed and 10,000 were ill.[174]

CHAPTER FOUR

THE STRUGGLE FOR BATAAN

W ELL BEFORE THE Japanese invasion of Luzon, the Japanese planned to conquer Bataan as part of their strategy to capture Corregiidor. They were convinced Allied plans included a defense of the peninsula. The Japanese decided to utilize the east road of the peninsula as the main transportation route and Bataan as a stepping stone toward the Island of Corregidor. As a consequence, only a minor portion of the Japanese invasion force was assigned to Bataan's West Coast that was unpaved in many places. General Nara organized his force around the 122nd Infantry and added a field artillery battalion, a platoon of engineers, and a labyrinth of support units. Colonel Watanabe was assigned as commanding officer with the initial primary goal of Bagac.[175]

Watanabe encountered little resistance as he moved south and west into Olongapo City on 10 January 1942. A couple days later, a small Japanese force in landing craft took over Grande Island, which protects the entrance to Subic Bay. Meanwhile, artillery and anti-tank units departed Manila for Olongapo to support the effort on the West Coast. General Homma assembled an armada of small vessels in Manila and transported the support units to Olongapo. He planned on using the 122nd to proceed down the west road and the 20th Infantry to attack the inland flank of I Corps.

A handful of Filipino soldiers were positioned in the small barrio of Moron. The Japanese 26th Cavalry moved into position on the seaward end of the "minor line of resistance" running eastward to the mountains. Many maps do not show the triple peaks with Mount Natib in the center, Mount Santa Rosa to the north, and Mount Silangan to the west which anchored the inland resistance line. The 3rd Infantry held the MLR that also ran from the beach to the mountains, specifically Mount Silangan. It was the top of these peaks that I Corps and II Corps failed to permanently attain or retain contact through the rough terrain.

The east side of the mountains was rough whereas the west side was impossible. Steep and ragged rock outcroppings broke the dense tropical forest which was so uninviting, the Filipinos had not inhabited the area in centuries. Between Moron and Bagac, there was a break in the jungle and a crushed rock road joined the two barrios. Mount Silangan rose through the jungle canopy into the sky and overlooked Moron. I Corps laid land mines along the road and the trails leading toward the road. The defenders also built gun emplacements, cleared lines of fire, dug foxholes, trenches, and strung barbed wire.[176]

The Japanese marched southward toward Moron on 14 January. The Philippine 31st Infantry Division's Artillery Unit was located atop the western slopes of the mountains acting as infantry since they no longer had any artillery pieces. In fact, there were few artillery pieces in I Corps and what was available was antiquated such as the old British Mountain howitzers called Vickers. They overlooked the west road. K-Company of the 1st Infantry was assigned the gap in the mountains between the two corps but never achieved contact with II Corps. To Wainwright, no communications with II Corps was a minor annoyance since he was convinced the mountainous terrain between the two Corps was impassable.[177]

Wainwright ordered C-Company of the 194th to move forward and challenge the Japanese advance down the west road. Mansfield and his company of tanks were dispatched from II Corps to help I Corps that had no tanks. "Every time they need a fire put out, they call out old Charlie Company," muttered Mansfield as the tankers headed west. He spent the remainder of the Battle for Bataan in Stuart tanks; his days in the half-tracks were past. The tanks crept slowly up the twisting and hilly road north of Moron when a few horseback riders of the 26th Cavalry reported Japanese anti-tank guns were located ahead. Wainwright was notified and immediately recalled the tanks.

In the morning of 16 January, the Japanese crossed the Batalan River into Moron and quickly over ran the Filipino defenders. The defenders scattered into the surrounding jungle. General Segundo, a West Pointer and Commander of the Scouts immediately coun-terattacked. The move surprised the celebrating Japanese, and ran them out of the barrio. Reinforcements returned the following morning and the Japanese recaptured Moron, leaving the barrio in smoldering ruins.

Wainwright was surprised when the Japanese surmounted the inland jungles and mountain slopes to the east. Infiltrators at-tacked the 1st Infantry from the rear and remained entrenched on the mountainside of the 1st's position along the slopes of Mount Silanganan. At this juncture, the Philippine 31st Division departed for II Corps.[178]

The 31st's positions along the beaches were replaced by the 91st. The 91st was not well trained and carried lighter weapons. The division carried tons of .50 caliber ammunition even though they had no machine guns. The 72nd Infantry was pulled back from the beach to back up the inland flank alongside the Pilar-Bagac Road seven miles south of the Japanese lines.

On 18 January, the Japanese struck again, this time at the outposts along the forward line of resistance and dispersed the defending Filipinos. The victory by the Japanese made the Allies nervous, especially when four Japanese ships north of Moron shelled the west road. The vessels attempted to land supplies but B-Com-pany of the 92nd Artillery fired down on the ships with 155mm guns from atop Mauban Point.

The Japanese buildup and pressure continued on the 19th but managed no gains. It was only a precursor for the main offensive

9-HARM

the following day. The Japanese 122nd attacked the Philippine 1st Division's MLR and infiltrated through and around the lines. Many of the infiltrators were stopped along the beaches but the tactic worked in the foothills.[179] The fighting continued for another day and the Japanese established a roadblock on the west road behind, to the south, of the MLR utilizing only infiltration tactics. The Allies were cut off from their own supplies and reinforcements from the south. They attacked the roadblock again and again with vigor but in vain.

C-Company of the 194th entered the fray but was thwarted by land mines. They slowly navigated the narrow and treacherous road surrounded by forests. Mansfield and the gunner preceded their tank looking for mines. This was the case for all the tanks with the commander issuing orders to the driver utilizing only hand signals from the crew walking the roads. Despite virtually no infantry support, the tankers passed the minefield and raced toward the roadblock. A few tanks were caught in tank traps made of logs. Filipino soldiers raced to the aid of the tankers and eventually cleared the logs. A few tanks had mechanical problems but the remaining tanks pulled them out of trouble with cables and towed them to an area for repairs. The tank effort also proved futile at the roadblock and was temporarily called off.

For the next few days, every unit in I Corps assisted in the attempt to clear the roadblock but the Japanese were well entrenched. End runs and frontal attacks all failed and the roadblock remained in place. The MLR was attacked a number of times by the Japanese but held. A total of six Allied battalions fought to open the roadblock but there wasn't a single machine gun among them. Most of their weapons were single shot bolt action rifles which couldn't cope with the Japanese automatic and semi-automatic weapons. Then the Allies ran short on food and ammunition so they left a shell of men to defend the MLR and began a withdrawal south. The 91st went first followed by the Constabulary forces and then the 26th Scouts. The withdrawal in I Corps was conducted professionally and successfully with a minimum loss of lives. Unfortunately, a lot of military equipment was lost including the few remaining artillery pieces.[180]

Following the initial phase of the defense of Bataan, the Allies performed well. They fought valiantly and presented a stiff opposition to the advancing Japanese, which resulted in a stalemate of the battlefront by the end of January. The Japanese losses were high with the defenders inflicting eight casualties for every one suffered.[181]

To the east, II Corps withdrew to the Pilar-Bagac Road requiring I Corps to keep pace moving to the south. On the morning of 25 January, I Corps began its retreat with most of the infantry units moving down trails along the sea. Without jungle and forest coverage, the troops were warm and thirsty from the march and discarded most of their equipment. The tankers negotiated through the jungles and around the roadblock, thence back to the west road. Being a tanker did save on footwear.

The Japanese made a move on I Corps with amphibious landings in four areas beginning on the 17th with the idea of cutting the Allies in half along the west road. General Selleck commanded the area and was ordered to defend the coastline against attacks from sea. His staff assumed Agloloma Bay was the logical place for a landing. He placed remnants of artillery, the Navy Battalion, and survivors of other units into defensive positions around Agloloma Bay. His plan was good but resources meager.

A reinforced Japanese battalion departed from north of Moron at Mayagao Point on the 22nd. They traveled in barges with members of the 2nd Battalion of the 20th Infantry but ran into trouble quickly. Barges, in this sense, are motorized landing craft. The PT-34 with LT Bulkeley was steaming south along the coast following an attack in Subic Bay when he encountered the Japanese motorized troop barges. He took the barges under fire, sinking and setting afire most of the craft. 300 Japanese survived the attack and landed undetected but mistakenly on Longoskawayan Point only 1.5 miles west of Mariveles Harbor. Sitting on the narrow little beach, the Japanese were a mile south of the 60th Coast Artillery's

E Battery with its brand new radar. The radar watch spotted the Japanese at sea but nearby Army Air Corps radar could not verify the contacts and the search was given up. At sunrise on the 23rd, lookouts on Mount Pucot sighted the Japanese and sounded the alert.[182]

Another portion of Colonel Tsunchire's landing force inadvertently landed on Quinamuan Point north of Apploloma Bay. The tankers were ordered into the breech on the beach and Mansfield was thankful he was inside the relative safety of his tank. He swept his machine gun in giant arcs across the beach in front of him, periodically dropping an enemy on the run. Before the enemy was totally killed or captured, the invaders leaped from the cliffs to the beach and sea below. It was a turkey shoot as the Allies picked off the men in the water or on the open sand. Some Japanese managed to get into caves in the face of the cliffs as a temporary haven. The enemy was removed with some difficulty. The Battle of Quinauan Point and the encounter at Caibobo Point to the north resulted in the death of 900 Japanese of the 2nd Battalion, 10th Infantry. The Allies suffered casualties as well but there were none among the 194th that day.

Bridget's Naval Battalion was the first Allied unit to confront the Japanese as they raced for the height of Mount Pucot. The Japanese got to the summit first but Bridget surrounded the mount and wiped out a couple patrols headed for the west road. The Japanese retreated in two groups ending up in a dense forest at Lapiay and Longoskawayan Points. Guns and mortars failed to budge the Japanese from the points so Bridget called for assistance from the huge mortars on Corregidor. Battery Geary unleashed the fury of 12-inch mortars, devastating the enemy late on 25 January but they maintained their positions. Bridget's Battalion charged again but failed to move the Japanese.[183]

The remnants of the 34th Pursuit Squadron played infantrymen and were in the perfect defensive position when the next Japanese barges tried to land. They sprayed the barges with automatic weapons and drove the surviving Japanese into the cliffs. The *USS*

QUAIL, a minesweeper, arrived on the scene and took the caves in the cliffs under fire with her 3-inch gun. With the pilots at the top of the cliff swinging sticks of dynamite into the caves and the *QUAIL* blowing them out of the caves with her gun, most of the invaders were soon eradicated from the cliffs. The *CANOPUS* sailors got involved too as they cruised around the base of the cliffs in an armored motor whaleboat, spraying the fleeing Japanese with rifle fire. The Scouts remained near the top of the cliffs, executing any Japanese attempting escape by climbing to the top. Nevertheless, a significant number of the invaders did manage a foothold near the top of the cliffs where they met the wrath of Mansfield and the 194th.[184]

In II Corps, the efforts of the Allies became more futile. As the war waged, the Japanese managed supplies and some reinforcements while the Allies saw no relief manpower and zero food and ammunition supplies. General Sutherland inspected both Corps and reported to MacArthur the positions were untenable and a withdrawal was mandatory. On the night of 22 January, Field Order #9 was issued ordering both Corps to retreat to a line along the Pilar-Bagac Road.[185]

In I Corps, the Allies moved south well ahead of the advancing Japanese but trouble was expected in the east vice west. The initial problem in II Corps was moving the remaining heavy artillery. Stockpiled ammunition had to be broken down and loaded on wagons and trucks. Each artillery piece required a tractor and tow bar to move the gun and only half the required number was available. It was another failure in advance planning. The 11th Division moved west to support Wainwright as did the 45th Scouts. In case the Japanese broke through the defensive line, a huge supply of meat and C-rations was shipped to Corregidor which was critically needed in Bataan. A couple rice mills in Pilar and Orion were dismantled and moved south. The next move was the field hospitals and wounded.[186]

In II Corps, fighting units moved back on 24 January. Part of the 31st Infantry Regiment with the self-propelled guns of the

194th acted as rearguard again. The 194th formed a sparsely spaced defensive shield until late on the 25th after all the other units had safely moved south. Mansfield remained on the West Coast with I Corps while Manny and K-Company nervously patrolled the thin defensive line. When the other units safely passed, the 31st climbed in trucks and slowly headed south. The trip was annoying at best with the roads cluttered with vehicular traffic, all moving south. Clouds of flies followed slow moving traffic while the air was filled with a fine dust that had men coughing up mud. The sky was filled daily with Japanese observation aircraft so it was no surprise the Japanese advanced shortly after the withdrawal commenced. The next battle took place near Abucay Hacienda where the Japanese were stopped initially by the 41st but the line was broken later.

Prior to pulling out, Manny and the 31st busied themselves with sabotaging vehicles unable to make the trip south. Precious sugar went into gas tanks, bombs were placed on drive shafts, engines dismantled, anything to render the vehicles useless to the Japanese. Once the 31st got underway, they quickly ran into other withdrawing units. A traffic jam of massive proportions formed on the road to Balanga and Back Road. The crushing mass of vehicles and humanity on the roads played hell with organizational control as men intermingled with any convenient or passing unit.

Manny and his driver started off earlier than the rest of the 31st since they were to find and prepare food for K-Company that evening. They departed from the far western end of the Hacienda Road late on the 24th and arrived on the crowded junction with Back Road. Both men wore bandannas over their faces in a vain attempt to keep out the dust. Their truck crawled in first gear through Abucay and headed south on Highway #110.

They reached Balanaga around sunrise of the 25th, covered in dirt and dust. Manny and the driver took turns driving through the throngs all night with occasional stops at "gasoline stations" which consisted of a few gasoline barrels lying alongside the road. Exhausted and filthy, they stopped by a small pond to wash and bath. For a moment, the stress of the day vanished like the dust from their bodies as they soaked in the pond. Suddenly, Balanga was struck by a series of Japanese aircraft. Manny stood up to see what was happening and saw dozens of huts catch fire and heard the scream of injured coming from every direction. Luckily, the pilots failed to shoot into the pond so Manny and driver survived unscathed. They quickly dried themselves, dressed, and were back on the road heading south toward Orion.[187]

The 31st's Third Battalion covered the Regiment's departure so K-Company remained in foxholes on a low ridge overlooking a cane field as Manny headed south. Their wait for activity was short lived as the Japanese staged a full-scale "bonsai" attack along the line in front of the 31st, particularly at I-Company. The cane field was set afire which roared in flame and the 31st's gunners mowed down the charging Japanese by the dozens. The men just kept firing, round after round, clip after clip, at the fanatic silhouettes racing out of the burning fields. The 1st Battalion of the 41st Artillery was called upon to support the 31st with their 75mm canons. The charge ended as a complete disaster for the men of the Rising Sun and quiet reigned temporarily again. Then the 3rd Battalion withdrew south.

It wasn't the first sugar cane encounter for the 31st. At the Asbucay Hacienda, the sugar cane fields were ready for harvesting, tall and full. The 31st was sure the Japanese were in the field. "Major, I seen some Nips back in that there cane, sir!" "Could be Sarge. Any guess on how many are in there?" "Saw a whole pile of 'em sir," yelled a private, "how we gonna get 'em out Major?" "Hell man, I don't know. Let me think on it." One of the men was from Hawaii and recalled how they burned the fields following a harvest "Why not burn 'em out sir?" "Damned good idea private. Get me a couple gallons of gasoline." The major poured a line of gasoline along the front of the field and set it afire. The field caught fire in a huge and immediate conflagration and the major disappeared in the flame and smoke. The Sarge yelled at the men to keep their eyes open for the major. The troop's eyes strained in

9-HARM

vain for their officer and hope for his survival waned. Suddenly, right in front of them, the major stepped out of the flames. Most of his cloths had been burned from his frame with only a pair of .38 pistols around his waist.[188] An Oklahoma Cherokee in his company looked at the officer and said, "Me call him Major with three gun!"

The 194th waited patiently south of Hacienda Road, a crooked dirt road. A column of Imai's Japanese 141st Infantry pursued the general withdrawal down the same road. It was in the middle of the night but a full moon was setting as the Japanese rushed down the road in pursuit of the Allies with little caution. The 194th turned off their engines to save fuel and tank commanders ordered their men to button up their shirts to reduce the chance of burns. Flying hot brass often caused burns and clogged the tank floor and clutch linkage. "Commence firing!" shouted the tank commanders. Each Stuart tanks barked and belched its first round of 37mm canons in unison at the advancing column, then fired at will. The .30 caliber machine guns joined the canons while the acrid smell of gunpowder filled each tank and the tanker's eyes watered in the gray smoke. The first dozen or so Japanese in the column flew backwards as if catapulted with the first volley of rounds. The Japanese lost dozens in a few minutes and wildly retreated to the rear only to run directly into a large group of Allied stragglers heading south and behind the Japanese. Caught in a deadly crossfire, the remaining Japanese infantrymen ran for cover in surrounding woods.

On 25 January, the 31st was hit hard by Japanese dive-bombers who bombed the vehicles and strafed the men. It was a lengthy attack and some vehicles were lost but the men all survived with only a few scratches. The 194th moved back up the road to the north looking for stragglers, despite headquarters reports that all units had passed to the south. The tankers didn't want to leave any Allies behind enemy lines. Luckily for the groups, some up to 200 men, the tankers found men still wandering north of the old defense line plus the entire 2nd Battalion of the Provisional Air Corps Regiment that never received the order to withdraw.

Light rain fell at sunrise on 26 January and the 194th moved south a few miles to take up their new positions north of the Pilar-Bagac Road. Their orders were simple; delay the Japanese as long as possible. There was a lull in the action and the men took advantage of the inactivity to stretch out on the tanks and take a nap. One member of each crew made breakfast while the other men slept or washed in the warm rain. For the moment, the war seemed distant with only an occasional rumble of guns in the distance.

A few self-propelled 75mm mounts arrived to support the tankers. "Come and get it," cried out a few young gunners turned cooks. The men looked at what was prepared and choked a bit. It looked like fried powdered eggs and some sort of fake meat but they ate anyway. No one had eaten for over a day. As the tankers slid off the Stuarts for breakfast, a Filipino civilian ran into the camp screaming, "Dem Nips are right behind me and a head'n dis way!" Breakfast was forgotten as the crews slam-dunked themselves into the tanks. "Here they come," shouted a tank commander as another column of Japanese infantry marched down the road toward them. The tanks took the formation under fire and the Japanese scattered off to the sides of the road. The 75mm gunners were in excellent positions to blast the enemy out of their hiding spots back onto the road. "Easy does it men, slow your fire or you'll melt the barrels," ordered Col. Miller as he paced back and forth in front of his tanks. Between chews on tobacco he assigned new targets and the machine gunners claimed many enemy lives.

Japanese aircraft joined the fray but were ineffectual but enemy artillery slowly closed in on the 194th units. Two tanks were crippled so Miller decided to pull his battalion back and head south. The withdrawal was complete and the men remained hungry. Meanwhile, MacArthur reported the situation to Washington on the 25th and 27th indicating complete success by the Allies despite the fact the Allies were in withdrawal.[189]

9-HARM

The 31st moved south another five or six miles until they were behind the reserve line of resistance (RLR). The line ran between Orion and Bagac. They had been at the front for eleven straight days of combat and were exhausted. The Japanese spotter aircraft were out again and dropped thousands of propaganda leaflets. The message predicted gloom and doom but offered free passage to a place of surrender. Other notes asked the defenders what their wives were doing while they fought in the jungles. The most popular means of leaflet disposition was at the latrine as a toilet tissue substitute.

Life for the 31st and other units arriving at the Orion-Bayac Line was reminiscent of Abucay with no preparations made for the arriving units. There was neither organization nor supplies for the defenders. The men immediately dug foxholes again, strung barbed wire when they found some material, and built gun emplacements. There was good news for the men though as a handful of P-40s surprised the Japanese held air bases at Nichols and Nielsen Fields, destroying aircraft, supplies and killing 300 Japanese.

"Fearless Freddy" Warder in USS SEAWOLF departed Darwin on 16 January and steamed 1,800 miles to Corregidor, arriving on the 27th. He discharged .50-caliber ammunition and some 3-inch antiaircraft rounds, back-loading submarine spare parts, 16 torpedoes plus 25 passengers. The passengers consisted of intelligence personnel, pilots and a Navy yeoman.[190] The USS TROUT arrived late in January to remove gold and silver bullion belonging to the Treasury of the Philippines. [191]

USS SEADRAGON crept into Lingayen Gulf and raised hell for awhile and then was chased out. She slid down the west coast of Luzon and into Corregidor where she took aboard "Cast" code breakers and torpedoes on 4 February. She was alongside the USS SEA LION when bombed at Cavite[192] and was badly damaged but repaired sufficiently to submerge.[193] USS SARGO arrived at Corregidor on 4 February. She brought 40 tons of ammunition, removed 24 nurses, B-17 specialists, and a special communications group and equipment. USS SWORDFISH arrived on the 19th

to refuel and took on torpedoes, departing with Philippine President Quezon and party to deliver to Panay, 300 miles to the south. *SWORDFISH* immediately returned to Corregidor to pick up more passengers. During the month of February, submarines also participated in the defense of Java in a losing battle but the *USS S-37* picked up 60 survivors. *USS PERCH* was sunk but most of the crew escaped and were taken prisoner to spend the rest of the war in the mines at Ashio.[194]

During preparations at the RLR, the 31ˢᵗ managed some rest. They pitched their tents under a coconut palm grove and a windstorm the first night brought down the nuts, the tents, and some headaches. At another time, the men were given permission to hold swim call which was a welcome respite. Unfortunately, the spot chosen for swimming was filled with purple Portuguese men-of-war, a lethal jellyfish. Luckily, none of the men were seriously hurt.

The Japanese conducted small amphibious landings on both coasts. The small scale landings had proved successful in Malaya. Meanwhile, as the 31ˢᵗ was resting, their orders were changed to a reserve status while the 31ˢᵗ Philippines replaced the Americans including the beach defenses from Pandan to Limay.[195]

The Japanese converted a dozen or more inter-island passenger ships into gunboats. Gradually, they built a small fleet of gunboats the Americans called "wooden battleships." Added to the small fleet were tugboats, barges, and other small craft. Every few nights, the Japanese used the craft to harass the coastline of Bataan, remaining just outside of allied gun range. The craft moved daily between Manila, Guagua, and Orani.[196]

The "Bataan Ration" took its toll on the men after weeks on the reduced diet. Malnutrition was widespread and the men often relied on food seized from dead Japanese for sustenance. It took a few weeks for the stomachs to shrink and the pangs of hunger to become painful. Fighting, and particularly hand-to-hand combat, temporarily eased thoughts of hunger as adrenaline coursed through the men's bodies. The stench of rotting dead also helped suppress the thought of food. Nevertheless, stamina and strength of the Allies became critically low. Dysentery took its toll among the Allies, especially the Americans. Yet the men got up daily and moved forward to fight, some barely able to stand.[197]

Abucay fell during the withdrawal as Japanese artillery fired volley after volley at the Allies and attacked in repeated banzai wave attacks. Barely sufficient Allied artillery covered the retreat and the 194th was called in again to block the Japanese advance while the infantry moved south. Hospital #1 was moved to Little Bagio and the 31st dug foxholes for the nurses.

Some units of the 192nd joined C-Company of the 194th in I Corps which gave the Americans a total of 23 tanks on the west coast. Three of the 192nd's tanks entered the fray on the third day of the Battle for the Points but backed away from severe anti-tank gunfire. The tanks of both battalions were utilized intermittently for the following week but no gains were achieved. The jungle was too dense for the tanks. After a couple of weeks of fighting, the jungle was virtually denuded of vegetation whereupon the tankers could see their way around and the battle shifted in favor of the Allies. Unfortunately, the defoliation also made the tanks more visible and sounds inside the tank changed from the scratching of branches to the tinkling sound of small arms fire hitting the steel plates.[198]

After the Navy rounded up the surviving Japanese in the caves and cliffs, the Battle of Quinauan Point, Longoskawayan Point and Caibobo Point to the north was over with over 900 Japanese dead of the 2nd Battalion, 20th Infantry. The severest Allied casualties occurred at Quinauan Point. The War Department announced on 25 January, "A heavy enemy attack was made on the left flank of General MacArthur in the Bataan Peninsula (the west coast and MacArthur was already secure on Corregidor) . . . Among the hostile troops participating in the assault were many who landed at night . . . on the west coast of the peninsula. There were heavy enemy infiltration along the beaches and in the mountains. Defending troops were forced to give ground with considerable losses."[199]

The Japanese Command knew they lost a battalion at the Points so Homma ordered the 16th Division in Manila to send assistance. Only one infantry company answered the call, traveling by truck to Olongapo on 26 January then boarded landing craft for Quinauan. The Japanese got lost again and landed a mile short and a fiasco resulted on both sides. I Corps was confronted with amphibious landings one after another behind the MLR.

The airmen and sailors were not jungle fighters and the battle went badly until the Scouts arrived. Homma again ordered reinforcements for his amphibious troops and this time received a 500-man battalion. The reinforcements had orders to support the remnants of previous landings in taking the west road and Mariveles Mountain. Intelligence informed Wainwright of the invasion plans and he immediately took steps to repel the amphibious landings.

The landing came late on 1 February with roughly 1,000 Japanese infantry in 13 landing barges in Aglaloma Bay. Navy lookouts spotted the flotilla and reported to Wainwright. Shore batteries illuminated the barges and the few remaining P-40s attacked the vessels. The P-40s shredded the barges with fragmentation bombs and .50-caliber machine guns while Allied artillery joined in the slaughter. The Scouts and Naval Battalion met the remnant barges on the beach. The Japanese mine laying vessel *YAEYAMA* supported the flotilla but was waylaid by *PT-32*. Only 400 Japanese made it ashore and only three of those Japanese survived the landing.[200] Mansfield and C-Company supported the defense with machine gun fire.[201]

The remnants of numerous Japanese amphibious landing attempts left many Japanese along the coast. The battle along the coast lasted throughout February with the Allies unable to beat the Japanese off the beach area and the Japanese not able to evacuate their stranded men.

The Japanese fought valiantly and fanatically, clearing mines from roads and fields by throwing themselves on the explosives.

9-HARM

They surmounted barbed wire with human bridges across the wires and charged the Allies in human waves of the banzai charge. The Japanese were experts at infiltration and ambushes.[202] Savagery by the enemy at times was unbelievably cruel particularly on captured Allies. Bayoneting tied up prisoners and cutting off genitals was a favorite source of entertainment that infuriated the Allies to the point where the Allies rarely took prisoners.[203]

On 15 February, the *USS HOUSTON* was battered by Japanese bombers to the south as she escorted the transports *MEIGS, MAUNA LOA, TULAGI,* and *PORT MAR,* filled with American and Australian troops headed for Timor. Bombers attacked the gunless transports so *HOUSTON* placed herself between the transports and bombers, successfully beating off the attackers. *HOUSTON* received a standing ovation following the battle by the thousands of men who had been saved. Unfortunately, *HOUSTON* was sunk on the 28th in the Battle at Sunda Straits. She and *HMAS PERTH* took on a large Japanese amphibious force and were sunk after running out of ammunition and with multiple casualties. A third of her crew survived to become POWs and many of the crew received revenge torture.[204]

LT Dorsey stole the tugboat *RANGER* and some barges and returned to Cavite to rescue remaining equipment. On the 20th, he lead 60 officers off Corregidor on the Inter-Island ferry *LEGASPI,* then the men used an open motor launch and navigated successfully to Australia.

The 31st Infantry Regiment was involved in the Battle of the Big Pocket and the Tuol Pocket. Some Japanese who landed on the West Coast and infiltrators from the north got behind the RLR. Battles and numerous skirmishes waged for over a week until over 1,000 Japanese were encircled and trapped. The 2nd Battalion closed the circle on the invaders, then the "head hunters" were sent in. Negritos and the blowgun hunting Igorets, pigmies from northern Luzon, rode astride tanks of the 194th.

Mansfield and his fellow tankers weren't too keen about the natives riding on their tanks but the natives got the job done.

Japanese fell one after another to the arrows of the jungle warriors while Mansfield just watched the slaughter. He couldn't control a slight shiver every time he looked at the natives on his tank. The Japanese attempted surrender to the Filipinos only to be shot as the Filipinos felt turnabout was fair play for the numerous atrocities committed by the Japanese. The hierarchy of Japan never forgot the "pockets" and heads literally rolled following the surrender of the Philippines.[205]

General Nara's men found a map of Allied defenses in an old storeroom in Manila and discovered the two lines of resistance across the Bataan Peninsula. Nara assumed he was facing the same situation as at Abucay with the northern line a delay line and the southern line the main defense. He calculated the main defensive strength of the Allies to lay along a line roughly from Limay to Mariveles Mountain. The terrain was rugged and covered with underbrush six to nine feet in height that provided excellent coverage for Allied equipment. This time, the two Corps were not separated physically by large mountains as along the Orion-Bagac Line.

The new defensive line was tested on 26 January 1942. The Allies were in total disarray again with units shuttling back and forth with a seemingly continuous change of orders. Units of the 32nd Infantry, who got into position moments before the attack, managed to stem the first attack. The first major attack came the following day when the Japanese 9th and 141st backed by the 142nd Infantry charged toward Mount Samat. The Japanese had their problems as unit strength was cut almost in half with a dire shortage of officers due to previous battles. Supply movement was hampered as the Allies watched every move from atop Mount Samat and directed effective artillery fire on supply truck convoys. Then the 65th Brigade became ill with severe diarrhea.

The Japanese managed to slowly correct their problems and continued to pressure the Allies. The 9th Infantry was recalled and the 65th lost more than half its number to illness and casualties. On 8 February, Nara prepared yet another attack when Homma withdrew him north of the Pilar-Bagac Road. In San Fernando, Homma met with his staff to discuss progress of the battles. Things were not going well. Homma decided to rest his men and call for reinforcements while keeping the blockade tightened against the Allies.

The stubborn defense on Bataan caused uneasiness among the Japanese as the Allies fought with bravery and for the cause to save the Philippines. The military might of Japan ground to a halt in Bataan and resistance by the Allies stiffened throughout Southeast Asia and the Pacific. In January, Homma's 14th Army lost 2,725 killed with about 12,000 men ill. The 14th no longer existed as a fighting unit while the 16th Division and the 65th brigade no longer were effective. In mid-February, Homma withdrew to the north of the battle lines a few miles. Meanwhile, a food rationing system was initiated in the Japanese homeland which was to last for the duration of the war.[206]

Through February and most of March, fighting was relatively quiet and the battle a stalemate. The 31st and 41st Divisions fought their way back to the original lines of resistance at Abucay. Despite poor health, the morale of the Allies skyrocketed with confidence by stopping the Japanese. The men managed an occasional smile, momentarily forgetting the daily pain of malaria, dengue fever, dysentery, jungle rot, and starvation. Their daily diet included geckos, iguanas, snakes, and anything else they could get their hands on. Most of the men lost twenty to thirty percent of their body weight during the defense of Bataan. Some Allied units claimed more men to get extra rations. It was a hell of a way to survive.

The men no longer spoke of women and booze for their only thought was food. Food was an all-consuming state of mind and commanders kept their men from expending unnecessary energy. On the coastlines, the men fished with hand grenades and dynamite. In the 31st, the men ate rice and their pack mules and horses. Manny's skills as a meat cutter were in high demand.

One day, Manny was ordered to take a jeep and proceed to a

specific location to kill and butcher a carabao or water buffalo. This was not the first time Manny was sent on such a mission. Many times he butchered horses, mules, cats and dogs, and even monkeys. He drove down a dusty back road to an intersection under repair by Construction Engineers who were also directing traffic. The road was riddled with bomb craters and the engineers were filling the holes. An engineer held up traffic going Manny's way for an agonizing long time and faced away from Manny. With patience running out, Manny shouted at the traffic controller, "Hey Corporal. Ya going to wait till the end of war to let me pass. Man, I've got important business here!" The corporal wore the insignia of the 809th Engineers National Guard.

The engineer turned his head, ready to give Manny a mouthful back when their eyes met. "Holy shit, is that you Manuel you crazy son of a meat butcher?" "Salvadore, you son-of-a-bitch. What the hell you doing on this island. Who's taking care of the goats?" Manny forgot about his meat and Salvadore forgot about the traffic. Manny almost fell down when jumping out of the jeep and the two met in the middle of the road. They hugged each other and danced around yelling and shouting in joy like little children. Salvadore called another engineer to direct traffic, jumped off his box, hurdled a bicycle, and ran to Manny's jeep. Manny moved the jeep off the road and the two talked with gusto. Salvadore had a can of vegetables so the two chowed down as they told stories and asked questions. "So what the hell are you doing here Manny? Ya crazy or something?" "Hey goat breath, I'm a soldier now with the 31st!" "What's a butcher doing in the infantry anyway?" "I carry a rifle, don't direct traffic, but at the moment I'm on my way to butcher a water buffalo for the troops. So I'm still cutting meat. I didn't even know you hitched up." "When you left, I decided you had the right idea so I hitched up with the National Guard and joined the 809th Engineers. We went to Hawaii and then got sent here." Then Manny dug out a can of soup and between sips they caught up with the last year of their lives. Every few minutes they hugged and then went on talking. Over an hour went by and they both had to go. In unison they said, "See ya. Keep your head down!" It was 31 March 1942.

As in any military organization, rumors ran wild each day. One day, the word was two American troop ships landed just south of Manila with replacement troops for the Americans. The present defenders were to be sent back to the States for a well-deserved rest. There was always "more food" stories which kept morale from crash-landing. Help was on the way but was not to effect the Battle for Bataan. Admiral King ordered three submarine squadrons from the Atlantic to the Pacific.[207]

During the stalemate and pause in fighting in March, the Allies rebuilt and added to defenses and communications. By the end of the month, the Allies were better prepared than in January. Even the medical personnel were in an improved status with the two hospitals in full operation, restricted only by the availability of medicine. Food remained scarce and continued to cause suffering among the defenders. Small coastal freighters and blockade-runners attempted to land food but usually failed on Bataan but with a little success on Corregidor.

Despite the food shortage, pilots were well fed in case aircraft were delivered even though the Allies held no operational airfields. The food shortage was so acute, front line soldiers fainted in chow lines due to hunger. A medical analysis of the Allied fighting man's combat efficiency on 1 April approached zero. Gasoline and tire shortages curtailed most vehicular movements. A 27 March War Department communiqué indicated increased activity was expected in Bataan shortly.[208]

By 1 April 1942, the Japanese were finished fooling around and determined to complete the conquest of Bataan. The first step was to take Mount Samat, the highest peak behind the Bagac-Orion Line. At 1000 on the 3rd, Good Friday, the Japanese opened the offensive with a 5-hour artillery barrage. General King commanded the Bataan Forces consisting of 79,000 soldiers, 6,000 civilians, and roughly 20,000 refugees. The soldiers were made up of 11,796 Americans, 8,270 Philippine Scouts, and 59,000 Philippine Army. The defenders faced bomber and dive-bomber attacks by day and massive artillery pounding at night. The 31st lost every heavy gun, truck, and piece of equipment they owned.[209]

The peninsula south of the battle line in II Corps was an open and rolling terrain sprinkled with numerous trails. Following the loss of a regiment in I Corps, the Japanese decided to concentrate its effort in II Corps. General Lough placed his few remaining artillery pieces atop Mount Samat, hiding them in the sparse woods to avoid the probing eyes of Japanese observation aircraft. King's reserve force was his most experienced unit, the 31st Infantry Regiment.

Zero hour was set at 0500 on 3 April and the Japanese moved up to make contact with the Allies along the entire length of the front. Quickly, II Corps outposts fell and at 0900, 196 Japanese heavy artillery pieces shattered the quiet in Bataan. The artillery concentrated on Mount Samat. As the artillery fire slackened, aircraft picked up the onslaught. Following the bombing and strafing, the artillery barrage resumed. Tree coverage on Mount Samat slowly disintegrated revealing the guns and bunkers. The 42nd and 43rd crumbled and dissolved as General Nara's 65th Brigade, led by tanks, overran their positions.

MacArthur made it clear there would be no surrender. "If it is to be destroyed (his command) it should be on the actual battlefield taking full toll from the enemy." The Japanese were so successful on the 3rd, they repeated their strategy on the 4th. The 21st Infantry retreated and the Japanese 4th Division reached Mount Samat's foothills before nightfall. The physical condition of some of the Allied soldiers was so bad, a number of them died in their foxholes prior to the arrival of the Japanese.

In the morning of the 4th, as things were going from bad to worse, King committed his reserves, the 31st. At 1600, Manny and the 31st headed north for the San Vicente River. Even in the waning days of the battle, rumors continued in a vain effort to lift morale. Two members of Manny's 3rd Battalion were treated for self inflicted gun shot wounds, frantically attempting to get away from the Japanese onslaught. The battalion struggled along narrow and ragged trails and paths, heading north to face the enemy. Manny slipped and fell a few times on the rocky trail. He told himself to concentrate on his walking and not to worry about the Japanese. Maybe a miracle would happen before the fight started – oh how he prayed for the miracle.

As the east began to glow with morning twilight, Manny and K-Company was halted and told to dig foxholes. They were positioned near the top of Mount Samat with a counterattack by the 31st scheduled for 0700. The Allied artillery barrage to precede the counterattack never occurred for Japanese artillery zeroed in on the few remaining pieces first and destroyed the guns. The attack by the Japanese also destroyed the Allied communication system but the 31st nevertheless advanced. They moved about 500 yards when they were stalled by Japanese defenses. The 31st answered with a mortar attack, firing the old 2.95-inch Stokes rounds. The Japanese line, only 150 yards ahead, buckled amidst the cries of anguish from the wounded. Unfortunately, just as things seemed to be going well for the Americans, they ran out of mortar ammunition. The Japanese responded with their mortars with uncanny accuracy. Suddenly, a strange and loud swishing sound was heard in the sky that passed overhead and exploded with fury on the Japanese line. It was the sound of 12-inch mortars, with their rotating bands, fired from Corregidor ten miles distant. The mortar round had a killing range of 400 yards and created havoc with the Japanese infantry. Manny watched in awe and danced with glee until a few nearby rifle rounds brought him back to reality.

The 31st dug in again and when a trench was finished, Manny sagged to the bottom in exhaustion, trembling with hunger. There was no food and little ammunition. A scouting party returned to the trench with hands full of rice balls and a type of sausage that looked similar to "Slim Jims." The men came across dead Japanese and robbed them of their food. There were even small balls of sugar candy. It wasn't much when spread around the company but it was food. There was a temporary lull in the fighting so the men sat down to enjoy a Japanese lunch. One man starting singing and the rest joined in

"Dugout Doug MacArthur lies a shaking on the Rock,
Safe from all the bombers and from any sudden shock;
Dugout Doug is eating of the best food on Bataan,
And his troops go starving on.
Dugout Doug is ready in his Chris Craft for the flee
Over the billows and wild raging sea.
For the Japs are pounding on the gates of Bataan,
And his troops go starving on."[210]

No sooner was the food gone and song finished, than the battle resumed. Despite a somewhat poor reputation as misfits and troublemakers, the 31st knew how to fight and fight they did.[211]

On the night of the 4th, the Japanese regrouped. It was Easter Sunday and when the Japanese resumed the offensive, they caught numerous Allied soldiers observing Easter services. The mountain was hit by 56 Japanese bombers at first light while another 81 bombers struck Mount Orion. The Japanese infantry advanced up the north side of Mount Samat and the Philippine 21st Division was destroyed.

Manny's spine tinkled and his hair stood on end at the sound of Japanese bugles. The battle on Bataan had waged for four months and each fight was preceded by the wails of bugles yet Manny cringed at the sound. It was precisely 2000 on the 5th when the bugles blared as the sun set with a particularly eerie sky. Manny felt God was preparing hell for someone and he hoped it wasn't him.

General Wainwright boated to Bataan on Easter Sunday to view the situation personally. It was not a satisfying tour and he organized a counterattack utilizing the 31st and remnants of other units. Most of the groups that were to join the 31st couldn't make it to the rendezvous area. On the morning of the 6th, the decimated Allies tried the counterattack. The 45th Infantry, with only 300 men left, the 41st Infantry, and the 194th C-Company headed north on the west road. The counterattack ran directly into the

9-HARM

Japanese offensive. The Japanese 65th ran into the remainder of the 42nd and 43rd and decimated the Allies. Mansfield and his tankers chugged up the west road until their infantry support melted away. Everywhere Mansfield looked, he saw Japanese and his machine gun barrel glowed cherry red. As the Filipinos ran into the jungle, the 65th Brigade ran unchecked to the south until they encountered the Scouts of the 57th. The offensive temporarily slowed.

The final phase of the Allied counterattack was the role of the 31st. The 31st's commander, Colonel Brady, ordered a hot meal for the men, asked the chaplain for a prayer, and issued each man three C-rations. Manny's stomach almost revolted at the feel of hot food and he hungrily packed his C-rations. He didn't have to cook the meal either. "My God, I may live after all. Thank you!" He didn't have much time to relish a full stomach for they were ordered back to the front within the hour. They were to retake a position previously abandoned by the 21st along the Reserve Defense Line. The meal felt good but it didn't abolish the exhaustion each man felt and they struggled forward in darkness toward for the front. To make conditions worse, fleeing Filipinos from the battlefront kept running into the men of the 31st. Resolutely, the men of the 31st moved forward.

With retreat and flight rampart along the entire battlefront, the 31st moved forward against unbelievable odds. Colonel Brady appreciated the situation and reported the problem to General Lough, who, in turn, ordered the advance halted. The 31st was ordered into a defensive posture. Manny and the 3rd Battalion were held in reserve, just behind the defense set up by the rest of the 31st. As dawn arrived, the 31st faced the brunt of the Japanese offensive which was the Japanese 4th Division. The Americans held off the onslaught until ordered to withdraw in mid-afternoon. Manny, with K-Company and L-Company, served as the rear guard to cover the regiment's withdrawal. They 31st used the last of the 81mm mortar rounds to disengage the enemy.

As the 31st withdrew, General Kitano committed his reserves, including tanks, to enforce the Japanese 4th Division and attack the front. The 31st fought desperately and knocked out a few tanks before their guns were silenced. An hour after the withdrawal began, II Corps received orders to continue falling back until the reached the east bank of the San Vicente River. All units still in reserve were moved to the river to cover the withdrawal of the 31st and the 57th Infantry. As 6 April ended, the Japanese had destroyed the 21st and 41st Divisions and the 51st Regiment.[212]

The fall of Bataan was evident and most of the Allied units moved forward to the crumbling line of defense in one last desperate effort to shore up the line. Patients in the two hospitals that could walk got up and joined the men at the front. Over 4,500 patients were in the two field hospitals and preferred to die fighting than lying in a hospital bed. Many of the patients were too weak to make it far and fell alongside the road. These men were tagged and called casualties in the hope someone would help them.[213]

The fighting reached the coast where the Japanese came ashore in landing craft and boats under the cover of a huge smoke screen. On the nights of the 5th and 6th, the two gunboats from China saw action. The USS MINDANAO and USS OAHU managed to get out of Corregidor and arrived along the Cavite coastline in time to raise hell with the Japanese amphibious landing. Pyrotechnics and ammunition lighted the sky for miles as they scored heavily on the amphibious craft.[214]

On 7 April, the day began with ten bombs exploding on Hospital #1, strewing bodies and parts over the entire hospital area. Over 70 patients were killed and things grew worse on the battle line. The Scouts were ordered to help the 31st but when they arrived at the last known position of the 31st, they heard fighting raging to the south and assumed the 31st escaped. The 31st was stranded.

By mid-morning, the Japanese located a hole in the Allied defenses along the San Vicente River. The Japanese 61st Infantry plunged through the gap and General Bluemel responded by send-

9-HARM

ing the remnants of the Philippine 31st to assist. The situation degenerated rapidly and Allied units began destroying ammunition and burning documents. One Allied unit after another broke and ran from the front, often leaving what little equipment they had behind. The A-Company and B-Company of the 194th moved north to breech the gap with C-Company moving east to cover the retreat.[215]

General Bluemel desperately attempted to reorganize the 31st but it was virtually impossible. The 31st was shredded and the survivors spread asunder. Manny and the 3rd Battalion moved in to protect the rest of the regiment whereupon they came into full view of Japanese artillery. As the artillery rounds exploded nearby, the men crawled across the terrain, providing some fire support to the withdrawing two battalions. The 33rd Infantry attempted to help the 31st, was spotted by Japanese artillery and obliterated. Then orders arrived from Bluemel for the entire regiment to retire.

Manny was scared to death and sure the end was at hand. His fellow soldiers felt the same way. Manny and a handful of K-Company members scrambled southward, scampering between bushes and rocks. Suddenly, the remainder of the regiment was caught in the open on an old road by Japanese dive-bombers. Mansfield and the 194th saw the action and tried to come to the aid of the 31st but were hammered by the aircraft. Communications between units failed to exist except for a few telephone lines but the Japanese were monitoring the circuits and even joined in the conversations. The main or East Road became a giant parking lot of burning Allied vehicles and equipment.

By the end of the day, the 33rd Infantry was gone. It had been the only intact Allied unit west of Mount Samat. Wainwright was appraised of the dire situation but rather than permit surrender, he ordered the defenders to continue the fight. He had no choice with MacArthur's direct order to fight to the end. On Bataan, General King placed every man along the Mamala River. In I Corps, the men withdrew to the Binuanga River, five miles to the south. By the time Bluemel and his men arrived in position, the Japanese were already on the north bank of the river. The situation was untenable so the men moved further south to the Alangan River. This was the situation at the beginning of 8 April with nary a soul in reserve.

The main players along the river were the 300 remaining functioning members of the 31st and the Scouts of the 57th. The 26th Cavalry arrived around midnight on the 7th. None of the defenders made physical contact with anyone on their flanks. Everyone dug a foxhole and Manny feared it might be the last time he had to dig a hole. He was partially correct; he would dig no more foxholes but plenty more holes.

Just after noon, the Japanese 8th Infantry moved into the sights of the 57th Scouts. To their right, a couple American Infantry companies withdrew a short distance to the Paalungan River because they simply ran out of ammunition. The 31st anchored the defensive line in the center. A couple hours later, Japanese tanks appeared on the north bank of the river and fired point blank at the 31st. Once the infantry joined the tanks, they crossed the river and forced the Scouts and the 31st to retreat. At this point, General King notified General Wainwright the end was near and if men were needed on Corregidor, now was the time to move them to the Rock.

King ordered the 45th Infantry to Mariveles for transportation to Corregidor, which further reduced the number of defenders. Then he ordered another withdrawal, this time back to the Lamao River. All that was left was the equivalent of a couple companies of scouts and less infantrymen from the 31st. That evening, 8 April, General King decided to negotiate surrender with the Japanese. Unaware of King's decision, Wainwright issued an absurd order; move I Corps north and retake Olanagapo. The entire Allied force moved south with no leadership nor discipline. Bluemel was asked to hold the line on the Lamao River until sunrise when a car carrying a white flag would pass through the lines. The die was cast.

Around 2130, Mother Nature objected to the torture of the

peninsula with an enormous earthquake that stopped the war for an instant. Even the submarine *USS SNAPPER* a hundred miles at sea felt the quake. At 2200, King ordered everything of value destroyed. An hour later, the Navy destroyed all assets in Mariveles. The *DEWEY DRYDOCK* was sunk and the minesweeper *BITTERN* scuttled. They moved all remaining fuel and ammunition to Corregidor. Likely the saddest event the night of the 8th was the destruction of the *USS CANOPUS*. She provided support to the defenders to the last hour. A skeleton crew took her out to Lilmbon Cove and scuttled her in 14 fathoms of water. At dawn on the 9th, the last boat cast off with her seacocks open. Her crew joined the Marines for the last gasp battle and many of her crew died in the last few hours of fighting.

Bluemel moved his men and looked for a safe area for the last few hours to eat and rest. At dawn, he stopped his men and ordered fires started for a hot rice breakfast. Most of the medical personnel were moved to Corregidor during the night. Around 0200, the Army commenced destruction of TNT in warehouses and many people believed it to be an after shock earthquake. At 0330 on 9 April 1942, General King's Staff headed for the Japanese line under the white flag of surrender. Unconditional surrender came nine hours later.

CHAPTER FIVE

THE SURRENDER AND THE MARCH

THE UNITED STATES Forces, Far East (USAFFE) fought a good fight – an outstanding fight in fact – but the defenders had too little too late. II Corps defenses crumbled on 7 April 1942 and the rest of the Bataan defenders gave up their last small glimmer of hope on 9 April. The troops were on reduced or no rations of food and water for weeks yet performed Herculean tasks despite their diminished physical condition. On 6 April, the Allies attempted one last counterattack but their physical strength failed them. As rumors continued the U.S. Navy was anchored in Mariveles to evacuate the men to Australia, the 31st Infantry Regimental colors were burned.[216] In POW camps later, Japanese veterans admitted the defense of Bataan was the fiercest fighting they experienced during the course of the war. The Defenders of Bataan fought much better than the resistance in Singapore and Malaya.[217]

The entire military communications system failed in the final week that resulted in more chaos and disarray with groups and individuals wandering about without guidance. By the 9th, little organization remained as illustrated by the surrender in small groups and units.[218] By 7 April, the only general on the line was Clifford Bluemel who led a slow retreat of the remnant troops to the Alangan River. They were less than seven miles from the southern tip of the Bataan Peninsula and despite the slow pace of retreat, many men were lost from fatigue. By nightfall, the Japanese had the defenders on the run and the roads were clogged with retreating men. The southern tip of Bataan was a mass of confused defenders who no longer were capable of a thought process and on the very verge of delirium. The majority of nurses were removed from the two field hospitals and boated to Corregidor.

The CANOPUS was a sad sight as she was towed out to sea by the tugboat MANAPALA. The tug cast off her lines as the sea valves were opened above her final resting-place. Activity on the sea and shore ceased as everyone paused for a moment to watch the old lady sink. The submarine tender had been a bright light in the defense of the peninsula and then the light was out.

General King sent a couple officers to find the Japanese lines and arrange a surrender meeting with General Homma. Colonel Ernest Williams and Major Marshall Hurt were instructed to barter for surrender terms themselves if Homma refused to see King. They were to inform Homma of the number, the terrible condition of the defenders, no military organization remained to aid in the surrender, but some vehicles were available for transportation of the Allies. Major General Nagano eventually met with King and accepted an unconditional surrender although King was unable to negotiate for other Allied forces in the Philippines. King saved fuel and vehicles to move the prisoners but was never asked by the Japanese to utilize the vehicles. The Allies eventually destroyed the equipment that directly led to the Bataan Death March.[219]

At dawn on 9 April, every road, path and trail was clogged with fleeing defenders while Japanese aircraft viciously attacked the men and equipment, including the two hospitals. Added to the turmoil, Corregidor opened fire in support of the hospitals with their huge mortars only to have the Japanese move their artillery into the hospital areas. The carnage caused panic but Chaplain Bill Cummings rose to the occasion in prayer at the hospital which settled the men but cost him an arm by shrapnel. Without either food or hope, General King surrendered 78,000 men, ignoring his potential for court-martial. The fighting stopped except for a few hours of continued battle by General Bluemel while

General King ordered the troops moved out orderly and to utilize their own vehicles.[220]

Most defenders knew of predetermined surrender areas. When the word of surrender arrived, the men headed to their assigned areas to meet the Japanese. Most units destroyed all equipment, including the vehicles to be used for prisoner transport. No one liked the thought of surrendering and a few, regardless of physical condition, took their chances in the jungles and forests. A few survived by joining guerrilla groups while most failed the tests of the cruel environment and were captured, turned themselves in, or died in the countryside. Unfortunately, Homma was not prepared for King to surrender so soon and the men in such poor physical condition.[221]

Japan was inundated with prisoners with no way or plan to cope with them. Bataan presented the conquerors with over 78,000 men; Hong Kong coughed up another 10,000 men; in Malaya over 100,000 POWs were taken; and the Dutch East Indies added thousands more. Tojo took the bull by the horns and made a policy statement that was to govern the treatment of prisoners for the duration of the war. Everyone in the "Greater East Asia Co-Prosperity Sphere" must keep working for the war effort including all prisoners of war.[222] He sent Lieutenant Colonel Tsuji to the captured countries in the name of the Emperor to explain the treatment policy for POWs. One of his ploys to make a point was to shoot the first POW he saw with his pistol and state, "This is the way to treat bastards like this."[223]

Most of the defenders in the south and west of I Corps were informed to muster at the abandoned airstrip near Mariveles to surrender. Thousands of desperate defenders gathered in a clearing near the airstrip and fell into a loose formation; and surrendered. The Japanese pushed the prisoners into columns of a few abreast and a hundred or two to a group. Other units and groups surrendered on the main road or anywhere they found Japanese military. Eventually, all the men were herded on roads and paths and marched to the east and the south. They were marched around the southern tip of Bataan, picking up stragglers as they progressed. Slowly, the prisoners marched or staggered north up the east side of the peninsula.

Mansfield and the 194th spent the night of 8 April breaking off gas tank valves and setting their tanks afire. Captain Kadel, A-Company Commander, offered to lead his men in an escape by moving north but only nine men accepted his offer. The destruction of equipment continued until sunrise. Grenades were exploded in each engine compartment but a month later, at least one of the Stuarts participated in the invasion of Corregidor. Mansfield and a handful of other tankers were ordered to make a Japanese flag from bed sheets with the rising sun colored by using brake fluid and iodine.[224]

The defenders faced the surrender with mixed emotions for they were grateful the fighting was over but felt guilty of surrendering. Some of the 194th came across abandoned trucks containing food. They ate creamed peas on toast that was a culinary delight for the starving men. The first Japanese Mansfield and the tankers encountered were as exhausted as the defenders. They were Japanese infantrymen who just walked by the tankers without a look or a word. Dirty and exhausted, they wore sweat stained uniforms with cloth flaps on the back of their caps. Their lower legs were wrapped in wool puttees akin to the "Dough Boys" of WWI. A young Japanese private fell to the ground in exhaustion and was summarily shot on the spot by his fellow riflemen. Mansfield and the other defenders witnessed the incident and shuttered in terror. If the Japanese treated their own men that way, how would they treat the prisoners? Meanwhile, American officers were trucked away while the men remained in the area before beginning the march to Balanga.[225]

The antitank company of the 31st fared well with their first encounter with the enemy. They also contacted an infantry unit but both sides seemed to share a mutual respect for each other. They met in a flat dry field near Mariveles. The Americans were ordered to strip to their shorts and place all their possessions on top of their cloths. LCOL Calyer, executive officer of the 31st and West Point graduate, was not about to give up his class ring; an emotion only an academy graduate can appreciate. He successfully secured the ring to his testicles under his shorts.[226] A search was conducted but none of the Americans were beaten or shot. Instead, they were directed down a trail to Little Bagio on the road to Mariveles.[227]

A doctor with the 31st, Captain Hibbs, was confronted by Japanese soldiers who searched him and found his medical bag. They pointed into his bag and yelled loudly, apparently wanting medicine. The doctor vigorously gestured to the negative only to be threatened by a bayonet to his throat. He reached into his bag and gave them a bottle of apomorphine tablets used to induce vomiting.[228] A soldier grabbed the bottle and walked off, sharing the contents with his companion. Within minutes, both Japanese soldiers were violently ill and emptied the contents of their stomachs.[229]

The 31st's officers mustered at Cabcaben at dawn on the 9th but no Japanese were present. Around 0630, three Japanese arrived to handle the surrender of the officers. The officers were pushed, stabbed with bayonets, and robbed of all valuables. Following the gross treatment, the officers were pushed down a road to the south and to the west toward Mariveles. As the officers walked toward Mariveles, one of the officers carried a duffel bag full of personal belongings not considered valuable by the Japanese. Under the relentless sun, the bag weighed heavily on the officer and his gait staggered. He was prodded by bayonets by the Japanese but could go no faster. The Japanese guards pushed him off to the side of the road – a single shot was heard.[230]

A few Japanese infantrymen found an old American ambulance with the keys in the ignition. The three climbed in, started the ambulance, and took off down the road. They hit the "zigzag" nearing Mariveles at a high speed. A few days later as the death march progressed, the ambulance was found overturned with three bodies inside. An American ambulance won a small victory.[231]

Many of the men entertained thoughts of escaping but their poor physical condition persuaded most of them to surrender. Some men held out but without food and no knowledge of how to reach the Filipino guerrillas, they eventually succumbed and joined the long column of prisoners. One such prisoner from the 803rd returned to the march and when searched, was found with a can of sterno. A small group of guards took the sterno and strode off down the road, spooning sterno down their throats. They later convulsed and died a horrible death; another small victory, this time from a can of sterno.[232]

Forty-two Japanese prisoners were recovering from injuries in Hospital #1. After the surrender, they refused to leave the hospital once the defenders departed on the march.[233] When the Filipino and American medical personnel left, the injured Japanese were summarily shot.

The Allied prisoners were strung out along the dirty and dusty road as far as the eye could see. Not only did defenders come out of the brush to join the column but also Japanese soldiers. A few soldiers and the guards were friendly but most of the Japanese were angry and vindictive men, intent on harassing the POWs and stealing everything they could find from them. Common items stolen were wristwatches, lighters, and wedding rings – sometimes with the ring still attached. For some strange reason, a few POWs kept their Japanese souvenirs. It was a certain invitation for trouble and retribution was instantaneous. Manny recalls seeing a couple American officers carrying Japanese Yen. The supposition was anything Japanese was taken from a dead Japanese soldier which did not sit well. The two officers were summarily beheaded on the spot. Beheading with a samurai sword caught on like the flu and Japanese seemed to thoroughly enjoy the activity, yelling with excitement at each event. The beheading was horrible and inhumane but even worse was the apparent enjoyment by the captors.

Manny took off his high school class ring and surrendered it along with his watch. Amidst the killing and brutality of the minute, the Japanese did appear to honor religious items and permitted Manny to continue wearing a rosary around his neck. The guard that permitted him to wear the rosary wore a Buhidt pouch.[234]

Most Japanese guards were anything but understanding. Many of the guards were men unfit for duty in the regular army, mentally and/or physically. They demonstrated delight in dealing pain to the Americans and bragged about how they hurt the prisoners. One POW begged for water but the guard waved him away from an artisan well and prodded him with his bayonet. The blade passed into the POW's bowels. As the American screamed in pain, the guard was furious over his dirty bayonet and made the POW clean the blade with his shirt. The POW continued to plead for water whereupon the guard shot him in the mouth. The guard achieved the silence he sought. In another case, a POW was drinking out of a ditch when caught by a guard. The guard ran him through with his sword and pinned the poor man to the ground. He struck a pose of the conquering hero with his foot on the POW's back, pulled out his sword, and urinated on the writhing prisoner.[235]

One night during the march, it rained. It was a blessing from above and undoubtedly saved many lives as most POWs literally received no water during the march. Both Manny and Mansfield observed junior officers forced to stand at attention for hours while guards used the officer's faces as punching bags. Flag officers were handled separately but did suffer some brutality. Officers were a target for brutality followed closely by tall Americans and any POW wearing a helmet.[236] Later, it was generally agreed that such Japanese action was a result of an inferiority complex stemming from the subservient position of the Japanese lower rated enlisted man.

Homma won the Battle for Bataan but total victory required the capture of Corregidor as well. Bataan was a stepping stone to Corregidor, the ultimate goal in the Philippines. With the fall of Bataan, Homma was faced with an enormous logistics problem with all the prisoners of war. He had to clear the roads of the POWs before he could move his equipment and men in position to attack Corregidor. He managed to get 150 gun batteries into position in southern Bataan to bombard the island fortress.[237]

A month earlier, the Japanese developed plans to truck all the POWs to San Fernando, then rail them to Camp O'Donnell. Unfortunately, the plan called for the movement of no more than 40,000 healthy men in Allied vehicles. The received 78,000 walking wounded and sick with no vehicles. Their only option was to walk the men to San Fernando, a distance of about 60 miles from Mariveles. A final and detailed plan for handling the prisoners was never completed

The infamous march began in Mariveles and throughout the Southern Bataan area. The little port overflowed with humanity and destroyed equipment. People, military and civilian, milled about in no particular pattern. No one knew where to go or what to do. All the Japanese equipment and troops were committed against Corregidor while the wounded and relieved troops from the Japanese 14th Army headed north for Manila.

About 1100, orders reached the on-scene Japanese and the POWs were lined up, 4 to 8 abreast, in groups of 100-200, and the march began. Slowly, the men shuffled down the road and out of Mariveles and up the grapevine of the Mariveles Mountains. Mansfield looked down the road to the south at the remnants of the 194th's location in absolute horror. As far as he could see was a long column of struggling POWs heading south towards him. It was the first day of the march and most of the men still had canteens and headgear. Mansfield seriously considered heading back into the woods and jungle but he was hungry as hell and his officer explained he would be better served to remain with the prisoners and receive food and first aid.[238]

The dust and flies descended on the column as the 194th joined the column. The guards fell on the 194th like birds of prey and stripped them of their valuables while roughing up the men. Colonel Miller led his men onto the road and the 194th was soon in the same cadence as the column; a pace of death and suffering.

Mansfield looked around as they walked east and he read his own thoughts in the eyes of each prisoner; it was humiliation, shame, hunger, hurt, and thirst. Injured and ill were given no quarter by the boisterous guards who kept busy with beating and pushing. There was a wide variety of brutality and injury rendered by the guards but by the end of the day, they settled, for the most part, in prodding POWs with bayonets and clubbing them with rifle butts. Hopes for survival dimmed when five more truckloads of guards arrived to supplement the 20-30 guards with Mansfield's group. Most of the guards were positioned in the rear of the group column to prevent stragglers from leaving and slowing down progress. When stragglers failed to keep up with the column, they were bayoneted. The killing of POWs began in earnest.[239]

Mansfield and his fellow tankers were in one of the lead groups and joined another small group to make up a unit of about 200 men. Meanwhile, Manny and a part of the 31st were about in the center of the column, miles astern of Mansfield. To call the odyssey a march is a misnomer as not one POW was capable of real marching. Many men were not with their units and the situation worsened as men slowly joined the column from the woods and jungles. They were punched and thrown into the column no matter the unit moving past. Most POWs desperately looked around for a friend or member of his unit.[240]

Hospitals #1 and #2 were hit by Japanese bombers and the surviving patients and Filipino medical personnel forced into the march. Most of the patients failed to keep the pace in the column and eventually were shot or bayoneted to death.[241] The ambulatory cases remained in the field hospitals for a couple months. Some cases between ambulatory and walking wounded were transported to Bilibid Prison in Manila.

As the march continued, the severely injured and sick fell back in the column. A few paused for a rest but were quickly knocked back into ranks or killed. The column turned into a giant mixer and the ruthless activity of the guards caused the ranks to move. It wasn't long before Mansfield no longer was with his fellow tankers. He would never see the tankers again; not on the march, not in the camps, and not in Japan.[242]

An elderly colonel, not in good physical shape, had difficulty staying with the column. As he struggled to keep from falling behind, he was stabbed in the buttocks a number of times and his trousers became caked in dry blood and a swarm of flies. When his column crossed a small bridge above a dry creek bed, he jumped off the bridge and landed on his head on the rocks 100 feet below. He suffered no more.[243]

The sun merciful set but the Japanese guards continued to press the POWs onward until around midnight. None of the POWs knew the exact time since no one was left with a watch. An apparent planned stop ceased motion of the entire column at the same time. The POWs were permitted to rest but ordered to remain on the road. Although no food or water was forthcoming from the Japanese, many of the men still carried some water in their canteens. A number of the prisoners could take no more and attempted to escape but bullet or blade killed most of them.

In the morning of the 10th, well before sunrise, the POWs were forced back on their feet and resumed the march. The column met a Japanese truck convoy heading south near Cabcaben which was within range of the guns on Corregidor. Shortly after sunrise, the POWs were marched onto the Cabcaben Air Field and lined up on the seaward side of the field, well within the range of the long glasses on Corregidor. Japanese artillery was positioned on the field behind the POWs. The artillery opened fire on the island fortress, assuming the Americans would not return fire with the POWs in the line of fire. Such was not the case as the big 12-inch mortars returned fire immediately, hitting behind the POWs and slowly walking toward the Japanese guns. The POWs hit the deck and scattered into nearby woods. Considerable difference of opinion exists on how many POWs were killed or injured.

The majority of the POWs were rounded up during the artillery exchange and the march resumed. The march passed the beach near Cabcaben and the guns from Corregidor fell quiet. The guards continued to push the column faster so they could clear the road for a Japanese military convoy led by General Mutsuobe with two divisions of tanks. The POWs were pushed off to the side of the road so the military equipment and fresh troops from Singapore could pass.

For an unknown reason, the men of the 200th and 515th Anti-Aircraft Regiments were overlooked. The men assembled near the airfield in Cabcaben but the Japanese ignored them. When the Japanese artillery barrage of Corregidor was complete and the march resumed, the men were finally noticed and loaded into troop trucks and moved to Orani. The following day, they were fed, put back in the trucks and delivered to Camp O'Donnell. The men were lucky and did not suffer through the march.

Mansfield came to a rise in the road and dared a glance fore and aft at the column. He couldn't believe the sight but was jarred back to reality as a rifle butt found the small of his back with an appropriate litany of words from a guard. "You son-of-a-bitch, I ought to kick . . . " and the rifle butt found him again, this time in the face.

A gross incident occurred as the convoy passed the column. A Japanese soldier in a truck flipped a grenade into the column of POWs. Men died and were injured which marked them for death in the column gauntlet. The Japanese laughed in glee at the carnage as the convoy continued southbound.[244]

The POWs looked forward to seeing a clearing in the jungles or woods as a potential resting-place since the few rests were in such areas. As the second day progressed, the guards were replaced with fresh troops who had no opportunity to steal their fair share of POW valuables. The POWs were rousted at every opportunity and frisked for valuables. If they found nothing, the individual POW was beaten. A sergeant next to Mansfield violently protested the loss of his wedding ring. He swore at the guard and made a threatening gesture. His voice stopped in mid-sentence as his head was cleanly dispatched from his neck.

The third time Mansfield was searched, a guard pushed his hands deep into Mansfield's pockets and fondled him, jabbering away in Japanese. It took every shred of self-control Mansfield could muster to keep from busting him in the mouth – but he would have lost his life on the spot. The POWs were stopped on occasion to rest but made to stand in the baking sun; the prisoners began to crack and break.

The prisoner's physical and mental stamina gradually failed which prompted increased adverse action by the guards in the form of bayoneting and beheading. Torture and death became a contest among the guards who performed the more gruesome killing ranked highest in entertainment value. To escape notice and trouble from the guards, the POWs eased their anguish of diarrhea and dysentery by relieving themselves in their pants rather than stepping out of ranks to relieve themselves.

Midway in the column, Manny and his group struggled in an encounter with Japanese tanks. The POWs were forced from the center of the road by the iron behemoths. Just in front of Manny, a guard grabbed a POW and threw him in front of the oncoming tanks. Before the POW could regain his balance, the first tank, then a second tank, and another, and another hit him. Troop carrying trucks rolled over the body and then again by more tanks. His image was later described by Americans who walked past him as nothing more than a skin deep image covering the dirt and cobblestones looking akin to well aged road kill.

The Japanese troops in the trucks had a sport of their own. The struck POWs from moving trucks with their rifles or caught a man with long snake whips, dragging the unsuspecting POW down the road behind the truck. The prisoners had to be aware at all times of the Japanese game playing for failure to do so could cost them injury or worse. The rifle swinging and whip usage was prevalent for the duration of the march when Japanese troop convoys passed them headed south.

When part of the column passed Field Hospital #2, the POWs were granted permission to get water from a small stream near the hospital. The patients yelled at the POWs to join them in beds as patients but the Americans refused and returned to the column. A number of the POWs were heard mumbling they wanted to get the hell out of Bataan, not remain.

An estimated 86,000 Filipino civilians were caught in the Battle for Bataan. Most of the civilians fled south when the Japanese invaded Luzon. Following the surrender, only 31,000 were accounted for with the remainder probably killed by battles, starvation, or at the hands of the Japanese.

LT Hadley Watson was walking in a column with some of his fellow 57th Infantry of the Philippine Scouts when a young Japanese officer approached him. The Japanese wanted to ride on one of the motorcycles lined up along the road rather than continue walking. Colonel Tranell of the 57th shouted, "anyone know how to run of one of these things?" "Hell yes," responded Watson. He walked over to the motorcycle, started it, put the Japanese on the seat, shoved the cycle into 1st gear, and showed the officer where the accelerator was located let him go. A bloody scream and stream of profanity came from the Japanese as he went roaring down the side of the mountain with no idea where the clutch or brake was. No one saw him again.

General Parker's Corps headed up the East Coast of the peninsula while General Jone's men remained on the West Side waiting to continue the fight. Jone's men hid in foxholes in the jungle until the Japanese arrived under a white flag and explained the battle was over. The Allies were directed eastward across the peninsula on jungle trails and an old cobblestone road going to Balanga. Field grade officers were eventually removed from the column along the road, placed in trucks, and transported to Balanga.[245]

The initial phase of POW evacuation was completed in Balanga and the first to arrive was General King and staff. They arrived in the afternoon of 9 April that prompted a large photographic session for propaganda usage. Then the inquisition began with the main subject being Corregidor. Some Japanese were convinced the Malinta Tunnel on the island led to southern Bataan. Then the officers were taken to Orani to await other American flag officers.

On the evening of the 12th, the officers were driven to Camp O'Donnell to become the first POWs in the camp.[246]

Balanga turned into a giant disorganized mess as the West Coast POWs joined the column from Mariveles. The weather was hot and there was little shade covering the roads. The men in the column hoped they could obtain water from the Talisay River but as they approached, they found the riverbed filled with dust. The column continued north out of Balanga led by General Jones. It was the first time in history an American general was forced to walk to a prison camp.[247]

Soon the sides of the road became littered with dead and dying men from the column. The bodies quickly bloated in the heat. On the same day, crows and ravens tore into the bodies while flies hung in clouds over the remains. The poor physical condition of the POWs caused problems and attracted guard attention. Unfortunately, the attention received often resulted in death for the failing POW. [248]

In Manny's group, the guards permitted the POWs to drink water out of ditches and carabao wallows. Within hours, the men who drank the water were violently ill. Near Orani, a member of the 31st collapsed and two of his soldier friends carried him until they became too weak. A guard forced the two Americans to kill the ill soldier with shovels. Needless to say, the Americans refused until the guard pointed his pistol at them. The terrible deed was done. Two Filipinos were ordered to do the same thing to an American, leaving the fatally injured half-buried, still beckoning for help. In another incident, POWs were forced to bury faltering prisoners alive.[249]

Filipina mothers feared what the Japanese might do to their daughters. They muddied their faces and bound their breasts to make them look less desirable. Unfortunately, many Japanese soldiers sneaked up on young girls and dragged them off into the woods or their camp.[250]

A new Cadillac on a small bridge a few miles north of Cabcaben stopped the column of POWs. The Japanese Press arrived and forced

Robert K. Harmuth

the POWs to raise their hands in surrender and to look forlorn. The latter was not difficult. Later, the picture appeared in "Life" magazine.[251] The march continued and by the afternoon of the 10th, all the POWs were out of water. The canteens were empty. Most of the road had a ditch alongside which held stagnant water from past storms and runoff. The water was green with algae and alive with mosquito and fly larvae. The dehydrated POWs attempted to quench their thirst in the ditches but were literally beaten or bayoneted to death for leaving the column. At sunset, the guards confiscated all POWs canteens and any other vessels for holding water.

The march continued well into the night. In numerous places, artisan wells pumped cool, clear water onto the ground. There were a number of incidents where the POWs were stopped and made to face the water, yet not permitted to drink. The torture continued throughout the next day and intermittently during the remainder of the march. Some POWs were led into an old Philippine estate enclosed by brick walls. One of the POWs lost control next to one of the walls in the dark but his screaming was quickly silenced by a single rifle shot. The following morning, some of the POWs were unable to stand, let alone walk. Stiff from laying down following days of marching, they could not rise. They were picked up, thrown into the back of trucks and never seen again.

Early in the morning of the 11th, the third day of the march, the lead column group reached the barrio of Orani. The countryside and road flattened which made walking easier. The march continued north while the POWs were rendered to walking robots, their senses numbed by hunger, thirst and pain. The thought process seemed impossible and the brain refused to acknowledge the experience. Mental strength drained, the POW's desire for self preservation waned. The weakest in each group were placed in the front of the column so their fellow POWs could help them from reaching the rear where they were at the unrelenting mercy of the guards.

Mansfield hurt and literally shook with malaria chills. His stomach felt afire and when he tried to speak, his thick tongue was out of control. Each step brought agony and he prayed for help. Suddenly, his group was shoved off the road and into a field. His prayer was answered as he collapsed to the grassy ground. Over 100 exhausted men fell to the ground, some so exhausted they passed out from the heat and others were in a semi-delirium. Twenty or more guards stood watch over the men but offered neither food nor water. Occasionally, a guard noticed a man or two in severe agony and sympathized with a kick or punch. Pleas for water usually resulted in laughter, a guard pouring his canteen of water on the ground, or a favorite was urinating on the POW. A few men could take no more and attempted to escape into a nearby jungle. They were shot or dragged back and bayoneted.

Cruelty was administered to civilians as well as the POWs. Many of the civilians tried to help the POWs and were punished if caught by the Japanese guards. A farmer and his wife near Limay tried to give prisoners some water and food but were caught by guards. As a column walked by, the couple were tied to stakes and burned to death. A Filipina mother and infant were beaten when caught passing a ball of rice to a POW. Some of the column almost broke ranks at the sight but managed to refrain and save their lives.[252]

Mansfield's rest abruptly ended with the jar of a rifle butt. His muscles screamed in pain as he struggled to his feet and forced himself to walk again. He didn't realize it at the time but he was lucky. He and his group had no Formosan or Korean guards who were more brutal than the Japanese. The march continued along the winding coastal road and through a multitude of small villages and barrios. Mansfield recognized the area since he and the 194th had retreated along the same road. Many of the villages were vastly altered by the course of the battles. Where once stood peaceful villages and homes now only smoldering ruins remained. Smoke and death replaced the smell of food cooking and the salt air. However, the beating taken by the buildings was not reflected in the people. They lined the road and cheered the POWs as the limped northward. When the guards weren't looking, they passed prisoners small napkins made of banana leaves with food and cups of water. As the columns passed through areas like Balanaga and Orani with the large sugar plantations, the locals passed them short stalks of sugar. Balls of rice were cooked and passed to the men for they were small enough to hide in one's hands. When the guards detected the passing of food, they grabbed the food and threw it in the road which no longer was paved. The guards took delight in watching the POWs desperately scoop rice grains up out of the dirt and gravel road. The gravel, rock, and dirt road hurt the men's feet and particularly bothered Mansfield's bad foot.

The Philippine Scouts were another favorite target of the Japanese guards. The Japanese sought revenge for the terrible beating the Scouts gave them at Abucay Hacienda. While detained in Orani during the march, the Japanese forced some of them to dig a trench then kneel in front of it. Each Scout was slammed on the head with a shovel. While stunned, the Scouts were pushed into the trench and buried alive.[253]

Filipinos were handled the best of all the Allies for the Japanese envisioned the Philippine Island becoming a part of their empire. When the prisoners stopped, the Americans often were made to stand while the Filipinos were permitted to lay down and sleep. That is not to imply the Filipinos were treated well; just better than the Americans. "It was the mistreatment by the majority of the Japanese troops which shocked the civilized world."[254]

Not every guard was cruel. Seiichi Nishida was a member of a water purification unit and he watched in disbelief as the POWs marched past him. Hundreds of POWs stumbled by, scorched in the baking sun, half-naked, and mumbled something he didn't understand. He moved closer and learned his first English word: "water, water." He filled his mess kit lid with water and gave a POW some water. From under the sunburned face, a tear flowed down the POW's check and he heard two more words, "thank you, thank you."[255]

Mansfield thought he was in one of the lead groups until one night his group was led into a vacant and fenced field to rest. The field was littered with cast off clothing and human feces. An officer in his group complained to the guards about the terrible conditions and the entire group ended up standing for additional hour.[256]

The remnants of the 31st struggled north on the same road a few miles back of Mansfield and came across a cool mountain stream crossing below the road. It was almost impossible for Manny to control his urge to jump into the water. The men were stopped at the stream's bank, ordered to face and listen to the bubbling cool water. Manny stiffened in anticipation of getting a drink but it was not forthcoming. A young lad, younger than Manny, could take it no longer and fell to his knees on the stream bank to drink. A guard with a sword rushed to his side and a swishing sound was heard. The head fell into the stream and floated away while blood poured from between his shoulders, turning the water red.[257]

Local Filipina women visited the fenced POWs and wept openly at their treatment. When the guards saw the women, the women were summarily shot. Soldiers continued to filter out of the woods and join the groups despite being warned off by the POWs. They too were hungry and thirsty. Somehow, they missed the willing assistance of the villagers and guerrillas.[258] The 12th of April, the 4th day of the march, brought continued suffering and death. At the next rest stop, some men could not avoid sitting in previously deposited feces. Only one water spigot dripped water for hundreds of the POWs. Invariably, fights and pushing started and an officer stepped in to restore order. He received a 6-inch bayonet blade run up his butt. He attempted to escape the guards but they grabbed him and threw him into a slit trench filled with human feces. The poor officer tried to crawl out but was pushed back and clubbed by the guards. Eventually, he drowned in human waste.

Mansfield's group neared San Fernando and passed a large sugar cane field in full bloom. Suddenly, without a word spoken, the entire group broke ranks for the field, completely catching the guards unaware. The guards didn't know how to cope with the problem so they permitted the POWs to gather sugar cane for an hour. The guards rounded up the men and got them back on the road. The men gorged themselves on the cane having no idea what it would do to their innards later. Never the less, the sugar provided them with badly needed energy.[259]

The heat continued and the column kicked up huge choking clouds of dust as they neared Lubao. The guards walked on the windward side of the column to avoid the dust leaving the leeward side unguarded. One of the POWs took advantage of the opportunity and rolled off the road and into a ditch. He leaped a hedge and dashed, in a manner of speaking, into a marsh and lay in tall grass. Blair Robinett met Chaplain Father Duffy who had the same idea. That night, they were befriended by a Filipino youth who gave them food and drink.[260]

Near sundown, Mansfield's group reached the village of Lubao near San Fernando. The group joined other groups in a larger room made of chicken wire in a sheet steel warehouse. Mansfield learned from Filipino POWs that the structure was a theater for cockfights before the war. Multitudes of locals awaited the POWs arrival with bananas, coconuts, water, and other foods. Again, the villagers were battered by the guards and forced to depart the area. Garbage was thrown into the wire arena like slopping hogs. It was a pathetic sight as the starved men groveled for food remnants and picking chicken droppings from the food. The POWs absolutely needed nourishment. Then a Japanese guard walked among them with the head of an American on a bayonet followed by more guards and more bayonets.[261]

The final leg of the march from Lubao to San Fernando was in daylight under a unmerciful sun and nary a tree or bush lined the road. A handful of Americans broke ranks and eventually joined local guerrillas.[262] Thousands of POWs no longer had shoes or useful footwear and were tortured by the hot asphalt. Burns were added to blisters and sores on the feet.[263] As the POWs neared San Fernando they were greeted by troop filled trucks that lined the sides of the road. The Japanese troops swung rifle butts at the POWs. It was gauntlet, Japanese style.[264]

Manny's group arrived in San Fernando a few days later but his group was permitted to rest and purchase food from the local villagers. The only food Manny could find were balots for a peso each. He shared a couple with a doctor and forced down the Filipino delicacy.[265]

Day five of the march or the 13th began no differently for the lead groups. Mansfield stood in a long line awaiting water. He prayed for the strength to make it through yet one more day. Impatiently he waited for his turn and received water in his cupped hands. It was the day's water ration. He learned the day prior that picking up wet mud was not looked upon kindly when he received the proverbial rifle butt in the back. Mansfield tried to think positively – he still had his feet and the remains of his shoes. He no longer took them off when he rested for his feet swelled beyond the ability to get them back on.

With his handful of water came a few grains of rice that served as breakfast. Then the POWs were hustled out of the arenas and back on the road. Mansfield walked for a couple of hours when they were diverted off the main road and into a small town. During this part of the march, there were Japanese guards on both sides of the column and only a few feet apart. There would be no escape from the town. Mansfield had no idea why such heavy security was in effect until the answer came into view. The POWs were herded into a railroad yard and shoved into boxcars. They were to receive a railroad ride to Capas.

The train cars were smaller than American trains, a three-quarter-gauge line railroad.[266] A hundred or more POWs were stuffed into each car although a few men were permitted to sit atop the cars. Mansfield managed to crawl in a car while many men were unceremoniously thrown into the rail cars. The men had no room to sit and were packed into the cars like standing sardines. The doors were locked and the temperature immediately skyrocketed with a proportionate loss of oxygen. When all the POWs were loaded, the train got underway.

For over two hours, the POWs stood in the stifling heat and gasped for air. The last moisture in their bodies sweat out. In some of the cars, the POWs shifted positions periodically to permit the men to breath easier near the doors and walls of the car. In other cars, some men went mad in the heat and fought with each other to get near a crack in the sidings. The cars smelled badly from the men's sweat and lost body functions. There was no choice if one had to relieve himself – it had to be done standing side by side and butt to butt in the car. Men became sick in the heat which added to the horrible conditions in the car.

Finally, the train stopped and the doors were opened. Blinded by the sunlight, the men handed each other to the ground. Each car had dead, held up by the mass of standing men. Many men collapsed when the pressure of all the men eased and were beaten out of the cars by guards. The POWs were beaten and shoved into a column and the march resumed. Mansfield could barely stand let alone walk. To add to their misery, the men were forced to carry their dead that turned out to be about 7-8 men per rail car.

The POWs struggled out of the rail station and into the streets of Capas. Benevolent villagers met the POWs and gave them some food and drink but Mansfield was already beyond the point where citizens aided the POWs. They turned westward and out of the city. It was the final leg of the infamous journey and only a few miles in length but in the POWs condition, it seemed thousands of miles. As the sun set with the relative coolness of evening descending upon them, they reached the final goal – O'Donnell Prisoner of War Camp.

Mansfield and fellow POWs literally collapsed once inside the camp gates and fell into a deep sleep approaching a coma. Minutes later, they were awakened by guards to bury the dead. There would be no water forthcoming until the dead were buried. The group of anti-aircraft POWs trucked earlier served as a reception committee and helped the arriving POWs as much as they could. The long odyssey was complete after almost two weeks for all the POWs to arrive in Camp O'Donnell. Approximately 55,000 Filipinos and 8,000 Americans walked 60 or more miles depending on where they surrendered.

Back on Bataan, patients in the two hospitals and the prisoners unable to work were moved to Bilibid Prison in Manila. Bilibid was an old civilian prison built by the Spanish decades earlier. It was surrounded by 20-foot walls with electrified wires on top. The prison was built in the shape of half a wagon wheel with the hub being the guard's quarters and watch station. The spokes were large numbers of barracks.[267]

CHAPTER SIX

LIFE IN CAMP O'DONNELL AND
CABANATUAN CAMPS

COLONEL TOSHIMITSU TAKATSU and his staff surveyed potential sites for POW camps in late March 1942. The search began in Tarlac Province and Camp O'Donnell. Takatsu was responsible for finding confinement facilities and quarters for an expected 25,000 American and Filipino POWs when Bataan fell. Camp O'Donnell was hurriedly built in early 1941 at the direction of General MacArthur to house Filipino recruits to be trained by American instructors. The camp consisted of multiple poorly built shacks with one of the better shacks named a hospital. When Takatsu completed his tour in O'Donnell, he headed for Cabanatuan.[268]

A few miles northeast of Camp O'Donnell was another abandoned Philippine Army training center located near the small village of Pangatian. The camp was in better condition than Camp O'Donnell and the colonel was certain the two camps could handle the anticipated numbers of prisoners. The report went to General Kawane who was responsible for transporting all POWs to camps and clearing the peninsula for the Japanese effort against Corregidor. The plan was to march the POWs to the East Road where Allied trucks were to transport the men to San Fernando. There the POWs were to be railed to Capas with an eight-mile walk to Camp O'Donnell.[269]

The POWs were a pitiful sight. Outwardly, they were unshaven, covered in sores, and severely sunburned. They were skinny, nothing more than skin and bones, after months of living on half rations or no food. The men were clad in remnants of uniforms and their footwear was ragged or nonexistent. But worst of all, the men were literally dying of thirst. The tankers from the 192nd and 194th averaged a weight loss of between 45 and 55 pounds per man. Some of the men were so weak, when injured they lost conscience before anesthetic could be administered.[270]

The POWs passed through the main gate into Camp O'Donnell, flanked on either side by high towers equipped with machine guns. A barbed wire fence led from the gate in both directions as far as the eye could see. Mansfield opened an eye and looked around. It took him a moment to figure out where he was. He collapsed after entering the camp compound and didn't know how long he had been out when a kick to his foot made him scream in pain. It had not mended before the march and was swollen and bruised from the walk. A few days later, he was carried to the "hospital" with malaria and dingue fever.[271] His temperature skyrocketed to over 104 degrees and didn't recede until a medic found some atabrime, also used to treat symptoms of malaria. Dingue Fever causes acute cerebral diseases or severe headaches and swelling, rashes, and wild tumors. The fever is transmitted by the common mosquito.[272]

Camp O'Donnell was a labyrinth of broken and incomplete buildings. The decrepit barracks buildings were actually elongated nippa huts with palm fronds and branches used to cover the structure. The camp was located eight miles west of the Manila Railroad Line at Capas. The POWs were held at O'Donnell until the fall of Corregidor. The camp was located on the central plain of Luzon, covered in high cogan grass which rolled like the waves at sea in a wind. There were no trees in the god-forsaken land with the only shade provided by tall wood gun towers that surrounded the camp between strands of barbed wire. There was one small stream running through the camp, which was initially the only source of water. The Americans and Filipinos were split into different areas separated by a small dusty road.

The Japanese promoted working with the Philippine People in a New World order, administered by Japan. All East Asian countries were to be brought under the roof of Japan, which eventually translated in the early release of most Filipino prisoners.

On a small knoll in the middle of the camp was the camp commandant's residence where he addressed the POWs when all the men arrived from Capas. The men stood under a beating sun and awaited his appearance. A short swarthy interpreter came out in the commandant's stead and saluted a fluttering Japanese flag on a tall roughly hewn pole. He smartly did an about-face and addressed the assembled POWs. "The captain, he say Nippon has captured Java, Sumatra, and New Guinea, and will soon own Australia and New Zealand. The captain, he say Nippon and America are enemies and always will be till Nippon victorious. He say you are not prisoners of war; you will be treated like captives. He say you not know how to act as soldiers. You have no discipline. He say you not stand at attention to talk so he say you will have trouble from him."[273]

Most of the Americans in the camp hospital suffered from streptococci bacteria in addition to their other ailments. Mansfield struggled with his illnesses and was assigned to a work detail in the hospital. Despite fever and weakened by malaria, he labored daily hauling water and swabbing the wood deck in the makeshift hospital. He was reminded daily how fortunate he was to be in the hospital and alive. Living in one of the barracks was not lucrative due to the shabbiness of the structures so many POWs lived outdoors. "You like treatment here, nay? Much better than other prisoners!" Mansfield mumbled, "Don't know how it could be much worse. Wormy rice and a cup or two of water every day. Dumb Jap!" in a whisper.

After a few weeks in the hospital, Mansfield was sent back to his barracks. He had been forced to sleep on the hospital floor but in the barracks, he had a straw mattress, an inch thick. It made little difference in comfort. He met his barracks roommates for the first time and was aghast at the disheveled and tattered bunch of men. Only a few of his roommates had the strength to stand and shake his hand. Most of the men lay outside on their mat in the blistering heat and stared aimlessly into space. Manny made the same observation at his barracks and noted most of the men didn't care enough to brush off the flies.

Mansfield wasn't pleased with his assignment to the grave-digging detail until a fellow prisoner reminded him it was much better to dig the graves than to go into the grave. POWs died in such large numbers, Mansfield and his detail found it necessary to dig large holes for mass graves. Bodies not buried in a day were buried the following day along with the new dead. The dead were buried quickly for the intense heat degenerated the corpses rapidly. Initially, the POWs stood to salute the dead as they were carried to the burial site. Unfortunately, the procession of dead became so commonplace and the survivors so weak, the practice eventually ceased.

One of the better work details was stevedoring on the docks of Manila, which reflected relative civilized and humane treatment. The treatment was thought to be decent since the Japanese commandant and the POW Officer-in-Charge were friends before the war in San Francisco.[274] Mansfield was to see the docks in this detail shortly.

Local villagers assisted the prisoners with small portions of food through the barbed wire on occasion but were of little help to the injured and ill that could not move to the fenceline. Guerrillas made their presence known in the barrios and villages where the work details toiled but rarely in the camp. The guerrillas stole supplies from Japanese truck convoys and passed the food and clothing onto the POWs. They kept the ammunition and fuel for themselves but the little extra food helped men like Manny and Mansfield stay alive.[275]

Then there were the flies . . . everywhere there were flies; the big blue and green kind frequently found in garbage and sewage.

ROBERT K. HARMUTH

Stories were told of bushes bending under their weight. It was impossible to eat without flies in the food. Nary a meal was eaten without some fly consumption.

Manny also stumbled into Camp O'Donnell and collapsed after the march. There were only 80 or so remaining in his marching group when they arrived in the camp. The exhausted, sick, and filthy men also were permitted to rest for a brief period. They were then assigned to barracks and the hospital as had Mansfield's group. The remnants of the medical corps served in the hospital, doing what they could for the POWs despite a pitiful shortage of medicine. What medicine survived the march was soon depleted. POWs died at the rate of 300 to 400 per day. The worst day was 27 May 1942 when 471 Filipinos and 77 Americans gasped their last breath. Colonel Duckworth, an Army doctor, was then assigned to the hospital and the death rate dropped drastically to about 125 per day.[276] Some sources estimate 700 Americans and 10,000 Filipinos died in Camp O'Donnell in less than two months. Men's weights dropped from 200 to 90 pounds..[277]

General King wasn't held with the rest of the POWs although the majority of his staff was present at Camp O'Donnell. The POWs were divided into groups of ten men and placed in a singular section of each barracks. The barracks had a captain, usually a sergeant, while the officers were housed in barracks near the main gate. The officers had their own brig with Marines manning the facility.[278] Colonel Beecher, USMC was the senior American officer present.

The fresh water supply was desperate with only one (some remember two) faucet which slowly dripped water and couldn't be turned on or off. A couple ingenious POWs found an old Model T-Ford that they got running. The men hooked up a pulley to a rear wheel and the water pump. Soon, water flowed from the spigot that improved the water situation to unsatisfactory.[279]

The guards looked and acted mean. A real soldier did not desire prison guard duty and the billet was looked upon with disdain. As the Japanese Army became more committed and involved, guard duty was relegated to the old, crippled, and challenged. Many of the camp guards were suspected insane, alcoholic, and perverts. These guards were to govern Manny and Mansfield's lives for the next three and a half years.

On the Filipino side of the camp, an estimated 3,000 Filipinos arrived from Corregidor who were in relatively good physical condition compared to the survivors of the Death March. They were permitted to carry personal effects in duffel bags including some food, cloths, and medicine. The new arrivals were aghast at the sight of the POWs from Bataan and quickly shared whatever they had with them.

It mattered little which camp one was in when it came to insects. The mosquitoes were everywhere and quickly spread malaria throughout the camp. Manny and Mansfield constantly slapped flying pests and brushed off ants. Bugs were everywhere. Lice were a continuing problem no matter the conditions in the camp or weather. The men followed the example of monkeys and picked lice and fleas from each other. Although there were no beds, there were plenty of bed bugs that disappeared during the day into the wood and dirt to reappear at night in full force. [280]

USS SPEARFISH was in the area before Corregidor fell and ordered to pick up passengers from the rock on 3 May. When the submarine surfaced off Corregidor, she was fired upon by Japanese artillery located in South Bataan. The USS PERRY stood out from the island and transferred a number of personnel to the submarine, including 13 nurses. They were spared the agony of becoming prisoners of war.[281]

The nippa hospital was overwhelmed with dysentery patients but the medical staff had no soap or rags to clean neither the structure nor the patients. The building was infested with insects and feces dropped by the ill. The building and area was so filthy, a scratch of the skin festered into huge ulcers, often causing the loss of a limb. One of the medics suffered an agonizing and embarrassing problem when he became constipated while also having bleeding hemorrhoids. The opening literally healed shut.[282]

A large number of deaths occurred because the prisoner just gave up on life. They just stopped eating the meager rations and soon all pain disappeared. The mainstay of the POW daily food ration was lugau, a watery rice soup normally filled with worms and other vermin. Some POWs hid their cup of lugau until darkness when they couldn't see the contents. Others just closed their eyes and ate but all the men knew the taste of a worm. Men, who didn't give up, spent time and energy desperately attempting to get others to eat and move. They even tried beating the demoralized POWs into activity but usually in vain.

In June, Manny became violently ill with malaria. His chills gave way to a high fever. It wasn't his first malaria attack so he immediately knew what was wrong. His skin felt on fire and dry followed by delirium and convulsions. He physically and mentally reached the brink of death. He had enough of the hell and torture and was ready to surrender his life. A Catholic Chaplain found Manny in this state and took him under his wing. For days, the chaplain force fed Manny and managed to beg quinine pills from the Japanese. Manny recovered and forever would be in debt to the wonderful man in the Chaplain Corps. It mattered not at all what the faith, chaplains came to the aid of everyone.[283] The chaplain may have been Father Cummings who was known to often forsake his own food ration and give it to the dying. He was world renowned for his statement, "there are no atheists in the foxholes."[284]

At the height of the prisoner population in O'Donnell and Cabanatuan Camps, there were 37 known chaplains. By denomination, the largest number of chaplains were Catholic probably because the majority of the Filipinos were Catholic. The chaplains said mass daily before sunrise so it didn't interfere with daily work details. Rosary services were conducted nightly while confessions were heard prior to morning mass. Chaplains held comparable services from other faiths and the chaplains were credited with saving the lives of hundreds of POWs.

Water remained the critical item in the camp and the men spent hours in line waiting their turn to fill a canteen. Mansfield stood for hours in the sun waiting and when he reached the faucet, it took five minutes for the canteen to fill. It was a good day when he reached the faucet without seeing a prisoner die in line. Water from the faucet was only used for drinking, not for cooking or washing. Without water to wash, the POWs suffered from numerous skin disorders and oozing wounds. Showers were only available during the rainy season. When he wasn't in line for water, Mansfield sat in front of his barracks, passing from reality to day dreaming and back again.

A helpful occurrence was the arrival of the monsoon season in May 1942. The rain fell in torrents so there was some relief in drinking water and washing a month after the POWs arrival in camp. The rain almost destroyed what was left of barracks as roofs and sidings collapsed. The men slept outside rather than chance part of the roof falling on them. They huddled together to keep warm and fought with knee high mud when they moved during the day.

A few mechanics got a break in O'Donnell and were assigned to a work detail repairing vehicles. The detail remained active for the duration the Americans remained in the camp. Mechanics and truck drivers were permitted to move around in their work. This gave them the opportunity to bargain and beg for food in the villages and barrios. Truck drivers actively sought medicine for their sick comrades when out of the camp and a few became black marketers.

A work detail was sent to Capas to repair a bridge destroyed during the Allied retreat south. Another detail, comprised of Signal Corps personnel, was detailed to recover telephone cables cut during the battles and restore the telephone system. Although officers were not required to work, many volunteered for work and avoid torture or death. An idle POW was an invitation for trouble from the guards. A detail of hundreds of men was sent into the jungles and woods to build a road. Conditions were so grim for the detail, over 70% of the men died in the first month, mostly from pneumonia. A water detail spent the day filling canteens and carrying them back to camp on bamboo poles. The good part of this work was the men in the detail always had plenty of water to drink.[285]

Gerald Wade of the 93rd Bombardment Squadron was assigned to the water detail and bailed water from a nearby creek for cooking. The doctors decreed the water safe as long as it was boiled. One day, Wade and a companion went to the creek for water and decided to take a swim before returning to the camp. With the guards in the distance, they made a break for freedom and escaped. Wade came down with malaria that night but a Filipino youth found the pair and led them to a schoolteacher and a Philippine Scout for help.[286]

The Japanese did not take kindly to escape attempts and took drastic action to halt escape efforts. Ten men were caught outside the camp one night and hanged the following day. Since it happened to be the Emperor's birthday, the sentence was commuted to hanging by the thumbs vice the neck. The ten men hung for days and when they were cut down, only one of the men was still alive so he was shot. The event did capture the attention of the POWs. The big persuader against escapes was the assignment of all prisoners to groups of ten. If any man escaped or attempted escape, the remainder of the ten men was executed. If all ten men escaped, 100 other prisoners were killed. At the Davao Penal Colony, a handful of officers decided to take the chance and escape. They manufactured tools from Red Cross box contents and on 4 April 1943, they made a mass escape. They reached the north coast of Mindanao, made contact with local guerrillas, and were removed by submarine to safety. Only one officer failed to make it to freedom.

Manny was assigned to the burial detail. The depressing duty was split into two groups; one dug the holes and the other transferred the bodies to the gravesite. The bodies were buried 15-20 to a hole and the detail worked a full day every day. The death rate

)-HARM

was so high, there was no time for prayers, chaplains, or officers. If members of the burial detail saw a friend or acquaintance, they thought prayers for the man then continued on with their work. A disgusting chore was straightening out the bodies so they would fit into the grave. The water table was so high, the hole was dug quickly and bodies buried before water seeped in and floated the bodies. During the rainy season, it was difficult to keep the bodies from floating out of the hole.

The Japanese didn't anticipate burials and initially no tools were available for the work. For the first week, the burial detail scrapped out holes with their hands and plates but they fell behind on the burials. The dead stacked up and the smell was unbearable; the sweet ugly odor of rotting dead. The dead were pulled out of barracks every day and stacked in a line and body upon body. The wall of bodies became many feet high and in the hot sun, the decay process moved quickly. The camp became a haven for maggots, flies, vultures, and wild dogs.[287]

Most POWs felt guilty they surrendered and wished they had fought to the last man rather than succumb to the treatment of the Japanese. General King was overheard to say he would have to stand court martial some day for disobeying Wainwright's orders. He told his listeners they had not surrendered but rather had been surrendered and followed his orders. It didn't make the POWs feel much better.

As time passed, POWs continued to die but a pattern developed. Survival appeared to depend more on mental attitude than physical condition. Men gained strength from their belief in God while others survived from a fear of death or anger toward the Japanese. However, the trend of the men surviving seemed to depend on having a family or others to love as well as self-pride. It was the man who had something to live for that remained alive.[288]

The Japanese occupied nearby Clark Army Air Base and sortied aircraft out of the field on a daily basis. The POWs counted the Japanese planes flying over head, headed south to Corregidor. Later, they counted the aircraft returning, carefully hiding smiles when the count of returning planes was less than the number departing.

An area of relaxed rules was religion. The POWs were permitted a certain amount of latitude and permitted priests from local parishes to visit the camp on Sundays to say mass. The padres often smuggled mail, money, and medicine into the camp under their vestments. Mail from home was a precious commodity, especially since the Japanese delivered virtually no mail for the first couple years of the war. What little mail arrived was highly censored and made little sense. Mail was non-existent in Camp O'Donnell and slightly improved at Camp Cabanatuan.[289]

It was imperative the POWs move around to keep their bodies functioning properly. A common activity for Manny and Mansfield, as many others, was to walk among the thousands of POWs looking for a friend or former soldier mate. Finding someone among thousands was difficult at best because everyone looked different. The men that couldn't or otherwise didn't move about steadily lost their battle for life. If they remained in the damp barracks, scratches didn't heal and wounds grew larger and rotted. Soon the wounds became tropical ulcers and the flesh rotted to show bright white bone that turned yellow with lymph, ooze, and blood.

Things went badly on Corregidor and the Japanese celebrated the Emperor's birthday with a massive bombing and bombardment. The rock was left ablaze but that night, a couple PBY's landed and removed 50 Americans of which 30 were nurses.[290]

The POWs started to work for a wage of about 10-yen per day or roughly 3-cents per day. Officers received slightly higher pay whether they worked or not. They had their own galley and were able to purchase sufficient meat to live above the baseline of starvation. Manny was acutely aware of officer's resources since he was often hired to butcher meat. Manny managed to work a deal where he was paid for his services by receiving food. For example, he used parts of chickens for soup such as the head and feet while saving the feathers for making a pillow.

9-HARM

Occasionally the POWs had an opportunity to get in a lick of their own against their captors. Ed Fisher was assigned to a small work detail called the "tea detail." The Japanese truly enjoyed tea with their meals and as a refreshment. When the tea mug was empty, the detail carried two 5-gallon buckets to the creek. Ed and companion filled the buckets and since they weren't escorted, came up with a wonderful scheme. "Hey Ed, what do you think about pissing in the buckets?" In uncontrolled laughter, his friend answered, "sounds good to me." The two drank heavily of the water then relieved themselves in the buckets. If they were caught, it meant instant death. They returned with the full buckets used to make ten gallons of tea. The Japanese thoroughly enjoyed the tea and one guard yelled at them, "This is great tea. Want some?" He was shocked when the two hungry POWs turned down the generous offer.[291]

In early May, the POWs were told Corregidor surrendered. At Camp O'Donnell, things didn't change much as work detail after detail continued working throughout Central Luzon. Most of the heavy work was the repair of roads and bridges destroyed or damaged during the war.[292]

Seven weeks after arriving in Camp O'Donnell in early June, the American POWs were moved to Camp Cabanatuan. Of the 12,000 Americans who fought so gallantly in Bataan, 9,000 battered and starving Americans made it to Camp O'Donnell. An estimated 1,500 Americans died on the Death March and 1,000 Americans were moved to Corregidor prior to the fall of Bataan. Only 7,000 Americans walked out of O'Donnell.[293]

By August 1942, only 100 patients and five medics were left at O'Donnell when the last group of Americans left the camp by truck for Camp Cabanatuan. Of the 55,000 Filipinos to arrive at O'Donnell, 28,000 perished. In a desperate effort to win the hearts of the Philippine People, the Japanese released the remaining Filipinos in December 1942.

Malaria struck the Japanese Army while Homma was preparing to invade Corregidor. The supply of quinine disappeared and two-thirds of his army was out of commission at one point. Invasion plans continued, however, although under duress. Landing craft assembled and departed Lamao for Corregidor where they were pounded by the ancient island defenses and WWI vintage rifles. The invasion effort was a slaughter for awhile but eventually, the Japanese put their men ashore. Slowly the tide turned and Corregidor fell.[294]

Of six mine sweepers assigned to the Asiatic Fleet, only the *USS QUAIL* remained. Three were sunk by Japanese aircraft in Manila Bay and two went south to the Netherland East Indies. Despite severe damage to *QUAIL* and many of her crew involved with repairs in the fortress, she managed to get underway on 5 May to clear a path for the submarine *USS SPEARFISH* who evacuated personnel, mostly nurses. *QUAIL* watched in horror as the Japanese unleashed a devastating artillery barrage and bomber attack on Corregidor shortly thereafter. Near the end of the bombardment, a round penetrated an underground magazine.[295] The explosion caused landslides onto the defensive beach emplacement and *QUAIL* was ordered to move and assist Fort Hughes on Caballo Island. When the vessel arrived, the fort was in shambles so *QUAIL* was ordered scuttled. As the old ship sank, white flags were observed over Corregidor, Fort Frank, and Fort Drum but not Fort Hughes.[296] LCDR John Morrill and his men from *QUAIL* slipped away from Fort Hughes the night of 6 May in a 36-foot launch. They carefully negotiated the Japanese patrols and set off for Australia. Averaging 5-knots, they safely completed the voyage to Port Darwin.[297]

The Fort Frank garrison was forced aboard a transport ship and taken to Nasugbu where they labored on the docks and nearby facilities. Without food or drink, the work was finished in two weeks and the POWs were transferred to Cabanatuan.[298]

Some POWs ended up in Bilibid Prison. It was used to house badly wounded prisoners although most Allied POWs were summarily killed if unable to work. The prison had American medical personnel and rudimentary medical supplies that helped keep the prisoners alive. Some of the POWs were assigned work details on the docks as stevedores. These men were given full food rations daily plus they were normally able to pick up useful items on the docks. One of the favorite commodities was tobacco that could be used to barter for almost anything.[299]

In the summer of 1942, General MacArthur organized a group of spies and saboteurs. It was established as the Allied Intelligence Bureau (AIB) and played a critical role in MacArthur's return. In one of the AIB's initial adventures, the submarine USS GUDGEON transported members, as did the USS THRESHER a few months later. Soon agents on the Philippines communicated regularly with the AIB and the AIB disseminated the "Bataan Fortnightly" to the Philippine People. It was an informational pamphlet intended to keep the population advised of progress in the war and lift morale.[300]

It was mid-summer 1942. It was difficult to be certain since there were no watches, clocks, or calendars. Since Philippine winters were rarely cold, seasons were guessed by the amount of rainfall. Mansfield guessed it was the middle or late summer.

It was close to high noon and Mansfield was standing in the water line to fill his canteen. Suddenly, a large number of Japanese military cars and trucks roared through the camp gates and stopped near the knoll in a cloud of dust. The lead car stopped in front of the Commandant's quarters and Mansfield watched the customary exchange of salutes. The officers entered the quarters and POWs gathered in small groups and spoke in hushed voices. Something big was up with so many brass visiting. Moments later, the officers came out of the Commandant's Quarters and the vehicles departed.

The commandant summoned his personnel, including all guards. They huddled on the knoll for a few minutes then called all the POWs to quarters for muster. It didn't make Mansfield happy since he was near the head of the water line. Grudgingly, the prisoners fell in at quarters. The lines of POWs looked like rows of scarecrows in a cornfield and the men were a bit testy. Without a word of explanation and no opportunity to pick up their meager belongings, the American POWs were pushed into a column of four abreast and marched out the main gate and into the countryside. They walked, limped, and struggled eastward. Since 11 April 1942 when the first contingent of prisoners arrived at Camp O'Donnell to that moment, 30,172 men died in the camp.[301].

The men struggled down the road until they were close to the halfway point to Capas, the old railhead. They were met by a long convoy of troop trucks and ordered into them. The loading took an hour or more as many of the men were lifted into trucks. The trucks carried the men through Capas and continued further to the east. The road was dirt and rock, radically changed directions that caused the POWs a great deal of discomfort in the back of the trucks. The truck convoy slowly crept down the road and into the next day. The light from the rising sun shown dimly through the choking dust when the trucks abruptly halted. The prisoners were unceremoniously dumped and pushed out of the trucks onto the ground. The Americans had arrived at POW Camp #1 at Cabanatuan.

Cabanatuan Camp #1 was located about six miles from Cabanatuan, a city of 100,000 people. Cabanatuan means "rock" and was the capitol of Nueva Ecija Province in northeast Luzon and a part of the central plain. The camp, akin to O'Donnell, was built by the Allies prior to the outbreak of war for training Filipino troops. The camp was surrounded by rice paddies at the base of the Sierra Madre Mountain Range with the Quezon Mountains separating the city from the Philippine Sea. A road led eastward to the village of Baler while to the west were the sugar cane fields of Tarlac and the China Sea further west of the Zambales Mountains.[302]

Like O'Donnell, Cabanatuan was surrounded in barbed wire and a guard tower every few hundred yards. The camp was well organized with plenty of barracks, its own food farm, a hospital and an American headquarters building. Each barracks building had built-in wood bunk bed tiers although there were no mattresses. The barracks had swing up windows made of bamboo, which provided air circulation. The camp was activated in August 1942 and used to consolidate POWs from O'Donnell and Cabanatuan Camps #2 and #3 also near Cabanatuan.

Water availability was better and its source was a deep well pumped to a holding tank thence to faucets. Bathing was still forbidden but the waiting time in the water line was reduced to a half-hour.

The camp was a half-mile long and a third-mile wide. A small knoll rose in the center of the camp as in O'Donnell with Japanese headquarters and a guardhouse called "posay bodega" located nearby. Captain Mori was the camp commandant who had been a reserve officer, lived in Manila, and ran a bicycle shop prior to hostilities. Japanese officer and enlisted housing was situated inside the camp with all housing, including the POW's barracks, on 3-foot stilts. Keeping the barracks off the ground was a big improvement and helped keep the men dry during monsoon seasons. The barracks were about 65' X 20' with the roofs thatched with nipa palm fronds.[303] Each building held around 125 POWs. A raised walkway went the length of the barracks between rows of bunks with bamboo slat bottoms and roughly a yard wide. The nipa roof kept out most of the sunlight and some rain. The officers were berthed in lean-to type structures with 12-15 officers per building. The only dominant structure was a water tower near the Japanese officer's quarters. LCOL Curtis Beecher, who was sent back with his Marines from Shanghai, was the ranking POW officer.

A small pond near the main gate was home to a flock of white ducks and geese that drew hungry glances from the POWs. Guava trees grew inside the camp, were later used by corpsman to make tannic acid for diarrhea cases. The entire camp was surrounded by three separate barbed wire fences.

The Japanese paid dearly for their victory on Corregidor and left bodies strewn on the beaches and waters of the island. Guards ordered the Corregidor POWs to pick up the bloated bodies of fallen Japanese with dog tags then cut off the body's arm. The tags were attached to the arm and sent back to Japan to the next of kin.

The POWs were marched to the dock area at Bottomside on 23 May and literally piled into three old cattle ships for transportation to Manila. The vessels anchored in Manila Bay the same night off Dewey Boulevard. The following morning, the sun beat unmercifully on the steel decks of the ships and the POWs nearly roasted. Around noon, the men were pulled out of the holds and placed on barges that took them to shallow water. The men were pushed off the barges into the water and made to wade ashore. They were corralled on the beach and mustered.

The men were pushed into a column of eight men abreast and marched to Bilibid Prison. A number of the prisoners collapsed during the march but were picked up by guards and trucked to the prison. The Filipinos lined the streets and were permitted to give food and assistance to the men.[304] The prison was clean, the decks polished, flush toilets, bathing and shower facilities, and an unlimited supply of water. The POWs were served three meals a day for the 5-6 day stay at the facility. Flag officers were placed in a separate group and shipped off to Formosa the following week while the first 1,500 men were assembled for their trip to Cabanatuan.[305]

Generals Wainwright and Beebe were held captive inside the University Club in Manila during the last days of organized resistance in the Philippines. Wainwright was awakened one morning by the sound of cheers and clapping outside. He peered out his window to see his old command from Corregidor marched down Dewey Boulevard to Bilibid Prison.[306]

Early in the evening of 27 May 1942, the first contingent of POWs from Corregidor arrived at the railroad station in Manila from Bilibid. It was a typical warm and windy night with heavy rain as the guards slammed the POWs into steel boxcars. Belittling the Americans failed again as the Philippine population cheered the prisoners and jeered the Japanese.[307] The ride was hot, tight, and unsanitary but a far cry from the trip suffered by the Bataan Death March POWs. The trip took four hours and when they reached Capas, the men were given a rest before starting off for the camp.[308]

The prisoners hiked 14 miles in the rain to Camp Cabanatuan #3 and they found the usual unreadiness. No arrangements had been made for the POWs arrival and though there were barracks, they weren't ready. There were no functioning utilities and the men were told if they wanted water, drink out of a puddle. Two meals were served daily; breakfast was mushy rice or lugao and a mess kit of rice in the evening with a tablespoon of rock salt. Conditions were untenable for captor and captives alike so the commandant marched the POWs out of the camp and down the road a few miles to another camp. This time the walk was tougher and the men from Corregidor received a taste of what the Bataan POWs received on their march.[309]

The men arrived in Cabanatuan Camp #1 and were assigned barracks the following day by rank and rate. The water system was intact and a welcome sight to the dirty and exhausted prisoners. The men relaxed a bit with water and a bunk but were amazed there was virtually no security for the camp. A quick look around gave them the answer. Where could they possibly go?[310]

A common torture used by the Japanese was to make the prisoner kneel with hands tied behind his back. A two inch diameter pole was placed and tied behind the knees. A wire was strung between the hands to the ankles, behind their back and around the neck. Any movement by the POW tended to cut into the neck. The POW was left in the position, sometimes for days.[311]

The Corregidor POWs suffered and their living conditions were poor but they gasped in disbelief and horror when the lead contingent of the Bataan POWs from O'Donnell arrived in camp on 6 June. In front with the lead group was Mansfield.

After all the men settled in, the O'Donnell medics set up shop in the barracks designated as the hospital. They finally had some medicine the men Corregidor brought with them and immediately began treating the severely ill. Dysentery led the list of

diseases which caused a gas to develop in the stomach with resultant diarrhea and undigested food in the bowels. Beriberi was prevalent caused by vitamin B-1 deficiency and came in the wet and
dry variety. Dry caused a wracking pain in bones and joints while
the wet was painful and caused extreme swelling of the body. Scurvy
was indicative of vitamin C lack and attacked the gums of the
mouth and lining of the mouth and nose. Malaria was possibly
the worst malady especially without the availability of quinine.
Diphtheria was very contagious and brought the only medical assistance from the Japanese. Fungus like athlete's feet and "jock"
itch plagued many and most men developed a type of tropical
ulcer on parts of their body.[312]

Wainwright and his senior staff were trucked from the University Club in Manila to Tarlac on 9 June where they joined other
senior officers from Bilibid and O'Donnell. They were stuffed into
crowded barracks of 180 men each with conditions little better
than at Cabanatuan. The customary camp rules were read and the
Japanese thoroughly enjoyed observing American generals and colonels salute and bow to Japanese privates. Food was worse than in
Manila yet better than O'Donnell and Cabanatuan.[313]

On 11 August, the general and other senior officers were forced
to spit polish their barracks then loaded aboard a train. They arrived in Manila later in the day and loaded into trucks. An American POW was Wainwright's driver who informed the general the
Marines had landed on Guadacanal. Nothing could have pleased
the general more than to hear the Americans were already on the
way back and he quietly passed the word to his fellow officers. The
morale of the men skyrocketed. The truck driver was in Mansfield's
work detail and told the detail the story that night on the docks.

The officers were shoved out of the trucks on Pier #7 in the
Port of Manila and loaded aboard a Japanese merchant ship. The
officers would later call the "hell ship" the *STINKO MARU*. The
ship got underway that night for Karenko, Formosa.[314]

Conditions at Cabanatuan improved as cooler weather arrived
in the autumn months but it came too late for 2,339 Americans

that had died in O'Donnell since early May. As life in the POW camp settled into a routine, a demand for manpower was generated to help the war effort in Japan. A movement of POWs from camps began to provide slave labor on the Japanese homeland. A few of the POW camps provided better living conditions such as the Davao Penal Colony. Food was grown on farms for camp use but the POWs received little of their labor. Overall, prisoners who came from farms in the States fared better than city dwellers. It wasn't so much the toughness but the men who grew up on farms were used to injuries and coped much better.[315]

The Japanese Code of Honor taught the soldier to fight to the death and never surrender. If a Japanese soldier was taken captive, he was to end his life as soon as possible or be disgraced. This code may account for the Japanese eagerness to end the POW's lives and to look upon the prisoners with such contempt.[316]

Shortage of water continued to plague the POWs in Cabanatuan until the Filipino prisoners were released and thousands of Americans were shipped to Japan. As the population of the camp diminished, Americans were billeted 100-men to a barracks with a captain or lieutenant in charge and a sergeant to act as a master-at-arms. However, the officers usually did not live in the barracks but in officer's quarters. He controlled the lives of the POWs, the warehouses, and food supplies. There even was an American guardhouse inside the camp for offenders.[317]

There was no soap available so the POWs made their own from lard and ash. It smelled bad and felt worse but it worked. However, the lard was worth more as food than soap so the soap making ended. Late in 1943, soap arrived in limited quantities in Red Cross packages. Some POWs wore "quan" buckets on their waists in which anything edible was placed. "Quan" has been defined by some as "thing-a-ma-jig." They found food such as insects, snakes, frogs, weeds, etc.[318]

In a variety of ways, small amounts of food and information found its way into the camp from outside the fence. When a can of food arrived, the POWs covertly checked the label for messages from the Filipino underground. Messages for individual POWs were often sent on evaporated milk cans. General information was quickly passed around the camp by mouth.[319]

Late in 1942, three officers were caught retrieving food from outside the fence line. They were forced to dig their own graves prior to the administration of torture. They were tied to a wood frame and beaten in the crouched position with wood behind their knees. They could live if they survived the torture for 72-hours. The first officer begged to be shot in a day, the second went blind and was shot, and the third was forced to self-amputate both legs before he asked to be shot.[320]

The division of POWs into groups of ten to deter escapes didn't work so three extra strands of barbed wire were added to the surrounding fence and some of the strands were electrified. In some areas, there were three rows of fences. One night, the inward fence line was electrified and the guard in the watchtower answered the urge of nature. He relieved himself over the side of the tower and his stream hit the charged wire. By the time the guard hit the ground, he was dead.[321]

Some work details actually aided the POW's health and welfare. One party traveled twice a week to Cabanatuan to pick up rice for the camp. Members of the work detail often were grateful recipients of handouts from the local villagers. Other work details worked in local barrios and villages that provided the POWs an opportunity to smuggle goods back into the camp. The men sewed pouches in their cloths in which to carry goods. Japanese surprise searches failed to stop the smuggling. Many equipments used by the Japanese and Philippine equipments ran on alcohol which was a source of smuggling and entertainment. The POWs often filled their canteens with "white lightning."[322]

Another group worked on the camp farm and their health improved markedly. But the most significant contribution to the POWs well being was news received during the work and brought back to the camp. As time progressed, it became obvious the United States was turning the tide of war. The news instilled hope, which cured a variety of ills, especially despondency. About the same time, the Japanese began releasing Filipino prisoners in the hope of a propaganda coup. Unfortunately for the Japanese, the released Filipinos did not back the Japanese and many turned to assisting the POWs still in the POW camps and guerrilla activities.

During the march from Bataan, a few POWs managed to escape by hiding under the long and flowing skirts of Filipina women who lined the road. During some of the walks by working details, the same skirts were utilized to smuggle food and money to the POWs.[323]

In January 1943, Manny was assigned the burial detail. His health had improved somewhat and as his duties took him about the camp, his thoughts centered on his old and dearest friend, Salvadore. He asked his fellow POWs if they had seen or knew the whereabouts of Salvadore but in vain. At the time, there were approximately 32,000 prisoners in Camp Cabanatuan. One day, Manny headed for "Zero Ward," or the building of the dead. It was a storage building for the dead until the bodies were buried. His route took him between a couple hospital wards and he observed with pity and frustration the prostrate human beings that were so very ill. Suddenly, he stopped in his tracks for lying before him was a naked body with the tattoo of the 809th Engineers on his arm. Manny gasped a short prayer the man was not Salvadore

The man had given up all hope and Manny shed a tear as he looked at the wretched skeleton before him. He was filthy and covered in sores and flies. As a leaned over to get a closer look, a guard struck him with a rifle butt and ran him off the ward. The sight of the man remained etched in Manny's mind so he returned to the ward the next day. He carefully searched the area for guards, then moved to the side of the poor man. Gently, Manny turned the man's head to look at his face. "Oh my God, Salvadore, is it you Salvadore?" His eyes opened slowly and blankly stared at Manny. A few minutes passed, then ever so slowly, a look of recognition appeared in his eyes. His mouth moved but he uttered nary a sound and a small trickle of tears rolled down his cheeks.

"Salvadore, speak to me. Say something!" Salvadore's head dropped and his body slumped, his head resting on Manny's lap. "Medic, medic," screamed Manny.

"So what the hell ya want man?" spoke a man who looked no better than Salvadore. "This is my best friend Salvadore. Can you help him? He looks very ill, " Manny pleaded. The medic quietly explained there was nothing he could do to help his friend, then walked away leaving the two alone. Manny cradled Salvadore's head and stroked his hair while he prayed. "Is that you Manny?" "Yes Sal, its me. What's wrong?" That was a foolish thing to ask and Manny felt stupid. It was easy to see his friend was near death. "I'm dying Manny. I just can't take it any longer." Manny hugged him tightly and said, "Oh no you're not going to die. I'm going to take care of you. You stay here and I'll be right back," Manny spoke quietly and again felt foolish. Where the hell was Sal going to go? Sal didn't have the strength to roll over let alone walk somewhere.

Manny headed back to his end of the camp and gathered his barracks mates around him and told them of Sal's plight. "I need your help guys. I know none of us have a pot to pee in but just a few crumbs will help." By early afternoon, Manny was on his way back to Salvadore with a small ragbag in his hand. Salvadore had not moved a bit but was in the shade of the barracks window flap. His skinny arms were clasped around his knees and his chin rested atop the knees. His body language was poor and displayed unmitigated defeat. "Hey Sal, I'm back and brought you a few things." "Manny, just leave me alone buddy. I just want to die in peace." "No way am I going to let you do that Sal, I'm your best friend and we'll work through this thing together," spoke Manny. "Here, try some quan and water. Come on damn it! Get your head up and open your stubborn mouth!"

Manny carefully pulled Sal's head back and fed him some rice and water soup. He dribbled water into the parched mouth and Sal almost choked to death on just a few drops of water. Ever so slowly, Sal began to respond and took nourishment willingly.

Manny and his friends dug a slit trench near Sal's barracks since all the men in the building were in bad shape. They swept out the barracks, cleaned up generally and brought more water and food for the sick men. "Hey goat man, you going to make it through the night okay? Need a cigarette?" "Hell, I'd probably choke to death on a smoke." "Okay, now take it easy Sal, remember I have to keep you alive since I'm going to marry your sister." "No shit," mumbled Sal, "I'll drink to that man, never had a butcher for a brother before."

The guards showed up again and ran Manny and friends back to their own barracks. "Sal, I'll be back in the morning. You hang in there, hear! Just ask God for some help."

The following morning after burial detail, Manny went back to see Sal with some lugao rice and cigarettes. Sal managed to greet Manny weakly. They chatted briefly as Sal explained how bad he hurt. Tears again rolled down his cheeks and he bit his lower lip in pain. Manny encouraged him to keep trying and talked about the old days herding sheep. "Think of these little Nips as just another kind of goat. You can handle them Sal." Then the guards arrived and ran Manny away again.[324]

Manny was back on the burial detail the next day but his mind was completely with Sal. The early afternoon burial followed the assembly of corpses in a dirty building designated as the "morgue." Every body had everything removed if the living could use it. Only the genitals were covered with grass, dirt or whatever was available. In the morning, the burial detail went to the burial site and dug graves that were usually large holes for multiple bodies. Anything available was used for stretchers to move the bodies, which were virtually unrecognizable following starvation, disease, and brutality. There was no registration of the dead except the guards removed the man's dog tag following death.[325] In August 1942, the Japanese required the POWs to erect a large marker in the cemetery with an inscription that read, "Dedicated to Americans, dead as a result of disease contracted in Bataan." One day, Manny was on burial detail and bent over while straightening a dead man's arm when he froze in horror. On the arm was the tattoo of the 809th Engineers. "Oh God, no!" He rolled the man over and stared into a beaten face. "Thank you God." It wasn't Sal.

Every day Manny returned to care for Sal. He kept him modestly supplied with water, tea, and food. He even made Sal a loincloth, which the men called "G-strings." Manny massaged Sal's muscles since he still had insufficient strength to walk. One of the chaplains came to the aid of Sal and between he and Manny, Salvadore began to recover. The monsoon season arrived which reduced the water and severe heat problem followed shortly thereafter by the arrival of the first Red Cross packages. Manny's friends chipped in some of their food to help Sal. God truly was with Salvadore.

During the two years Manny spent in Camp Cabanatuan, he was too ill and weak to work on many work details but gratefully spent a lot of time working in the fields on the farm. Raising crops and tiling the soil was tough but had the benefit of extra food, fresh air, and was well removed from the endless brutality of the guards. Prior to the Japanese invasion, the fertile Central Plain of Luzon was a breadbasket of agriculture. Only a few farms still produced a couple years later; one was run by the POWs.[326] Huge orchards and groves that once grew mangoes, papayas, coconuts, oranges, and bananas disappeared after being neglected. The fields were plowed and sowed with archaic picks and shovels. The POWs grew tomatoes, pechay, corn, onions, comotes, lettuce, watermelon, and other vegetables in sufficient quantity to feed the Japanese garrison. Unfortunately, a type of sweet potato on a vine was about the only vegetable to reach the POWs. Any bit of vegetable matter not consumed was mixed with human waste to create fertilizer. As many as 2,000 prisoners, including officers, worked the fields later in their captivity.[327]

There had been a number of large ranches on the plain but the owners and workers fled into the mountains leaving the stock to become feral and scattered. The American prisoners utilized a number of their own cowhands from cattle country and soon the

)-HARM

stock was rounded up and the ranches fenced. The POWs had their own slaughterhouse that butchered steers and water buffalo for the tables of the captors. Manny had the opportunity to work as a butcher but seldom benefited with any fruit of his work.

The POWs worked in the rice fields as well, doing most of the planting and paddy preparation. Filipinos were normally forced to cut and reap the rice. POWs, too weak to labor in the fields, were given buckets of tobacco juice and a brush to place on plants to kill insects. The system worked admirably.[328] The guards refused to permit the men to squat, kneel, or sit in the fields. The POWs had to bend from the waist to do their work.

Early in the occupation of Cabanatuan by the POWs, a commissary store was created and operated by the prisoners. Although the amount of money earned by the POWs was of negligible value for the enlisted men and modest for officers, it was sufficient at times to make the difference between life and starvation. Groups of POWs often pooled their earnings to purchase an item of sheer necessity. Cash also became available by selling smuggled goods and a black market flourished. An unfair advantage for officers at the commissary was rectified in 1944 by forming a slush fund for the enlisted men held by the commissary.[329] Cigarettes and alcohol were the basic units of barter. Gambling also had its niche in the camps. Once a gambler made some gains, he paid other POWs to do his work and often went months without any labor. The need or urge to get sufficient funds to buy necessities for life caused many men to become deplorably destitute to the gamblers.[330]

The prisoners controlled their own guardhouse. A POW caught stealing, fighting, etc. was placed in the detention facility as were any prisoner entertaining thoughts of escape. The time spent in the stockade was not all bad, however, as the building was located near the main gate. The guards used the men in the guardhouse to offload supply trucks that offered the opportunity to slip a morsel of food in their pockets. The bad side of guardhouse life was the men had latrine duty every day.

Eventually, Red Cross boxes arrived at Cabanatuan. Some boxes were mailed to individuals but most were to POWs in general. Millions of Americans packed boxes every month for pickup and delivery to the prisoners as well as the rest of the American Armed Forces. The boxes were shipped to New York where they were sent to Geneva for distribution. For the POWs in the Philippines, the boxes first went to Tokyo, then to Manila and finally to the individual camps. Along the box route, the contents were slowly stripped for Japanese use, often under the pretense of security inspections. In Cabanatuan, as in many camps, the POW officers were in charge of the Red Cross box distribution and storage. Manny received only one Red Cross package during his stay at Cabanatuan, mostly cloths and desperately needed cod liver oil pills.[331] Mansfield received no packages in Cabanatuan but did receive a couple when working in the Manila port area.[332]

More valuable than any commodity was mail and the Japanese appeared disinterested in getting it through to the POWs. The mail was delivered to each camp in huge bags, sorted, and placed in smaller bags, one alphabet letter per bag. In Cabanatuan, each day one bag was opened and fifty letters removed . . . end of the day's distribution. The daily mainstay that continued to feed survival seemed to be rumors and religion.[333]

In June 1944, guards informed Manny that he would be departing on a long trip. He was to be shipped to Japan and received new cloths from the guard. Manny and Sal got together for one last visit and Manny gave him every possession he owned. Sal had sufficiently improved in health to be removed from the binnacle list and assigned to light duty details. They reminisced about the old days and spoke hopefully of their future. Then it was time for Manny to leave.

Mansfield received a stroke of luck and was assigned a work detail that moved him from Cabanatuan to Fort McKinley south of Manila. Without forewarning, one morning Mansfield was ordered to get his gear together and move out in five minutes. Getting his "stuff" together took no time since there was little to gather. Seventy-three POWs joined Mansfield, were stuffed into a couple trucks, and taken to Manila. They were dropped at Bilibid Prison for an overnight stay then marched through Manila to Fort McKinley. They remained there for 13 months. It was August 1942.[334]

Mansfield's group lived at the fort in austere conditions but improved over O'Donnell and Cabanatuan. The POWs were drivers in a motor pool that worked all over the Manila area and Bataan Peninsula. Most of the work was conducted in the port area where they moved cargo from Japanese ships. Cargo nets and pallets were occasionally dropped and cargo boxes broken open to furnish food and other necessities to the workers nearby. Their favorite "drop" was saki, whiskey, alcohol, and candy bars. Often, the dock workers shared the goods with the truck drivers. The Japanese guards usually turned their heads and permitted the goods to be stolen but the POWs learned quickly they could not count on a consistent Japanese attitude. The Japanese guards were unpredictable and one day theft was okay while the next day heads may literally roll.

One of Mansfield's chores was hauling gravel and rock from Manila to Clark Air Base. Hundreds, if not thousands, of American POWs were assigned to the project of rebuilding the airstrips. The prisoners were chagrined and angered at the sight of rows of aircraft on the aprons and tarmacs with the "red meatballs" painted on the wings and fuselage.

Following 13 months at Fort McKinley, Mansfield was marched back into Manila to the waterfront alongside Pier #7. He was bunked in a large old office building across the street from the infamous pier. Mansfield started working the ships as a stevedore or longshoreman. Operating trucks and forklifts, he moved cargo from the ships to their first point of rest on or near the pier. He became a member of "G.G's 400 thieves" named for their leader, LCDR George G. Harrison. While the guards basked in the sun and drank, the POW stevedore gang was hard at work sabotaging ships and stealing cargo.[335]

Mansfield's work took him throughout Manila and surrounding area where he encountered a wide variety of people including guerrillas. In fact, guerrilla activity took place all over the Philippines. Activity near Cebu City resulted in the capture of Admiral Koga, the top Japanese naval officer. A submarine picked him up and shipped him to Australia.[336] They were constantly moving in and out of the suburbs and city. Mansfield had to be careful when talking to people because he often had a guard riding shotgun with him. The people managed to pass war information back and forth that was of great interest to the POWs. When he refueled his truck with alcohol, Mansfield always topped off his canteen so when he returned to their barracks, he brought back news, food, and drink. During his assignment in the port area, Mansfield and fellow POWs received some mail from the states although it was very tardy and heavily censored.

One day, Mansfield stole a handful of eggs. That evening, he gathered his squad's rice rations and cooked rice and scrambled eggs. He cooked them in a large iron skillet when a guard caught him. Mansfield refused to tell the guard where he got the eggs so he was forced to stand for hours with the skillet extended in one hand. "Who gave you the rice and eggs, answer me!" "Go to hell," retorted Mansfield. "That will cost you another hour out here. Where did the eggs come from?" "Chickens, of course," replied Mansfield. "You son-of-a-bitch. You'll pay for that remark." The guard went to the guardhouse for help. About a half dozen guards came out and walked into Manfield's barracks. They shoved his entire squad out of the building and made the men stand at attention next to him. Eventually, the guards tired of asking questions without answers and ordered everyone back into the building.

The underhanded work by the POWs wasn't confined to Mansfield's group. Everywhere the Japanese held territory, Allied POWs undermined the Japanese war effort. One of the details to Fort McKinley out of Bilibid loaded barrels of aviation gasoline onto flat bed trucks which were transported to a rail yard for loading into box cars. A quick half turn of the filler cap on every tenth barrel did the trick. Huge fires exploded on trucks and rail cars all over the yard but far from the nearest POW.[337] Fort McKinley's group also handled bombs and a couple of the POWs on the work detail knew how to defuse detonators. Most of the bombs they handled were captured American bombs and it is estimated that 10% of the bombs were rendered inert.[338]

After the time at O'Donnell and Cabanatuan, the prisoners were almost naked from deteriorating cloths but were reclad when sent on some work details. At both Fort McKinley and the port in Manila, Mansfield received new cloths to provide the locals with a good image of the Japanese. At Cabanatuan, the POWs weren't permitted to wash or clean cloths while at McKinley and Manila they had showers and real soap. At McKinley, the prisoners had real beds and sheets and the sick went to a real sick bay. The barracks were relatively insect free. At least one report indicated one of three patients in July 1942 in the O'Donnell "hospital" died. At McKinley and the harbor area, there were virtually no deaths. The Japanese took care of their slave labor in the Manila area.

Prior to the fall of Corregidor, tons of gold and silver was scuttled to prevent the Japanese from confiscating the precious metal. The Japanese discovered the fact from POWs at Cabanatuan and Bilibid. They located American divers working in the port and Fort McKinley and sent them to Corregidor. The divers found the silver and gold but hid the gold and only brought up a few silver pesos. The divers stalled for months and the Japanese eventually recovered only a tenth of the silver.[339]

At a number of POW camps, officers provided a great service to the POWs by staging shows and giving lectures. Subjects of the lectures varied widely, depending on the officer's skills, including language, travel, sports, and hobbies. The camp shows were roaring successes and served to entertain the prisoners and guards. The respite of shows and lectures took the POWs mind off their current situation and improved the mental and physical condition of the men.

Flies continued to plaque the POWs and were a major contribution to the epidemic of dysentery. The Japanese determined the source of flies came from open latrines and slit trenches. Rather than build sanitary facilities, the Japanese initiated a fly campaign. They encouraged the POWs to kill flies and to build fly swatters. When a prisoner killed a fly, he placed it into an empty Carnation Milk can and when the can was full, he turned it in for a cigarette. Ingenious POWs turned their entire economic status around by collecting vast amounts of flies and swapped the cigarettes for food and necessary items.[340]

Food remained scarce and hunger drove the men to eat almost anything. Items hunted included the snail and although not cooked to taste like true escargot, it was food. During the winter months, a small white worm about an inch long with a black head appeared in the rice and was consumed as a protein source. Weevils also were in the rice, impossible to separate, and consumed by the thousands.

A major uplifting of morale was provided by rumors and listening to a small radio built by one of the POWs. He listened nightly to short wave news and officers quietly and covertly passed the word daily to the rest of the POWs. Word of Allied victories in Africa and Guadacanal gave the men hope. It was good news following July 1942 by which time the Japanese had conquered the Philippines, Singapore, Hong Kong, Dutch East Indies, Malaya, Borneo, Bismark Islands, Siam, Sumatra, the Gilberts, Celebes, Timor, Wake, Guam, and most of the Solomons and half of New Guinea.

After August 1942, things improved somewhat at Cabanatuan as the Japanese started providing American medical personnel with basic medicines that included quinine that helped malaria and antitoxin which did little for diphtheria. The POW death rate sharply decreased. Simultaneously, favorable reports filtered back from Osaka about the work accomplished by American prisoners. The Japanese Home Ministery ordered thousands of more Americans to supplement the Japanese stevedoring and work force.

Cabanatuan Camp #1 was the worst of the Cabanatuan camps and severely overcrowded. The Japanese decided to relieve the situation by shipping a large number of POWs to Mindanao on the cargo vessel *ERIE MARU*. An interesting dialogue took place between the resident and newly arrived POWs. Finally, the Mindanao POWs knew the fate of the men on Bataan and Corregidor. With the call from Japan, another 1,500 POWs from Cabanatuan were shipped out in the lower holds of the *TOTTORI MARU*. Along with the call for more Americans, the War Ministry published food allowances for Americans in Japan: officers 420 grams of food daily while the enlisted who worked received 570 grams. All POWs had to work to receive a daily ration but officers were used primarily in supervisory roles.

At the end of 1942, estimated numbers of American POWs held by the Japanese were:

Philippine Islands	13,250
Japan	2,900
China	1,650
Manchuria	1,200
Malaya	450
Celebes	250
Burma	200
Formosa	150
Wake Island	150
Total	20,200[341]

About this time, survivors of the Philippine Army were released to their families, 28,000 of the original 55,000 captured had perished. As a response, the Secretary of State signed a formal protest of conditions and treatment of American prisoners on 12 December 1942 and forwarded the letter to the Swiss Government.

The fortunes of war shifted by the end of 1942 in the South Pacific. The Japanese planned another offensive in China but all extra men and supplies were sent south. Entire divisions from Korea and China were shipped into the South Pacific to halt the Allied advance. The evacuation of 17,000 troops from Guadacanal provided the only highlight for the Japanese in early February 1943.

The Battle for Guadacanal was over and America was on a comeback while Japan suffered its largest defeat in her history.

Admiral Yamamoto made an inspection tour of advance bases to uplift sagging morale and get a front line view of the war. On 18 April he was on an aircraft out of Rabaul when American P-38 fighters intercept his aircraft and killed the admiral. Possibly the most rational and realistic Japanese flag officer was dead.[342]

In early 1943, MacArthur's AIB organized the Fifty Group to provide supplies to guerrillas on Mindanao. The submarine *USS TAMBOR* carried the group and supplies to Pagadian Bay on the south coast of Mindanao and dropped off two Americans, three Moros, and 7-tons of supplies for the guerrillas. The submarines *USS NARWHAL* and *USS NAUTILUS* provided more supplies to the guerrillas utilizing instructions from the AIB. The British submarines *HMS PORPOISE* and *HMS TANTALUS* actively supported the AIB in reconnaissance runs until mid-1944.[343] On 29 September 1943, the *USS BOWFIN* evacuated escaped POWs from Mindanao to Freemantle, Australia including Captain Sam Grashio.[344]

POWs continued to be sent to Japan but on 21 September, the remaining prisoners at Cabanatuan and Bilibid were given a real treat. US Navy aircraft from the carriers *HORNET, WASP, INTREPID, BUNKER HILL,* and *LEXINGTON* flew sorties against Manila and major Japanese military bases in southern Luzon. The Americans had gained control of the skies and seas. The aircraft joined the submarines in sinking Japanese convoys unwittingly killing hundreds of POWs in the process. Over Cabanatuan, the POWs were treated to the sight of a US Navy aircraft shooting down a Zero. The camp morale skyrocketed and the men used a former Japanese cheer, "Ichiban American hikokio!" (American plane number one)

Cabanatuan slowly shipped the POWs to Japan or other camps. The original Davao Colony Group returned to the camp, departing Davao on 6 June 1944. They boarded a greasy and rusty little freighter, weighed anchor on the 12th and arrived in Moro Bay in

Zamboanga a couple days later. For a moment the POWs forgot about the war as they observed one of the famous Philippine sunsets. They sailed for Cebu and landed in a miserable camp until they were shipped out again on a smaller ship. A few days later they returned to Pier #6 in Manila and were herded into Bilibid Prison. They arrived in Cabanatuan on the 28th to be greeted by only 700 frail and ill POWs.[345]

The Philippine neighborhood had been anything but quiet since the Japanese invasion and became increasingly active as the trends of war shifted in favor of the Allies. An elaborate intelligence system was established by a number of individuals for numerous reasons but all led to the demise of Japan. Possibly the largest underground network was Miss U set up by Margaret Utinsky from St. Louis. Her husband was a Bataan POW and died in Cabanatuan so she dedicated herself to helping the POWs with food, medicine, money, and clothing. Her organization included Catholic priests who were able to enter and depart the camp unhindered. The effort was successful and included material items plus added mail and message service. Their efforts undoubtedly saved untold numbers of POWs from death by giving them hope.[346]

During WWII, Japan was electronically illiterate. Communication equipment had to be repaired by prisoners which permitted the POWs to eventually set aside sufficient parts to build their own radios. For some reason, the Japanese did not consider communications seriously which was not the case for Allied and Filipino locals. Dorothy Claire Phillips, an Italian, opened a large nightclub in Manila – the Club Tsubaki. She and her ladies entertained the Japanese, learned their language, and gathered intelligence from drunk officers. The total number of intelligence gathering groups is unknown but they all contributed to the war effort.[347]

CHAPTER SEVEN

OTHER PRISONERS OF WAR

THE WAY JAPAN conquered China was not pretty. As early as 1933, the Japanese promoted the cultivation and smuggling of heroin. The army protected the heroin dealers who in turn contributed profusely to the army for the Japanese army's assistance. The opium trade permitted by the Japanese literally raised havoc with the Chinese population.[348] Farmers and peasants were slaves to the Japanese but permitted to raise crops only for the Japanese Army. Army units were given Chinese women, known as "comfort women," for their personal pleasure when the Army units fought as a reward. Unfortunately at the "comfort stations," the women for pleasure were not volunteers and were raped, beaten, and often killed so they couldn't bear witness of the crimes at a later date. Almost everywhere the Japanese traveled, particularly in combat zones, they committed atrocities beyond civilized belief. The army was instructed to burn every building as the men advanced thereby permitting the officers to readily determine the exact location of the front. The captured Chinese soldiers were often used as targets for bayonet practice.

Chinese laborers were rounded up like cattle and forcibly shipped to the front or Japan to work. They were stuffed into freight cars, along with Chinese POWs, and moved to the closest port of embarkation on hell ships headed for Japan. Over 41,000 Chinese were sent to Japan with over 1,000 dying on the ships while another 6,000 died when working in Japan. Over 400 Chinese were killed at the Hanaika Copper Mine following a riot over slave conditions.[349]

A strange twist of submarine fate added a bazaar POW story. On 23 May 1939, the new *USS SQUALUS* conducted a test dive off the coast of Portsmouth, New Hampshire. A disaster resulted when a faulty main induction valve flooded the engine rooms. The submarine settled to the ocean floor at a depth of 240' with 33 officers and men trapped in the forward end of the ship.[350] The *USS SCULPIN* found the *SQUALUS* and the surviving men were rescued using the McMann diving bell. Navy salvage engineers raised the hull and she was recommissioned as the *USS SAILFISH*. *SAILFISH* and *SCULPIN* were assigned duty in the Pacific Fleet in WWII. Japanese forces sank *SCULPIN* on 19 November 1943. Survivors were transferred to a couple Japanese aircraft carriers for transportation to POW camps in Japan.[351]

Twenty-one *SCULPIN* crewmembers were aboard the Japanese carrier *CHUYO* when she was attacked off the coast of Hachijo Jima in the morning of 4 December 1943 by *SAILFISH*. *CHUYO* sunk and only one *SCULPIN* submariner survived the sinking. [352]

The Seabees were in the first group of POWs to reach Japan along with British civilians captured on the Gilbert Islands. They weren't Seabees yet but Civil Engineer Corps Officers in the U.S. Navy. They were officers in Public Works on Guam when taken prisoners during the first two days of hostilities. They remained POWs on Guam for a month and then were shipped to Japan on the *ARGENTINA MARU* on 10 January 1942 along with 400 other Americans. They were barged ashore off Shikoku in the Inland Sea and railed to Zentsuji Prison Camp.[353] Some of the men were moved to Mitsubishi Camp #1 in August 1942 following a relatively comfortable stay in Zentsuji. The new camp was located between Tokyo and Yokohama and comprised mostly of British soldiers from Hong Kong. The men worked as stevedores but the officers refused to work. Living conditions remained bearable.[354]

The *USS HOUSTON* and 13 other American ships early in

1942 blundered into a huge Japanese fleet in the Java Sea. Outnumbered and outgunned, six ships went down on 27 February and only three returned to Pearl Harbor. *HOUSTON* and *HMAS PERTH* attempted a daring dash through the Sunda Straits the following night but ran into a Japanese force. Both ships were sunk and of the 1087 *HOUSTON* man crew, only 366 survived the night. Of the surviving crew, 77 died in POW camps.[355]

Unlike women of other conquered countries, the Japanese did not physically abuse American nurses, for the most part. Following the fall of Corregidor, the remaining nurses were taken to Santo Tomas Internment Camp in Manila. Despite little physical abuse, the nurses suffered many of the same diseases as the men POWs due to lack of food and nourishment. They suffered beriberi, malaria, dysentery, pneumonia, and a wide variety of skin disorders.[356] The nurses were led by Major Maude Davison , the chief nurse on Corregidor. There were 89 nurses in the Philippines at the outbreak of hostilities. Twenty-two escaped Corregidor by submarine, PBY, and the hospital ship *MACTAN*. The remaining 67 nurses survived and were liberated on 3 February 1945.[357]

The Davao Penal Colony was initially a better camp than Cabanatuan but deteriorated rapidly in 1943. It was a site for frequent POW escapes resulting in a 200 Japanese guard force. About 1,000 POWs were sent from Luzon to Davao to slave on projects but the majority of the arrivals were too ill to work. Another 1,000 joined the Davao group from other areas of Mindanao with the camp population reaching 1,961 in April 1944.[358]

The *USS GRENADIER (SS-210)* was on her 6th war patrol deep in enemy waters between Sumatra and the Malay Peninsula. Targets were scarce but intelligence reports indicated Japanese activity near Penang so LCDR Fitzgerald looked in Malay Harbor. A couple targets were sighted but while making his torpedo approach, Japanese aircraft arrived on the scene. A tremendous blast shook the boat as a bomb exploded just above the watertight bulkhead between the Maneuvering and After Torpedo compartments. Power was lost and fires ignited in the cubicle as *GRENADIER* settled to

-HARM

the bottom 270-feet below the surface. Acrid smoke filled the boat but the crew managed to extinguish the fires. Unfortunately, propulsion was lost with the main induction valves knocked off their seats and leaking. A bucket brigade was formed and the drain pump repaired so the crew could dewater the boat.

The After Torpedo Room was a mess and the torpedo tubes forced off their foundations and bent to port thus bending the main shafts. Watertight integrity was lost and hydraulic lines ruptured. The crew worked all night and managed to get the boat to the surface the following morning. However, propulsion was impossible and the deck gun was inoperable. The GRENADIER could not move nor fight. The crew made a makeshift canvas sail in an effort to close a nearby island where the boat could be scuttled and the crew swim ashore to search out assistance. As the drifted closer to the island, they radioed SubPac of their situation and destroyed classified material. Suddenly, Japanese aircraft appeared on scene and the crew fought back with 20mm and .50 caliber machine guns to down the aircraft.[359]

Soon enemy surface units arrived in the area and the skipper abandoned and scuttled ship. The Japanese ships circled the submarine until she sank then picked up the crew. The crew was placed on a small inter-island steamer[360] that was converted into a gunboat. The men were beaten and interrogated unmercifully then placed ashore where the routine continued. Their time on Penang was reminiscent of other POW treatment until months later when they were shipped to Singapore. The daily routine there was public beatings on a parade ground. Finally, they were placed on a hell ship which was attacked by American submarines. Gratefully, their ship was spared.[361]

The GRENADIER was taken to Camp Ofuna near Tokyo for intense interrogation. Ofuna was not a work camp since they considered submariners and airmen murderers vice prisoners. As such, the Japanese did not report their status as POWs.[362] Following eight weeks of questioning, the crew was moved to Camp Omori. The men were placed into tiny cells, one man per cell on small man-made islands in Tokyo Bay known today as Forts #1, #2, and #3. Narrow bridges connected the islands with the mainland. The normal routine was questioning, beatings, and poor food.[363]

At Omori, conditions were similar to other POW camps and Norm Albertson worked as a stevedore in the port of Shimagawa, loading and offloading ships. Norm was later assigned to work at Nagigawa where he was forced to work in a rail yard. The work routine was ten straight days of work followed by a day off but the work was from sunrise to sunset. He also worked for a short period in the Mitsubishi steel mill.

The crew of the *GRENADIER* was joined by many airmen and submariners but a pleasant surprise was the arrival of the crew of the *USS TANG*, including their Medal of Honor Awardee, Captain O'Kane. *TANG* was sunk by a circular run of her own torpedo. Only 30 men of her crew survived the explosion including five whom escaped by a buoyant ascent from the sunken submarine. Among other notable internees in the camp was Pappy Boyington of the Black Sheep Squadron.[364]

USS PERCH (SS-176) was alongside *CANOPUS* on 7 December 1941 but got underway for sea. On her second patrol on 25 February 1942, she was depth charged off of Celebes Island. She proceeded to Java to assist in stopping a Japanese invasion force. Badly mauled, she surfaced to run for Australia. On the surface, she was attacked by two cruisers and three destroyers. Virtually destroyed, she was forced to scuttle ship and the crew of 62 were picked up by a destroyer and taken to Makassar City. Shortly thereafter, they were shipped to Japan on the hell ship *ASAMA MARU* in October 1942. They worked in mines near Ashio where nine members died of malnutrition and disease.[365] They spent the remainder of the war in Japan, some of which was in Omori.[366]

Months later, the submariners, like the other POWs held in Japan, noticed indicators the war was turning in favor of the United States as Japanese warships into Tokyo Bay in various degrees of damage and disarray. American bombers ruled the skies and the POWs observed huge columns of smoke rising from Tokyo and other cities on Tokyo Bay. The noticed a new aircraft, the large and silvery B-29s which some POWs recognized from designs seen before they were captured. The B-29s came in swarms and on a few nights the entire skyline of Tokyo glowed red from millions of fires.[367]

Fifteen Civil Engineer Corps Officers became guests of the emperor early in the war. Ten of the men were on duty at Cavite Navy Yard of which three were evacuated and successfully reached Australia. Four other officers were assigned to the Naval Station on Guam that was attacked on 10 December 1941. Three were taken prisoner. Four other officers befell the same tragedy on 23 December when the Japanese took Wake Island. Three of the men went through the hell ship rotation of the *ORYOKOK MARU, ENOURA MARU,* and *BRAZIL MARU.* The three from Guam went to Zentsuji Prison on Shokaku Island via the *ARGENTINA MARU.* The Wake Island officers went to a POW camp near Shanghai on the *NITTA MARU* where they joined the Marines from Peking and Tientsin. Of interest was all captured CEC officers remained on active duty and retired years later.[368]

The *USS TULLIBEE (SS-284)* attacked a convoy in the spring of 1943 while on the surface and was attacked by convoy escorts. During the fray, *TULLIBEE* fired numerous torpedoes and a nearby violent explosion shook the boat, knocking some of the crew from the bridge. The submarine sank and only one man survived the night and machine gunning. He was later picked up and followed a similar path at Ofuna and to Ashio.[369]

USS ROBALLO (SS-273) was on patrol in the South China Sea when she struck a mine on 26 July 1943 while making a torpedo run on a *FUSO*-Class battleship. She sank quickly and a dozen crew on the bridge were thrown into the sea. They managed to swim ashore at Palawan and searched for the local guerrillas. Instead, the Japanese found them and they became POWs in the Puero Princess Prison Camp. None of the submariners survived the war and may have died in the infamous POW gasoline killing on Palawan.[370]

The old *USS S-44* departed Attu on 26 September 1943 for a

patrol off Paramushiro. While on the surface and attacking a small merchant ship, they in turn were attacked by a Japanese destroyer. The old submarine took hit after hit and began to sink. They waved a white flag but the Japanese ignored the signal or failed to see it. The onslaught continued and only two crewmembers survived. They were also taken to Paramushiro, interrogated and beaten, then sent to Camp Ofuna. Later they were moved to a copper mine in Ashio.[371]

A group of four Americans and Filipino POWs escaped their camp at O'Donnell or Cabanatuan and made it to the Negros Island. They sought and received assistance from the local guerrillas under the commanad of Colonel Salvador Abcede. All four had survived the Bataan Death March. On 11 May 1944, the *USS CREVALLE (SS-291)* picked them up along with 37 other refugees, mostly women and children.[372]

South of Osaka was the "model camp" and headquarters for the Prisoner of War Bureau called Zentsuji. Following Tojo's instructions to his POW camps, "no work, no food," camp commandants tried to find a use for officers. They attempted to assign officers supervisory jobs but most American officers refused. Some officers were sent from Tanagawa and Umeda to Zentsuji for this reason.

Perhaps the most famous POW was Major Gregory "Pappy" Boyington. His squadron was anxious for him to shoot down his 26th enemy aircraft and create a new record. On 3 January 1944, he was jumped by a large number of Zeroes and his wingman shot down. His plane was seriously damaged and he ejected, landing in the sea. A Japanese submarine picked him up, transferred him to a destroyer whereupon he went through a litany of interrogation and POW camps. Eventually, he moved from Ofuna to Omori where he observed firsthand the onslaught of B-29s over Japan.[373]

As the American bombing continued to worsen, the POWs were utilized in cleanups and building bomb shelters. The POWs heard of the destructive atomic bombs from their guards but local

)-HARM

civilians never attacked the POWs as reported in other documents.[374]

On 6 June 1944, 1,200 POWs were bound, blindfolded, and force-marched to Davao Harbor to be placed aboard a ship. The vessel remained in port for days in unbelievable crowded and hot conditions. The men who were to make the trip were comprised of POWs who worked at Lieanan Field and Matina Field. A major group worked at Lansang Field on Mindanao even while under attack by American bombers. Eventually, the POWs were placed on an old freighter in early September 1944. The old ship was torpedoed on 7 September with only 87 survivors. The 87 men made it ashore, were contacted by Filipino guerrillas and finally returned to American lines.[375]

Bill Landreth was a typical fighter pilot who always wanted to fly. He joined the Navy in Deccember 1941 and became a member of fighter squadron *VF-17*.Carrier based, his squadron flew the first F4Us in combat and amassed 154 Japanese kills with Bill getting three Zeroes. He formed a new squadron and reentered combat on the *USS INTREPID* with *VF-10* in February 1945. On his first mission over Uwajima, he blew up an ammunition dump while flying at 300 feet altitude and 400 knots. His aircraft was struck by flying shrapnel. He managed to nurse the Corsair over Tokyo Bay where he landed dead stick. Bill was captured and his injuries nursed on the cold cement floor of the Tatami jail. Later he was moved to Omori to join fellow aviators and submariners.[376]

The AIB intelligence gatherers kept Navy fliers and submariners busy with reports of Japanese fleet and merchant activities. A few weeks after the Japanese were pushed off Guadacanal, a huge flotilla of eight troop transports and 7,000 troops with numerous naval escorts was found leaving Rabaul. American and Australian fighter aircraft caught the fleet in the Bismark Sea. When the smoke cleared, thousands of Japanese filled the sea. Allied pilots strafed the survivors and ten PT boats finished any surviving Japanese. "In the Pacific, the Japanese had set the ground rules: dog-eat-dog, no quarter asked, none given."[377]

SAN ANTONIO

PORAC

CARMEN

SAN FERNANDO

SUBIC

GUAGUA
LUBAO

DINALUPIHAN

OLONGAPO

CALUMPIT

HERMOSA

GRANDE IS

▲ MT SANTA ROSA

ORANI
SAMAL

▲ MT NATIB

ABUCAY

▲ MT SILANGANAN

MORON

MAUBAN

FILAR

ORION

BAGAC

▲ MT SAMAT

LIMAY

BATAAN

MARIVELES
MOUNTAINS

LIMAY

MARIVELES

CABCABEN

BATAAN
REFERENCE
MAP

CORREGIDOR

CAVITE

-HARM

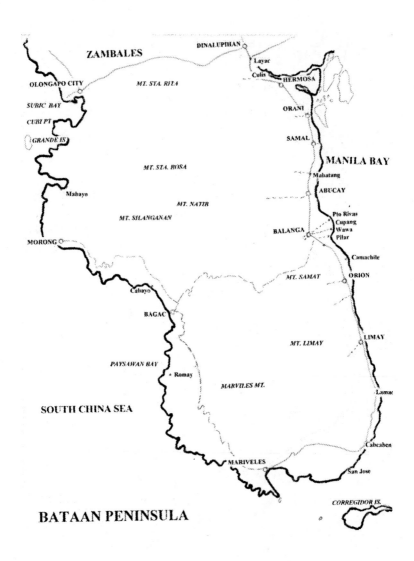

ZAMBALES

DINALUPIHAN

Layac

Culis

HERMOSA

OLONGAPO CITY

MT. STA. RITA

SUBIC BAY

ORANI

CUBI PT

SAMAL

GRANDE IS

MANILA BAY

MT. STA. ROSA

Mabatang

ABUCAY

Mabayo

MT. NATIB

Pto Rivas

MT. SILANGANAN

Cupang

Wawa

BALANGA

Pilar

MORONG

Camachile

Cabayo

MT. SAMAT

ORION

BAGAC

LIMAY

MT. LIMAY

PAYSAWAN BAY

Romay

Lamao

MARVILES MT.

SOUTH CHINA SEA

Cabcaben

MARIVELES

San Jose

CORREGIDOR IS.

BATAAN PENINSULA

"Manny Eneriz at age 76 in Camarillo, California" from author's file.

"Mansfield Young during boot training at San Lois Obispo,
California 1949" from author's file.

ROBERT K. HARMUTH

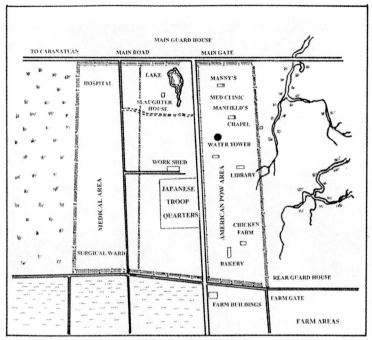

PRISONER OF WAR CAMP
CABANATUAN CAMP # 1

"Camp Cabanatuan as explained by Manny Eneriz, Mansfield
Young, and other Ex-POWs and sketched by author."

"The Bataan Death March" from National Archives web page.

"Two POWs following release from POW and Internment Camp at Santo Tomas" from National Archives web page taken by UPI photographer.

)-HARM

NOTHING is to be written on this side except to fill in the data specified.
Sentences not required should be crossed out.   IF ANYTHING ELSE IS
ADDED THE POSTCARD WILL BE DESTROYED.

I am well ~~(sick~~ ~~(Serious~~
~~I have been admitted to hospital as (wounded~~ ~~(not serious~~
~~Am getting on well   Hope to return to duty soon.~~
I have ~~received your~~ ~~(Letter dated~~ ....
~~(Telegram dated~~ ....
~~(Parcel dated~~ ....
Letter follows at first opportunity.
I have received no letter from you (for a long time
~~(lately.~~

Signature *John F. Cote Jr.*
Date *Dec. 9-1941*
Sub.ron 4 Standard Form No. F.4   471-A—S/M Base, PH.—7-15-41—26M.

"A post card distributed by Commander, Submarine Forces, Pacific in July 1943 to be sent home in case of war" from Polaris Magazine, Submariners of WWII.

"USS BATFISH (SS-310) flying battle flags returning to port following war battle" from Naval History Magazine.

"Nagasaki three days following the atomic bomb drop." Photograph taken Eugene Sutherfield after being dropped offshore for 24-hours probably by USS CATFISH (SS-339).

ROBERT K. HARMUTH

"Manny Eneriz (left) and Mansfield Young in 1999 in front of Seabee Memorial, Naval Construction Battalion Center, Port Hueneme, California." Photograph by James Daly, retired combat photographer, US Navy.

"Americans who will not be POWs rescued at sea by US submarine." Photograph from US Naval Institute Press.

Robert K. Harmuth

"US submarine USS TROUT retrieving gold bars belonging to the Philippine Government at Corregidor just prior to its surrender." Photograph from US Naval Institute Press.

"American refugees picked up by US submarine USS CRE-VALLE in the Philippines enroute Darwin, Australia." Photograph from US Naval Institute Press.

ROBERT K. HARMUTH

CHAPTER EIGHT

A FREE TRIP TO JAPAN

M ANPOWER WAS PARAMOUNT among the dwindling
resources of Japan. Prisoners of war of all nationalities were shipped
to Japan to perform hard common labor. One important reason
for labor need was the rapidly diminishing imports of coal. The
input of coal declined from approximately 2,750,000 tons a year
in June 1941 to less than 250,000 tons a year in April 1945.[378]
Ships moved POWs from Mindinao to Luzon and then to Japan as
well as taking most of the POWs held on Luzon to Japan or other
labor camps. In July 1944, a group of 500 prisoners left Manila
from Cabanatuan and Bilibid on the *CANADIAN INVENTOR*
including Manny Eneriz. Coincident with the Cabanatuan contingent, 350 men were shipped out of Shanghai and 1,500 men
followed shortly thereafter from Manila on the *NISSYO MARU*
including Mansfield Young. It was obvious, Japan not only wanted
slave labor in Japan but wanted to leave no prisoners behind in the
Philippines. The Japanese senior officers desired no one left to provide firsthand proof of atrocities leveled on the prisoners.

Mansfield awakened with a jerk as a sharp pain pierced his
side. A Japanese guard prodded him with a bayonet. "Get up and
get out," he screamed at the POWs in the barracks. "Screw you,"
Mansfield mumbled which earned him another jab in the side
from the bayonet. "God almighty, it's the middle of the night for
christ sake," someone muttered in the dark. They got up and the
guard ordered them to take their belongings, be that as it may.

With rags and a few items in hand, Mansfield was pushed outside with hundreds of other prisoners and shoved to the assembly area for muster.

They mustered and walked in a column to the Cabanatuan main gate where a long line of trucks awaited them. Pushed, jabbed and hit with rifle butts, they were forced into the trucks. Within minutes, the trucks were full and underway. The trucks slowly rumbled away from the camp and headed into the countryside. "Now where the hell are we going? This another big work detail?" "Hell no! Too many of us for that. Man there must be hundreds of us in these trucks."

The seats were hard and damp while the air was warm and humid. It was a typical Luzon summer night. The men recognized the countryside, which they had traveled before on various work details. They were driving toward San Fernando where their infamous march ended so long ago with a trip by rail to Capas near Camp O'Donnell. They drove through the streets of San Fernando, then turned off the road to Bataan. Maybe it was going to be a huge working party.

Months earlier, other groups were transported to various prison camps and details, many of them to Japan proper on ships like the *ERIE MARU*. She took 1,000 POWs from Cabanatuan to Mindanao in November 1942. The *SAIKA MARU* took 300 men to Pawalan in July 1942, the *TOTTORI MARU* moved 1,202 POWs to Pusan on 2 October 1942, and the *HOKKU MARU* departed with Cabanatuan Camp #3 POWs on 9 October 1942. The *NAGARA MARU* took General Wainwright and senior officers out of Manila on 14 August 1942 and the *NAGATO MARU* shipped out 1,700 POWs on 7 November 1942. *UMEDA MARU* left with 1,500 POWs and the *MATE MATE MARU* carried 500 more POWs from Cabanatuan on 24 July 1943. The *ARISAN MARU* took 1,869[379] out of Bilibid on 21 October 1943 and the *CORAL MARU* took 800 plus in October 1943. These were just a few of over a hundred "hell ships." (see listing at the end of this chapter)

Years earlier on their way from Bataan to the camps, the POWs had walked and struggled the five miles the trucks now traveled to the San Fernando railhead. It was heart warming to Mansfield when he witnessed how the Filipino People reacted to their presence. The Americans were beaten and humiliated before the locals. With defeat, came the abuse from the Japanese toward the Filipino for being a friend or ally of America. The fear of a Filipino change of heart toward the American was quickly dispelled as the prisoners were greeted at every step by cheers, food and encouragement; and even renditions of "God Bless America." Mansfield felt considerably better and a little proud as he listened and watched the reaction of the locals. Maybe it was going to be worthwhile to stay alive after all![380]

It was still dark as the men were driven through Manila but Mansfield recognized the area. The trucks headed for the waterfront area where he had driven trucks and forklifts for months. "Hey guys, we're headed for the harbor," yelled Mansfield. "Think they've got a big ship discharge job, eh?" "Don't need this many guys to off load a ship. "I know where we are. This is Pier #7," some one shouted.

The trucks pulled up to a large ship. It was the *NISSYO MARU*. The POWs were ordered out of the trucks and mustered, again. The men walked, some crawled, up the gangway to the main deck of the ship and were directed to one of the forward cargo holds. Mustered again next to the hold, they were ordered down a long cargo net secured to the top of the hold. "One man down; ten men down; a hundred and another hundred . . . my god, how many do they think they could crowd into this damned dark hole?"

Mansfield looked up and observed the sky changing from a dull gray color to one of pink tint. It was near sunrise. He heard a commotion on the main deck above him, then another hundred or so men climbed down or were hurled into the hold. There was scarcely room to stand let alone breathe heavily. Some of the men yelled and panicked whereupon the Japanese crew lowered the hatch cover into place and the POWs were plunged into total darkness. Imagine the hysteria of the situation. Some men screamed and others were angry and swore. What was their destiny or destination? It was July 1943 and in another month, the *NISSYO MARU* was to make port in Japan. The men would become another company of working slaves.

Within a couple hours, the hold became stifling hot and many prisoners passed out from the heat. "I think Jake is dead guys. What should we do with him?" "Well for damn sure, we aint goin ta dig a hole in here to bury 'em." Then someone began screaming for help, air and water. Shortly, the hatch cover was removed and cooler air, only around 100 degrees flowed into the hold and the men breathed easier.

The men sat or stood in their own filth and the ship's crew did little to remedy the situation. Daily around noon, groups of a few men at a time were permitted topside for some fresh air and to wash down with salt water. Food was thrown down to the men like slopping hogs and the half-starved prisoners fought over the garbage like animals.

Mansfield and the *NISSYO MARU* arrived in Japan in early August. The men were divided into five groups and sent to camps and mines to work. These men were in the Osaka Group and Mansfield's group was sent to Kameoka to work in a lead mine. Others went to work in coal and copper mines.[381] Mansfield's voyage was one of the safe trips made by the POWs to Japan, as the *NISSYO MARU* was never attacked during the transit.

In September 1943, the *USS PADDLE (SS-263)*, an American submarine, torpedoed the *SHINYO MARU* off the coast of Mindanao that carried hundreds of Allied POWs. The prisoners were in the lower holds of the vessel and when the ship began to sink, the Japanese crew abandoned ship without giving any assistance to the POWs. Many American POWs managed to escape their holds and into the water whereupon they swam toward other Japanese vessels in close proximity. The Japanese freighters and destroyers stopped to pick up the Japanese crew but refused to aid the POWs. They pushed the men back into the sea as they attempted to climb on board. Out of hundreds of prisoners, only 82 made it ashore the next morning. The men were assisted by Filipino guerrilla bands and later carried to safety by the *USS NARWHAL (SS-167).*[382]

The first group of POWs shipped out of Cabanatuan was sent to the Davao Penal Colony and treated relatively well. The food was better on their "hell ship" and they actually had elbow room and fresh air. Unfortunately, when the sea voyage ended, they experienced the same treatment as in Cabanatuan. However, they did receive Sundays off.[383]

The medium sized freighter, *ARISAN MARU*, quietly got underway from Pier #7 in Manila on 21 October 1943 (or 11 October) with two holds crammed with prisoners headed for Japan. She carried over 1,800 POWs who sat and lay on each other in the holds. Among the prisoners were the men who originally were sent to Davao from Cabanatuan a few months earlier. The sun rose and the temperature exceeded 120 degrees in the holds. No human waste facilities were offered except for a few wood "honey dew" buckets and with the sweat, the stench became unbearable. Additionally, the *ARISAN MARU* ran into a typhoon and the holds soon filled with sick POWs and vomit.[384]

About 1500 on the 24th, *USS SHARK II (SS-314)* fired three torpedoes at the *ARISAN MARU*. One slammed into the hell ship's side.[385] The prisoners were terrified but did not panic. Another torpedo exploded in the forward hold that held half the POWs. Hundreds of men were killed and maimed. Thirty minutes later, the POWs in the second hold managed to climb out since all the guards had abandoned ship. The men were torn between getting into a life jacket and joining the guards in the water or running to the galley for food. Some accounts relate the crew putting hatch covers in place over the hatches preventing any POW from exiting the holds. As evening set, the vessel settled deeper into the water and sunk. By nightfall, a couple hundred POWs remained alive in the water as a Japanese cruiser passed by but did not stop to pick up a single POW. A Japanese destroyer stopped to pick up the

-HARM

Japanese crew and pushed the Americans back into the water. Only 9 men survived the ordeal. Five men found a lifeboat and made it to China and were saved. Four others reportedly survived, 2 of which were picked up by a Japanese destroyer and returned to Takeo while two others made a raft and were picked up by a Japanese merchant ship. The 4 were together on Formosa but knew of no other survivors.[386] U.S. submarines had directions to search for American survivors in the vicinity of ships sunk when headed toward Japan. *SHARK II* was not heard from after the attack so it is probable she surfaced to look for survivors and was sunk by a Japanese destroyer. Japan reported an attack on a submarine in the area with a sinking indication.[387]

In some hell ships, death was almost a blessing as treatment on board the vessels was unbelievably cruel. In most cases, the men were crammed into the closest of quarters in holds often-used prior for the storage of coal, hazardous materials, or cattle. The POWs suffered temperature extremes while sitting in their own waste with virtually neither food nor water. Even when ships were strafed and bombed, no medical assistance was rendered to the prisoners.

In June 1944, the Japanese ordered three chaplains to accompany a group of 1,000 American prisoners to Japan. It was the first time chaplains were permitted to accompany outbound prisoners. Prior to the voyage, laymen were trained by the chaplains to fill the void or lack of religious leaders. The layman conducted burial services, prayers for the sick and Sunday services. Copies of the Service Book for Ship and Field were smuggled out of Camp O'Donnell by Chaplain Sam Donald who in turn issued them to the temporary "chaplains." The three chaplains selected were Stan Reilly, John Curran, and Sam Donald. They may have been on board the *NISSYO MARU* with Mansfield. More chaplains were called after their first voyage probably for their calming effect on the POWs in the holds. After all, the Japanese were looking for laborers, not dead bodies.

The Japanese began the war without ships designed to protect convoys or merchant vessels. They understood the requirement before the outbreak of hostilities but took no action until after 7 December 1941. The Japanese never recovered and commerce shipping suffered severely throughout the war. The shortcoming affected the "hell ships" that usually traveled in convoys. They were at the mercy of the American Submarine Force that almost single-handedly brought Japan to her knees without the ability to import food and raw materials.[388] The first convoy escort forces protected ships only in the Moji, Takeo, Manila, and Singapore areas. However, the effort was so austere, merchant and hell ship losses to American submarines, and later U.S. Navy carrier aircraft, was significant. Due to the shortage of escort vessels, convoys were often delayed for days or weeks while awaiting escorts. As a consequence, the import of supplies and slave labor was delayed much to the chagrin and anguish of the POWs.[389]

Perhaps the most clever escort vessel devised by the Japanese was the "Q-ship" and "Super Q-ship." The vessels were disguised as merchant ships and equipped with guns and the best anti-submarine detection devices available at the time. The *DELHI MARU* of 2,000-tons was the first vessel so designed. Similar efforts were common knowledge via Hollywood movies such as "Bongo Pete" in the Bongo Straits with a Japanese submarine to surprise attacking American submarines.[390]

Manny Eneriz's story differs little. The POWs were awakened at dawn as usual in Cabanatuan and mustered. Manny and his group were pushed into troop carrying trucks and driven to Manila. It was early in the morning in June of 1944 as he watched the gates of Cabanatuan Camp #1 gates pass behind him. The trucks stopped and the men were ordered out. The men looked at the front door of the ancient prison of Bilibid as a crowd of Filipinos surrounded them. "Where you go Joe? Corregidor, you Corregidor Americans? You must be Bataan men." Someone told the crowd they were from both Bataan and Corregidor. "Ooh, from Bataan Joe. We told you all dead, uh Joe?" Many in the crowd had American friends and deluged the POWs with questions and names. "Do you know John, he at Bataan.? "Have you seen . . . " and the queries continued.

The crowd cheered the POWs, clapped their hands, and told the men how they loved and cared for Americans. It was a touching moment and the first praise the prisoners heard in years. The Filipinos patted the men on their backs and helped the weak and crippled. Some of the POWs returned the "V" for victory hand signs shown by the crowd. Then a scream, "Get your asses back in line!" followed by rifle butts in the backs. "Screw you yellow prick!" "Stuff it asshole."

The men were marched into old Bilibid Prison, shoved to the ground in the courtyard, and made to squat. Eventually, they were assigned a space and sent to their quarters. Despite its old age, the arrangements were a quantum leap improvement over Cabanatuan and the prisoners actually ate a decent meal. The following day, the summer sun beat down unmercifully on Manila but the POWs remained cool. The huge old building absorbed the sun's heat while the prisoners sat in the cool shade. Unfortunately, the men remained in Bilibid for only a few days.

Manny's group felt comfortable after a few days and at home in Bilibid but their group was mustered again along with a few other groups in the prison. Then the POWs were marched out of the prison and through the streets of Manila to the waterfront. They marched, or straggled, through the business district and past the old Bureau of Posts, down Dewey Boulevard and toward the docks. It was night and a heavy fog lay over Manila Bay. It was a long walk and Manny noticed a glow of lights in the distance. As they closed the lights, he realized they were walking down a long wharf in the Port of Manila. At berth alongside the wharf was the *CANADIAN INVENTOR*, a dingy and rusty old freighter captured earlier from the British. The guards stopped them at the foot of the gangway and two Japanese officers ran up to the quarterdeck to talk with the crew. Then came a wave of the arm from one of the officers.[391]

Theoretically, the Japanese prevented the import of dysentery to Japan by checking the stool of all the POWs prior to boarding each ship. Prisoners not desiring to make the trip asked another POW with dysentery for a positive stool sample and the man never left the POW camp. However, every account of voyages of the hell ships included numerous accounts of dysentery cases.

The guards ordered the men to climb the gangway in a single file. One after another, the prisoners started up the bouncing gangway that flexed to the step of each man. They were greeted at the top of the gangway on the main deck by more guards who roughly pushed the POWs forward to Hatch #2. Once there, the men were clubbed and forced down a long, cold and slippery steel ladder that led to the bowels of the hold. There were a number of hatches but the entire vessel forward of the deckhouse was one large compartment with no watertight integrity what so ever. Manny knew he was at the bottom of the ladder when his foot alighted upon a soft material. There were no lights in the hold. The entire space was filled with bulk salt, piled to within 10-15 feet of the hatches. The air smelled stale, acrid, and foul. More POWs followed until there was no room. In the dark, he felt his way around until he found a little space and sat down on the salt and waited. When he put his hand on the bulkheads, it felt gritty. Not only was the hold damp and cold, it was still full of coal dust from the ship's previous voyage. Gradually, his eyes became accustomed to the dark and he saw shadows in the little light coming through the hatch opening. Some prisoners fell over Manny as they looked for a place to park their bodies, swearing and yelling at each other and the Japanese.

The demand for prisoner slave labor was precipitated by the loss of many skilled and unskilled Japanese workers to the military and civilians near the war front. The most sought after skill in the prisoners was dock workers, commonly called stevedores. Few POWs had waterfront experience and most POW work on the waterfront resulted in pilferage and sabotage. One in five workers in shipyards were male Japanese with the remainder made of women, students, criminals, and POWs. The POWs didn't help the war effort as they overheated rivets to brittle uselessness, defecated in equipment, lost tools, and generally hampered orderly construction. The Japanese had their own problems as they often interchanged the use of feet and meters within their metric system with expected consequences.[392]

Wood buckets shaped like bathtubs were lowered on ropes and used as heads, toilets, rest rooms, and a place to deposit bodily waste. The hatch cover was lowered into place and covered the entire opening. Groans and moans came from the POWs, which reflected their thoughts. Their fears concerned another railroad ride except in a cargo hold. The hatch cover was battened down for sea and total darkness blanketed the hold. The crew did remove a small part of the hatch that gave the prisoners some fresh air in the bottom of the hold and a little light. Then they were ordered to rest and sleep, a difficult feat since many had to stand.[393]

The men quieted down and rumors began. "Where the hell do you think they're taking us?" "Probably to Japan." "Naw, I'll bet they're going to take us to some place like China." "I got the word on the dock, we're going to salt mines in Manchuria." "That can't be right, damn it. You can bet your ass it'll be a slave camp or factory."

The sun rose and a shaft of light reached down to the prisoners. A couple barrels of water and two pots of rice were lowered into the hold while waste buckets were pulled up, dumped, and returned. It was not to be a luxury cruise.

Manny felt a bump alongside the ship in the afternoon as a tugboat made up their lines to move the ship to sea. Then the ship was underway and most of the men agreed they were headed for Japan, a trip that should take four or five days. She joined a convoy of 13 to 18 ships.[394] Within the hour, the old merchant ship rolled, yawed, and pitched gently in the sea but it was sufficient movement to make some of the POWs ill. The situation in the hold deteriorated rapidly by nightfall. The guards lowered the men rice but as hungry as they were, it was virtually impossible to eat in such a putrid environment. Most of the POWs were soldiers who did not adapt well to rough seas. Buckets overturned, the men were sick, and it was a hell of a mess. The men screamed in anguish and the crew responded by closing the only small opening in the hatch.

The following morning, the hole in the hatch was reopened and the POWs welcomed the blast of fresh, cool air. A few prisoners died during the night, which was sad, but it provided a bit more room for the survivors. The Japanese respected all people's religion, including rites for the dead and they permitted some of the POWs topside for a brief funeral service. An Army Chaplain performed the service for the deceased. Soldiers among the POWs shuttered in disbelief as the rag wrapped bodies were rendered to the deep for they were not accustomed to the ways of the sea.

Life at sea continued miserable but the seas settled a bit after a couple days. A few prisoners were permitted topside for a few minutes each morning and afternoon. When Manny was permitted on deck, he looked out to sea and saw a number of Japanese ships. He was impressed with the sleek lines of the Japanese men-of-war and how lethal they appeared.

A couple sergeants organized the prisoners and ordered the men to clean up the hold. Some were reluctant but they got off their haunches and agreed the activity was beneficial and certainly improved living conditions. On the 5th day of the voyage, Manny noticed a land mass on the horizon to the northwest during his brief visit to the head on a 2" X 4" frame. He had no way of knowing but thought it likely was Japan. It was Formosa (Taiwan). The ship made a number of course changes and anchored in Takao Harbor (Kaoshung) to await the arrival of another convoy they joined for the final leg of the journey.[395]

The POWs were grateful for the protection offered by the harbor and the motionless ship. But the cool waters of the sea and the sea winds also disappeared and the hold grew progressively hotter. The harbor was protected from the westerly winds by a high seashore cliff and the refreshing aroma from the bay waters was akin to a benjo ditch. The POWs gave the *CANADIAN INVENTOR* the nickname *"BENJO MARU."* The outside smell differed little from the conditions in the hold. The temperature in the hold increased markedly and was aggravated by the heat emitted through the single steel bulkhead between the hold and boiler room. The prisoners became dehydrated and pleaded for water but in vain until more prisoners died. When the men asked for more food and water, the ship's crew explained their own rations were frugal and couldn't afford to give the POWs more.[396] They suffered in Takao for days before the ship returned to sea. Once underway, the holds cooled down and the men began to feel better but the ship reversed course and returned to port. American submarines in a wolf pack were lurking outside Takao.

A few days went by before *CANADIAN INVENTOR* got underway again. The makeshift 2" X 4"s head was replaced by large flower a pot which was an improvement and somewhat humorous as a man sat on a flower pot on a rolling deck. The ship joined a huge armada of Japanese warships and cargo ships. Manny estimated between 80-90 ships in the convoy. The few prisoners that made it topside, reported seeing ships as far as the horizon. The weather remained calm and ship's motion minimal. The men worked out a rotation where half the men laid down to sleep while the other half stood. It worked well.

A couple of nights out of Takao, the POWs were alarmed at the sound of sirens and they saw searchlights sweeping the skies through the hole in the hatch cover. It became a nightly occurrence as the Japanese convoy fought off American submarines and carrier aircraft. A number of deep and thunderous explosions were heard some nights, indicative American submarines were finding their targets. A nearby tanker was torpedoed and exploded. The POWs cheered at the sound of the explosions until they realized their ship could be next. Immediately, Manny enthusiastically joined the others in prayer to God to avoid the ire of the submariners.

ROBERT K. HARMUTH

The convoy continued at sea for weeks and was attacked daily. Guns fired and depth charges exploded. Suddenly, the entire ship shook from stem to stern as a nearby ship exploded after being torpedoed. The men panicked thinking the CANADIAN INVENTOR was hit. That night, more Americans died and the chaplain again took charge. Amid the gunfire and explosions, his voice rose loudly like a bosun and he led the men in saying the Lord's Prayer. Quickly the hold quieted as the men joined in prayer.

The following night, the convoy ran into a severe typhoon and the sea turned into mountains of angry waves and tossed the ships about like corks in a washing machine. Few POWs became sick however, as they were too frightened to worry about seasickness. Huge waves slammed into the ship and on the main deck, funneling green seawater into the hold through the small opening. The CANADIAN INVENTOR's refrigeration system was damaged and soy sauce turned bad. The next day, the POWs were issued ample soy sauce, which looked like light brown baby poop, with rice. It didn't taste bad but set badly in the stomach.

The prisoners took a beating in the hold as they were hurtled one way and another. More men died and others broke limbs. Funeral services became a gruesome daily activity. After 63 days out of Manila, the ship berthed in Japan with the surviving POWs near exhaustion and death.

As the Allies hit the beaches at Normandy on 6 June 1944, 1,239 prisoners on Mindanao were trucked to the port at Davao. They were tied together, blindfolded, and thrown into the backs of trucks to be unceremoniously dumped at Davao. Still tied, they were forced up the gangway of the YASHU MARU. When they reached the quarterdeck, they were issued a Red Cross package and sent below into a hold.[397]

Six men escaped prior to boarding the YASHU MARU and another man escaped while the vessel was moored in Zamboanga. The last escape cost the POWs dearly as they were confined below decks and the main deck rails were blocked with equipment to prevent escape. However, the next night another POW escaped so

-HARM

the guards cut off all food and water rations. The following day, the vessel stopped at Cebu and discharged the POWs. They loaded onto another hell ship, identified only as the "824." On 26 June, the ship arrived in Manila and the POWs were removed. The 500 men from Mindanao joined 500 Americans from Cabanatuan via Bilibid. The entire group was then embarked on the *CANADIAN INVENTOR* on 2 July 1944. The remaining men from Davao were trucked to Cabanatuan.[398]

The *CANADIAN INVENTOR* departed 3 July but returned the next day for an unknown reason but it was likely a submarine warning. The ship remained in Manila for two weeks under the baking sun while the POWs suffered miserably in the holds. She finally departed on 16 July followed closely the next day by the *NISSYO MARU*. The *CANADIAN INVENTOR* arrived in Moji on 1 September 1944. She also anchored for two weeks in Takeo to avoid a storm then spent the remainder of the voyage dodging between islands to avoid the ever present American submarine. The POWs renamed her from *BENJO MARU* to "*MATI MATI MARU*" – mati means "wait." From Moji, the largest group of POWs were railed north to Yokkaichi and then to Nagoya POW Camp. There, the men were forced to labor in a copper smelting plant with Dutch and British prisoners. Another group of 256 men went to a camp at Omine Machi on the southern tip of Honshu where they worked in a coal mine for the next two and a half years with British prisoners. A third group of 200 men joined Americans working a coal mine at Fukuota Camp #17 at Omuta near the southern tip of Kyushu. This camp became the largest single concentration of Americans in Japan and was Manny's temporary home.[399]

On 20 August, 750 Americans boarded a hell ship and sailed that night for Japan via Zamboanga. They were moved to the *SHINYO MARU* following a month of labor near Lasang building two airstrips. They departed on 5 September in company of a small convoy including two destroyer escorts. The convoy was attacked on the 7th by the *USS PADDLE (SS-263)*. She hit the tanker

EIYO MARU that was sunk later by naval aircraft. The *SHINYO MARU* was hit by two torpedoes, which terrified the POWs and caused severe damage. Many POWs and crew were killed or maimed by the blasts. The ship listed to port and many of the POWs managed to climb ropes out of the holds and clamber topside to jump off the starboard side. It was a difficult task for the men, in their decimated physical condition. As the POWs arrived on deck, remaining guards fired on them but numerous POWs survived the massacre and got into the water. The remaining Japanese ships in the convoy left the men in the water to fend for themselves. About 500 Americans went down with the *SHINYU MARU* and those in the water attempted to swim ashore. The *EIYO MARU* went aground before she sank and fired upon the POWs swimming for shore. Some of the prisoners survived this onslaught and made it to the beach where they contacted guerrilla units. Arrangements were made to evacuate them to safety on the *USS NARWHAL (SS-167)*.[400]

American submarines enjoyed a hay day on 12 September 1944 as the *USS GROWLER (SS-215), USS SEALION (SS-315),* and *USS PAMPANITO (SS-383)* intercepted a Japanese convoy about 200 miles east of Hainan Island in China. *PAMPANITO* sent the *KACHIDOKI MARU* to a watery grave and the *SEA LION* sent *RAKUYU MARU* to Davey Jones Locker while *GROWLER* was busy sinking convoy escorts, the frigate *HIRADO* and destroyer *SHIKINAMI* plus a few other unverified ships. On board *KACHIDOKI MARU* were 900 British POWs from Singapore, all crammed into #2 hold with a possibility of a few men on deck. As was the rule, the hell ship was not marked with any identification to indicate she carried POWs or injured. The only men that survived jumped within the first ten minutes after the torpedoes hit. Almost all the POWs were lost.

American submarines were busy evacuating personnel from the Philippines throughout the war. The *USS SHARK (SS-174)* evacuated Admiral Hart and his staff from Manila on 26 December 1941 and on the same date, the *USS SEAWOLF (SS-197)* took

Captain Fife and his staff from Corregidor to Darwin. *USS SWORD-FISH (SS-193)* departed Manila with Captain Wilkes and staff on the 31ˢᵗ bound for Surabaya. She returned to Corregidor on 20 February 1942 to remove President Quezon. In May 1942, the *USS SPEARFISH (SS-190)* evacuated nurses from Corregidor. There were many more missions in the next few years.[401]

On *RAKUYU MARU*, the POWs heard the submarine attacks on the convoy a couple miles ahead of them. The horizon was littered with burning ships and survivors in the water. The *SEA LION* nailed the *NANKAI MARU* and then hit the *RAKUYU MARU*. The first torpedo struck Hold #1, just 30 feet forward of the hold with all the POWs. *PAMPANITO* also sank the tanker *ZUIHO MARU*. The *USS BARB (SS-220)* and *USS QUEENFISH (SS-393)* were also in close proximity to the convoy which added to the Japanese confusion. The *RAKUYU MARU* went down slowly while Japanese frigates picked up the Japanese crew. Once the survivors were rescued, the frigates repeatedly steamed through the POW survivors in the water, killing many. Among the groups of POWs on the *RAKUYU MARU* was the surviving crew of *HMAS PERTH*.[402]

Life was a miserable and monotonous routine at Camp Cabanatuan as the remaining prisoners lived one day at a time just to exist. On 7 October 1944, word was passed the men were to ship out to points unknown soon. By then, the prisoners heard stories about the men from Davao and had no desire to go any-where by ship. The grapevine talked about advances by the Allies and the Philippines were ripe for invasion. The grapevine was be-lievable as the men often spotted American naval aircraft overhead. The next day, 1,619 men were crowded into trucks, 35 men per truck, and motored to Manila. This left only about 500 prisoners behind in Cabanatuan who were physically disabled.[403]

The men were housed in Bilibid Prison in Manila where they met several hundred other American POWs with a few Dutch and British. They remained there for weeks as naval aircraft pounded the nearby Manila port area while the prisoners prayed no Japanese vessel made port to take them away to Japan. Food and water rations were small and the men continued to lose weight.

28 November 1944 in the early evening, the largest aircraft carrier in the world departed Tokyo. The *SHINANO*, displacing 71,000 tons fell game to the *USS ARCHERFISH* at 0300 on the 29th and was soon on the ocean floor. Built to withstand as many as twenty torpedoes, her watertight integrity was incomplete and succumbed to the attack of only one American submarine.[404]

On 13 December 1944, the 1,619 men were marched out of Bilibid Prison and counted. It turned out to be a practice run and the men returned to the prison after standing for hours in the sun. A day later, they repeated the exercise but after muster, they were marched through the streets of Manila. How the Filipinos knew more prisoners were being marched to the docks is unknown but they were out to cheer the POWs. They wore clean white shirts called barong tagalogs in a tribute to the POWs. As the men walked, unknown to them, 200 miles to the south Americans were on a march across Leyte.[405]

The column of POWs stretched a mile in length and as they entered the port area, they viewed the skeletal remains of dozens of ships lying on the bottom or banks of Manila Bay. The infamous Pier #7 was half destroyed as was most of the waterfront facilities. American flyers had been busy. Two vessels remained at the pier, their hulls gutted by fire while another two merchant vessels remained afloat and undamaged. The men grinned at the damage and mumbled a few words of cheer about the damage. Then reality returned and they realized they soon would be boarding one of the Japanese ships. One of the two ships was a passenger vessel by the name of *ORYOKO MARU*, likely the most publicized of all the hell ships. She was built in 1939, was 10,000 tons, and well known in the Sea of Japan as a greyhound among passenger ships. The POWs noticed she was not marked in any way they could see to indicate she was another hell ship.[406]

The usual lack of organization was present as the POWs and guards milled about the wharf. The men were finally mustered and left to stand in formation waiting to board the ship. There were hundreds of Japanese civilians on the wharf as well who were waiting to board the same ship. The Japanese civilian population on Luzon was nervous and abandoning the captured land of the Philippines as the Allies drew ever closer. The civilians packed hastily, many carried cloth bags and luggage tied with string. Finally, the civilians boarded the ship followed by herding the prisoners into three groups who were pushed into three cargo holds. For some reason, the officers were sent into the holds first followed by the enlisted on top of them. There were 850 men in the after Hold #5, 500 into Hold #1 forward, and the remaining 250 or so men into Hold #2, the least crowded. The men sat on sacks of grain used to feed horses on the trip to Manila. There was a ventilation system used to cool the horses but was not turned on for the POWs. The grain and the nauseating residue of horse manure remained in the holds.[407]

The *ORYOKO MARU* got underway that evening and stood out to an anchorage in Manila Bay where they joined four other merchant ships and a cruiser. The POWs were given no water or food during the evening and night. The prisoner's shouts for food and drink annoyed the passengers and the crew placed a cover on the cargo hatch. Fifty or more POWs died the first night due to suffocation.[408]

Just before dawn, the *OROYKO MARU* and her escort weighed anchor and headed for North Channel between Corregidor and Bataan. She transited the channel with no problem and headed north along the west coast of the Bataan Peninsula. As they progressed, the temperature in the holds rose and the dead were stacked in the corners of the holds. A few of the men were crazed and ran about in the holds out of self-control. Commander Bridget was in one of the holds and managed to calm the situation. The men removed their tattered clothing and fanned the air that revived some of men who had passed out from the heat.[409] The cargo holds had wood tiers built around the periphery about three feet high and nine feet deep. The POWs were expected to reside on the shelves but it was difficult to breathe.

In the afternoon, the prisoners were fed some rice and water but the sound of aircraft and the reply of anti-aircraft interrupted their "feast." *ORYOKU MARU* was strafed repeatedly and a multitude of bombs narrowly missed the ship. Suddenly, a huge explosion rocked the ship. A bomb hit the civilian's quarters. Then more strafing raked the hull, adding ventilation to the holds. A bomb near miss jarred the hatch covers loose permitting additional air into the holds and some light. Soon, the four 3-inch guns of the ship were silenced. The ship turned into Subic Bay and grounded herself off the shore of Olongapo. Then it was dark as night fell.

On the morning of 15 December 1944, the word was passed to the prisoners they were to be taken ashore. BMC Clarence Taylor made it topside and lowered a lifeboat to take the wounded ashore. The movement was interrupted by the arrival of the first wave of Navy aircraft of the day. Within minutes, a bomb exploded on the ship's fantail. The *ORYOKU MARU* caught fire and the Japanese abandoned ship. Most of the POWs escaped the holds and some of the POWs recognized Olongapo as the old naval station. Word was passed to the POWs where the lifeboats were located and to abandoned ship. The men jumped over the side and struck out for the shoreline.

Navy pilots eventually recognized the POWs in the water and ceased firing. Most of the men made it ashore, recaptured immediately, and herded into tennis courts near the shore.[410] The men were mustered and the head count was 1,340 POWs still alive out of the original 1, 619. Dead prisoners were stacked near the entrance to the tennis courts. As the men looked out into Subic Bay, they witnessed the Navy's first use of rockets in combat from F4Us and F6Fs. The *ORYOKU MARU* 's fires intensified and then she exploded and sunk. The men cheered at her demise only to be smacked with rifle butts. The sun beat on the men unmercifully and thirst became intolerable. For five days and nights, the men blistered in the sun and shivered in the cool of the night. At the end of the fifth day, the head count dropped below 1,300.[411]

LCOL Curtis Beecher, USMC took charge of the surviving POWs and he stood atop the tennis referee chair, directing activities. A tiny field hospital, be it as it may, was set up under a couple blankets to provide a respite in the shade for the more severely injured. Even an amputation without anesthetic was performed. On 20 December, a convoy of Japanese trucks arrived at the tennis courts and loaded the POWs. The convoy moved inland over the Zamabales Mountains toward San Fernando. That night, the men were stuffed into an old theater and a jail. Eight of the most ill were trucked off for medical help but bayoneted and beheaded. The POWs remained in jail and the theater until the 24th when they were moved out by truck to the railhead in San Fernando. The train ride was a repeat of the days from Bataan to Camp O'Donnell, hot and dirty. The POWs trembled in fear of their destination. They didn't head for Capas and rode past the ruins of Clark Field. The men could see out of the top of the boxcars through cracks and open seams. They witnessed Navy aircraft in dogfights with Japanese planes and cheered enthusiastically as pieces with red meatball insignia fell from the sky. The periphery of the airfield was a series of trenches and foxholes filled by Japanese defenders-what a wonderful Christmas gift for the prisoners.[412]

The train passed Lingayen Gulf and stopped in a small barrio where the men were stuffed in an old schoolhouse. On Christmas morning, only the very sick were permitted to remain in the schoolhouse while the rest of the POWs were forced to sit in the sun outside. A small portion of rice and a cup of water was the ration for the day with some rotting banana stalks thrown in for desert. The next day, the POWs were marched to the sandy beaches of Lingayen Gulf and permitted to cool off in the ocean. The salt water stung the sunburn but the cool water felt good. Unfortunately, no fresh water shower was available so the dry, crusted salt eventually caused more sores and irritation.

They remained on the beach and the following day a huge storm hit the area. The POWs dug holes in the sand in a vain effort to get out of the high winds coming off the China Sea. On the 27th, they were marched to a small nearby port and boarded the 10,000 ton *ENOURA MARU* with a large "#1" painted on the stack. About 1,000 men were herded on board while the remaining 236 men were loaded on another ship, the *BRAZIL MARU* with a large "#2" on her stack. A final count or guess was made of 1,305 men. On the 28th, the two rusty vessels got underway with at least one American a day dying in the holds. The crews didn't permit the dead brought topside until a large group was gathered. It did not add to the environment in the holds. The bodies were line-hauled out of the holds, feet first with ankles tied and covered in feces and filth. The survivors became violently ill at the sight.

In the following weeks, the vessels only moved during daylight and anchored near islands at night. They were beyond American aircraft range but not the ever present American submarine. Ships were sunk in their convoy but the two hell ships continued unscathed. On New Years Day, the convoy reached Takeo on Formosa. Both ships berthed at a pier and the dead were brought topside for disposal ashore. 37 British and Dutch were taken ashore while the living prisoners on board were about 1,262. An estimated 314 men died on the *ORYOKU MARU*.[413]

Early on 9 January, an air attack struck Takeo and was intercepted by Japanese aircraft. The air battle waged for hours and both hell ships were hit by bombs. The vessels lost power and lighting, plunging the entire ship into darkness and terrifying the POWs. Numerous deaths and injuries occurred in the holds and the prisoners were helpless to assist each other. On the 12th, a cargo net was dropped into the holds and the dead lifted out amidst prayers from the chaplains and men. About 150 men were dead and placed on a barge and deposited ashore. A burial detail went with the dead where a common grave became the final resting-place. A memorial now marks the site. The head count dropped to 930 scarcely living POWs.[414]

The *ENOURA MARU* was damaged beyond repair so her POWs were moved to the *BRAZIL MARU* for the final leg of the journey to Japan. Once loaded with the added men, the *BRAZIL MARU* got underway. On the 13th, the convoy of 5 destroyers and 7 merchant ships moved into the Formosa Strait and moved toward Japan on a zigzag course. On the first night, 46 more men died including a dozen on deck before they got into the hold. The trip took more than two weeks and two bastions of strength throughout the imprisonment failed to see Japan – CDR Bridget and Father Cummings.[415]

As the trip progressed, the weather turned cold and uncomfortable in the holds. During the night of the 17th, the ship threw a towline to another vessel that was dead in the water then resumed the transit. The last week of January 1945, the prisoners averaged 25 deaths per day. Finally, the crew got the picture and gave the Americans water daily. The ship was under the umbrella of air coverage from Japan that flew overhead continuously.

The *BRAZIL MARU* moored in Moji, Japan on 30 January 1945. A final roll call was taken and only 435 of the original 1,619 POWs remained. The temperature dropped below freezing as the men were off-loaded and marched a few blocks to a warehouse containing a huge community bath. The men were permitted to bathe and given a canteen cup of rice, seaweed soup, and a hot cup of tea. After a nights rest, the men were placed on a train and sent to work camps; 100 to Fukuota Camp #1, another 100 to camp #3, and the remainder to Camp #17. Thirty days later, 161 of the 425 who reached Japan were dead, leaving a total of 264 of the 1,619 who began the voyage.[416]

ROBERT K. HARMUTH

SUMMARY OF HELL SHIPS AND OTHER
POW CARRYING VESSELS:

(A NUMBER OF the hell ships were given nicknames as Hotsy Maru, Byoki Maru, Stinko Maru, Diarrhea Maru, Dysentery Maru and Benjo Maru.)

AKI MARU – The 11,409-ton passenger-cargo vessel departed Singapore on 10 January 1943 with 74 POWs to Formosa. The ship was sunk by the USS CREVALLE (SS-291) on 26 July 1944 at 18-24N, 118-02E.[417]

AKIKAZE – A Japanese destroyer departing Wewak on 17 March 1943 with 60 German and Chinese civilians. Reported sunk with all POWs lost although some records indicate she wasn't sunk until 3 November 1944 by the USS PINTADO (SS-387) northwest of Manila.[418]

AMAGI MARU – A 3,165-ton passenger-cargo ship that transferred 1,071 POWs on 22 April 1943 from Soerabaja, Dutch East Indies and arrived in Haroekoe, Ceram Island, Dutch East Indies 17 days later.[419] She was sunk by HMS TANTALUS on 2 April 1944 at 10-52N, 93-12E[420]

AMERICAN MARU – USS NAUTILUS (SS-168) received an "Ultra" intelligence message indicating a large convoy was departing Saipan. NAUTILUS blew the stern off the 6,000-ton transport on 6 March 1943 loaded with 1,700 elderly, women, and children who were construction workers on Saipan. They were ordered back to Japan and the number of casualties is unknown.[421]

ARGENTINA MARU – She was a high-speed passenger liner that departed Guam on 10 January 1942, one month after Japan captured the island. 400 POWs were carried in a hold but permitted topside during good weather. The men were given fish and wormy rice in buckets. Navy boatswain's mates took charge of food distribution after fights for the food. The maru arrived offshore Shikoku on 16 January in the Inland Sea. The POWs were taken ashore in barges, then moved by streetcar to Zentsuji that housed Russian prisoners in 1904-1905. POW treatment was relatively good in the camp.[422]

ARISAN MARU – The vessel took the second detail out of Bilibid numbering 1,775[423] men. She departed Pier #7 in Manila on 21 October 1944 after remaining at berth for 10 days. Few officers were in the group since emphasis was placed on workers. She joined a convoy of 13 ships when Navy aircraft bombed Manila and returned to Manila as MacArthur landed on Leyte. She completed loading. The maru was torpedoed 225 miles off Hong Kong on 24 October by *USS SHARK II* (originally thought to be *USS SNOOK*). The crew cut the Jacob ladders into the holds and the hatch covers were secured. The 6,886-ton cargo vessel sank at 20-54N, 118-19E in the Bashi Straits.[424] She was hit by one of three torpedoes fired and the stern disintegrated. Only 9 POWs survived, 5 in a boat that made it to China and 4 others who were reported as picked up by the Japanese. She possibly was hit first by *USS SNOOK* before sinking.[425]

ASAKA MARU – She departed 4 July 1944 with 738 POWs from Singapore to Manila. She carried the same or another group of 738 POWs on 9 August 1994 to Takeo. She was hit by a typhoon while in port on the 13th and sunk on an island of the Bashee Group south of Formosa. 31 POWs. were lost in the grounding. They were in the water for days before being picked up by a Japanese destroyer and taken to Keelung, Formosa. The *HAKUSAN MARU* moved them from Formosa to Japan. There was at least two other *ASAKA MARUs*, one a converted light cruiser and the other a passenger-cargo ship, which was sunk by Navy carrier aircraft on 12 October 1944.[426]

ASAMA MARU – The large 16,975-ton transport departed Wake Island in May 1942 with an unknown number of injured and sick POWs.[427] The vessel originally participated in a political prisoner exchange that consisted primarily of diplomats and civilians including Ambassador to Japan Joseph C. Grew. The exchange was with the US Charter vessel *GRIPSHOLM*, a Swedish liner, on 23 July 1942. She departed Wake Island again 1 November 1942 with 20 POWs.[428] She moved 71 POWs from Singapore on 21 September 1943 enroute to Japan. They were survivors of the lost *USS GRENADIER*.[429] In early October 1942, she distributed Red Cross food to POWs throughout the Pacific. On 10 October 1942, she departed Makassar with about 1,000 POWs, some survivors of the *EXETER*, bound for Nagasaki. The *USS SUNFISH* damaged her. The POWs worked in a Kawaminami Zozen Shipyard until 25 April 1945 when many were transferred to Camp Hoten in Manchuria. She was sunk on 18 January 1943 by the *USS GRAYBACK (SS-208)* at position 24-15N, 122-19E during a daytime attack. She carried the survivors of the *USS PERCH* of which 51 survived the war. Another *ASAMA MARU* was sunk by the *USS ATULE* on 24 October 1944.[430] (see picture)[431]

AWA MARU – She was an 11,600-ton passenger-cargo ship that moved 525 Australians from Singapore to Moji on 26 December 1944. The U.S. was concerned about the treatment of American POWs and asked Switzerland to intercede and transport Red Cross packages to the POWs. On 17 February 1945, the U.S. gave the maru safe passage to deliver the packages. *AWA MARU* departed Moji bound for Singapore and Indonesia to return to Hong Kong and Takeo. She carried hundreds of tons of spare aircraft parts, ammunition, rubber, and 1,700 passengers. ADM Lockwood sent a message to all submarines three days running, "LET PASS SAFELY THE AWA MARU CARRYING PRISONER OF WAR SUPPLIES. SHE WILL BE PASSING THROUGH YOUR AREAS BETWEEN MARCH 30 AND APRIL 4. SHE IS LIGHTED AT NIGHT AND PLASTERED WITH WHITE CROSSES. She did carry some supplies for the POWs but was sunk by *USS QUEENFISH (SS-393)* in the fog on 1 April 1945 at 25-25N, 120-07E.

She displayed none of the signs of her special mission nor was seen in the low visibility. CAPT Laughlin, skipper of QUEENFISH was court martialed but only received a letter after rescuing 13 airmen enroute Guam. Navy carrier aircraft sank another AWA MARU, a small cargo ship, on 14 July 1945.[432]

BENJO MARU – A well-known name for the HARO MARU. She carried 230 Americans to Hosakura in January 1945 from Manila. Little is known of the voyage. The POWs were in very poor physical condition upon arrival in Japan. She stopped in Hong Kong then proceeded for a two-month stay in Takeo. The POWs were eventually placed on another ship for the trip to Japan.[433]

BRAZIL MARU – Also known as Hell Ship #2, she took POWs from ENOURA MARU and made port in Takao. The 5,859-ton cargo ship sailed 14 January 1945 leaving Lingayen Gulf in a convoy for Japan and left almost 300 dead. Of the original 1,619 POWs, 630 survived by some accounts[434] – others are much lower. Details are found earlier in this chapter. She arrived in Japan 2 February 1945. A mine sank her on 12 May 1945. A previous BRAZIL MARU was sunk on 5 August 1942 by USS GREENLING (SS-213) at 09-04N, 150-54E.[435] She was a 12,752-ton troop transport and ex-passenger liner carrying 600 passengers and 400 troops bound for the Solomons. This maru was sunk later by an unknown submarine.[436]

BROOKE YACHT – A small boat belonging to the Brooke Clan moved 8 escapees from Sandakan on 4 September 1943 to Kaochung.[437]

BYOKI MARU – (its real name was the RASHIN MARU) On her infamous voyage, she was at sea for 70 days while transporting Australians from Singapore to Japan. In the same convoy was the TOYOFUKU MARU. The BYOKI MARU was sunk by the USS PARGO (SS-264) on 8 August 1945. The 5,455 ton cargo vessel went down at 41-15N, 131-19E after being hit by three torpedoes.[438]

CANADIAN INVENTOR – 1,200 POWs were returned from the Davao Penal Colony of which 700 were sent to Cabanatuan and the other 500 loaded on board the *CANADIAN INVENTOR*. Another 500 American POWs departed Manila after arriving from Cabanatuan and Bilibid. She was a freighter captured by the Japanese. She departed Manila on July 1944 and arrived in Moji on 2 September 1944.[439] Conditions were so grim for the POWs, they killed and slashed each other to drink their blood and eat the flesh. The ship was one large hold and not compartmentalized like most vessels. The one huge hold was already half full of bulk salt on which the POWs resided for 63 days. Bad weather, submarine evasion, and convoy problems delayed the ship. The largest group was moved north by train to Yokaichi. They worked in a copper smelting plant. 256 men went to Omine Machi on the southern tip of Honshu to mine coal. The remaining [440] 200 or so were sent to Omuta thus becoming the largest single group of American POWs in Japan.[441] See also *MATTI MATTI MARU*.

CELEBES-Departed 15 May 1942 and was underway for 9 days with 1,983 POWs.[442]

CHO SAKI MARU – Carried 1,000 POWs from Java on 22 April 1943 to Ambon.[443]

CHUKA MARU – This maru moved 1,200 POWs in April 1944 to Batavia, Singapore, and Sumatra. During the 6-day trip, 5 men died on board. Navy carrier aircraft sank the 2,189-ton cargo ship on 24 September 1944. Army aircraft sank another *CHUKA MARU* on 20 August 1944.[444]

CHUYO – A 20,000-ton Japanese escort aircraft carrier that carried 22 POWs from the *USS SCULPIN (SS-191)* sunk 19 November 1943 by the Japanese destroyer *YAMAGUMA*. The carrier was sunk by the *USS SAILFISH (SS-192)* on 4 December 1943 and only one of the submarine POWs survived. He was taken to Asio copper mine to work.[445]

CLYDE MARU – The 5,497-ton passenger-cargo maru carried 500 POWs from Manila on 23 July 1943 to Moji. She was sunk in January 1945 by the *USS PICUDA (SS—382)*. A namesake ship was sunk by the *USS SAWFISH (SS-276)* southeast of Toizaki.[446]

COASTAL CRAFT – Moved 100 POWs from Celebes on 11 November 1944 enroute Java. 27 POWs were killed during a P-38 attack.[447]

COASTAL CRAFT – Transported 50 POWs on 13 April 1945 from Muna to Makassar.[448]

CORAL MARU – The ship carried more than 800 Americans from the Philippines to Moji, Japan in October 1943. 400 men went to the Osaka Group to labor in steel, mining, and transportation. A small group went to Sakura-Jima to assist the British POWs working in a shipyard. 350 Americans were railed to Niigata. The remainder went to Hirohata, 60 miles west of Osaka to work at the Seitetsu Steel Company.[449]

DAINICHI MARU – She ran 1,000 POWs on 23 September 1942 from Timor to Surabaya. Another trip she conducted took 1,000 POWs from Java on 11 October 1942. The maru departed Singapore on 30 October 1942 with 1,200 POWs of which 500 were Dutch and British POWs from the *YOSHIDA MARU*. She stopped over in Saigon thence Takao, reaching Kitokyushu, Japan on 25 November with 80 dead on board. The trip took almost a month. She also carried some survivors from the *YOSHIDA MARU*. Her next trip was on 20 February 1943 with 86 Chinese and European internees from Hankow to Nanking. She was later sunk by the *USS GURNARD (SS-254)* on 8 October 1943. The 5,813 ton cargo ship was hit by 3 torpedoes and sunk at 18-24N, 119-09E.[450]

DEKLERK – Left Singapore on 28 March 1943 with 1,000 POWs on board bound for Kuching. She then departed Kaochung for Jesselton and Sandaken with another 760 POWs.[451]

824 – Carried POWs off the *YASHU MARU* who later were moved to the *SINGOTO MARU*.[452]

EIYO MARU #2 – A former British ship, she carried 1,846 POWs from Singapore on 10 October 1942. She steamed for 9-days and 10 men were lost enroute Kuching and Jesselton. An *EIYO MARU* was sunk by American submarine on 20 February 1945. She was a 8,673-ton tanker. Yet another namesake, a 5,061-ton tanker was sunk by Navy carrier aircraft on 7 September 1944.[453]

ENGLAND MARU – The vessel carried 500 POWs in mid-May 1942. The voyage was 9 days from British Sumatra to Burma. She later carried General Percieval and 400 officers to Formosa. The 5,829-ton cargo ship was sunk by the *USS GRAYBACK (SS-208)* 17 May 1943 at 00-45N, 148-30E.[454]

ENOSHIMA MARU – She moved 564 POWs from Keelung to Moji on 25 January 1945.[455]

ENOURA MARU – The ship loaded over 1,300 POWs that survived the sinking of *ORYOKU MARU* in Subic Bay. She was also known as Hell Ship #1. She departed in late December 1944 and the prisoners received no food and spoonfuls of water. Off Formosa on 8 January 1945, she was jumped by Navy fighter-bombers. The maru was shredded and sunk with 500 POWs killed. The survivors were transferred to *BRAZIL MARU.*[456]

ENURI MARU – The hell ship took some survivors from Takeo on 14 January 1945 and arrived in Moji on 29 January 1945.[457]

ERIE MARU – The maru took over 1,000 Cabanatuan Camp #1 POWs to Mindanao in November 1942. The maru arrived at Lansang, Mindanao on 7 November 1942. She was later sunk by *USS STURGEON (SS-187)* on 11 January 1944. She was a 5,493 tanker torpedoed at 32-56N, 132-02E.[458]

EX-BRITISH SHIP – On a 9-day cruise, the ship carried 1,846 POWs leaving Singapore on 10 October 1942. Ten men died enroute Kuching and Jesselton.[459]

FRANCE MARU – Reportedly carried POWs on 5 November 1943 from Batavia to Palembang. A *FRANCE MARU* was reported sunk by the *USS HADDOCK (SS-231)* on 6 and 13 November 1943. The second date, the 13th, fits the scenario. The patrol report of the *HADDOCK* states her torpedoes ran under the target on the 6th. The maru either survived or another *FRANCE MARU*, a 5,828-ton passenger-cargo ship, was sunk by Navy carrier aircraft on 12 January 1945.[460]

FUKKAI MARU – The 3,829-ton passenger-cargo ship departed Singapore on 12 August 1942 with 1,100 men, spending 41 days in transit and make the ports of Takeo and Pusan. She carried high ranking military and civilian officials from Singapore and Malaya. The troop transport was later sunk by the *USS POGY (SS-266)* at 07-06N, 134-40E on 13 December 1943.[461]

FUKU MARU – She was also known as the *HOFUKU MARU, TOYOFUKU MARU,* and *FUUJI MARU.* A 5,325-ton passenger-cargo ship, she sailed out of Manila on 20 September 1944 with 1,289 Dutch and British POWs. Navy carrier aircraft sank her on 21 September 1944 near San Narcisco in Subic Bay. There were 1,226 casualties and 63 survivors were placed aboard the *ORYOKU MARU* which was also sunk on 13 December 1944.[462]

FUKUJI MARU – The maru transported 354 POWs on 9 November 1944 from Moji to Fusan, Korea. A couple weeks later the 5,293-ton cargo was sunk by the *USS PICUDA (SS-382)* at 34-14N, 128-28 East.[463]

GO MARU – She took approximately 74 officials from Batavia on 28 December 1942 to Singapore.[464]

HAKUROKU MARU – The vessel left Singapore on 4 July 1944 with 609 POWs enroute Manila and then on to Japan. She was believed sunk by an unknown submarine.[465]

HAKUSAN MARU #5 – The 2,211-ton cargo maru picked up 2,500-tons of US Red Cross packages from the Russians in Nakhodka and followed a route of POW camps, delivering the packages and supplies. She eventually returned to Osaka via Moji. On a later trip, she carried 707 POWs from Takao to Japan with the survivors of the *ASAKA MARU* on 17 August 1944. She picked up supplies in Nakhodka in October 1944, stopped for supplies for POWs in November for Korean Camps, thence to Kobe with the bulk of the food. She was sunk by the *USS CREVALLE (SS-291)* on 11 June 1945. There was a number of other *HAKUSAN MARUs.*[466]

HARU MARU – A rusty old 3,040-ton freighter from Manila carried 1,100 Americans, 100 British and Dutch POWs who survived a torpedoed ship ten days earlier. They boarded 1 October 1944 and made the trip in 120-degree temperatures in the cargo holds that were half filled with coal. She got underway on 3 October in a convoy of 18 ships. Nearby ships were sunk by American submarines, including the *HARUGIKO MARU,* but she made it to Hong Kong 11 days later. It remained there for 10 days then got underway for Takao, arriving 25 October 1944. The POWs were kept in the holds for 12 days, then moved ashore for two months. Eventually, they sailed to Japan. Many of the POWs were from the 192nd Tank Battalion. 39 POWs died during the voyage and many more died following the trip due to their weakened physical condition. This was one of the examples where the POWs fought in the holds in their heat-crazed state. Conditions were so severe, she was given the nickname "Benjo Maru." 500 of the POWs were sent to Hanawa Camp, better known as Sendai Camp-6B. This vessel may have been the *HISHIGATO MARU* which was sunk by Army aircraft on 2 January 1945. Some references to this ship list her as the *HARO MARU.*[467]

HARUKIKU MARU – The ship had 730 POWs on board when she was sunk by the submarine *HMS TRUCULENT* in the Malacca Strait on 26 June 1944. The 3,040-ton vessel departed Medan, East Sumatra destined for Singapore. 178 men did not survive the sinking.[468]

HARUYASA MARU – The vessel departed on 31 January 1945 from Singapore with 2,500 POWs on board for Saigon. The trip took 9 days.[469]

HEI MARU – The vessel took the surviving crew of the submarine *GRENADIER* following starvation, torture, and beatings as POWs. The trip to Singapore was typical of a hell ship. The

POWs were later boarded on the *ASAMA MARU*. She was an 11,621-ton ex-supply ship, sunk by the *USS DRUM (SS-228)*.[470]

HEIYO MARU – She moved 200 civilians in July 1942 to Japan. The 9,816-ton troop transport was sunk by the *USS WHALE (SS-239)* on 17 January 1943 at 10-10N, 151-25E. Navy carrier aircraft sank another small 973-ton cargo *HEIYO MARU* on 9 August 1945.[471]

HIOKI MARU – The ship transported 315 POWs from Singapore on 3 June 1944 to Moji.[472]

HOFUKU MARU – The ship's real name was the *TOYOFUKU MARU* that moved 1,287 POWs from Singapore to Japan on 21 September 1944. 950 of the men were lost on the trip when Navy aircraft from the *USS HORNET* and *USS WASP* sank the ship. [473]

HOKKO MARU – The maru departed Manila with Cabanatuan Camp #3 POWs. She was attacked by the *USS SPEARFISH (SS-190)* on 9 October 1942 during her transit to Formosa but all the torpedoes missed. The POWs ended up in Pusan where they were shipped to Manchuria. The maru carried another 1,287 POWs on 4 July 1944 from Singapore to Manila. The 5,385-ton troop carrier and cargo ship was sunk later by the *USS HARDER (SS-257)*. Another *HOKKO MARU* cargo ship of 5,346-tons was sunk 28 November 1943 by the *USS RATON (SS-270)*. Another namesake was sunk by a marine casualty on 23 March 1944.[474]

I-8 SUBMARINE – The submarine carried 103 POWs on 2 July 1944 from Tjisalak but was sunk. Only 5 POWs survived the sinking. She was sunk by Navy surface craft on 30 March 1945.[475]

I-37 SUBMARINE – The submarine sunk the *HMS CHIVALRY* and took 62 prisoners on 22 February 1944. Later she apparently laid a minefield on 18 April. She was sunk on 27 April 1944 by the *USS POGY (SS-266)* near Penang and the Japanese managed to kill 61 of the 62 POWs. Postwar Army-Navy records attribute the loss to Navy surface ships.[476]

ICHI MARU – The vessel moved 32 officers from *EXETER, ENCOUNTER, POPE,* and *PERCH.* on 7 April 1942.[477]

IKOMA MARU – On 21 January 1944, the 3,156-ton passenger-cargo ship departed Palau with 611 POWs for Hollandia. The maru was sunk by *USS SEAHORSE (SS304)* on 21 January 1944 at 03-25 North, 137-06 East. 418 of the 611 POWs were lost.[478]

INAZUMA – The vessel departed for Bandjermasin on 2 March 1942 with 376 survivors of the *EXETER* and *ENCOUNTER.* Later on 4 March, she carried another 143 survivors from *POPE.* The 2,000-ton destroyer was sunk by the *USS BONEFISH (SS-223)* on 14 May 1944 at 05-03N, 119-36E.[479]

INTER-ISLAND STEAMER – She moved 200 POWs in July 1942 from Manila to Davao.[480]

ISLA PRINCESA – The ship transported 346 POWs from Manila to Palawan on 29 July 1942.

JU MARU – She moved 300 POWs in May 1945 from Fukuoka to Pusan. One POW died during the one-day journey.[481]

JUNYO MARU – The 5,065-ton cargo ship carried 6,520 passengers; 2,200 POWs and about 4,320 Javanese laborers. She departed Batavia, West Java on 15 September 1944 enroute Padang, West Sumatra. She was torpedoed on 18 September 1944 off Sumatra by *HMS TRADEWIND.* She sank with 5,620 deaths; 1,377 were Dutch and Indo-China POWs, 64 Australian and British; and a handful of Americans. There were 723 survivors. Many survivors had their hands hacked off for trying to escape. She was sunk at 02-53N, 101-10E. The number of POWs carried and lost do not quite equate. This was the largest marine disaster in history.[482]

KACHI MARU – She moved 600 POWs out of Ambon to Batavia on 25 August 1944.[483]

KACHIDOKI MARU – (see RAKUYO MARU) The American submarine wolf pack, "Ben's Busters," comprised of

GROWLER, PAMPANITO, and *SEALION* lay in wait of the convoy from Singapore to Formosa in early September 1944. In the convoy was the *RAKUKO MARU* with 1,350 American and British POWs who had been laboring on a railroad in Malaya. *GROWLER* sank the destroyer *SHIKINAMI* and *SEALION* sank the transports *RAKUYO MARU* and *NANKAI MARU,* 9,400 and 8,400 tons respectively. The *RAKUYO MARU* lost 1,159 of 1,500 POWs she was carrying. *USS PAMPANITO (SS-389)* sunk the *KACHIDOKI MARU* on 12 September 1944 at 19-25N, 112-23E. She was a troop transport of 10,509 tons and 430 of her 950 POWs were lost. She was the former *SS PRESIDENT HARRISON* recovered by the Japanese near Shanghai. It was repaired and initially named the *KAKKO MARU.*[484]

KAISHUN MARU – The hell ship left on 17 September 1944 from Mindanao for Luzon with 150 POWs on board. On the 3-day trip, 4 men died during an air attack.[485]

KALGAN MARU – She carried 1,974 POWs on 4 September 1942 from Timor to Java and on to Singapore.[486]

KAMAKURA MARU – A troop transport of 15,000-tons, she was involved in a second POW swap, this time between the British and the Japanese. She departed Singapore on 29 November 1942 and arrived in Japan 8 December 1942 with 2,200 men; 563 Australians, 500 Americans, 950 Dutch, and 200 British. Later, she carried 696 POWs on 26 February 1943 from Makassar to Singapore. She was sunk by *USS GUDGEON (SS-211)* at 10-18N, 121-44E in the Sulu Sea near Panay on 28 April 1943. The maru was sunk at night indicating for the first time to the Japanese that American submarines were radar equipped.[487] She was large at 17,526 tons and was programmed for conversion to an aircraft carrier. A beautiful passenger liner, she called at Pearl Harbor prior to the war and was known as the pride of the Japanese merchant marine. She had carried 2,213 POWs, leaving Singapore on 28 November

1942 and sailing to Nagasaki 9 days later. She lost 10 dead at sea during the voyage.[488]

KENKON MARU – The maru departed Java 8 October 1942 with 1,500 POWs , losing one man. The 4,575-ton troop transport was sunk by the USS GATO (SS-212) on 21 January 1943 ENE of Buin.[489]

KENZAN MARU – The ship carried 300 POWs on 6 September 1944 from Makassar to Surbaya. A previous namesake was torpedoed in November 1943.[490]

KENWA MARU – The 6,384-ton tanker departed Manila on 6 March 1944 enroute Japan with 200 POWs on board. On 23 May 1944, she was attacked by the USS RAY (SS-271) who left her sinking. A few hours later, the USS CERO (SS-225) sank the maru shortly after sinking the TAIJUN MARU. There is no indication any POWs lost their lives.[491]

KIBITSU MARU – A 9,575-ton transport, she moved 677 POWs from Hainan to Japan on 10 September 1944. The 18-day voyage cost the lives of 8 POWs. The maru sunk on 8 August 1945 after striking a mine.[492]

KING KONG MARU – This 5,000-ton ship carried about 1,500 POWs from Batavia on 8 October 1942 and reached Singapore on 11 October 1942. Upon arrival in Singapore, the group received 300 more men and the entire group was shipped to Moulmein, Burma on the MAYEBASSI MARU and YINAGATO MARU.[493]

KOKUSEI MARU – She was a 5,396-ton cargo ship that moved 456 POWs beginning on 3 June 1944. She was sunk by the USS HAMMERHEAD (SS-364) on 1 October 1944 at 06-30N, 116-15E.[494]

KORYU MARU – The vessel carried 235 POWs from Shanghai on 4 March 1943 to Nanking. A small tanker of only 589-tons, she was torpedoed first by the USS FLYING FISH (SS-229) and then sunk by the USS RASHER (SS-269) on 31 October 1943 at 01-25N, 120-46E. Another sinking date is listed as 22 April 1943. Two other marus of the same name were also sunk; one by Navy carrier aircraft on 10 October 1944 and another small tanker sunk by a mine on 14 June 1945.[495]

KOSHU MARU – The *KOSHU MARU* departed Batavia on 29 July 1944 with 1,513 POWs enroute Makassar. She was met by the *USS RAY (SS-271)*. The 2,812-ton cargo ship was sunk with 1,239 of the men lost. The maru sunk at 04-05S, 117-40E on 4 August 1944.[496]

KU MARU – She transported 150 POWs in September 1944 from Palawan to Manila.[497]

KUNITAMA MARU – The maru took 1,000 POWs from Java to Ceram on 22 April 1943. The 3,127-ton cargo ship was sunk by the *USS CAPELIN (SS-289)* on 11 November 1943 SW of Ambon.[498]

KUNISHIMA MARU – The 4,083-ton cargo vessel moved POWs on 23 December 1943 from Ambon to Makassar. She was sunk by the *USS SUNFISH (SS-281)* on 23 February 1944 at 34-11N, 136-48E.[499]

KURIMATA MARU – The hell ship left Soerabaja, East Java on 22 April 1943 with about 1,500 POWs for Ambon in the Moluccas, arriving on 29 April 1943.[500]

KYOKKO MARU – She transferred 2,000 POWs; 1,500 Dutch, 300 British, and 200 Australian. The vessel left on 26 April 1943 from Singapore and arrived in Japan on 21 May 1943. She was a 6,783-ton passenger-cargo ship sunk by the *USS CREVALLE (SS-291)* on 15 November 1943 at 14-53N, 119-56E. A small merchant maru of the same name was sunk by a mine on 1 January 1945.[501]

KYOKUEI MARU – She moved 1,200 Dutch POWs from Sumatra on 16 May 1942. The trip took 5 days. The 10,570-ton tanker was sunk by the *USS BLUEFISH (SS-222)* on 8 November 1943 at 17-00N, 116-17E.[502]

LIMA MARU – The 6,989 cargo ship left Manila 21 September 1942 with 500 American POWs. She arrived in Takao on 24

September. She was sunk later by an unknown submarine but it may have been *HMS SEA ROVER* [503]

LISBON MARU – The 7,053-ton transport began her journey with 1,816 British POWs on 27 September 1942 from Hong Kong and lost 842 enroute Japan via Shanghai.[504] She was sunk on 1 October between Hong Kong and Tokyo by *USS GROUPER (SS-214)*. The maru sunk at 29-57N, 122-56E after being hit with 2 torpedoes.[505] 846 men were lost when the survivors were used for target practice in the water. 970 survivors were mustered in Shanghai and moved to Japan on the *SHININSEI*. Three POWs escaped via China and found their way back to the UK.[506]

MARU #760 – The maru carried 1,000 POWs from Bugo to Davao on a 5-day trip beginning 18 October 1942.[507]

MAEBASHI MARU – She took 1,700 POWs from Kinkon on 14 October 1942 to Burma.[508] On a later trip, she carried 1,800 POWs from Singapore to Burma transiting from Moluccas to Java. She was sunk by *USS POGY (SS-266)* on 30 September 1943. She was a 7,000-ton cargo and troop carrier and was sunk at 06-10N, 139-08E.[509]

MAKASSAR MARU – She moved out of Batavia on 26 September 1943 with 3,500 POWs on board, bound for Singapore. The 4,026-ton troop carrier was sunk by the *USS POMFRET (SS-391)* on 2 September 1944 at 21-02N, 121-36E.[510]

MAROS MARU – The small 600-ton ship carried 500 Dutch and British POWs from Ambon, the Moluccas plus another 150 survivors from another sunk ship on 17 September 1944. She laid over for more than 40 days for repairs in Makassar, South Celebes. Half the POWs were lost. The voyage took 127 days from July to September. Other records indicate it was out for 67 days and 325 of the men died on the trip.[511]

MATE MATE MARU – (former British vessel *CANADIAN IN-VENTOR*. *M*ati-mati means "wait") The hell ship departed Manila on 24 July 1944 with 500 POWs from Davao and another 500 from Cabanatuan who had been examined and judged fit for heavy duty, including Manny Eneriz and Dr. Thomas Hewlett. The ship's crew lashed a 155mm cannon on the forecastle which represented a anti-aircraft battery. The POWs had 2 doctors and a medical warrant to care for the sick and injured. The maru stopped at Santa Cruz and took on manganese ore then proceeded to Tapei on 31 July 1944. The vessel was already carrying bulk salt in the POW's hold. She arrived in Moji on 1 September 1944, completing the longest hell ship journey.[512] The POWs remained in a quarantine status for a few days then were railed to Omuta where residents stoned the men. This was the first contingent of POWs into Omuta.[513]

MAYEBASSI MARU – This maru departed Singapore near the end of 1942 and headed for Moulmein, Burma. She carried 1,500 POWs from the *KING KONG MARU* and 300 more from a camp in Singapore. The POWs were later transferred to the *YINAGATO MARU*.[514]

MELBOURNE MARU – The vessel moved 500 POWs on 18 January 1945 from Formosa to Japan.[515]

MISSYO MARU – She loaded 900 POWs on 4 July 1944 in Manila, all in one cargo hold. They were divided into 2 holds later. The convoy was attacked by a submarine in the Formosa Straits and other vessels were sunk. With the skies glowing red with ships on fire, the POWs were terrified and Father Reilly rose and led the men in prayer. Immediately serenity quieted the POWs.[516]

MIYO MARU – (possibly the *BIJOU MARU*) On 3 June 1944, the vessel moved 208 POWs from Singapore to Formosa. The ship was damaged and the POWs transferred to the *TAMAHOKO MARU*.[517]

MOJI MARU – The 3,831-ton combination passenger-cargo vessel departed Penang on 11 January 1943 with 800 POWs bound for Moulmein. She had 25 men die on the 5-day trip. She was later sunk on 12 June 1945 by Navy carrier aircraft.[518]

MONTIVIDEO MARU – The 7,267-ton transport carried 1,053 Australian POWs, 840 of which were military. Almost all were killed during an 8-day voyage from Rabaul on 22 June 1942.[519] The USS STURGEON (SS-187) sunk her on 1 July at 18-37N, 119-29E off the coast of Luzon.[520]

NAGARA MARU – She was a small 856-ton cargo maru that gave 180 POWs, including General Wainwright and officers, a trip to Formosa departing Manila on 12 August 1942. She was an old 1934 10,000 ton freighter, sunk by the USS SEA ROBIN (SS-407) on 5 March 1945 at 05-42S, 114-02E. She made another POW trip, departing Singapore on 7 November 1942 with 600 men going to Rabaul thence to Ballale. She had one man die. Another NAGARA MARU was sunk by the USS CROAKER on 7 August 1944 and yet another 7,148-ton transport was sunk on 14 November 1944 by Army, Navy, and Marine aircraft.[521]

NAGATO MARU – The ship departed Manila 7 November 1942 with 1,660 (1,400 to 1,700 by other estimates) American POWs and arrived in Japan on the 25th with 157 dead; 7 died enroute and 150 were left to die on the dock. They were as-signed to the Osaka area in Umeda, Yodogawa, and Tanagawa. Conditions were horrible in the camps, the worst being at Umeda where 1 in 4 died of cold and malnutrition. She was sunk by the USS SALMON (SS-182) on 28 October 1943 at 43-50N, 145-40E. She was a 2,969-ton cargo ship.[522]

NANKAI MARU – A 8,416-ton passenger-cargo ship carried 500 POWs in the same convoy with the RAKUYO MARU. She was sunk by the USS GROWLER (SS-215) which was a part of Ben's Busters wolf pack. POWs trying to escape the cargo hold were shot.[523]

NANSHIN MARU – The maru picked up 3 pilots and took them to Davo. There were many namesakes of this vessel, number-ing to at least #31, and most of them were sunk by American submarines.[524]

NANSHIN #17 – She departed 18 July 1945 from the Celebes to Makassar thence to Batavia. She lost one POW on the trip. She is not one of the *NANSIN MARUs* listed as submarine sinkings.[525]

NARUTO MARU – The ship carried 60 Australian officers, 6 nurses and 13 Australian women from Rabaul to Japan in July 1942. The 7,149-ton aircraft ferry was sunk by *USS WHALE (SS-239)* at 24-03N, 142-45 E on 8 August 1943.[526]

NATORU MARU – The vessel departed New Britain on 15 July 1942 with 60 POWs and 19 women including 6 Australian nurses. She sailed to Yokohama, Japan.[527] It may be the same ship as the *NARUTO MARU*.

NI MARU – The maru departed Java 4 June 1942 with 500 POWs arriving 5 days later in Singapore. Forty men died on the 4-day voyage [528]

NICHIMEI MARU – The 4,704-ton cargo ship moved 1,000 POWs departing Penang on 11 January 1943 for Moulmein.[529]

NISSYO MARU – The vessel departed Manila on 17 July 1944 with 1,500 POWs including Manfield Young. Most of the men were sent to Bilibid a few days earlier to assemble with other groups to be shipped to Japan. 1,000 men were placed into the after hold and 500 in an amidships hold. She arrived in Japan on 5 August after numerous attacks by American Naval Forces. The men were sent to five locations: the largest group of 300 went to steel mills at Fukuota #3 near Tobata on Kyushu; 200 went to a coal mining group at Fukuota #10 near Moji; 200 went to Oeyama, an Osake Camp to work in a nickel mine and processing plant; smaller groups went to Kameoka and Funatsu which were also in the Osaka Group to mine lead. Apparently a common name for a Japanese vessel, a number of *NISSYO MARUs* were sunk during the war by American submarines. This *NISSYO MARU* likely survived the war.[530]

NITTA MARU – (possibly known as the *NITTO MARU*) She was a converted Matson liner made in Japan. She departed

Wake Island on 12 January 1942 with 489 POWs and 746 civilian workers and contractors. The maru arrived in Yokohama on 18 January 1942 where she laid over a few days before moving out toward Shanghai (Woo Sung). She left behind 400 civilian construction workers and badly wounded 300 civilians. Surviving wounded were taken to Japan later leaving 100 civilians to work for the Japanese. Five Marines were beheaded amidst extremely cruel conditions.[531] Four days out of Yokohama and 12 out of Wake, she arrived in Shanghai. She traveled up the Whangpoo River to Woosung. The POWs were marched to the Shanghai War Prisoners Camp. Within the week, the POWs were joined by Marines from Peking and Tienstsin. There were 1,400 Americans in the camp.[532] If the vessel was the *NITTO MARU*, she was sunk by the *USS SEAHORSE (SS-304)* on 3 July 1944 at 19-20N, 115-50E. The *NITTA MARU* was later converted to an auxiliary aircraft carrier.[533]

NITIMEI MARU – She departed Singapore on 10 January 1943 bound for Moulmein-Rangoon, Burma with about 1,000 POWs. Navy aircraft attacked her on 15 January 1945 about 80 miles from Burma in Martaban Bay[534].

NOTO MARU – The 7,191-ton cargo ship transported 1,035 POWs (estimates between 985 – 1,035) from Manila to Japan on 24 August 1944 to Japan, losing one man on the voyage. 150 men came from Bilibid, 517 from Cabanatuan, 345 from Clark Field, and 150 from Nielson Field plus some fill-ins. They were all placed into a 60' X 40' hold. They arrived in Takao on 31 August and Moji, Japan on 6 September 1944. 500 POWs arrived in September 1944 at Hanawa in Northern Honshu and were sent to the Mitsubishi Copper Mine, Sendai, Camp #6. She was sunk by Army aircraft on 2 November 1944.[535] A previous *NOTO MARU* was sunk on 31 October 1942 by the *USS GRAYBACK (SS-208)*.[536]

OP TEN NOORT – She was sunk on 4 March 1942 with 900

-HARM

POWs and underway one day with Java Sea survivors from Bandjermasin to Makassar.[31]

ORIANOKA MARU – The maru left Manila 15 December 1944 and arrived in Japan 25 January 1945.[537]

ORYOKU MARU – She was the last transport out of Manila, loading out at Pier #7 with 1,619 POWs from Cabanatuan and Bilibid. They were marched through Manila to the harbor and ship. She departed at 0300 on 14 December. She was a 16,000 ton converted ocean liner known to some as hell Ship #1. 1,035 of the POWs were officers. The maru was attacked by Navy aircraft from the *USS HORNET* off Subic Bay and about 100 POWs were killed. She slipped out of the area under the cover of night but was attacked again and hit in the after hold where 150 POWs were killed. The ship went aground and the POWs tried to escape but were machine gunned in the holds and the water. 286 POWs were killed and 1,333 survived. The men were rounded up and placed in the *ENOURA MARU,* known as Hell Ship #2. Prior to her demise, she had carried high-ranking officers and civilians from Formosa to Manchuria.[538]

OSK FERRY – It ferried 1,000 POWs from Java to Singapore beginning on 8 January 1945.[539]

OTARU MARU – A small rat infested inter-island passenger vessel that took senior officers, including General Wainwright, from Takeo to Karenko, arriving 17 August 1942.

PANAMA MARU – The 5,287-ton cargo ship took 130 Chinese to Truk departing on 20 December 1942. She was sunk by Navy carrier aircraft on 23 January 1944.[540]

RAKUYO MARU – A 9,419-ton passenger-cargo ship that departed on 12 September 1944 from Singapore to Japan with 1, 318 Australian and British prisoners from Singapore. She was torpedoed by the *USS SEALION (SS-315)* off Hainan on 12 September enroute Formosa. She sank along with the *KACHIDOKI MARU, KAIBOKAN HIRATO,* and the destroyer *SHIKINAMI* which was sunk by the *USS GROWLER (SS-*

215).[541] 158 POWs were picked up by submarines; 72 by *USS PAMPANITO;* 54 by *USS SEALION;* 18 by *USS QUEENFISH;* and 14 by *USS BARB.*[542] 2,218 POWs began the voyage and 1,500 were lost. There were an even 900 POWs on *KACHIDOKI MARU.* The survivors managed to lash pieces of floating wreckage together as rafts.[543]

RASHIN MARU – see *BYOKI MARU.* She departed Singapore on 4 July 1944 with 1,065 POWs and headed for Manila. On a later trip, she left Manila on 9 August 1944 with 1,065 POWs enroute Moji. The trip took 30 days and 15 men died on the voyage. She was sunk at 41-23N, 131-25E by the *USS PARGO (SS-264)* on 8 August 1945.[544]

RIO DE JANIERO MARU – The 461-foot maru hauled 200 POWs on 2 October 1943 from Makassar, South Celebes to Batavia, West Java. They arrived on 5 October 1943 to an empty harbor except for one ship and wrecks. Another name-sake was torpedoed by *USS SPEARFISH (SS-190)* on 27 July 1942.[545]

ROKKO MARU – The passenger-cargo ship departed Batavia on 9 February 1943 bound for Singapore. She was attacked by the *USS PIPERFISH (SS-388)* on 18 September 1944 but not sunk. The 3,038-ton troop transport was sunk a couple weeks later by Army aircraft between Takeo and Keelung.[546]

ROKO MARU – The vessel carried 1,184 Canadians from Hong Kong in January 1943 to Japan. The *USS TANG (SS-306)* sunk the 3,328-ton cargo ship on 11 August 1944 at 33-58N, 136-19E.[547]

ROKYO MARU – The 9,419-ton ship departed Singapore and probably headed for Japan. She carried about 1,318 American and British POWs. She was torpedoed on 5 September 1944 near Hainan by the *USS SEALION.* All 1,318 men probably died in the sinking.[548] (not confirmed by Alden nor NAVEXOS)

RYUKYU MARU – It was a transport-cargo ship of some type between 3,000 and 6,000-tons. Little is known of the maru except around 41 POWs were killed when she was torpedoed. Waterford reports the sinking on 17 November 1943 while Alden/NAVEXOS reports 12 January 1944 by the *HMS TALLY HO*.[549]

SAMUNUSAN MARU – The ship transported POWs from Timor on 27 July 1942 to Java on a 10-day voyage.[550]

SAN MARU – She carried 100 POWs from Mindanao to Formosa beginning 15 August 1942.[551]

SANDAKAN SS – The maru transported 320 officers from Sandakan on 16 August 1943 to Kuching.[552]

SANKA MARU – The 2,495-ton cargo ship departed Manila on 27 July 1942 for Pawalan, arriving on 31 July with 300 POWs. She was sunk later by the *USS KETE (SS-369)* at 29-31N, 127-55E on 10 March 1945.[553]

SEIKYO MARU – A 2,608-ton gunboat that took three enemy nationals to Canton on 21 May 1943. If the spelling is *SEIKYI vice SEIKYO,* she was sunk by *S-41 (SS-146)* on 28 May 1943. Army aircraft sank a *SEIKYO MARU* on 5 February 1944. It must have been a second *SEIKYO MARU* since the *USS KING-FISH (SS-234)* sunk another on 23 October 1942.[554]

SHI MARU – The vessel departed Timor in October 1942 with 1,000 POWs on a 12-day voyage to Singapore.[555]

SHICHI MARU – The ship left Singapore on 5 November 1943 for Japan.[556]

SHINIYO MARU – A small vessel enroute Manila thence Japan from Zamoanga, Mindanao, carrying 750 American POWs from work on the airstrip at Lasang. She departed on 3 September 1944. She was torpedoed 7 September 1944 by *USS PADDLE (SS-263)* at 08-11N, 122-40E. The maru was originally built as a 5,061-ton tanker. Only 81 POWs made it ashore (85 according to Breuer, 83 by Playter). 500 men went down with the ship and many were machine-gunned in the water. The survivors contacted Filipino guerrillas and were later rescued by the submarine *NARWHAL* and taken to Biak.[557]

SHINSEI MARU – The ship took 840 British survivors from the

LISBON MARU departing Shanghai on 5 October 1942 to Japan, losing 5 on the trip. The 4,746-ton cargo vessel was sunk by the *USS TARPON (SS-175)* on 28 August 1943 at 33-39N,139-28E. There were many other *SHINSEI MARUs*.[558]

SHINYO MARU – She originally departed Zamboanga, Mindanao Island on 3 September 1944 probably bound for Japan via Manila. She carried 750 American POWs. She was torpedoed by *USS PADDLE* on the 7th near Sindangao Point with only 83 survivors or 668 dead.[559] Just during the autumn of 1944, American submarines caused the death of over 4,000 Allied POWs.[560]

SHOZAN MARU – A 2,838-ton old cargo ship that took senior officers and some enlisted from Karenko to Tainan. The POWs were taken by rail to Shirakawa on Formosa. This was General Wainwright's group. The vessel was sunk later by the *USS THRESHER (SS-237)* at 41-40N, 129-52E in December 1942.[561] The second *SHOZAN MARU* was sunk by the *USS JACK (SS-259)* on 26 June 1943.[562]

SIBERIA MARU – A large white 3,461-ton transport with a green stripe and red crosses pulled into Takao and anchored near the *TOTTORI MAR'U*. It was a hospital ship. She was sunk by Navy carrier aircraft on 24 September 1944.[563]

SIBIJAC MARU – The maru carried 8 POWs in March 1944 from Kuching to Singapore.[564]

SINGAPORE MARU – The vessel departed Batavia for Singapore on 17 October 1942 with 1,100 POWs. She continued the trip from Singapore with 1,100 POWs to Moji, arriving with 60 dead on 20 November 1942. Another 80 men died within a few weeks of arrival in Japan[565]

SINGOTO MARU – The maru took 1,194 men from *YASHU MARU* in Cebu on 21 June 1944 to Manila. One man died on the 4-day voyage.[566]

SMALL STEAMER – The craft took 62 civilians from Berhala on 12 January 1943 to Kaochung.[567]

SONG GIANG MARU – A 1,065-ton cargo maru carried 504 POWs from Hong Kong on 15 December 1943 to Takeo. She was later sunk by the *USS FLASHER (SS-249)* on 29 April 1944 near Hone Cohe.[568]

SUBAH MARU – She transported 75 POWs on 25 October 1943 from Sandakan to Kaochung.[569]

SUEZ MARU – A 4,646-ton cargo vessel, she departed Ambon Island, the Moluccas on 25 November 1943 with 1,150 POWs on board bound for Soerabaja, East Java. She was sunk by the *USS BONEFISH (SS-223)* on 29 November 1943 at 06-20 South, 116-30 East. 540 POWs were lost.[570]

SUGI MARU – The ship carried 200 POWs on 6 September 1944 from Makassar to Surabaya. 55 POWs were lost on the 23-day trip. The *HMS STATESMAN* sank a namesake #5 on 22 August 1944 near Port Blair. There may be confusion on the dates of sailing.[571]

TACHIBANA MARU – She left Wake Island on 20 September 1942 with 200 POWs for Japan. The 6,521-ton tanker was attacked a couple of times before the *USS SAWFISH (SS-276)* sunk her on 9 October 1944 at 19-30N, 116-38E. A *TACHIBANA* was a small destroyer sunk on 14 July 1945 by Navy carrier based aircraft which was more likely to carry 200 POWs than a tanker.[572]

TAGA MARU – The 2,868-ton cargo ship departed Manila on 20 September 1943 with 850 American POWs, stopping briefly at Takeo. She arrived in Moji on 5 October 1943 with 70 dead,[573] It was sunk by the *USS SARGO (SS-188)* at 21-40 North, 131-19 East on 9 November 1943. Another *TAGA MARU* was sunk by *USS FLYINGFISH (SS-229)*on 9 June 1945.[574]

TAIKO MARU – She transferred 530 POWs on 25 October 1942 from Ambon to Hainan. Later, she carried 700 POWs on 27 February 1945 from Keelung to Moji. Four previous namesakes were sunk by American submarines. The 1,925-ton cargo ship was sunk by *USS GURNARD (SS-254)* on 11 July 1943.[575]

TAKA MARU – The small 887-ton cargo ship carried 500 POWs from Kuching on 9 April 1943 to Sandakan. She was sunk by Navy carrier aircraft on 14 July 1945.[576]

TAIKOKU MARU – The 2,633-ton cargo ship departed Manila destined for Japan on 24 March 1944 with 305 POWs on board. She was sunk by the *USS SAND LANCE (SS-381)* on 17 May 1944,[577]

TAMAHOKO MARU – The obsolete and ill-maintained 6,780-ton passenger-cargo vessel left Gagayan, Mindanao on 1 October 1942 with 268 POWs for Manila. The maru was 250 feet in length with 3,000 shp. It mounted a 75mm gun on the bow and carried 3 landing craft on deck. She also took on 208 POWs from the *MIYO MARU* when she was damaged. Although hot and crowded, the chow was decent with rice, fish, squash and tea. She berthed at Pier #7, Manila at 1830 on the 4th. The bay was filled with burned and sunken hulls. The POWs remained in Bilibid until the 7th when they returned to the port. They joined 1,600 men from Bataan and Corregidor plus 11 officers from Negeros Island. Then the men were crammed on the *TOTTORIE MARU*.[578] She took 772 POWs on 18 June 1944 from Takeo to Japan but was waylaid by the *USS TANG (SS-306)* on 24 June 1944 near the *TOTTORIE MARU*. 560 of the POWs died.[579]

TANGO MARU –The vessel departed Java on 24 February 1944 with 3,500 POWs on board and headed to Ambon. She barely had been underway when she was torpedoed by the *USS RASHER (SS-269)*. The 6,200-ton cargo ship went down quickly and 3,000 POWs lost their lives.[580]

TATSUTA MARU – She carried 200 POWs from Japan to Wake Island as laborers leaving Japan on 12 March 1942. The 16,975 troop transport was sunk by the *USS TARPON (SS-175)* on 8 February 1943 near Mikura Shima.[581]

TATTORI MARU – Another Manila departure, this time on 8 October 1942 with 1,202 American POWs. 14 Americans were transferred to a hospital in Takao, and 585 at Kobe. The maru arrived in Mudken, Manchuria on 11 November 1942 with 11 dead during the 30-day journey from Mergui to Tavoy.[582]

TATURA MARU – She was involved in a British and Japanese prisoner swap.

TEIA MARU – A 17,537-ton transport involved in a prisoner exchange in October 1943, then proceeded to Shanghai to deliver supplies. She returned to Manila in early November where American POWs discharged the cargo; a likely chance Mansfield Young was involved in the off load. The vessel carried Red Cross supplies from the Portuguese colony of Mormugao via the Swedish liner *GRIPSHOLM*. She was sunk by the *USS RASHER (SS-269)* on 18 August 1944 at 18-09 North, 120-13 East. She was one of eight ships sunk by RASHER on that single day.[583]

THAMES MARU – The 5,871-ton cargo vessel departed Singapore on 5 May 1943 with 2,022 POWs and bound for Babelthuap Island, Palau north of New Guinea. She arrived on 8 June 1943 with 200 dead. An earlier namesake was sunk by the *USS SILVERSIDES (SS236)* on 17 May 1942 with the loss of 200 men at 33-28 N, 135-35E. This *THAMES MARU* was sunk by *POMPON (SS-267)* on 25 July 1943 at 02-40N, 148-35E. *POMPON* also sank *KINSEN MARU* moments earlier.[584]

TIESEN MARU – The 5,050-ton cargo maru took 180 officers from Sandakan on 16 October 1943 to Kuching. She apparently experienced a near miss when she was attacked a year earlier by *USS FINBACK (SS-230)*. She was sunk by the *USS FLASHER (SS-249)* on 3 May 1944.[585]

TOBA MARU – A 6,995-ton transport sunk by the *USS SPEARFISH (SS-190)* on 25 April 1942.[586]

TOGO MARU – A small 800-ton merchant that moved 6 POWs

from Cape Jacquinot on 12 February 1944 to Rabaul. She was sunk by the *USS PARCHE (SS-384)* on 11 April 1945 near Todogasaki.[587]

TOKO MARU – Known by some as the *TORO MARU*. The vessel carried 500 men from Manila to Japan beginning on 5 September 1942 and ending 32 days later. The 2,747-ton cargo ship was sunk by the *USS SEAHORSE (SS-304)* on 30 January 1944 and another namesake was sunk by a submarine a year later.[588]

TOMOHUKO MARU – The ship received 766 POWs (267 Australian, 196 British, 43 American, and 266 Dutch) from *UNKNOWN MARU PS#2* in Takao for the trip to Japan. She was sunk by the *USS TANG* on 24 June 1944 near Nagasaki with the loss of 559 POW lives.[589]

TONE MARU – The hell ship carried 111 POWs on 26 February 1944 from Behar but lost 72 men on the 6-day voyage. Other namesakes were sunk by submarines, Army aircraft, and Navy land based aircraft.[590]

TOTTORI MARU – The maru was an obsolete and rusty ship. She got underway at 2000 on October 8th. The ship carried 1,994 POWs and 3,000 Japanese with one urinal and one water faucet for everyone. She headed for Formosa. A near miss torpedo exploded near her stern on the 9th and she fell out of line in the convoy. Food was scarce and conditions were miserable. The maru anchored in a busy Takao harbor on the 12th. The men were joined by 2 British POWs from Singapore. Three of the most ill were transferred, likely to the *SIBERIAN MARU*. She got underway on the 18th after a submarine scare. On the 20th, they were anchored off Bohko, it was cold and men began dying. She returned to Takao on the 28th then back to Bohko to join a convoy, heading for Japan on 1 November. On the 7th, she stopped at Fusan, Korea where 1,420 POWs got off to go to Mukden. 580 were taken to Moji, arriving on the 9th. They went to Osaka on the 11th while 74 men and 14 officers were railed to Tokyo, thence to Kawasaki to work in a chemical plant. Eleven men died during the voyage. She was sunk 15 May 1945 by the *USS HAMMERHEAD (SS-364)* at 09-21 North, 102-25 East. She was a 5,978 cargo vessel. Another *TOTTORI MARU* , known as the 5,937-ton *TOBA MARU,* was sunk in April 1942. A *TOTTORI MARU* was torpedoed near Manila by the *USS SILVERSIDES (SS-236)* in May 1942 but the sinking was not confirmed.[591]

TOYAMA MARU – The maru moved a number of Canadian POWs from Hong Kong in December 1942 to Japan. She moved 504 POWs on 26 December 1943 from Formosa to Japan. She was sunk on 29 June 1944 by the *USS STURGEON (SS-187)* at 27-47 North, 129-05 East.[592]

TOYOFUKU MARU – She was sunk 21 September 1944 off Manila by Navy torpedo bombers. She departed Singapore in June carrying British and Dutch POWs. Less than 200 of the POWs made it ashore. The men in the holds were starving to death and the Japanese crew believed the POWs had cholera so she put into Manila. When she departed to join a convoy, she was hit by bombs and sunk within 3 minutes of being struck.[593]

TOYOHASHI MARU – The hell ship carried 1,017 POWs in mid-May 1942 for 5 days. The *HMS TRUSTY* sunk the 7,031-ton cargo ship in the Malacca Strait on 4 June 1942.[594]

TRADING VESSEL – The vessel moved 450 POWs from Ambon to Celebes on 8 October 1944.[595]

UME MARU – On 7 July 1942, the maru carried 1,494 POWs in 10 days from Siingapore to Sandakan via Kaochung. It is thought she was captured in Southeast Asia early in the war. *UME MARU* was 3,100-tons with the usual discomforts of living at sea, particularly in a hold. The prisoners were forced to build an airstrip. The camp was actually good in comparison to other POW internment camps. She was sunk by the *USS SEAHORSE (SS-304)* on 4 November 1943 and sunk at 28-40 North, 135-25 East.[596]

UMEDA MARU – The ship left Manila 7 November 1942 with

1,500 American POWs. She arrived in Japan 25 November with 15 dead.[597]

UNKNOWN MARU – There are 23 documented "unknown marus" but few were known to be involved with POWs. She departed Manila on 16 October 1944 with 1,100 POWs from Cabanatuan and Bilibid on board. Torpedoed on the 24th by an unknown submarine, all but 5 POWs were lost and they managed to make it to China. It was possibly the *EIKO MARU* sunk by the *USS SEADRAGON (SS-194)* or the *SHINSEI MARU #1* sunk by the *USS SNOOK (SS-279)*.[598]

UNKNOWN MARU – Listed as Prison Ship #1,[599] this vessel departed Batavia, East Indies on 30 December 1942 and arrived in Takao on 1 February 1943. She carried 74 high ranking military officers and civilians of the Dutch and British. The ship was an old rusty 4,000-ton steamer and conditions, including food and drink, was the same for the Japanese soldiers on board as for the POWs.

UNKNOWN MARU – Listed as prison Ship #2,[600] the vessel departed Singapore on 1 June 1944 bound for Japan. However, when she arrived in Takao, the 766 POWs (267 Australians, 190 British, 43 Americans, and 266 Dutch) were transferred to the *TOMOHUKO MARU*.

UNKNOWN MARU – Listed as Prison ship #3,[601] the place of departure is unknown but the likely destination was Singapore. She carried about 1,100 British and Dutch POWs. She was sunk by Navy aircraft in Manila Harbor on 22 September 1944 and over 900 POWs died.

UNKNOWN MARU – Listed as Prison Ship #4,[602] this vessel was known as the *OCTOBER SHIP* by the POWs on board. She departed Manila on 11 October 1944 and headed for Japan with 1,800 men on board. She was torpedoed and sunk on 25 October 1944 between Hong Kong and Formosa. Only four POWs were picked up out of the 1,800.

UNYO – A Japanese escort carrier, which carried 20 submariners of 42 taken prisoner after the destroyer YAMGUMO, sunk the *USS SCULPIN* on 19 November 1943. The remaining submariners were placed on the carrier *CHUYO* following an interrogation on Wake Island. The men were taken to an Ashio copper mine for the remainder of the war. The 17,830-ton carrier was sunk ESE of Guam by the *USS HADDOCK (SS-231)*.[603]

URUPPU MARU – She picked up 5 American pilots on 5 September 1944 and took them to Davao and Manila.[604]

USHIO MARU – The maru carried 62 *PERCH* survivors to Makassar on 3 March 1942.[605]

USU MARU – She left Batavia on 4 January 1943 with 1,978 POWs and took them to Singapore.[606]

WALES MARU – The ship moved 950 POWs from Singapore on 16 May 1943 to Japan. She was attacked in April 1944 by the *USS JACK (SS-259)* and sunk a month later by *USS LAPON (SS-260)*.[607]

WEILLS MARU – The vessel departed Singapore 6 May 1943 and arrived in Japan on 7 July 1943. She carried about 950 POWs (300 Australian, 600 British, and 50 American).[608]

YAMAGATA MARU – The ship steamed from Maebashi to Moulmein on 23 October 1942 with 1,000 POWs. The 3,807-ton cargo ship was sunk by the *USS REDFIN (SS-272)* on 16 April 1944 at 06 51N, 123 37E.[609]

YAMAGUMO MARU – The ship carried the 42 survivors from *USS SCULPIN* to Truk in November 1943. She was sunk the following year on 25 November 1944 by the *USS HALIBUT (SS-232)* near Leyte.[610]

YAMAKAZE – The warship carried 300 POWs from *EXETER,* departing Encounter on 2 March 1942. It was a one-day trip to Bandjermasin. The 1,685-ton destroyer was sunk by the *USS NAUTILUS (SS-168)* on 25 June 1942 off Katsuura. [611]

YASHU MARU – She moved 1,239 POWs from Davao on 12 June 1944 and joined a Japanese convoy to Zamboanga City. She made port on Cebu after 6 days and the POWs were shifted to a second, smaller ship known only as "824." This ship docked in Manila on the 25th at Pier #7. Half of the prisoners were sent to Cabanatuan. She moved 1,250 POWs on 12 June 1944 from Davao to Cebu. 56 of the men died on the 5-day trip.[612]

YINAGATA MARU – The ship took 1,799 POWs from the *MAYEBASSI MARU* in Rangoon to Moulmain, Burma.

YOSHIDA MARU – The ship departed Batavia, West Java on 22 October 1942 with 3,000 POWs and Javanese prisoners bound for Singapore, arriving 25 October 1942. The cruise lasted 4 days and 10 men died during the trip. The POWs and Javanese were then transferred to the *DAI NICHI MARU.* The 2,920-ton ship was one of a number of cargo vessels rebuilt as a tanker and sunk by *USS FLASHER (SS-249)* on 18 January 1944 at 23-46N, 151-30E. She may have been torpedoed by the *USS SUNFISH (SS-281)* and damaged on 20 February 1943.[613] Another *YOSHIDA MARU,* a combined cargo-passenger vessel of 5,425-tons, was sunk by the *USS JACK* on 29 April 1944. The vessel burned and sank rapidly with an entire regiment of Japanese infantry on board.[614]

GENERAL INFORMATION.

Most of the POWs located in the Philippines departed from Manila. POWs in Southeast Asia were usually shipped out of Singapore utilizing Keppel Harbor to Japan via Takeo and Saigon. POW hell ships were known to arrive and depart ports in Java, Sumatra, Burma, Ambon, Haruka, Timor, New Britain, etc.

Each "hell ship" had a standard set of orders while carrying prisoners of war. The following is an order issued by the Prisoner Escort Navy of the Great Japanese Empire to the POWs on the *NAGATO MARU* on 7 November 1942. It is typical of what was issued on all "hell ships"

-HARM

"1. The prisoners disobeying the following orders will be punished with immediate death.

Those disobeying orders and instructions.

a. Those showing a motion of antagonism and raising a sign of opposition.

b. Those disobeying the regulations by individualism, egoism, thinking only about themselves, rushing for your own goods.

b. Those talking without permission and raising loud voices.

c. Those walking and moving without order.

d. Those carrying unnecessary baggage in embarking.

e. Those resisting mutually.

f. Those touching the boat's materials, wires, electric lights, tools, switiches, etc.

g. Those climbing ladder without order.

h. Those showing action or running away from the room or boat.

i. Those using more than one blanket.

2. Since the boat is not well equipped and inside being narrow, food being scarce and poor, you'll feel uncomfortable during the short time on the boat. Those losing patience and disordering the regulation will be heavily punished for the reason of not being able to escort.

3. Be sure to finish your 'nature's call.' Evacuate the bowels and urine before embarking.

4. Meal will be given twice a day. One plate only to one prisoner. The prisoners called by the guard will give out the meal quick as possible and honestly. The remaining prisoners will stay in their places quietly and wait for your plate. Those moving from their places reaching for your plate without order will be heavily punished. Same orders will be applied in handling plates after meals.

ROBERT K. HARMUTH

5. Toilets will be fixed at the four corners of the room. The buckets and cans will be placed. When filled up, a guard will appoint a prisoner. The prisoner called will take the buckets to the center of the room. The buckets will be pulled by the derrick and be thrown away. Toilet paper will be given. Everyone must cooperate to make the room sanitary. Those being careless will be punished.

6. Navy of the Great Japanese Empire will not try to punish you all with death. Those obeying all the rules and regulations, and believing the action and purpose of the Japanese Navy, cooperating with Japan in constructing the 'New Order of the Great Asia' which lend to the world's peace will be well treated."[615]

-HARM

CHAPTER NINE

WORKING IN THE MINES

M OJI, JAPAN WAS a primary destination port for prisoners shipped to Japan. Moji was located on the Island of Kyushu, across the Straits of Kammon from Honshu. In 1963, Moji, Kokura, Tobata, Yahata and Wakamatsu combined into the City of Kitakyusku resulting in the largest city on Kyushu. Moji, now the westernmost ward or district of Kitakyusku, was originally a leading fishing village and developed into a leader in foreign trade and a commercial port.[616] It has a huge coal-shipping installation that predates the days POWs helped mine coal during the war. The Moji and Sasebo/Nagasaki areas are blessed with large coal deposits with zinc and lead deposits near the center of the island. These resources played a major role in Mansfield and Manny's lives for the next year. Fortunately, the Island of Kyushu's climate is moderate with warm summers and mild winters but includes snow. The weather cooled with increased altitude in the mountain ranges of Kyushu where many of the mineral mines were located.

One of the major POW camps in Japan was Kawasaki #5, known to many as the Dispatch Camp, located on the Island of Honshu between Tokyo and Yokohama. It was an enormous steel manufacturing complex with Japanese and Korean laborers, both men and women. It held American and Philippine prisoners including groups from Wake Island and Guam. Late in the war, Dutch POWs from Java were added to the labor force. A work group of a hundred men were sent to the Sendai area in Northern

Honshu. There, many old mines were placed back into operation particularly those rich in zinc, copper and lead. One such place was called Sendai #7B near Odate. For some reason, the civilian contractors from Wake Island received cruel and punishing treatment in this POW camp.[617] A common occurrence was the severity of treatment of American POWs who surrendered easily vice those who fought desperately before surrender. Guam POWs were treated well in comparison to survivors from Wake. Possibly, the worst treated were the survivors from Bataan.

Meanwhile, the release of Japanese-Americans interned in California was held in abeyance. Following reports of atrocities by Japanese on American POWs and reports of Japanese-American and Japanese assistance to Japan's cause in Hawaii and the West Coast. In reality, the major fear in California was for the internees' lives.[618]

In Korea, it was commonplace to parade the "laborers" before the civilian population along with their Korean guards to promote the feeling that Korea participated in the war alongside Japan. This was not done with Bataan prisoners sent to Korea for they were in such poor physical condition. The Japanese feared the Americans would gain sympathy from the Koreans.[619]

One of the major camps where POWs mined coal was Fukouka #17 at Omuta on Kyushu. The City of Fukouka is the tenth largest city in Japan and located on the Bay of Hakata.[620] The coal mine was closed during World War I. The camp was inhabited by the first American prisoners from Cabanatuan brought to Japan in the freighter *MATE MATE MARU*.[621]

There was a typical procedure for prisoners shipped from Luzon. The prisoners were trucked or marched to Manila to spend a night or two in Bilibid Prison. When the vessel was prepared for the voyage, the prisoners were marched through the streets of Manila to demean them in front of the Filipinos and demonstrate the power of the Japanese. Manny barely sensed the cheering Filipinos lined on both sides of the street for he was in severe pain. He couldn't march because of his severely injured feet and legs. He performed a shuffle as he blindly followed along in the column of men toward the dock area. He was void of sense and emotion as were most of his fellow American prisoners.

Once on the docks, the POWs were mustered and forced up the gangway to the main deck of the ship, which in the case of Manny was the *CANADIAN INVENTOR*. A Japanese soldier hollered, "Eneriz!" "Ere I am" muttered Manny. Then he was poked and prodded up the gangway, long and steep, which swayed and bounced as the prisoners struggled to the top. He stopped about half way up to catch his breath and was punched by a guard and hit with a board when he reached the quarterdeck.

On the main deck, the POWs were mustered and searched again despite the slight chance any prisoner would still have any-thing of value. "What the hell do you expect to find you dumb shit!" Then Manny was beaten and clubbed again as he descended a wood ladder into a cargo hold. He peered down into a dark pit and shuttered with fear. "It's a freggin black cave of hell for gods sake."

Manny received a rifle butt in the small of the back when he paused a few rungs down the ladder to catch his breath. More and more prisoners were pushed down the ladder until there wasn't sufficient room for another man to get on the ladder let alone descend into the hold. He stood with the other men, unable to sit or lay down on piles of bulk salt in the bottom of the hold. The men cursed and cried in panic as claustrophobia and fear took hold in the dark. The men shoved and pushed in frustration to find space to rest, but in vain.

Manny said a prayer as he looked up at the glaring beam of light coming through the open cargo hatch from a floodlight on a cargo davit. The scene took him back to his youth and a picture in his Catechism that depicted the damned to eternal darkness. Prior to the hatch cover replacement, a guard threw a couple wood buck-ets into the hold to use as latrines. One bucket struck a prisoner in the head and knocked him senseless. Manny grit his teeth in anger and swore silently, "two buckets for five hundred men; you've got to be shitting me"-a poor play on words and a follow-on to his prayer.

Men hyperventilated in the close, dark quarters of the hold. The Japanese response to the screams for help was to place the cover over the hatch, plunging the men into total darkness. Panic became widespread immediately as men screamed and clawed at each other as a means of relief. When it seemed all was lost due to due to fright, a strong and deep voice shouted out of the darkness. "Please follow me, Our Father, who art in heaven, hallowed be thy name . . . " It was one of the chaplains and like a miracle, the hold quieted and the men's breathing eased.

The men might have felt better if they knew less than a thousand miles away, a huge American armada was descending upon Formosa like a flight of locusts as well as Leyte and points north and west. Admiral Kurita was losing his shirt and fleet to American submarines as he fled headlong with no submarine defenses in front of his fleet. Submarines *DACE* and *DARTER* welcomed him in the Palawan Passage and took out his flagship *ATAGO*, her sister ship *MAYA* and the *TAKAO*.[622]

The *CANADIAN INVENTOR* remained at Pier #7 in Manila for a few days prior to getting underway for Japan and the Port of Moji. A sparse amount of food and water was thrown down to the prisoners like one slopping hogs. Most of the food was lost on the bottom of the hold where it mixed with feces, urine, and the piles of salt. Mealtime was conducive to fighting among the men which kept the chaplains busy.

Once the *CANADIAN INVENTOR* was underway, the daily routine changed a bit in favor of the prisoners. Days passed into weeks and the *CANADIAN INVENTOR* remained at sea. The cruelty and hardships of the POW camps hardened the prisoners to adapt to almost any condition but they were severely weakened. The Americans adapted to life at sea, even in a hold, though the poorest of health died. A few at-sea burial ceremonies were permitted and chaplains officiated with a few kind words and prayers. Then the bodies of the deceased, wrapped in rags and bags, were dumped over the side of the ship. The POWs watched the event in disbelief by what was perceived as callousness. Most of the POWs were not sailors and did not understand the way of the sea. Not a tear was shed at the burials and the chaplains fought desperately with the men against despair and surrender of the will to live. "God almighty! They just dumped the bodies in the ocean to become fish food," Manny mumbled. He struggled for self-control for he had the horrible urge to strangle the nearest Jap. Then he became numb and oblivious to thought.

Through fair and stormy seas, the *CANADIAN INVENTOR* plunged onward at a snails pace, often changing course to avoid the ever pursuing American submarines. Midway in the voyage, the ship stopped in Takao for a few days. The sun beat down unmercifully on the ship's decks while the POWs were retained below decks in the holds for the entire time in port. The men suffered heat prostration and dehydration. Eventually, the ship departed and the winds and cool seas gently cooled the holds and her precious cargo.

Manny tried to sit down and as his buns hit the deck, there was a "squishing" sound as he sank into a few inches of excrement on the salt. For a brief moment, it was relief as the semi-liquid cover seemed cool to the touch. Another prisoner sat behind him and without a word, they put their backs together and managed a mutual back support system. They sank into a deep slumber, only to be awakened every few minutes by another prisoner crawling over them or a loud scream of anguish from nearby.

On the *CANADIAN INVENTOR*, as most "hell ships," the prisoners were kept in their cargo hold for a couple days after they docked. In this case, the ship docked at Nagasaki vice the usual Moji. The POWs suffered again from the heat as in Takao. Eventually, the cargo was discharged and the first POWs were permitted topside. The hatch cover was removed and bright sunlight beamed into the hold, temporarily blinding the men below. Fresh air rushed into the hold, pushing out a brownish haze of foul air and clouds of flies. For the first time in weeks, the men breathed fully and began an ascent up the ladder to the main deck. It was a laborious struggle and a team effort as the men, covered in filth, salt, and human excrement, crawled onto the main deck. Despite the prisoner's poor health, the men were beaten and punched into ranks for another muster. Manny screamed, "where the hell could we have gone?"

The men stumbled and fell down the same accommodation ladder they climbed nine weeks earlier. Once on the wharf, the men were led to a number of waiting buses. The men were mustered again on the buses and as Manny listened, many men weren't there to answer up to roll call. These were the men who only answered to God's muster.

It was a bumpy ride in antiquated buses. A few hours later, the buses stopped in front of a barbed wire encampment, known as Fukuota Camp #17 located at Omuta on the Island of Kyushu. The camp already had a number of POW residents. The camp eventually contained two hundred Dutch from Sumatra and Java; another two hundred Aussies from Singapore; four hundred Americans from Bataan and Corregidor; and two hundred English from Hong Kong. The POWs primarily slaved in a coal mine with the Dutch topside and the Americans and Aussies below in the mine. It was September 1944. The coal mines were treacherous since the coal seams in Northern Kyushu are thin, faulted, and contorted leading to small, individual basins or pockets of coal. The area is filled with small water springs that filled the mines and undermined the mine walls. Coal gas and earthquakes served as additional hazards.[623]

Life in Japan's POW camps was miserable but an improvement over the suffering in O'Donnell and Cabanatuan. The living conditions were austere and antiquated but the men lived in real barracks that held a hundred men each. The heads were clean and functional. The camp was circumvented by a ten-foot tall fence topped by electrified barbed wire to keep out the local Japanese.[624]

Every camp or prison had its own idiosyncrasy and at Camp #17 all prisoners were expected to march past the gate guard in

-HARM

cadence, swinging their arms widely as in the British military. The arms had to reach shoulder height and reach beyond the back. Failure to comply with the required performance resulted in a beating to the offender inside the guardhouse.

Upon their arrival in Camp #17, the POWs were given the first two days to familiarize themselves with the camp and get settled. The facilities were an improvement but the mere thought of working for the Japanese war effort stuck in the prisoner's craw. Surrender was an embarrassment but to aid the enemy was too much. Manny's group became miners for the Mitsui Coal Mining Company. The group's daily routine was to walk three miles every morning to the coal mine. The walk took them down a country road and through a small village. Initially, the townspeople looked at them with suspicion and even stoned the prisoners. The adverse reception wasn't so much hatred for he POWs as worry about losing jobs to the prisoners but the POW slave labor only supplemented the work in the mine.

Half of the walk to the mine was through the countryside that was primarily agricultural. Small farms dotted the countryside and lined the road with occasional small orchards intermingled between the farms. Manny found the walk refreshing and watching the farmers momentarily took his mind off the current situation. The small farming community brought back memories of the countryside in California. The locals were told the POWs helped the war effort so many of the peasants befriended the POWs, waving and smiling at them as they walked past.

The prisoners worked twelve to sixteen hours a day for ten days then received the following day off. The Japanese provided them with clothing that was the standard Japanese Army uniform without insignia. Unfortunately, the uniforms were only to be worn when the International Red Cross made an inspection tour. Inadequate but heavier outer garments were provided during the winter months.

When the prisoners arrived at the mine gate, they were lined up, checked in, and sent through the mine entrance. They walked single file with a hand on the man in front of him to the main mine shaft. Inside the mine, the prisoners stripped to a G-string or loincloth that was typical laborer wearing apparel. They wore no shoes in the mines since the moisture caused mildew and rotted the canvas or leather. Bare feet provided better gripping power than shoes in the wet and slippery tunnels. Unshielded incandescent light bulbs and kerosene lanterns were sparsely spaced giving the illusion of shadows working vice men. "Damn, I wonder if whoever wrote 'into the valley of death they rode' ever visited this place," one of the men whispered.

A conveyor belt system called a "traveyor" moved coal from the tunnels to a small rail car system. The rock and ore was shoveled onto a conveyor belt that carried the ore to a dumping location near parked coal rail cars. The conveyor was powered by a small boiler and flywheel controlled near the rail cars. As each car was filled, a prisoner pushed the cart to an adjacent track where it joined other full cars to be towed out of the mine.[625]

When the tunnel was extended, the prisoners drilled holes into the tunnel walls three feet deep and three feet apart. Dynamite was placed in the holes and plugged with clay. A Korean POW or worker was in charge of the blasting. Following the blast, the Korean checked all the tunnel walls for safety and shored up any weak spots. He carried a pouch on his hip that contained dynamite and tools of his trade. The blast filled the entire mine with a fine black coal powder and smoke that choked the workers for hours. The Japanese used the proverbial canary in a cage to insure the air was breathable. One of the American POWs was an experienced coal miner who kept his eye on the Korean to insure he did his job well. His skills were tested a couple of times by U.S. Navy aircraft who bombed the mountain top mines.

The Japanese used one Korean to monitor or supervise each five American and Australian prisoners. Each prisoner was required to extract five carloads of coal per day or twenty-five loads per day for each group. The Korean kept score on the loads so the POWs were careful not to alienate him.

-HARM

Not far into the mine was a tool room where the prisoners checked out equipment every morning before descending deeper into the mine to work. The tool room was run by Korean women who flirted with the prisoners. They were friendly and often had news or rumors of the war. But speaking to the Korean women was akin to talking with a madame of a bordello.[626]

Manny and his fellow prisoner, Jake, arrived at the tool room one morning and, "Manny, I think I'm gonna see how good these gooks really are." "You best be careful Jake. You get caught and you'll end up losing a lot more than your manhood," mumbled Manny. "Shit Manny, I've been saving these cigarettes for a month just for today. Sure you don't want to come along?" "Hell no. I've got more than enough problems to tend to let alone come down with lover's nuts." When Jake got to the head of the line, he nodded and smiled broadly at the young Korean woman who winked back at him. It was the "okay" sign. Jake looked around to insure no one was watching him and stealthily pulled a package of "Old Golds" from his pocket. He pushed it toward the woman who gave him an affirmative nod and smile.

Jake was issued a pick and Manny a shovel. They shuffled off in the direction of their group and Manny grinned as he noticed Jake walked with a bit of a spring in his step. Any prisoner who felt the urge for sex could show cigarettes and get an affirmative nod from the Korean women. Later in the mine, the prisoner broke his tool and walked back to the tool issue room for a replacement. For the cigarettes, he was invited into a back room for a quick tumble. Manny felt he needed every ounce of energy just to exist.

A day earlier, the mine gang blew another section of tunnel before knocking off work so there was plenty of shoveling and picking to do. Less than an hour transpired when Jake slammed his pick across the top of the conveyor and the handle broke. With a wry smile, "well, I guess I better go back to the tool room and draw another pick. Be back in a flash." One of the crew chuckled, "better make it a quickie! Don't want to work overtime again." Jake returned later with a wide grin and the group resumed work.

ROBERT K. HARMUTH

The meanest guard was a Japanese-American who was a UCLA Riverside graduate. This was not unusual as more than 8,500 Japanese offices were educated in the United States.[627] He spoke flawless and accent-free English and learned how Americans think and feel. For some reason, he hated Americans and took every opportunity to give them trouble. He would cover lights so he could sneak up on the working POWs in the hope of catching one doing something wrong. The slightest word spoken by a POW against the Japanese gave the guard liberty to beat the prisoner. Another Japanese was equally hated. He lost an arm in the China War and carried a grudge against everyone and everything.[628]

The coal mine shaft followed a vein which took a twenty degree down slope from the entrance. Moisture dripped from the tunnel roof and made the floor slippery and treacherous. The coal cars were pulled out of the tunnels by rope and pulley manned topside by the Dutch prisoners.

Suddenly, kawoom! The entire tunnel shock violently and rocks, coal, and dust filled the area. The lights flickered and went out. In the darkness, the men checked the lights on their helmets and made sure everyone in their crew was okay. The Korean miner checked his shoring and tapped a few pieces of wood back into place with his hammer. The tunnel remained intact in their section of the mine. Another threat to mine integrity was American air raids that was routine near the end of the war. A favorite target for the aircraft was the generating plants providing power to the mines. Loss of electrical power stopped work in the mines and the water pumps that removed water from the lower tunnels. Flooding was a threat and quick exit rendered impossible since the elevators did not work without power.[629]

When a work shift was completed, the prisoners moved to a location near the mine entrance where they removed their cloths. It was an unconventional locker room with a large four-foot deep pool fed by a warm underground river. Here the prisoners bathed to rid themselves of the coal dust and to wash a small towel they wore across their nose and mouth in the mine. After washing, they

HARM

were permitted to soak in the pool for awhile. The group moaned with pleasure as they soothed their aching muscles. After drying off, they walked to the entrance, checked out, and began the three-mile hike back to the camp. As they walked down the road, Manny noticed Jake was beginning to scratch a bit.

Manny returned from the mine one evening, early in his stay at Camp #17, exhausted and weak from the day's work. As he passed the main gate, he was stopped and dragged out of the line of returning prisoners. His marching was unsatisfactory and his bow to the guard wasn't sufficiently low. He received a crushing blow to the mouth from the gate guard that knocked him to his knees. Then he was dragged to another room and made to kneel upright with a log on his legs behind the knees and a heavy rock on his head. Eventually, his stamina and strength ebbed and the rock fell to the floor. He was whipped and punched. He was made to repeat the exercise and the beatings continued. At each recurrence, he was made to lean further back on the log which caused excruciating pain and cut off circulation to the lower portion of his legs. After numerous attempts to balance the rock, he passed out in pain and exhaustion. He was unceremoniously dumped in his barracks where his fellow POWs tended to his wounds as best they could. Manny suffered multiple bruises and a broken jaw that limited his ability to take any nourishment for days. The incident occurred again a few months later and Manny received a broken nose.[630]

Initially, the weather remained hot and humid with rain every few days, typical of the Japanese Islands. Manny had no idea where he was except somewhere in Japan and had no idea about the cold winters that would soon follow with snow commonplace, even on the southern island of Kyushu. During the winter months, the prevailing winds come from the northwest, which draws cold air from Korea and Manchuria.[631]

During their stay in Japan, prisoners were identified by POW ID numbers – Manny was #1220. Each prisoner was responsible to check himself in and out of the barracks and to document their destination within the camp on a black board inside the guard-house.

An Army doctor by the name of Captain Thomas H. Hewlett and a few other Allied medical personnel kept the POWs as healthy as possible and performed numerous surgeries utilizing dental Novocain and sharpened butter knives. The senior officer in the camp was Major John Mamerow but the most influential man was Navy Lieutenant Little who was appointed mess officer. He was overly enthusiastic with his responsibilities and refused extra food or supplies to the prisoners. Many were sure he reported fellow POWs for stealing food. Following the war, he was tried by Court Martial but found not guilty of war crimes.[632]

By mid-1944, the prisoners at Camp #17 heard aircraft at night high above the mountains and headed toward the western or southern coast. Occasionally they heard anti-aircraft fire in the distance and the rumble of gunfire rolling up the valleys and canyons of the mountains. It was a wonderful sound and raised the POW morale as they realized the course of the war had turned against Japan. Sometimes they heard fighter interceptors roar over-head toward the bombers but never heard an aircraft crash.

Early in 1945, the prisoners heard bombers day and night. Manny looked into the sky a number of times to see the silvery specs heading for Japanese targets. A number of times when he walked to or from the mine during an air raid attack, he saw bomb-ers, likely B-29s or B-25s, get hit and plummet to earth in fiery balls of flame and smoke. The POWs stopped and screamed for the aircrews to get out of the aircraft. They cheered the sight of parachutes but tensed at the sound of machine gun fire with the sight of a slumped form in the harness. On rare occasions, they watched a live American descend to earth or below their line of sight. Some were captured but none were brought to Camp #17. The Japanese didn't want the airmen near the POWs to talk about the fortunes of war in the Pacific.

A limited amount of information about the war was smuggled into the camp in old newspapers. A few guards asked large amounts of money for an old newspaper so only the officers could afford the papers. Fortunately, the officers passed the news on to the rest of the men.

Meanwhile, Mansfield Young was located in a POW Camp near the small town of Kaneoka, also on the Island of Kyushu. He and three hundred other prisoners occupied the camp to work a nearby old lead mine. He survived the voyage from Manila on the *NISSYO MARU* through the South China Sea and docked at Moji, Japan (known currently as Kita or Kitakyushu). Like Manny's experience, the prisoners were mustered and placed on buses that transported them to Fukuota. Fukuota was a distribution point for many prisoners to work camps throughout Japan.[633]

Mansfield's camp was located two blocks from the lead mine. The barracks buildings were similar to Cabanatuan but sturdier. Sixteen men were assigned to each room and each man had a single bunk-like structure with a single cloth pad for a mattress. The camp was located atop a huge mountain where the snow fell all winter and didn't disappear until summer. It was common for the depth of snow to reach twenty feet. The camp was probably located on or near Aso Mountain.

The prisoners were relatively well clad with simple but heavy clothing that kept a man from freezing but little more. One blanket was issued to each man which, when combined with the clothing and burning some charcoal in the room, kept them alive at night. By morning, the charcoal was used up and the prisoners met the coldest part of the day by moving around to keep warm. Most of the men, including Mansfield, suffered from pneumonia and double pleurisy, an affliction that recurred throughout his life.[634]

Each morning before first light, the men were roused out of the barracks, lined up and mustered, then headed out for a full day's work at the mine. The trek, although short, was difficult in the winter for the snow was deep. When they reached the mine shaft openings, the prisoners were issued miner's caps with a carbide gas light. A chemical reaction in a canister of the light emitted gas which was lighted for visibility.[635] Mansfield looked at the mine and felt he was carrying on family tradition. His father was a coal-miner in a small mining town in Wyoming.[636]

The men were separated into squads of ten groups of four men each who worked in the mine. The men entered the mine and slowly descended a long and sharp incline of the shaft to a depth of about three hundred-sixty meters. As in the coal mines, the tunnels were dark, damp, and cold.

Each four-man gang was required to fill four ore cars per man by the end of the working day. Each ore car held about two tons of ore. Two men worked a drill or water gun that slowly ate its way through the rock until a hole was roughly six feet deep. A few sticks of dynamite were packed into the hole and exploded. Everyone ran for shelter since the explosion often loosened or knocked down tunnel shoring timbers. Once the tunnel was judged safe, the men returned to shovel the rock and gravel into an ore car and pushed to the mine exit where it was dumped into large buckets held by a cable. When the bucket was full, it was pulled by pulley down the mountainside to a smelter. At the smelter, the bucket was dumped and refilled with mud or tailings and pulled back up the mountain to be dumped on the side of the mountain.[637]

Between drilling and shoveling, the men had few minutes to collect their breaths. A half-hour was permitted at noon for lunch which was usually a mess kit of old rice and hot tea. Hot tea was always available to the men. Often, the Japanese ran out of rice and substituted putrid barley. When the barley ran out, the men were given soybeans that couldn't be cooked.

The mineshaft was ten to twelve feet high and the tunnels were dug in a network with rooms at the end of each tunnel. The ore was mined in the rooms. The mine was little more than a series of manmade caves with little supports and shoring. The cold and dampness got to Mansfield who was severely ill a good share of the time.

In the barracks, the exhausted men collapsed in their bunks. They received no news of the war progress although they heard bombing in the distance in early 1945. By mid-1945, the bombing drew closer and louder. Near the end of the war, the prisoner population included Americans, Dutch, British and Javanese.[638]

Since the camp and mine were located high on a mountain in the Honshu Mountain Range, the views were often spectacular. On rare occasions, the men were given a Sunday off and permitted to rest. The men walked around the mountains for exercise and on a clear day, Mansfield could see the ocean on both sides of the island; the Pacific Ocean to the east and the Sea of Japan to the west. On one such day while the men were marching from the mine, the prisoners sighted a lone silvery B-29 high in the sky. After the war, the prisoners figured it had to be the B-29 bomber "Enola Gay" enroute to its history-making mission.[639]

Even at this date, the number of POWs held in Prisoner of War Camps is only estimated due to a lack of thorough record keeping. The camp locations and names, however, are known. Unlike Manny and Mansfield, the POWs, often times, used wood, bamboo, or anything available in the area to build more camp facilities.[640]

For a period of two years ending in 1944, the Japanese moved over 70,000 Allied POWs from the Philippines, Malaya, and other South Pacific areas northward, usually to Japan. Koreans were often employed to act as guards or for other menial tasks so the Japanese men were available for militarily employment. In general, the Japanese POW camps were much more hazardous to the prisoners than the German POW camps. Over 192,600 Allied personnel were captured and interned.

Following is a list of the majority of known POW camps in Japan only and some camps pertinent to this book which is representative of Japanese POW camps throughout the war area. Both Manny Eneriz and Mansfield Young were interned and forced to labor in camps in Japan proper:[641]

> BAGUIO – Located in northern Luzon where a small force
> of Americans and Filipinos were trapped behind en-
> emy lines in December 1941. The camp was infamous

for the "water cure." Most of the men were sent to Cabanatuan. Camp Holmes was nearby and held 500 civilians in the Bontoc Mountains.

POW#1 Hakodate #2: On the Island of Hokkaido, 18 miles southwest of Takikawa. Opened in early 1945 for 130 Americans from China and 150 British from Singapore to mine coal.

POW#2 Hakodate #3: Outside the town of Utashinai, the camp opened a month before war's end for 285 Americans and 45 British from Hong Kong to mine coal. A number of Marines, originally from Wake Island, were added on 6 July 1945.

POW#3: Asahigawa

POW#4: Bibai-Machi

POW#5: Hokodate Main Camp

POW#6: Hokodate Divisional Camp

POW#7: Kamiso Subcamp

POW#8: Mitsuishi

POW#9: Muroran

POW#10: Otaru

POW#11: Sappo Penitentiary

POW#12 Teniya Park Stadium

POW#13: Tomakomai

POW#14: Sendai Camp #11: South of Aomori, the camp opened a month before war's end. It held 198 Americans from Fengtai Camp, China (POW#207), 186 civilians and 12 military from Wake Island to work an open-pit iron mine. It was located near Peking and the POWs were moved to Korea in June 1945.

Sendai #5 at Kamaishi was located near the harbor and the work included labor in a steel mill.

POW#15: Hanawa Sendai #6: Near the northern tip of Honshu Island, it opened in the fall of 1944 with 500 Americans and 50 British POWs to work a copper mine.

POW#16: Matsusima Camp #2-D: Along the Tenryu River, it opened in November 1942 for Americans, British, and Dutch to work for local contractors.

POW#17: Hitachi, Ibargi-ken Camp #D-12: On the western side of Mount Juragaki. It was only open for a few months in 1944 for 300 American POWs to work in a coal mine.

POW#18: Niigata, Subcamp #5: A small port on Honshu's west coast. 350 Americans worked in the Niigata Ironworks and labored at coaling ships and stevedoring on the wharves.[642]

POW#19: Omori Main Camp: Tokyo area where pilots and submariners were held for interrogation and not listed officially as POWs. This is the camp where "Pappy" Boyington was held. It was a primary arrival spot for POWs in 1942.

POW#20: Achi Yamakita

POW#21: Akasaka

POW#22: Akita

POW#23 Aomori

POW#24: Ashikago

POW#25: Atami

POW#26: Chiba

POW#27: Chugenji

POW#28: Furumaki

POW#29: Futatsui City

POW#30: Fuji

POW#31: Franciscan Monastery

POW#32: Hakkone

POW#33: Hiraoka, Subcamp #3

POW#34: Hayashi Village

POW#35: Hitachi Motoyama

POW#41: Kawasaki #1 located south of Tokyo, received many general purpose laborers to work in Tokyo in 1942.

POW#54: Ofuna was a camp primarily utilized to hold and interrogate fliers and submariners. The *USS GRENA-DIER* crew was sent here, some remained and the others were sent to Shimoda Saki to work in a steel mill.[643]

POW#55: Five miles inland from Kamaishi, the American POWs worked with the Dutch.

CIC#69: Santo Tomas on Luzon that held 4,000 civilian men, women, and children from Manila. The camp was liberated in February 1945.

POW#77: Kobe POW Hospital, located in Kobe, primarily designed for prisoner-patients. Conditions were relatively good.

CIC#77: Tacoblan on Cebu held a few civilians from Cebu until they were moved to Santo Tomas. The camp was just west of the city and with its harbor and airstrip, it provided a great deal of work for the POWs.

POW#78: Kobe camp that held 300 prisoners which had 4 POW doctors, greatly helping POWs who were ill or injured. Most of the men were British who worked as ship fitters and laborers at Osaka Ironworks making steel for warships. The few Americans came from the *CORAL MARU.*

POW#79: Sakurajima Ichioka School interned 150 POWs from Guam in 1942.

POW#80: Umeda Bonshu was in a suburb of Osaka and held a total of 788 American POWs of which 118 died. Their work was in the Nippon Tsuun Kaisha rail freight yard.

POW#81: Akenobe, #6-B was 75 miles northwest of Osaka that held American, British, and Australian POWs. The men worked in a copper mine for Mitsubishi Mining Company. 115 POWs of the 458 men died in the first three months of confinement.

POW#82: Funatsu was near Osaka and housed 360 American and Australian POWs. The men worked in two smelting plants extracting lead, zinc, and tin.

POW#83: Notogawa #9B on the east bank of Lake Buva near Iba where 301 American, British, Dutch, and Australian POWs built dikes and irrigation systems.

POW#84: Oeyama, Osaka #3 on Wakasa Bay held 645 American, British, Canadian, Australian, Dutch, and Norwegian sailors. The men worked a nickel mine. Oeyama Bunsho in Suzo was a cruel camp whose camp commander was found guilty during war crimes trials.

POW#85: Roku Roshi near the Sea of Japan where 380 Americans and 15 British/Dutch were held too perform agricultural and road building chores.

POW#86: Tsuruga, Diivisional Camp #5B at the southern end of Wakasa Bay contained 400 American and Dutch POWs. The men performed stevedoring and longshoremen labor.

POW#87: Hirohata Divisional Camp was one of the cruelest of all POW camps.

POW#113: Tanagawa worked the POWs by digging and hauling dirt to construct wharves for submarines. 69 of the original 500 POWs died.

POW#116: Yodagawa Bunsho in Japan held 400 POWs who worked in a steel mill of which 87 died in less than five months in 1943.

POW#120: Zentsuji Headquarters Camp on the outskirts of Zentsuji held 957 men, mostly officers initially. It was one of the better camps.

POW#138: Kashi Camp #1 (Fukuoka #1) was moved around often in 1944 and held 913 Americans, British, Dutch, and Australians, including 100 civilians from Wake Island and 193 survivors of the *ORYOKU MARU*. The men worked a coal mine and built air raid shelters.

POW#139: Koyagi Shima (Fukuota #2) still held 1,422 American POWs in April 1946. The men worked at shipbuilding and watercraft repair. The camp lost numerous men killed and injured in industrial accidents.

POW#140: Tobata (Fukuota #3) was located near a huge power plant which confined 1,200 American, British, Australian, Indian, Dutch, Malayan and Portuguese POWs. The prisoners worked as stevedores, mechanics, machinists, etc. Conditions were inhumane and the camp rated "poor."

POW#141: Futase (Fukuoka #10) near Futase Village that held 552 American, Dutch, and British POWs where the men worked in coal mines.

POW#142: Camp #11 (Fukuota #11) in a small mining town 50 miles south of Moji. 590 Allied POWs worked in coal mines.

POW#143: Omuta, Camp #17 (Fukuota #17) was located 17 miles northwest of Kumamoto with a population of 812 American POWs in the camp, later joined by British, Australian, and Dutch prisoners. At liberation, there were 1,859 men working in coal mines and zinc smelters.

POW#144: Aokuma (Fukuoka #22) was 30 miles southwest of Moji with only 160 POWs.

POW#145: Beppu was located on the Bay of Beppu in northeastern Kyushu and housed POWs for a couple weeks in late 1944. There were 169 high-ranking and civilian men enroute Manchuria from Formosa, including General Wainwright.

POW#157: Nagasaki, Senryu #24 held only 135 Allied POWs who observed and felt the atomic bomb dropped not far away.

POW#158: Sasebo

POW#159: Subcamp #12 (Fukuota #12)

POW#160: Yawata, Camp #3 There were 33 civilian internment camps on the main islands.

POW#163: Shirakawa on Formosa was a temporary holding camp for tank soldiers including members of the 192nd and 194th Tank Battalions.

CIC#178: Serang was a small town on the west end of Java that held 350 surviving sailors from the *HOUSTON*.

POW#207: Fengtai, China received the Marines from Wake Island in May 1945 and sent them to Korea in June 1945. In May it held 1,000 Allied POWs.

POW#211: Naval POW Camp at Shanghai received Wake Island POWs 24 January 1942 and added many sailors from the *USS WAKE, HMS PETREL,* and *SS PRESIDENT HARRISON*.

POW#300: Bilibid Prison was built by the Spanish in 1805 and used as a holding camp and dispatch point for POWs shipped from Manila to other areas. At one time over 12,000 Americans and Filipinos were in the prison.

POW#302: Fort McKinley near Manila was an overflow for Bilibid and an operating base for some POWs working the Manila waterfront. Mansfield Young lived here for a number of months. The POWs here shared work in the port area with prisoners from POW#304, Engineer Island, and POW#308, Port Terminal Building.

POW#306: Nichols Air Field where POWs worked seven days a week building and repairing the airstrips.

POW#311: Cabanatuan #1 was divided into camps #1 and #2. Camp #1 held most of the officers from Corregidor. 5,000 were shipped out in late 1942 to Japan and 1,000 sent to Davao. That left 6,000 POWs who were moved to Cabanatuan #3.

POW#312: Cabanatuan #2 was four miles from Camp #1 and used primarily to intern American Navy personnel.

POW#313: Cabanatuan #3 was initially used for Corregidor POWs and the sick from other camps. All POWs in Cabanatuan Camps #1 and #2 plus O'Donnell were sent here when they closed. It became the largest POW camp in the Philippines. Both Manny Eneriz anad Mansfield Young were interned in #3 until shipped to Japan, except Mansfield spent sometime on the Manila waterfront.

POW#314: In Limay, Bataan held injured and sick POWs, many from Field Hospitals #1 and #2. They were to collect scrap iron and were treated well by the Japanese.

POW#317: Camp O'Donnell held 9,300 Americans and 50,000 Filipinos after Bataan fell but moved to Cabanatuan a few months later. Conditions were horrific and caused the death of 1,600 Americans and 25,000 Filipinos in one four-week period in April and May of 1942.

POW#319: Tarlac was used briefly to hold flag officers, including General Wainwright.

POW#326: Davao Penal Colony was used as a general purpose labor force.

POW#328: Palawan Barracks held about 400 POWs, mostly Marines, to enlarge an airfield on the island. It was the site of full-scale murder of POWs in December 1944 when MacArthur was threatening to retake the island. Only 9 of 350 men survived the massacre.

POW#347: First Infantry Depot, known by many as Makassar Camp, was located in the city of Bandoeng, West Java. It held 1,500 Dutch POWs, many from Makassar Camp in Makassar, South Celebes. Near war's end, the POWs were moved to POW#350 in Bandoeng. The population topped out at over 3,000 POWs on Celebes including 200 survivors from *PERCH* and *POPE.*

Woosung and Kiangwan-marines QUAN#49-3 Nov 1994
POW Hospital Shinagawa, Japan, QUAN #49-1, June 1994
Sugamo Prison, Tokyo QUAN #47-5 April 93
Ube, Motoyama, Omi Mache, Shinagawa, Omori,
    Sumidagawa, Karenko, Hanawa – QUAN, Nov '99

Robert K. Harmuth

CHAPTER TEN

AMERICA TIGHTENS THE NOOSE

FOLLOWING THE FALL of the Philippines, General Kuorda relieved General Homma who was unable to maintain the Japanese offensive schedule. Fortunately for the Allies, Kuroda commenced a lifestyle and attitude of the conquering hero and did little to strengthen the Philippine Island's defenses. His entire life centered on entertainment and womanizing. As the fortunes turned in favor of the Allies, the Japanese became concerned the United States might invade the Philippines. The Japanese Senior Military Staff inspected and found the islands exactly the way MacArthur had abandoned them in 1942. Kuroda was immediately ordered replaced by General Yamashita. Yamashita quickly assessed the situation and initiated improvements.

Yamashita had 410,000 soldiers with 20,000 staff and support personnel. His primary problem was the virtual blockade of the Philippines by the Allied navies and especially the American Submarine Force. The Americans controlled the skies and the seas thus cutting off replenishment convoys. Yamashita faced the identical problem faced by MacArthur a couple of years earlier.[725] Successful arrivals of cargo ships were so rare, Yamashita personally met and congratulated each vessel.[726]

The submarine *CAVALLE* detected a Japanese convoy on 17 June 1944 during the Saipan Campaign. While carrier aircraft destroyed the air arm of the Japanese Fleet in the "Great Marianas Turkey Shoot, the *CAVALLE* and *ALBACORE* sank the Japanese carriers *SHOKAKU* and *TAIHO*. [727] Freedom for the POWs drew a step closer.

The "Tokyo Express" was organized following Japan's failure to adequately reinforce Guadacanal and many Japanese merchant ships and troop transports found the ocean floor. As a result, Japan utilized destroyers and other warships to supply and reinforce Japanese held islands. Even the Japanese submarines conducted supply missions but the tonnage moved was insignificant. This removed a crucial offensive weapon from the Japanese arsenal and permitted the Allied convoys to move about the Pacific virtually unhindered by a submarine threat.

POWs were often used to perform stevedore and longshoremen work at advanced bases but as the war progressed, their labor became increasingly more important on the Japanese mainland. For the most part, utilizing POWs to supplement the rapidly decreasing work force in Japan was in vain. However, POWs in a controlled environment of mines was successful while in manufacturing and industrial endeavors sabotage was prevalent. With the help of POWs, coal production actually increased during the war over prewar outputs. [728]

The "Tiger of Malaya, " as General Yamashita was known, assumed command in the Philippines in the fall of 1944. The general correctly assumed MacArthur would invade the Philippines not only for its strategic importance but also because of his political promise to return. On the other side, MacArthur assumed Yamashita would be waiting for him on Luzon so he first landed on Leyte. MacArthur and Admiral Kincaid departed New Guinea for Leyte with a naval armada of 738 ships with the flagship, *USS NASHVILLE*. As the Battle of Leyte waged, the Imperial High Command in Tokyo ordered all physically fit POWs held in the Philippines be transported to Japan as soon as possible. The "physically fit" requisite was interpreted as anyone with a body still functioning and able to perform labor. Thus began the odyssey of Mansfield and Manny. [729]

ROBERT K. HARMUTH

By mid-1943, the intense propaganda program conducted by Japan in the Philippines began to show results. The Japanese owned all media sources in Southeast Asia and the anti-American campaign went uncontested. America's popularity slowly eroded and America's censorship program kept vital information from the American public such as the plight of American POWs and Japanese atrocities.[730] However, MacArthur's propaganda program advertising himself worked well as he utilized everything available going to the Philippines to carry his logo, "I shall return."[731]

The Japanese carried out covert activities, making substantial inroads into guerrilla activities and sabotage. Over 5,000 Filipinos joined the covert group called the "Makaili." Armed and trained by the Japanese, they were prepared to fight the expected return of the Americans. Meanwhile, America successfully penetrated Manila's society with spies that appraised MacArthur of everyone who arrived or departed Manila. With supply support from MacArthur, organized guerrilla groups in the Philippines grew to 182,000 men.[732] American submarines provided substantial food and ammunition to the guerrillas who in turn, smuggled food to the POWs in the camps.[733]

The newer American submarines could carry approximately 50-tons of supplies. The Silent Service covertly supplied thousands of weapons and millions of rounds of ammunition, tons of explosives, radio equipment and large supplies of medicine. For example, the *NAUTILUS* met Major Bob Lapham at Debut Bay with supplies that were used later in the raid on Cabanatuan. *NARWHAL* also was deeply involved in running supplies and personnel in support of guerrillas although dozens of submarines provided some support to the guerrillas throughout the war.[734]

Guerrillas rescued 85 POWs who escaped the sinking hell ship, *SHINYO MARU* on 7 September 1944. The ship carried 675 POWs captured at Bataan and Corregidor. Days later, Admiral Halsey launched carrier strikes against Luzon, shooting down 173 Japanese aircraft, destroying 305 aircraft on the ground, and sinking 59 Japanese vessels on one of the first air strikes. Halsey lost eight aircraft.[735]

Colonel Fred Bradsaw developed and organized a special unit to fight in irregular situations and conditions. The unit was known as the Alamo Scouts which had some members prior to the fall of Bataan. It was an all volunteer unit trained on remote Fergusson Island. The Alamo Scouts usually worked in teams of five or six with one officer. Each unit picked its own men and assignments were made by Army Intelligence of the 6th Army. They performed operations throughout the islands prior to the Cabanatuan rescue so the Scouts were not formed specifically for POW rescues.

In the morning of 21 September 1944, the POWs at Cabanatuan were conducting routine daily work details when they heard aircraft. They weren't the usual Japanese Mitsuibishis they heard almost every day. The men looked up to see hundreds of aircraft in a tight formation heading west. "They must be ours!" "Nay, can't be ours. There's too many of them." Wave after wave of aircraft passed overhead and then the men heard the rumble and thunder of explosions coming from the direction of Clark Field. "My God, they're ours!" The excitement continued when a Zero passed low overhead with a Navy Hellcat hot on its tail. With guns blazing burst after burst. The Hellcat hit its target and the Zero disintegrated and fell to earth a few hundred yards from the camp. A roaring cheer went up from the prisoners and the bayonet wielders ran all the POWs back into the barracks.[736]

It was the beginning of dogfights on almost a daily basis thereafter. Despite threats and beatings from the guards, the POWs continued to cheer on the Navy and Marine pilots. The POWs painted a huge red cross on a piece of cloth and pegged it down on the parade ground following an incident where a Navy pilot inadvertently strafed the camp. The senior American, Colonel Schwartz, and the POWs who painted the sign were severely beaten.[737] The bombing and strafing of the Japanese facilities on the Philippine Islands continued daily.

ROBERT K. HARMUTH

Admiral Toyada visited Manila at the urging of General Yashimida and found the defenses and attitude still not ready. He moved the last of his elite aircraft groups, the Second Air Fleet, in position to oppose the Americans when they invaded Luzon. With the First Air Fleet already in Manila, a formidable air force was posed to strike back at the Americans including kamikaze attacks. The Japanese fought valiantly in the air when the Americans hit Formosa and landed at Leyte.[738]

During the summer of 1944, the Japanese awaited the arrival of the highly advertised B-29s or "B-san." A few of the bombers appeared over Manchuria and Kyushu but the Japanese were deeply concerned when Saipan fell. The loss gave the Americans air bases for bombers less than 1400 miles from Tokyo. B-29's struck Kyushu on 25 October 1944 but minimal damage was inflicted. For some reason, they failed to obtain the results experienced in Germany. With General LaMay in charge, the pilots found a jet stream of great force flowed over Japan and blew the bombs off target. The relative safety of 32,000-foot altitude was sacrificed for better accuracy.

During the autumn of 1944, the Japanese moved POWs out of Luzon at a frantic rate. Their effort to move free labor by surface ship increasingly was hampered by Allied submarines and naval aircraft. Three major groups of about 2,000 POWs were moved out of Cabanatuan. They were trucked back to Manila and temporarily held in Bilibid Prison. Mansfield and Manny were in these groups as was Colonel Beecher, the former senior prisoner in the camp. Over 4,000 POWs were killed in hell ships during the three-month period. Somehow, the word got back to Cabanatuan that their fellow POWs were being killed enroute to be slaves in Japan. "Volunteers" for new duty in far away places dropped to zero. The last group of 2,000 POWs left Cabanatuan in December leaving only 500 of the sickest and injured behind. The final head count in the camp was 486 Americans, 3 Dutch, 23 British, and one Norwegian for a total of 511 men.[739]

Nearly coincident with the exodus from Luzon by the POWs was the deployment of the Japanese 23rd Infantry Division in nine troop transport ships from Manchuria, a voyage of 1,800 miles to Luzon. It was a seasoned and disciplined fighting unit deployed to help defend the Philippines. The troop transports were defended by the carrier *SHINYO* and four destroyers. On the night of 17 November, American submarines attacked the convoy and sent four transports and the carrier to the ocean floor. The surviving vessels fled in disorder to Manila where they were attacked by Navy pilots.[740]

As 1944 came to a close, American submarines was shredding Japanese convoys. Japanese voyages took two to three times longer than customary as the vessels desperately tried to avoid the submarine blockade around Japan and her few remaining holdings. When it wasn't the submarines, the remainder of the Navy and Marine Corps had a "turkey shoot" with the Japanese navy and merchant marine. General LaMay brought the fire bombing to Japan that had been so successful in Germany. By May 1945, Japan's industrial might was analyzed as

a. Steel production was a million tons per year, less than a third of what was required.

b. The 2,500 aircraft built per month was down to 500 or less per month.

c. Fuel supplies were so low the navy cut fuel oil with soybean oil.

d. LaMay's fire bombing program would destroy every city of 30,000 population or greater if continued by September.[741]

On 22 June, the Emperor ordered the Supreme War Command to discontinue the war.

On 6 February 1945, the *USS BATFISH* received an Ultra message about Japanese submarine movements. In the following few nights, she sank the Japanese submarines *RO-112, RO-113,* and *RO-115.*[742]

Early in 1945, the routine air raids on Japan abruptly ceased coincident with General Curtis LeMay becoming Chief of the 20th Air Force, the B-29 command. Precision bombing on military targets to avoid civilian casualties ceased and emphasis was placed on destroying the empire. Fire bombing was initiated and on 25 February, 231 B-29s hit Tokyo and obliterated one square mile of the city including 28,000 buildings. A larger raid was conducted on 9 March when 324 B-29s from the Marianas dropped 2,000-tons of firebombs on Tokyo. Over 200,000 people died in the insuing firestorm, three times greater than the atomic bomb at Hiroshima.[743] Following the fire bombing, the Allies asked Japan for an unconditional surrender but received no reply. With no surrender anticipated the Allies burned Nagoya, Osaka, and Kobe but Japan still refused to surrender.

As the POWs on Luzon were shipped off to Japan, the number of camp guards also diminished. At Cabanatuan, Captain Mori was relieved and the guard garrison halved. On 5 January 1945, the remaining residents at Cabanatuan heard muffled explosions to the north. They didn't realize the noise was the pre-invasion shore bombardment by the U.S. Navy 35-miles away at Lingayen Gulf.

The kamikaze concept spread quickly throughout the Japanese military. Soldiers carried explosives strapped to their bodies and threw themselves at American tanks. Soldiers from Okinawa's neighboring islands attacked the American Fleet with swords in hand. One-man suicide submarines attempted to ram Allied ships. Even civilians were readied to attack Americans in suicide attacks when the Allies invaded Japan. Meanwhile, the Battle for Okinawa raged for months with Japan losing 50,000 men in May and 60,000 in June prior to their surrender on 21 June.[744]

The effort by the U.S. Navy took its toll on the Philippines and the Japanese soldier's daily food ration was reduced by 50%. Unfortunately, the food shortage was reflected in the POW's food ration as they struggled to survive on a starvation diet. Fortunately, Red Cross packages were being belatedly issued by the Japanese on an irregular basis. As the Americans steadily advanced through the Philippines, the POWs were often punished for Allied victories. Probably the most abhorrent case was on Palawan. An Allied invasion at Puerto Princessa was imminent and the Japanese ordered all the prisoners into a 6-foot wide trench used for an air raid shelter. There were 150 Americans, Dutch, and British POWs in the camp. When all the prisoners were in the trenches, the Japanese poured gasoline on the men and set them ablaze. Some POWs managed to get out of the trenches but were shot and only a few escaped the inferno by jumping from a 75-foot high cliff into the ocean. They swam across the bay and found friendly natives and thence to a guerrilla group. It was an incredible feat of strength considering their poor physical condition. Two men survived and were picked up by a PBY seaplane to tell their stories of atrocities to Allied Command. The Japanese continued the killings to insure there were no witnesses remaining at the end of the war to tell of the atrocities and conditions.[745]

Leyte fell despite General Yamashita strengthening the island with five divisions from Luzon. By January, Luzon itself was invaded. Despite repetitive bonzai and kamakaze attacks, the Japanese were rapidly defeated. The area around Baguio was the site of wholesale slaughter of Japanese troops who fought to the final man.

An American convoy stole out of Leyte Gulf and into the Surigao Strait at darkened ship. In a single column, the ships sailed northward with Mindanao on the left and Negros on the right and on into the Sulu Sea. The following night, they cleared Mindanao and entered the South China Sea encountering rapidly deteriorating weather conditions. The troops soon lined the rails and emptied their collective stomachs while sailors kept a lookout for kamakazis. The convoy crept silently north along the coast of Luzon; close enough to see the lights from Filipino village.

On 12 January 1945, the American Fleet laid off Lingayen Gulf in calm seas, a little more than three years after the Japanese Fleet invaded Luzon at the same point. MacArthur's invasion plan was identical to the Japanese. He had insisted on landing at

Lingayen vice Manila because he required the Luzon Plain for room to maneuver and he didn't want to level his beloved city.[746] The convoy was pummeled by kamakazi and land based aircraft from Japan, Formosa, and Luzon. Fortunately, Navy and Marine Corps aircraft did well at keeping them at bay.[747] The American Seventh Fleet landed the Sixth Army in LSTs on the beaches. The soldiers ran ashore and quickly made their way across the low flats and beyond the lagoon at San Fabian. At first light, the men began to march toward Manila while the Navy fought off seventy plywood kamikaze boats and a fleet of midget submarines.[748] As the Sixth Army headed for Manila, the 32nd Infantry guarded the eastern flank and the 1st Cavalry moved toward Cabamatuan.[749] Manila was literally destroyed after MacArthur surrounded the city, Yamashita declared Manila an open city, but Admiral Iwabuchi decided to defend the city to the death.[750]

At Cabanatuan, the men could hear the rolling thunder of the war front increasing daily. Filipinos stopped by the fence line and yelled at the POWs. "Hey Joe, MacArthur is coming wid the Yanks. Dey got dem Nips running okay." The morale of 511 prisoners sky rocketed and many felt their years of prayers were about to be answered.

In mid-January 1945, intelligence reports indicated the location of Cabanatuan. Intelligence sources as well as rumors implied the Japanese might exterminate the remaining prisoners in POWs camps so the 6th Army Headquarters decided to rescue the prisoners. Lieutenants John Davis and Bill Nellists, both from California, led two companies of Alamo Scouts toward Cabanatuan. Captains Bob Prince and Frank Murphy led 107 Rangers, all volunteers, while Major Bob Lapham led 286 well armed guerrillas to the nearby POW camp.

On 28 January, ten Alamo Scouts moved into the camp area, lay in the rice paddies for hours on end, and observed the camp routine. A few Scouts mingled with the local Filipino community and watched activities from rocking chairs. They watched Japanese tank and troop movements later confirmed by P-61 aircraft.

The Rangers were in place by noon on the 30th, less than a mile away from Cabamatuan.

On 30 January 1945, LCOL Henry Mucci, Commander of the 6th Ranger Battalion, gathered his troops 30 miles inside Japanese lines. Slightly over a mile from Cabantuan, six Japanese tanks rolled into the area along with a couple platoons of infantry while another Japanese unit of battalion strength moved into position near Cabu. The tanks hid in warehouses across from he POW camp and the infantry moved into defensive positions inside the camp proper. A new "Black Widow " P-61 aircraft from the 547th Night Fighter Group equipped with infrared arrived and pointed out the targets to the Rangers.[751]

The POWs became uneasy at the sight of the Japanese infantry and were frightened about 2000 when all hell broke loose inside and outside of the camp. SGT Ted Richardson led the Rangers to the locked main gate. He broke his machine gun attempting to break the padlock then had his pistol shot out of his hand. He calmly picked up the pistol, shot the guard, and opened the gate.[752] The Rangers rushed into the camp through the gate.

POWs were convinced their demise was at hand. A group of Rangers took out the tanks in the warehouses with bazookas. Then all was quiet. The prisoners cowered under and behind anything they could find until a few Rangers emerged from the smoke and dust, "Hey guys, we're Yanks. You are all free! Come on men, get a move on it, we can't stay here long. Everyone head for the main gate, pronto."

Husky, brawny, and tough Rangers and Alamo Scouts gently lifted the living skeletons and carried them from the camp. Not an eye of the rescuers was dry as they experienced the unbelievable condition of the camp and the POWs. Carefully and warmly, the prisoners were led and carried out of the camp while Pajata and his guerrillas took out the remaining Japanese in the area. Over 500 Japanese would never listen to "Kimugayo" again. The entire camp was in flames as the men headed north for the American lines. The Rangers and Alamo Scouts encountered a number of Japanese patrols and units heading north to meet the advancing Americans. The operation went well with a very small loss of Allied life. All POWs were rescued except one British man who was deaf and died in the flames.

Fighting in Manila reached the walls of Bilibid Prison and the Yanks broke down the doors to find the central courtyard littered with dead Japanese. The POWs were still in their cells located in the spoke-like rows of barracks. The men were petrified with fright and unaware they were being liberated. The soldiers gently talked the men out of their cells where they cried in relief and hugged the repatriating Yanks. Meanwhile, the fighting for Luzon pushed southward and the Army was greeted by "veek-tory" by the local Filipinos. At Santo Tomas, The POWs were frightened as well but not as badly as their Japanese guards when nine Navy fighters roared over the camp a few feet off the deck. The guards didn't notice the pair of goggles tumble to the ground with a note attached. The note read, "roll out the barrel, Santa Claus is coming Monday or Tuesday.[753] As advertised in the note, the prisoners were released a few days later without a fight.[754] Some of the prisoners were survivors from Bataan and Corregidor. Gaunt Americans, Dutch, British, Russian and others were released and so pleased to be free, they tried to shake the hands of each soldier.[755] The Battle for Manila ended on 8 February 1945 with 100,000 Filipino citizens dead plus 6,500 Americans and 20,000 Japanese and the city reduced to rubble. [756]

Los Banos was located thirty miles southeast of Manila in the midst of Lake Laguna de Bay. The 11th Airborne Reconnaissance Team checked out the camp and found the Japanese close to butchering the 2,000 American civilians.[757] Thirty-two members of the 31st Airborne crossed the lake in bancas and a few hundred dropped in by parachute. Quickly, they quelled all Japanese resistance and all 2,147 internees and 412 paratroopers made it safely back to American lines.[758]

Bataan and Corregidor fell to he Allies. An American destroyer a mile off Corregidor was covered in debris and body parts when

HARM

the Japanese garrison blew themselves up inside one of the island's tunnels.[759] American PT Boats operating out of Mindanao upset a number Japanese counter-attack landings on Luzon, Panay, and Palawan. On 2 March 1945, General MacArthur returned o Corregidor on PT-373, almost three years after departing with Bulkely. [760] The Submarine Force continued to pressure the Japanese and dramatically reduced internment time suffered by Allied POWs in Japanese camps. The submarines obliterated the Japanese merchant navy, rescued American fliers before they became POWs, supplied guerrillas on islands hopped by the Allied advance, sunk Japanese hopes for developing their own atomic bomb and jet aircraft, and photographed the Japanese mainland for prospective invasion sites.[761]

Over 5,000 POWs suffered through the coldest winter of the century in 1944-45 in about thirty POW camps throughout Japan. Perhaps the greatest atrocities were leveled at American fliers. The Japanese were frustrated and angry by the devastation caused by American bombers and many fliers shot down were executed by beheading for their crimes. LaMay's fire bombing began in March 1945 over Tokyo. Prisoners in the Osaka Group witnessed firsthand the bombing of Nagoya and Kobe. Sixty-two American airmen died in the fire bombing of Tokyo which was so severe, Tokyo was removed from the bombing list.[762]

The war centered around Okinawa and the Japanese not only used all the kamikaze inventory but built a kamikazi fleet of ships centered around the huge battleship *YAMATO*, cruiser *YAHAGI*, and eight destroyers. The ships were given fuel for a one-way trip. They small fleet ran into the American submarines *THREADFIN* and *HACKLEBACK* who reported the Japanese position. The submarines couldn't catch the ships but followed until the *ESSEX* carrier task group caught up with them and sunk the group. It was the last significant Japanese Fleet sortie.

Fliers and Submariners received special treatment and torture carried out in accord with Kempei Tai procedures, equivalent in many ways to the Gestapo in Germany. They employed a wide variety of tortures such as removing fingernails, the infamous water cure, kendo sticks, iron bars, knotted ropes, wooden clubs, baseball bats, and thumbscrews. A favorite was to feed a POW rice until full, then forcing him to drink water until he swelled to the point of busting, then jumped on his stomach. They used cigarettes to burn noses, eyes, and ears. The most lethal of treatments were the medical experiments, usually resulting in death.[763]

With the fall of Okinawa, defense of the homeland was paramount for the Japanese. "Downfall Strategic Plan" was circulated to all senior Allied commanders in May 1945. The aim was to force unconditional surrender by lowering the will to resist by blockades and bombing. They would strike at Kyushu first, then Honshu. The invasion plan was called "Olympic" and scheduled for execution on 1 November 1945. In July, the Potsdam Declaration demanded Japan's surrender. Japan refused the terms of an unconditional surrender,[764]

HARM

CHAPTER ELEVEN

CLOSURE OF JAPAN AND THE BOMB

THE MAJORITY OF the American submarines in the Pacific operated out of Pearl Harbor where ample supplies and major repair facilities were located. A couple very active submarine bases were located in Darwin and Perth. Initially, Australia wasn't impressed with American submarines operating out of their waters since it prompted fear of a Japanese invasion. Failure of the submarines to stop Japanese progress due in large part to torpedo problems added to the uneasiness. The opinion changed radically by the end of 1942 and into 1943 as the old S-boats were replaced by the Fleet submarines which were faster and equipped with radar and electronics countermeasures equipment. By the end of 1942, the American submarines positioned a blockade around Japan and exacted a terrible toll on Japanese merchant and naval shipping. Japanese imports of raw materials dropped drastically yet they managed to maintain a 2,500 aircraft per month production. Japan's air war problem was not aircraft but the loss of pilots to U.S. Navy and Marine aircraft. Military manning became critical in Japan by late 1943 and all youth of draft age were ordered to report for five weeks of training no later than 1 December 1943.[765]

On 8 January 1944, the Japanese reissued guidance on the treatment of POWs to unit commanders that included the disposition of prisoners. On 28 January 1944, the American Press finally, after more than two years, released the news of what transpired on Bataan as related by CAPT William Dyess, LCDR Melvin

McCoy and MAJ Stehen Melnik.[766] The news of the atrocities turned American feelings to hatred and may have been influential in the use of the atomic bomb decision.

The decision to use the atomic bomb was a long and difficult one. It was agonized over by President Truman, his Cabinet, and the top military officers for months. Intelligence reports from Guam confirmed locations of numerous Allied POWs in camps near Nagasaki, one as close as a mile to the north. Despite the close proximity of the POWs, Nagasaki was retained on the secondary target list for Bomb #2 but the aim point was moved south to protect the prisoners. Americans expressed a fear for the potential loss of thousands of innocent Japanese citizens that Secretary of War Stimson relayed to General Groves. In Grove's memoirs he wrote, "I was not thinking so much about those (Japanese) casualties as I was about the men who had made the Bataan Death March."[767]

On 25 July 1945, the American cruiser USS INDIANAPOLIS stood into Tinian Island harbor near Saipan and offloaded components of the atomic bomb. The Potsdam Declaration demanded an unconditional surrender from Japan that disturbed General MacArthur. Regardless of MacArthur's ability as a military tactician or strategist, he did understand the Japanese and they would never accept giving up their emperor. His opinion to the Pentagon fell on deaf ears and Premier Suzuki's response to the surrender demand unintentionally used the word "mokusaatu." It meant to take no notice or threat with silent contempt. Although an inadvertent slam, Truman responded with the order to drop the bomb. A few days later, Tinian reported the bomb ready but Truman waited a few more days.[768] On 30 July, aircraft dropped thousand of leaflets over Japan telling of pending doom without surrender.[769]

In August 1945, the population of Hiroshima fluctuated hourly as many families departed at night and weekends to reduce the chance of being caught in an air raid. People moved into the heart of the city to work and attend school while another 10,000 workers constructed defense projects. Thousands of Koreans were forced to work at the Mitsubishi Heavy Industries and Hiroshima ship-building facilities. The population reached over 350,000 with army units included.[770]

Many foreigners lived in Hiroshima including Americans of Japanese descent, clergy students, and citizens of Germany, Russia, China, Mongolia, Korea and other Southeast Asian countries. No POW camp was located in Hiroshima but a captured airman foretold the use of the atomic bomb when trucked from Yahata Village to Hiroshima in early August 1945. No one listened.[771] Captain Marcus McDilda was shot down 4 July while on a strafing run over Japan and picked up by Japanese fishermen. Taken to Osaka, he was marched through the streets and beaten. He was interrogated and tortured, telling his captives of the atomic bomb that panicked his captors. Most residents of Hiroshima felt fortunate they had been virtually untouched by bombing, unaware the city was on the primary atomic bomb target list. Other than a few Navy attacks earlier in the year, Hiroshima only saw bombers pass overhead heading to or from other cities. A few felt their city wasn't bombed because of the high Japanese-American population in the city. In fact, Hiroshima was a large contributor to the war effort including industry, headquarters for the Second Army, home of the Chugoku Regional Army and site of the largest military supply depot with a large shipping port to the war front.[772]

The atomic bomb, Little Boy, was assembled on Tinian on Sunday, 5 August 1945 and readied for delivery on Hiroshima. The next morning, the B-29 "Enola Gay," escorted by "The Great Artiste," lifted off Tinian and crossed the Japanese coastline on Kyushu at 0730. They turned northward for Hiroshima.[773]

Atop the Honshu Mountain Range on Kyushu was the Kameoka POW Camp and lead mine. Monday was a rare day off for Mansfield Young and his work group was in the exercise yard on the beautiful clear morning. The prisoners heard the familiar drone of a bomber and looked up to see the silver body of a single B-29. Had they had telescopic vision, they would have read "Enola Gay" written on the aircraft's nose.[774]

The Ota River formed a fan-shaped delta that passed through Hiroshima, splitting the city into six spits of land. An air raid siren wailed shortly after 0700 amidst a major evacuation of people due to expected air raids. The population of the city dropped to less than 250,000. Children were building firebreaks prior to beginning school and workers were in the factories. Teachers moved the children to air raid shelters but the "all clear" siren sounded and life returned to near normalcy in the city.

Across Shikoku Island and the Inland Sea, Colonel Tibbits in "Enola Gay" made his turn to fly over Hiroshima. The weather was perfect and at 0815:17, Little Boy was on its way into the history books. The orange and black bomb fell earthward and at 1,870 feet, nine and a half pounds of cordite drove the uranium pieces together into a critical mass – 13,500 equivalent tons of TNT exploded. A brilliant purplish-white flash lit the skies just seventeen seconds behind schedule.[775] A brief but meaningful message was sent back to General LeMay on Tinian, "BINGO." Hiroshima no longer existed.[776] On the other side of the world, President Truman received a message as he ate lunch on the *USS AUGUSTA*. "BIG BOMB DROPPED ON HIROSHIMA AUGUST 5 AT 1916 WASHINGTON TIME. FIRST REPORTS INDICATE COMPLETE SUCCESS WHICH WAS EVEN MORE CONSPICUOUS THAN EARLIER TEST."[777]

Central Hiroshima was hit by a hot blast of hurricane force wind that leveled buildings and trees. No one downtown heard the explosion for they evaporated and the city became dark in a cloud of heavy smoke and dust. As the column of smoke rose, the color turned gray and the crown a bright orange and scarlet red. Almost 80,000 people were killed and another 80,000 injured while only three of forty-seven hospitals remained.[778]

Unfortunately, American POWs were killed by the bomb. Six airmen from the bomber "Lonesome Lady" parachuted after being hit by the Japanese battleship *HARUNA*. They were captured and taken to Hiroshima. Two fliers from a B-24 of the 494th Bomber Squadron were in Hiroshima as were two Navy fliers from the

HARM

carrier *TICONDEROGA* and one from the *RANDOLPH*. There were other unconfirmed stories of more American POWs in Hiroshima on the wrong day.[779] One American POW in Hiroshima survived the bomb only to be stoned to death by Japanese citizens.[780]

Japanese stubbornness to surrender after Hiroshima earned them a second bomb. Some Japanese and other world military leaders felt America didn't have another bomb. On 9 August, the Japanese Supreme Council met in a bomb shelter of the Imperial Palace – all the other rooms were burned out. They again refused the terms of the Postdam Declaration. After all, Hiroshima was small by comparison to the deaths and damage of the fire bombings of larger Japanese cities.[781] The Japanese had considerable knowledge of an atomic bomb since they were just days away from exploding their own atomic radiation bomb. General Groves and Admiral Purnell recommended the second bomb be dropped quickly to impress Japan the United States was mass producing the bomb. President Truman concurred.

Shortly after 2300, the crew of the B-29 "Bock's Car" gave their personal belongings to friends and reported to the briefing room. A large map circled Kokura in northern Kyushu as the primary target and Nagasaki, to the west, the secondary target. Unlike Hiroshima, Nagasaki had no industrial complexes surrounding the city so the diurnal shift of workers did not take place. Some military was stationed in the city; 6,291 men of the 122nd Brigade, 2,700 of the 134th Anti-aircraft Regiment, and 63 naval personnel. The atomic weapon to be dropped was called "Fat Man" and the B-29 "Great Artiste" was to fly instrumentation aircraft again.[782]

A typhoon drifted in the area of Tinian and Iwo Jima causing widespread bad weather and the flight crews had orders to drop only by visual observations. At 0156 Japan time, the B-29s took off amid thunderstorms and climbed to 31,000 feet. They reached their rendezvous point above Yakoshima at 0745 but as the B-29 "Bock's Car" approached Kokura,, visibility was obscured from smoke and clouds. A weather report indicated clear skies over Nagasaki so the aircraft headed for the secondary target.

9 August started as a beautiful day in Nagasaki. Tiny ringlets of smoke spouted forth from family homes as families prepared breakfast and then the air raid siren blared. Defensive positions were manned and the remaining citizens ran for shelters. The people waited until the "all clear" siren wailed and all the equipment was returned and people returned to their daily routines. Schools opened and factories started work. There were no reported aircraft over Kyushu.[783]

Chimoto-san was cutting grass on Mount Kawabira when he heard the drone of an aircraft high above. He looked up to at a huge cumulus cloud and a silvery object coming out of the cloud. He watched the graceful B-29 cross the sky when suddenly a black object dropped from its belly. "My God, a bomb," and he threw himself to the ground. "Bock's Car" had only sufficient fuel for one pass over Nagasaki.[784] Fat Man was released over the stadium and at an altitude of 1,540 feet, the firing and arming switches closed. There was a blinding flash and he looked down at Nagasaki. A huge column of fire, smoke and dust rose above the city, then a hot rush of air raced past him.[785] The railroad station clock stood at 1055.[786]

There were POW camps within the city which contained 350 men plus 2,500 Korean workers. The population of Nagasaki was estimated under a quarter million according to rice ration figures. Fukuota Camp #14 was located in Saiwaimachi less than two miles from the epicenter with 480 Javanese POWs and Camp #2 was four miles away.[787] None of the POW camps in the area were identifiable from the outside. POW Ensign Jolly of the Netherlands saved himself by diving under a table at the first glimpse of the flash. MN2 Jack Madison was knocked on his behind in a coal mine two miles away. Camp Fukuota #14 was completely destroyed with 60-80 prisoners killed and over 200 injured. Lance Corporal Jidayu Tajayu gathered up the fifty or so remaining POWs and carried them to the far off Taiheiji Temple. Koyagi Camp #2 had numerous casualties but no accurate estimate of deaths. There were 299 Japanese-American atomic bomb victims but only 11 were in Nagasaki.[788]

There was no one to sound the alarm nor was there an alarm to be sounded as a B-29 remained over the city and dropped a blizzard of leaflets which read: "Read carefully what is written in this leaflet. The United States has succeeded in inventing an explosive more powerful than anything that has existed until now. The atomic bomb now invented has a power equal to the bomb capacity of two thousand huge B-29s. You must reflect on this terrible fact. We swear that what we say here is the solemn truth. We have already begun to use this weapon against the Japanese Mainland. If you still have doubts, look at the destruction caused in Hiroshima by one single bomb. Before this bomb destroys all the military installations that are prolonging this useless war, we hope that you will petition the emperor to stop the war. The President of the United States has already given you an outline of thirteen conditions for an honorable surrender. We advise you to accept these conditions and to begin rebuilding a new and better peace-loving Japan. You must immediately take measures to bring to an end all armed resistance. If you do not do this, we are determined to use this bomb and other excellent weapons to bring this war to a swift, irresistible conclusion."

Not well written but to the point if there was anyone left to read the message. Outside aid did arrive and the message read. Secretaries Forrestal and Stimson tried to persuade Truman to cease further air attacks against Japan following the nuclear blasts as a humane gesture. Truman would have no part of it and only conceded there would be no more nuclear bombs if Tokyo responded affirmatively to the surrender demand. If Japan continued to be stubborn, he ordered two more bombs readied to be used on 13 and 16 August 1945.[789]

A few days prior to the atomic bomb drop on Nagasaki, SGT Eugene Summerfield boarded a submarine, possibly the USS CATFISH, in Guam. He was a photographer attached to Headquarters

Company in Guam. He was issued a camera and wet suit and told to take pictures where the submarine dropped him. The submarine surfaced off Nagasaki three days after the bomb drop and Summerfield paddled ashore to take pictures of the damage. He spent 24-hours taking pictures (see photos). He was approached only once by a Japanese man. Summerfield drew his pistol to defend himself but the man walked by, badly burned and in an apparent state of shock. The following night, he boarded the submarine and returned to Guam. His photos were made available to him fifty years later through the Freedom of Information Act.[790]

On 14 August, the Japanese War Ministry contacted all military commands to inform them of the pending surrender and instructed them to destroy all records concerning the treatment of POWs. The Emperor agreed to unconditional surrender on 15 August, a first in Japanese history. One minute before noon, the last notes of the Japanese National Anthem , "Kimagayo," concluded. Every Japanese person stopped and listened, even in Nagasaki where few radios were operational. Every vehicle and factory machine stopped and Japan was silent. " . . . We have ordered our Government to communicate to the Governments of the United States, Great Britain, China and the Soviet Union that our Empire accepts the provisions of their Joint Declaration. Indeed, we declared war on America and Britain out of our sincere desire to ensure Japan's self-preservation and the stabilization of Southeast Asia, it being far from our thoughts to infringe upon the sovereignty of other nations or to embark upon territorial aggranization . . . Moreover, the enemy has begun to employ a new and most cruel bomb, the power of which to do damage is indeed incalculable, taking the toll of innocent lives. Should we continue to fight, it would not only result in an ultimate collapse and obliteration of the Japanese Nation, but would also lead to the total extinction of human civilization. Such being the case, how are we to save the millions of our subjects, or to atone ourselves before the hallowed spirits of our Imperial Ancestors? This is the reason why we have ordered the acceptance of the provisions of the Joint Declaration of the Powers."[791].

The speech acknowledged the atomic bombs had forced the end of the war and saved millions of lives. It was a tough pill for most Japanese for Japan had not surrendered to a single nation in twenty-six hundred years and the previous news propaganda fed to the nation indicated anything but a losing cause for Japan. After the speech, most Japanese went home and awaited the Americans. The cabinet resigned in mass and prince Higashi-Kuni, Hirohito's uncle, became the new premier.[792]

At 0615 on the 15th off the coast of Japan, Admiral Bull Halsey launched another strike against the mainland. He received a message from CINCPACFLT, "Suspend attack air operations. Acknowledge." 176 planes were in the air and the carrier was only able to reach 73 and order their return. 103 continued on to carry out the last air strike of the war. The previous day, the *USS TORSK (SS-423)* made the final submarine attack of the war, sinking a medium size merchant ship and its 745-ton Kaibokan class corvette.[793] Sentiment ran high in western nations about the use of the atomic bomb but Truman answered the critics, "Nobody is more disturbed over the unwarranted attack by the Japanese on Pearl Harbor and their murder of our prisoners of war. The only language they seem to understand is the one we have been using to bombard them. When you have to deal with a beast, you have to treat him like a beast . . . "[794]

On 16 August, the officers of the Japanese Western Army Headquarters met to listen to the Emperor's broadcast in Fukuoda. Only four days earlier, the Japanese massacred American fliers. A message to officers read, "There will be an execution of enemy fliers. The fliers are being executed because they are being held responsible for indiscriminate bombings . . . " In reality, the fliers were killed because they knew too much of Japanese atrocities. Sixteen fliers were hacked to death by sword near Aburayama.

On the same day, OSS Major Jim Kellis heard the Emperor's speech and knew he had to move quickly to save the lives of prisoners. He demanded and received audience with the local senior Japanese officer in Peking, General Takahashi. He demanded and received cooperation on repatriation plans.[795] Later, Major Gus Krause, an OSS Commander, sent a crew of four over Manchuria northeast of Peking. It was a part of "Operation Cardinal" to save POWs. The four parachuted in and headed for the Hoten POW Camp at Mukden. They were confronted and taken prisoner by Japanese soldiers that didn't know the war was over. They were beaten and their lives saved at the last minute by a messenger on horseback that brought word of the war's end. The rescuers reached Hoten in time to save the prisoners. It was just a sampling of the OSS's effort to save POW lives throughout the remaining territories controlled by Japan.[796] The Submariner's primary objective in Yokosuka was to get submarine POWs out of the country. The *GRENADIER* and *PERCH* crews survived almost intact while the *SCULPIN* had 23 survivors and the *TANG* nine. There were survivors from only nine submarines of the fifty-two lost during WWII.[797]

The reply came from Japan: "I have just received a note from the Japanese Government in reply to the message forwarded to that government by the Secretary of State on 11 August." An army of reporters grew silent in the Oval Office as President Truman continued; "I deem this reply a full acceptance of the Potsdam Declaration which specifies the unconditional surrender of Japan . . . "[798] The same day, 16 August, Japan received acceptance of the surrender from the United States. Japanese nuclear scientists were saddened for they failed to achieve their goal in time although they did test fire their first atomic bomb just days after the Nagasaki bomb.[799]

Operation Blacklist went into effect immediately which was an Allied plan to retrieve all the POWs as soon as possible.

Manny Eneriz put in a full day's work at the coal mine near Fukuoka Camp #17. At the end of the work shift and after his bath in the underground hot spring, Manny and his fellow workers walked back to the camp. They departed the coal mine shortly after 1530 on 9 August and headed south toward the camp. Fukuoka Camp #17 was located roughly 30 miles north of Nagasaki.

The prisoners strolled down the road and conversed about the day's work. The subject of conversation shifted to the numerous American air raids in the past few weeks. They wondered why none of the bombing raids hit Nagasaki or surrounding area when suddenly, the men felt the earth shudder from two explosions. Manny immediately thought it was an earthquake. They looked south toward the sound of the explosions and saw a huge multi-colored mushroom cloud rising from the direction of Nagasaki. Then the men felt a soft but hot gust of air rush by them. As they continued walking, they puzzled over the cloud and hot air. The puffs of hot air continued for a few minutes and then an unseasonable warm rain fell.[800]

A mild breeze came out of the south from the direction of Nagasaki and gradually strengthened into a stiff wind. The wind carried a strange odor, a repugnant and nauseating smell none of them experienced before. By the time they reached the camp, the cloud had dissipated and the smell disappeared. The prisoners ate the usual watery rice and retired for the night.

The following morning, 10 August, the prisoners were up and ready to head for the coal mine. Manny slowly half-walked, half-stumbled out the barracks door for muster. The men forgot about their experiences the day before as they fell into ranks. The guards surprised the men by announcing there would be no work that day. It was the Emperor's Holiday for the following three days and the POWs were free to do their own bidding within the confines of the camp.

On the 14th of August, Manny and his fellow POWs fell into ranks and began the daily walk to the coal mine. The subject for discussion that morning was the strange blinding light of the previous week and the many rumors circulating among them and the Japanese guards. Following the blinding light incident, American air activity dropped to virtually nothing near their camp. A rumor started predicting a prisoner exchange with the Japanese.

The prisoners departed the camp for the coal mine with the usual Japanese guard escort. As they speculated on the rumor machine, a messenger suddenly roared up the road toward the work detail. The cyclist came to a sliding halt in front of the prisoners and excitedly spoke to the guards. Then, as quickly as the messenger arrived, he departed in a cloud of dust and roared back down the road. The column of prisoners was ordered to halt, about-face and return to the camp. Now the POWs were really curious about what was happening.

The following morning, 15 August, the Japanese Camp Commander ordered all the prisoners to muster in the center of the camp. With the officers and prisoners in ranks, the commander walked up to the senior POW and spoke quietly to him. He used his camp interpreter who was born in California and a UCLA graduate. Coincident with the commander's discussion, all Japanese guards who mistreated the POWs or were otherwise disliked, were ordered to depart the camp. Then the POWs were ordered back into their barracks while the unpopular guards disappeared into the countryside. Unlike many camps, the Japanese staff lived within the camp confines. The POWs pondered their fate as they wondered what was happening. They did not have long to wait.[801]

The senior POW officers ran all the prisoners back onto the parade ground for muster. Then the senior POW stood before the ranks of prisoners and announced in a booming voice, "Men, the war is officially over – and we won!" His announcement was met with a stony silence of disbelief for a full minute or two. It was an unbelievable period of silence. Manny looked into the sky, "my God Almighty, thank you for rescuing us from hell." Tears of joy poured from his eyes and when he looked around, he saw similar reaction by everyone. Then bedlam broke out and the men cheered and yelled enthusiastically. They slapped each other on the back and hugged as they congratulated each other for surviving the Japanese gauntlet. Privates hugged colonels, Americans hugged Aussies, and British hugged Dutch. In retrospect, it was an awesome display of emotions for a "bloom'n Limey."

Spontaneously, the men broke out in song, each singing their national anthem. The Americans joined the British in their version of God Bless America. With no more work in the mines, life looked brighter. Work was confined to housecleaning and the men painted large "POW" signs on the roofs of the camp buildings. On 27 August, the Allies resumed bombing but this time the bombers dropped food and cloths. The POWs saw more food in that week than they had seen in the previous year. Manny and the other prisoner's top priority was eating.

Most of the ex-POWs had yen that was as valuable as monopoly money. It was quickly replaced with military script which none of the local citizenry understood. After a few days of eating, Manny and his fellow prisoners felt better although most of them became ill from eating rich food they no longer were accustomed to. A few of them decided to take one of the nylon parachutes into town and have it sewn into shirts for some of the men. They stopped at a number of small shops but none of the merchants or seamstresses wanting anything to do with sewing the Americans anything. Their yen was useless and no one accepted the military script so the shopping trip ended quickly.

The men continued their slow stroll in town and came to a small railroad station. They talked and wished a train would come along to take them home when a long passenger train rolled to a stop in the station for a short stay. Manny stared in disbelief at the passengers. They were Dutch ex-POWs on their way to Nagasaki for transportation home. Manny and his fellows talked to the Dutch and they readily agreed to take them along. Quickly they were on their way for a destination far away from Fukuota #17. Manny never found out how the Dutch managed to commandeer the train with a Japanese crew.[80]

The old steam locomotive puffed its way slowly down the side of the mountain and hills toward Nagasaki. The locomotive belched puffs of black smoke which found its way into the passenger cars through the open windows. Only screens kept the larger pieces of soot from flying into the car. The men gagged in the gaseous smoke but didn't complain; they were homeward bound.

They passed through small towns and villages where the forlorn citizens watched the train in pain more than disdain. The Dutch cheered and yelled at the people, generally having a wonderful time that didn't endear them to the locals. Throughout the night, the train continued its trek to freedom, stopping often for track switching to circumvent destroyed sections of track. At first light on 16 September, the train reached Nagasaki and the men looked out the windows of the train in disbelief at the destruction. It then became apparent what the Japanese meant when they said, "one bomb, whole city gone." Manny pressed his face to the window screen and looked in utter horror. As the train moved slowly through the streets, he saw white spots on the pavements where persons once stood. He saw a masonry smoke stack which had been moved like a stack of checkers. Metal buildings had been melted like warm butter. He twisted his head to the left and toward the mountains from which they had come and noticed the denuded vegetation that was brown all the way to the green plateau. The tops of the mountains apparently remained above the blast.[803]

The train came to a stop on a spur near the wharves in the port area. The *USS HAVEN*, an American hospital ship and an escort aircraft carrier were tied up to a quay wall. The waterfront area was mostly intact. The Dutch and five Americans stormed out of the train in glee, shouting and yelling with joy when they saw American sailors and marines on the docks. Everywhere Manny looked, he saw Old Glory flying and a lump of pride stuck in his throat. Manny wore a beret with an American flag sewn to it which attracted the attention of some sailors. "Hey Mack, you guys Yanks?" "You can bet your sweet ass we are," shouted Manny. "Then follow me men and welcome to the Empire of America." When the sailors found out they were Bataan Death March survivors, they couldn't do enough for Manny and his four companions. They

HARM

were taken aboard ship, showered with hot water and given chocolate and coffee. Then they were deloused and given new clothing. Manny grinned as size ""small" completely engulfed his skinny frame.[804]

They received physical examinations and their Army affiliations logged. "Your folks will hear you are free and okay by this time tomorrow," explained a tough looking Marine sergeant. Manny and other "relatively" well ex-POWs were sent to the escort aircraft carrier for transportation. Manny reached the ship's quarterdeck and told them he was a survivor of the 31st Infantry Regiment from Bataan. The sailors logged him in and ushered him below to his own stateroom. The Dutch were given cots and slept topside. The liter cases and severely ill were taken aboard the *HAVEN* where the Navy medical staff gave them first class attention. A few days later, it was "Anchors Aweigh" and the ships were underway for Okinawa – the next stop on Manny's odyssey back home.[805]

The trip to Okinawa took a few days during which Manny was treated royally. The ships remained in Buchner Bay in Okinawa for about a week, awaiting the arrival of other ex-POWs before departing for Guam. A couple of days prior to the scheduled departure for Guam, a typhoon of enormous force approached the area and the Navy ships got underway to ride the storm out at sea. Manny didn't understand why the ships would go to sea to ride out the storm but the sailors explained the dangers of remaining at anchor in port during a typhoon. Following the storm, the ships returned to port and Manny was able to look around the island. Although quarantined, some U.S. Marines took the ex-POWs on a sightseeing tour in a truck. They visited the sites of numerous battles and the infamous Japanese caves. Manny, like many that followed, marveled the Marines were able to fight up the slopes and to the cliffs at White Sands Beach.

The ex-POWs were interviewed by Army and Navy Intelligence, and asked specifically what atrocities they experienced or witnessed. They also asked if they had witnessed any treasonous actions by Allied personnel. Lieutenant Little and the Japanese-

American from UCLA were noted. Both these men were eventually brought to Court Martial.

When Manny completed his stay in Okinawa, plans changed and he traveled to Guam via military aircraft vice the carrier. He flew to Clark Airfield in a B-24 light bomber and his seat was located behind and aft of the pilot and co-pilot. Once airborne, the pilot asked Manny to keep his eyes out for any aircraft. Manny took the assignment seriously only to find the pilots slipped the plane into auto-pilot and took up the serious business of reading comic books. Another series of intelligence queries was followed by Manny's assignment to a troop transport ship for transportation to San Francisco.

A day or two after Manny left the POW camp, the camp was deluged by a large group of journalists. Every man was interviewed and their stories told in their hometown newspapers. The ex-POW's family was notified of their well being by the press a day before the news was received from the War Department. No OSS Rescue Team was required in this camp and the actual departure of the men was filmed and recorded in Volume #24 of the Victory at Sea series. The men were loaded on military troop carriers and driven to Nagasaki. Once in the port area, the men from Fukuota #17 followed the same routine as Manny a few days earlier. The ships the ex-POWs traveled on kept the galley open 24-hours a day and by the time they reached San Francisco, most of the men regained some of their original weight.[806]

On 7 September, an American Recovery Team arrived in Fukuota #17 Camp. The rescuers were overwrought with emotion when they saw Manny's former fellow prisoners in the camp. They carefully gathered the ex-POWs together and escorted them to the little railroad station. On 8 September the ex-POWs arrived in Nagasaki and seemed to derive some satisfaction from the ruins. However, the most memorable sight was the American Flag flying over the city. The war was truly over.

At the Kameoka Lead Mine, news had not been received about the end of the war until the day after the surrender. One Monday,

Mansfield and the other prisoners got up as usual and fell into ranks ready to be led to the lead mine. The sun rose and the usual time to start the walk to the lead mine came and passed yet no guards appeared in the barracks area. Ever so cautiously, Mansfield opened the barracks door and peered outside. There was not a soul in the camp as far as he could see. The Japanese had abandoned the camp and disappeared. As in other camps, the POWs were paranoid and too frightened to attempt escape or even walk out of their barracks let alone the camp. The POW officers felt it prudent to sit tight for awhile and see what transpired. Finally, after a week and a half of no Japanese presence, the camp's senior prisoner, an Army Air Corps colonel, ventured out into the compound to ascertain what was happening. The camp was completely abandoned by the Japanese. He opened the main gate and disappeared from sight. He returned a few hours later on a railroad train. The station was not far away and a spur of the tracks was adjacent to the camp.[807]

Excitedly, the colonel gathered the POWs around him, "Men, the war has been over for two weeks. Haul that god damned Jap flag down. We won. We won!" The men stared at the colonel in utter disbelief while a sergeant hauled down the Japanese flag flying over the camp. "For real sir?" "Yes, for real men" and the colonel hugged the soldier who asked the question. A murmur rumbled through the ranks and then it rose to a crescendo of cheers as loud as the weak voices could yell.

The men found the energy to dance but the feelings of the men was best demonstrated by the smiles on their faces. They beat the odds. "Hey colonel, what happens now sir?" "Nothing but good news men. Tomorrow, we'll get some paint and place big red crosses on the roofs to help the fly boys find us to drop food and cloths. When you hear the airplanes, get inside so you don't get hit with falling food. We'll stay here a few more days until the Army gets sufficiently organized to ship us out of here and back home – back to America!" The celebration restarted and the men raided the Japanese barracks and buildings looking for food.[808]

Food and drink was initially dropped by parachute in 55-gallon steel drums. A few men were actually killed and others injured attempting to catch the drums while the drums were still in flight. Following flights dropped supplies wrapped in nets that proved less lethal than the drums. Eventually, the supplies were dropped with different colored parachutes to indicate the contents of the supply nets. Both Mansfield and Manny felt the supplies, in whatever form, was manna from heaven.[809] Some of the supply missions were described as the hairiest of the war by the aircrews. Close to 4,500 tons of supplies were dropped to an estimated 63,500 prisoners immediately following the war.[810]

True to their word, the Army bombarded the camp with food, drink and cloths the following day. For the first time since 1941, the men had bountiful food and drink. A few days later, a caravan of automobiles wound its way up the mountainside and picked up all the ex-POWs. The men were driven down the mountain to a waiting train at a small railroad station. They boarded the train and traveled to Osaka. They were given physical examinations, medicine and logged "in" as alive and well vice Missing in Action. Then they traveled by railroad to an air base near Yokohama. The train traveled through Hiroshima and the men stopped celebrating for a few minutes as they looked at the city with awe and disbelief. Mansfield remained ill on and off throughout the war including his trip through Japan.[811]

Recovery teams traveled throughout Japan and the remaining holdings of Japan to the ex-POWs camps to insure the safety of the men. Airlifts, sea lifts and hospital ships met the incoming released prisoners. Soon, most of the former POWs were on their way home. On 27 August, Operation Mission Pigeon landed on China's Hainan at Bakkli Bay led by Major John Singlaub. The OSS rescued 356 American soldiers and sailors thanks to the major who outwitted the uninformed Japanese guards. Regardless of the camp, the ex-POWs needed help especially in the camps where the word of surrender was received and the POWs took matters into their own hands. In some of the quieter camps like Nagoya, the men pooled their money to buy beef and in Kobe, the prisoners took over the camp and stores. On 29 August, a B-29, delivering food to a POW camp in Korea, was shot down by Russians.[812]

Lieutenant General Kawabe led a Japanese delegation to Manila to discuss the terms of surrender and restoration plans for Japan by the United States. The Japanese delegation was rightfully apprehensive throughout the trip that ended with a confrontation of thousands of very unhappy Filipinos. Their ire was understandable since the three week long siege of Manila in February resulted in the butcher of tens of thousands of Filipinos in the cruelest ways by the Japanese. Use of sword and bayonets was a favorite tool again but often entire columns of Filipinos were doused in gasoline and set afire. In hospitals, every female was raped and killed including nurses and nuns, reminiscent of Japanese earlier days in Nanking.[813]

Kawabe was not pleased with the schedule in which Americans planned to enter Japan but General Riley Sutherland insisted the U.S. Army land at Atsugi Air Base on 23 August, the Navy in Tokyo Bay on 25 August and the surrender to be signed on the 26th. Sutherland eventually conceded five days on the schedule.

Many of the ex-POWs boarded C-54 transport aircraft in Osaka for a flight to Okinawa where they remained until each individual was called out for transportation on the next leg of the journey home. Mansfield's experience was similar to Manny's as he faced hours of interrogation by Army Intelligence officials, answering questions about what happened following the fall of Bataan. Mansfield rested and ate for a couple of weeks then was sent to the air terminal for transportation to Manila. After waiting for over three days with no flight in sight, Mansfield decided to take matters into his own hands. Instead of waiting for his name to be called, he walked to the dispatch officer and gave him his name. Within hours, Mansfield was airborne and headed for Manila. Despite Manila being in absolute ruins, it was a free city again and Mansfield enjoyed another two-week rest and recovery period. He spent a lot of time looking around the Manila area pondering what a difference a couple years made. And then it was a bus ride to Clark Air Base and on an airplane to San Francisco. "San Francisco here I come. All 97 pounds of me!"

The POWs had feared mass murder if Japan lost the war, a fear prevalent in every camp. Many of the ex-POWs thank the atomic bombs for saving their lives. Fortunately, the end of hostilities was forced upon the Japanese so quickly, there was literally no time to execute the prisoners.[814] Treatment of POWs deteriorated gradually over the course of the war which is difficult to appreciate after O'Donnell and Cabanatuan. With guidance such as Hirohito's Privy Council and the Prisoner of War Information Bureau, the overall treatment of prisoners worsened. In some areas, the POWs were treated so badly, the possibility of survival was nil. When Tojo decreed that POWs were to work as laborers, untold numbers of POWs lives were actually saved.[815]

On 27 August 1945, the *USS MISSOURI* and her screen of destroyers, *USS TAYLOR, USS NICOLAS* and *USS NEW YORK,* steamed into Tokyo Bay followed by *HMS DUKE OF YORK* and two British destroyers, joined by the *USS IOWA* and *USS GOSSELIN.* At 1327, *MISSOURI* anchored in Sagami Wan, Honshu, Japan.[816] By 30 August, the Atsugi airstrip was filled with new C-54 cargo and troop carrying aircraft. C-47s with the 68th AACS Group arrived in Atsugi on 28 August loaded with communications equipment. MacArthur arrived a couple days later on a new C-54 and was online with the rest of the military and world.[817] [818]

It was a cool and overcast day in Yokohama on 2 September as four large limousines hurried toward the waterfront. Once there, eleven men impatiently awaited an American boat to take them out to the *MISSOURI.* They would have preferred a Japanese boat, but the dignitaries couldn't find a single boat intact.[819] The American boat turned out to be the destroyer *USS LANSDOWNE* who picked them up at 0730 for the 16-mile trip to the *MISSOURI* anchorage. Many boats came alongside *MISSOURI* that day but none more important than the one delivering General Wainright

HARM

or the boat bringing POWs from Ofuma. To add a little pageantry to the occasion, Admiral Halsey had the Naval Academy send out the flag flown by Admiral Dewey when he entered Tokyo Bay in 1853.[820] It was displayed behind the table on the 0-1 Level while the flag that flew from Washington, DC on 7 December 1941 flew from the ship's fantail.[821]

General MacArthur read the terms of surrender at 0902 and Mamoru Shigemitsu signed the document first at 0904 as a huge armada of B-29s in tight formation flew overhead. The procedure lasted 23 minutes, then MacArthur stated, "Let us pray that peace be now restored to the world and that God will preserve it always. These proceedings are now closed."[822] On 8 September, the 1st Cavalry Division led MacArthur into Tokyo to the new American Embassy and Old Glory rose and flew again – over the rubble that was once Japan. Admiral Spruance arrived in Japan in *USS NEW JERSEY* on 15 September to oversee the repatriation of all Allied ex-POWs held on Japan's mainland. His first stop was Wakayama on the eastern entrance to the Inland Sea. More than 1,300 ex-POWs were then received on board the hospital ship *USS SANC-TUARY* and a couple troop transports.[823]

Of interest was wherever there were Allied POWs, both before and following the surrender, not a single Chinese was seen. During the war, the Japanese often paraded POWs through the streets of cities but no one remembered seeing a Chinese POW.[824]

After Germany surrendered, MacArthur knew he finally had access to all of America's military assets. He and his staff planned an end to the war with "Operation Downfall," the invasion of Japan. Phase One was "Operation Olympic" which was the invasion of Kyushu set for 1 November 1945. Once the island was conquered, it was to be the jumping off point for the invasion of Honshu or "Operation Coronet." General Walter Krueger, Commander of the Sixth Army was to command the invasion of Kyushu with a force of three Army Corps and one Marine Corps or 14 combat divisions. It would include all 3,000 of Admiral Spruance's ships consisting of 66 carriers with 2,600 aircraft. Admiral Halsey was to prevent aid from Hokkaido or Honshu and could face 735,000 troops on Kyushu and 5,000 kamikaze aircraft.[825] Operation Coronet was set for 1 March 1946. An estimated five million men were to be involved in the Japanese invasion.[826]

Manny climbed up the gangway to the main deck of a USS CHENANGO (CVE-28) moored in Guam along with thousands of ex-POWs and other servicemen. He volunteered for duty as a steward and served as a waiter in the officer's mess. It wasn't bad duty as he feasted on the food prepared for the officers and was assigned to a stateroom all by himself. It was an enjoyable voyage, so good Manny barely recalls the stopover in Hawaii between the excitement of going home and the good life on the ship.

The ship berthed in San Francisco and Manny looked out over the huge homecoming crowd on the wharf. Everywhere he looked, he saw the American flag flying and his chest puffed in pride. Then he spotted his father Vicente and aunt Antonia, his cousin Felix and many of his neighbors. An agonizing long wait on board finally ended after the ship was secured and the men were permitted to disembark. Manny raced down the gangway and ran to his father's side.

Father and son, brother and brother, they hugged and cried with joy. A few quick stories were told, then as they started for home, Manny asked his father, "where's Betty?" "Oh, I don't know. Haven't seen her." "Father, she's my girl friend! You haven't seen her?" "Oh all right, she got married a few years ago and has a bunch of kids already." "God, she didn't wait for me very long did she?" "Sorry son." "Guess who was in the Philippines with me father?" "Who might that be?" "Salvadore was there with us. Have you seen his family lately? Has his family heard from him since I haven't seen him for a couple years and that was back in the Philippines." "Wait till you see my butcher shop Manuel, I've added on to the old building. You'll love it." "Father, where is Salvadore? What has happened to him?" Vicente's eyes filled with tears and in a sobbing voice, he said, " Manuel, Salvadore was killed." "No father, I took good care of him in a prisoner's camp. He was in good health when I last saw him." "Listen to me Manuel, Salvadore is dead. He died in one of those prisoner of war ships going to Japan. It was sunk by Navy airplanes. Apparently, the damned Japs never identified the ship as carrying prisoners. There was no way our airplanes could know."

After a few weeks with his family, Manny visited Salvadore's family. The family was renting the house on Washington Street where Manny grew up and all of Salvadore's sisters were there. It was a sad visit and many tears were shed. Then Manny went to the bar at the end of Washington Street and found Sal's father. He took Manny home and showed him Sal's Purple Heart and the telegram he received from the War Department. Sal's father also received $10,000 for Sal's death; a cheap price for a man's life – especially for his closest friend's life.

Mansfield followed a similar route back to San Francisco and was welcomed home as a hero by family, friends, and hometown. Many years later, his son was stationed in Japan in the Army at Eukuma. He visited the Hiroshima Museum to see some of his father's past but was distraught for what he found was a complete change in world history and details of the disaster. The fault for the war and the disasters belonged to the Americans according to the new Japanese history books. Mansfield attempted to fly back to the Philippines and Luzon on "Space-A" (available space on military aircraft) a few years later but was refused a Visa by the Philippine Government. The government wanted him to fly commercially and pay for a ticket and remain for awhile to spend his money. It was a hell of a welcome from a country for which he sacrificed so much. He did manage a brief stopover at Clark AFB during the Vietnam War when he was employed in country by Lockheed to work on helicopters.[827]

In July 1995, nuclear physicist Tatsusaburo Suzuki told the Associated Press about the Japanese adventures with an atomic bomb. Japan worked on the bomb during the war but had difficulty obtaining sufficient amounts of U-235. Assistance from Germany was sunk by the USS FLOUNDER in late

1944 when the American submarine torpedoed the *U-534* carrying two tons of enriched uranium to Japan. Some radioactive sources were found in Korea in time to test the first Japanese atomic bomb shortly after Nagasaki.[828] Suzuki did not address the test explosion that was documented by Wilcox and quoted from an "Atlanta Constitution" article in 1946 by David Snell who was a CID officer during the war. He interviewed Japanese officers in the nuclear program who described Japan's first nuclear explosion four days after Hiroshima in great detail. Weapons grade uranium, actually uranium oxide, was documented and retrieved on a Japanese submarine surrendered in Portsmouth, New Hamsphire following the war. The lab and testing was conducted in Korea and consequently many Japanese physicists were captured by Russia. There was also significant proof of a long-range delivery system for the bomb underway which was designed to reach the United States.[829] One nuclear laboratory and equipment was found by Americans and dumped into Tokyo Bay.[830] Suzuki did explain, however, that Japan had no "ethical qualms" about using their bomb against the Americans. Americans should feel relieved of any guilt for use of the atomic bomb against Japan.[831]

In the war trials following surrender, not every Japanese was to blame for everything. The Allies categorized the criminals into three groups: A Group was for officers who knew of the atrocities and made policy approving its conduct; Groups B and C was filled with Japanese who actually ordered or conducted the crimes. A list of over 300,000 Japanese was developed for Groups B and C. The list was stopped there only because it had to stop somewhere. On 3 May 1945, the International Military Tribunal convened to prosecute Group A war criminals. On 12 November 1948, judgment was reached on the 28 men tried. Twenty-five were sentenced and found guilty; seven to death, one was insane and two others died prior to the trials conclusion. Of the 5,700 Class B and C criminals that went on trial, 3,000 were convicted and 920 executed.[832] The first victim was General Yamashita who was hanged in an atmosphere reminiscent of a theater or football stadium. Despite the American defense counsel who felt he was innocent of war crimes, the British forced the issue since they were still seething from their defeat at Yamashita's smaller force early in the war. He was hung for the atrocity at Palawan even though he took command after the incident occurred. General Homma was found guilty and responsible for the Bataan Death March. He was shot while some of his officers, such as Colonel Tsuji, who were really responsible for the atrocities were never brought to trial. Tojo Hideki attempted suicide and the press dabbed pieces of paper in his blood for souvenirs. One wondered where the illness ended. General Araki was charged and found innocent of making war on China. He was the author of "bushido" which was not a war crime. Admiral Nagano died during his trial. Of 25 major war criminals, only General Matsui and Mamoru Shigemitsu escaped conviction.

Considering the tenacity with which a Japanese soldier fought, usually to the death, it was expected he would fight equally as hard in the defense of his homeland. Japanese citizens were prepared to fight whether with a bamboo stick or knife. Japanese men up to 65 and women up to 45 were formed into volunteer squads who drilled with old muskets, bows and arrows, and bamboo spears. There were one hundred million Japanese willing to die for their country.[833] The use of the atomic bomb eliminated the final confrontation thus saving millions of lives.[834]

Arguments followed the use of atomic bombs and continue today as to whether such power was necessary. Conventional bombing of Tokyo on 9 March 1945 killed 83,000 people, 12,000 more than the dead or missing after Hiroshima. Dresden, Germany was fire bombed and 135,000 people were killed. Unfortunately, conventional bombing did not persuade the Japanese to quit.[835] Some people concede the need for the first bomb but not the second such as former ambassador to

Japan, Edwin O. Reischauer. Unfortunately, Japan wasn't ready to surrender after just one bomb. There may have been a need for the first bomb but " . . . there was none for the second . . . The top American authorities did agonize over the decision to use the first bomb but seem to have given the little thought to the use of the second, 70,000 lives almost inadvertently."[836] He didn't read far enough.[837] Prior to dropping the second bomb, Nagasaki represented a large industrial complex. The Mitsbishi Shipyard consisted of 452 buildings supporting construction activities such as midget submarine construction, diesel engine manufacturing, ship repair docks, an oxygen plant, ship finishing facilities, etc.[838] "There's a widespread perception that the Japanese nation was the innocent victim of atomic warfare – that noncombatants suffered a fate reserved for soldiers, and that the punishment exceeded the crime. And maybe that's true. But it's also true that more POWs and soldiers, maybe as many as one million, would have died if the bombs were not dropped. In May of 1945, Supreme Japanese Commander, Field Marshall Terauchi ordered all POWs killed when the Allies landed on the Japanese mainland. Ironically, Hiroshima and Nagasaki averted that tragedy."[839]

Four times the rate of death occurred for Australian and American POWs at the hands of the Japanese than to the Germans. Of the 235,473 American and British prisoners captured by Germany and Italy, only 4% or 9,348 died in captivity whereas 27% of Japan's Anglo-American POWs or 35,756 of 132,134 did not survive. There were opposite incidents too such as the U.S. submarine commander that sunk a Japanese transport ship and spent an hour killing hundreds of survivors. On 4 March 1943, the day following the Battle of the Bismark Sea, American and Australian aircraft systematically strafed Japanese survivors.[840] But these were isolated incidents in retaliation for Japanese atrocities, not a national policy. The following table illustrates the death rates.[841]

COUNTRY	No of POWs	No. of Deaths	Death Rate
AUSTRALIA	21,726	7,412	34.1%
UNITED STATES	21,580	7,107	32.9%
BRITAIN	50,016	12,433	24.8%
NEW ZEALAND	121	31	25.6%
HOLLAND	37,000	8,500	22.9%
CANADA	1,691	273	16.1%
TOTAL	132,134	35,756	27.1%

MacArthur interceded on behalf of Japanese Unit 731 personnel at Pingfan who experimented on the human bodies of POWs. He felt the war was over and the United States needed all the assistance possible with the advent of the Cold War with Russia. This intervention, and others, left not prosecuted many other atrocities by the Japanese including bacteriological warfare and actual medical experiments on POWs.[842]

By the time post war Japanese born children were in school in the 1960s, the Japanese version of the history of WWII changed drastically. Gone was the attack on Pearl Harbor, the Philippines, the atrocities at Nanking, etc. In place of the truth was a war instigated by the United States and ended by nuclear weapons. References to the truth soon disappeared from bookstores and libraries.[843] Historian Saburo Ienaga sued the Japanese Government for removing atrocities committed by the Japanese before and during WWII but only managed to have the stories of medical experiments in Manchuria placed back into the text. The Rape of Nanking and other atrocities remain removed from the textbooks.[844] There was no feeling of dishonor nor need for forgiveness on the part of Japan.[845]

During the 50th Anniversary celebrating the Allied victory over Japan in June 1995, Japan declared "deep remorse" for its wartime actions against the other countries of Asia. Not one word was said to the United States about beginning the war nor a single word for what Japan had done to the Allied POWs. The United States quickly had re-established normal conditions with Japan following the war possibly because of the threat by communism in Asia and the U.S. needed Japan's support and bases.[846] America paid Japanese-Americans $20,000 in repatriation for those interned during the war. The American POWs were paid $2.50 for each day of captivity through a Red Cross administered fund and told to expect no more. No effort was made by Japan to pay the prisoners nor did the United States make a strong effort to claim such right.[847] The refusal by Japan to apologize or offer repatriation was based on the Treaty of Peace signed on 8 September 1951. The treaty ended all war claims against Japan effective 31 March 1952 and permitted the Allies to seize Japanese assets to settle war claims.[848] Since that time, an effort began to force Japan to reimburse ex-POWs for their labor during the war by Japanese firms conducting business in the United States.

Finally, in the midst of great controversy over no apology during the 50th Anniversary of V-J Day, Prime Minister Tomiichi Murayama stood up and spoke like no other Japanese was willing to do in the past. He extended his "heartfelt apology" for atrocities his country committed in WWII. "In the hope that no such mistake be made in the future, I regard, in a spirit of humility, these irrefutable facts of history, and express here once again my feeling of deep remorse and state my heartfelt apology."[849]

HARM

APPENDIX A

U.S. ASIATIC FLEET 1 DECEMBER 1941

CRUISERS:
USS HOUSTON(CA-30)*
USS MARBLEHEAD (CL-12)
USS BOISE (CL-47)
USS BLACK HAWK (AD-9)
USS CHILDS (AVD-1)
USS HERON (AVP-2)

TENDERS:
USS HOLLAND (AS-3)
USS CANOPUS (AS-9)*
USS OTUS (AS-20)
USS LANGLEY (AV-3)*
USS W. B. PRESTON (AVD-7)

SUB RESCUE:
USS PIGEON (ASR-6)*

SUBMARINES:
USS S-36*
USS S-37
USS S-38
USS S-39*
USS S-40
USS S-41

USS SEADRAGON (SS-194)
USS SEALION ((SS-195)*
USS SEARAVEN (SS-196)
USS SEAWOLF (SS197)*
USS SNAPPER (SS-185)
USS STINGRAY (SS-186)
USS STURGEON (SS-187)
USS SCULPIN (SS-191)*
USS SAILFISH (SS-192)
USS SWORDFISH (SS-193)*
USS PORPOISE (SS-172)
USS PIKE (SS-173)
USS SHARK (SS-174)*
USS TARPON (SS-175)
USS PERCH (SS-176)*
USS PICKERAL (SS-177)*
USS PERMMIT (SS-178)
USS SALMON (SS-182)
USS SEAL (SS-183)
USS SKIPJACK (SS-184)
USS SARGO (SS-188)
USS SAURY (SS-189)
USS SPEARFISH (SS-190)

DESTROYERS:
USS JOHN D. EDWARDS (DD-216)
USS ALDEN (DD-211)
USS EDSALL (DD-219)*
USS BARKER (DD-213)
USS BULMER (DD-222)
USS POPE (DD-225)*
USS PILLSBURY (DD-227)*
USS PAUL JONES (DD-230)
USS WHIPPLE (DD-217)
USS STEWART (DD-224)*
USS PARROTT (DD-218)
USS JOHN D. FORD (DD-228)
USS PEARY (DD-226)*

PATRON:
PATRON 101 – 18 PBYs
PATRON 102 – 18 PBYs
UTRON – 10 Utility Aircraft

PT BOATS:
SIX MOTOR TORPEDO BOATS

GUNBOATS:
USS ASHEVILLE (PG-21)*
USS ISSABEL (PY-10)
USS LUZON (PR-7)*
USS NAPA (AT-32)*
USS TULSA (PG-22)
USS OAHU (PR-6)*
USS MINDANAO (PR-8)*
USS LANIKAI (yacht)

TANKERS:
USS PECOS (AO-6)*
USS TRINITY (A0-13)

MINECRAFT:
USS FINCH (AM-9)*
USS TANAGER (AM-5)*
USS LARK (AM-21)
USS BITTERN (AM-36)*
USS QUAIL (AM-15)*
USS WHIPPOORWILL (AM-35)
* indicates vessel sunk

HARM

BATAAN INDEX

20th Air Force 211
21st Division 24, 25, 44, 45, 46, 47, 75, 76, 78
21st Artillery 45
21st Pursuit Squadron 16
23rd Field Artillery 37
24th Artillery 53
26th Cavalry 35, 38, 43, 48, 58
26th Scouts 35, 49, 58, 61, 68, 69, 73, 78, 79
27tht Bombardment Group 17
31st Philippine Division 22, 32, 35, 53, 54, 59, 68, 78
31st Infantry Regiment 11, 22, 24, 32, 35-39, 42, 46-57, 60, 62-69, 72-82, 85, 88, 89, 93, 96
31st Airborne 216
32nd Airborne 71, 213
33rd Infantry 79
34th Pursuit Squadron 16, 62
41st Division 24, 35, 51, 53, 54, 63, 72, 78
41st Field Artillery Regiment 35, 64
42nd Infantry 75, 76
43rd Infantry 53, 75, 76
45th Infantry Scouts 22, 54, 55, 56, 63, 77, 79, 80
51st Division 24, 35, 53, 54, 57, 78
57th Infantry Scouts 22, 35, 50, 51, 56, 70, 77-80, 92
60th Coast Artillery 61
68th AACS 233
71st Division 24, 32, 35, 37, 39, 46, 47, 48
72nd Infantry Regiment 37, 48, 60
88th Artillery Battery 37
91st Division 24, 35, 60, 61
92nd Artillery 60
93rd Bombardment Squadron 107
144th Field Infantry 12
192nd Tank Battalion 12, 14, 21, 32, 39-49, 69, 101, 164, 204
194th Tank Battalion 12-14, 17, 19, 22, 23, 30-33, 38-48, 50, 53, 54, 59-68, 70, 72, 77, 78, 84, 87, 88, 95, 101, 204, 205

200th Coastal Artillery 41
200th Anti-Aircraft Regiment 90
200th California 13
494th Bomber Squadron 221
515th Anti-Aircraft Regiment 90
547th Night Fighters Group 214
Army Engineers 41, 73
AIB 112, 129, 138
Cast Unit 52, 67
Far East Air Forces 15, 18
I Corps 35, 53, 58-63, 69, 70 78, 79, 80, 84
II Corps 35, 53, 58-63, 70, 75, 78, 82
Chaplain Corps 32, 33, 83, 97, 104, 106, 143, 147, 149, 156, 172, 190, 191
CinCPacFlt 3, 5, 35, 36, 132, 224
ComSubPac 15, 133, 144,
Ferry LEGASPI 71
GRIPSHOLM 159, 180
Dewey Drydock 80
HOSPITAL #1 33, 40, 69, 78, 86, 88, 89, 205
HOSPITAL #2 40, 78, 89, 92, 205
HMAS PERTH 70, 132, 152
HMS CHIVALRY 166
HMCS SAN JOSE 13
HMSDUKE OF YORK 234
HMS ENCOUNTER 166, 167
HMS EXETER 159, 166, 167, 174, 185
HMS INDOMITABLE 4
HMS PETREL 205
HMS PORPOISE 129
HMS PRINCE OF WALES 4
HMS REPULSE 4
HMS SEA ROVER 170
HMS STATESMAN 179
HMS TALLY HO 176

Robert K. Harmuth

USS INDIANAPOLIS 218
USS INTREPID 129, 137
USS IOWA 233
USS ISABEL 7
USS JACK 178, 184, 185
USS KETE 177
USS KINGFISH 177
USS LANSDOWNE 235
USS LAPON 184
USS LEXINGTON 129
USS LUZON 23
USS MACTAN 133
USS MANAPALA 82
USNS MAUNA LOA 70
USNS MEIGS 70
USS MINDANAO 23, 78
USS MISSOURI 233, 234
USS NARWHAL 129, 142, 151, 177, 209
USS NASHVILLE 208
USS NAUTILUS 129, 157, 185, 209
USS NEW JERSEY 234
USS NEW YORK 234
USS NICOLAS 233
USS OAHU 23, 78
USS PADDLE 142, 150, 177, 178
USS PAMPANITO 151, 167, 175
USS PARCHE 181
USS PANAY 2
USS PARGO 160, 176
USS PEARY 29
USS PENQUIN 23
USS PERCH 3, 44, 68, 135, 159, 166, 174, 184, 206, 225
USS PERMIT 3, 24
USS PERRY 105
USS PICKERAL 3

HARM

HARM

AMBON 161, 167, 169, 170, 171, 179, 180, 183, 186

HARM

HARM

ROBERT K. HARMUTH

HARM

HARM

LITTLE BAGIO 41, 69, 85

LIM, GENERAL 53

LINGAYEN GULF 8, 14, 18, 19, 24, 25, 29, 31-33, 35, 39, 48, 52, 155, 160, 212, 213

LIITLE BOY 219

LITTLE, LIEUTENANT 197, 229

LOCKWOOD, ADMIRAL 159

LONGOSKAWAYAN PT 62, 69

LORD NORTH 1

LOS BANOS 43, 216

LOUGH, GENERAL 74, 77

LUBAO 42, 98

LUZON 12, 16-18, 20, 23-26, 28, 31, 37, 39, 57, 58, 67, 71, 92, 102, 110, 112, 113, 122, 129, 132-142, 152, 153, 167, 172, 189, 200, 202, 209, 213

MABATANG 34, 51

MACARTHUR, DOUGLAS 2-8, 12, 13, 15, 17, 18, 20, 24-26, 40, 44, 45, 47, 53, 63, 66, 69, 75, 76, 78, 101, 112, 139, 158, 206-209, 214, 216, 218, 235, 235, 236, 240, 241

MADAME SAVORY'S 17

MAKASAR 44, 135, 159, 161, 167-171, 173, 175, 176, 179, 184

MAIN LINE OF DEFENSE 34, 35, 37, 38, 46, 50, 53, 162

MAKAILI 208

MAITLAND, COLONEL 14

MALAYA 68, 82, 83, 127, 128, 132, 133, 164, 167, 200

MALACCA STRAIT 165, 182

MAMALA RIVER 79

MANCHURIA 2, 128, 147, 159, 165, 175, 182, 197, 210, 211, 225, 230, 240

MANDATED ISLANDS 1

MANILA 1, 3, 4, 6, 8, 11, 13-17, 19, 21-23, 26, 29-34, 40, 41, 43, 44, 58, 68, 69, 71, 73, 88, 89, 99-101, 103, 111, 113-115, 117, 122-126, 129, 130, 138-140, 142, 143, 145, 149, 151, 152, 158, 159-185, 189, 190, 203, 205, 208-211, 213, 216

MANITOWAC, WI 25

HARM

ROBERT K. HARMUTH

I-37 166
I-173 25
ICHI MARU 166
IKOMA MARU 166
INAZUMA 167
INTER-ISLAND STEAMER 166
ISLA PRINCESA 166
JU MARU 166
JUNYO MARU 166
KACHI MARU 167
KACHIDOKI MARU 151, 167, 175, 176
KAGA 7
KAIBOKAN HIRATO 175
KAISHUN MARU 167
KAKKO MARU 167
KALGAN MARU 167
KAMAKURA MARU 167
KENKON MARU 168
KENZAN MARU 168
KENWA MARU 168
KIBITSU MARU 168
KING KONG MARU 168, 171
KINSEN MARU 181
KOKUSEI MARU 168
KORYU MARU 169
KOSHU MARU 169
KU MARU 169
KUNITAMA MARU 170
KUNISHIMA 169
KURIMATA MARU 169
KYOKKO MARU 170
KYOKUEI MARU 170
LIMA MARU 170
LISBON MARU 170, 177
MARU #760 170

HARM

RIO DE JANIERO MARU 176
RO-112 211
RO-113 211
RO-115 211
ROKKO MARU 176
ROKO MARU 176
ROKYO MARU 176
RYUKYU MARU 176
SAMUNUSAN MARU 176
SAN MARU 176
SANDAKAN MARU 176
SANKA MARU 140, 177
SEIKO MARU 177
SHI MARU 177
SHICHI MARU 177
SHIKINAMI 151, 167, 175
SHINANO 152
SHININSEI 170
SHINIYO MARU 177
SHINSEI MARU 170, 177, 183
SHINYO MARY 142, 150, 177, 209, 211
SHOKAKU 207
SHOKKA 7
SHOZAN MARU 178
SIBERIA MARU 178, 182
SIBJAC MARU 178
SINGAPORE MARU 178
SINGOTO MARU 162, 178
SMALL STEAMER 178
SONG GIANG MARU 178
SORYU 7
STINKO MARU 117
SUBAH MARU 178
SUEZ MARU 179
SUUGI MARU 179

HARM

TACHIBANA MARU 179
TACHIBANA 179
TAGA MARU 179
TAIHO 207
TAIJUN MARU 168
TAIKKO MARU 179
TAIKOKU MARU 179
TAKA MARU 179
TAKAO 190
TAMAGAWA MARU 52
TAMAHOKO MARU 171, 179
TANGO MARU 180
TATSUTA MARU 180
TATTORI MARU 180
TATURA MARU 181
TEIA MARU 6, 180
THAMES MARU 181
TIESEN MARU 181
TOBA MARU 181, 182
TOGO MARU 181
TOKU MARU 181
TOMOHUKO MARU 181, 183
TONE MARU 181
TORO MARU 181
TOTTORI MARU 128, 140, 178, 180, 182
TOYAMA MARU 182
TOYOFUKU MARU 160, 163, 166, 182
TOYOHASHI MARU 182
TRADING VESSEL 182
UME MARU 183
UMEDA MARU 140, 183
UNKNOWN MARU 181, 183
UNYO 184
URPPU MARU 184
USHIO MARU 184

HARM

HARM

ROBERT K. HARMUTH

HARM

HARM

BIBLIOGRAPHY FOR "BATTLIN' BASTARDS AND PIGBOATS

Abraham, Abie, *OH, GOD, WHERE ARE YOU?*, Vantage Press, New York, 1997.

A&E Television Biography Video tape, "General Douglass MacArthur,"New York, 1995.

Agawa, Hiroyuki, *THE RELUCTANT ADMIRAL*, Kodansha International Ltd., Tokyo, 1969.

Albertson, Norm, ex-POW from USS GRENADIER, personal interview.

Agramalian, George S., letter to editor, "Star Newspaper, " 6 August 1995, Ventura, CA.

Alden, John D., *U.S. SUBMARINE ATTACKS DURING WORLD WAR II*, Naval Institute
Press, Annapolis, 1989.

Alden, John D., Cdr, USN (Ret), "The Hell Ship of Convoy MATA-30 U.S. POWs and U.S. Submarines," The Submarine Review, Annandale, VA October 1999 issue.

Alden, Commander John D., USN (Ret), *UNITED STATES AND ALLIED SUBMARINE SUCCESSES IN THE PACIFIC AND FAR EAST DURING WORLD WAR II*, Self Published, Pleasantville, NY 1999.

Alexander, Colonel Irvin, *SURVIVING BATAAN AND BEYOND*, Stackpole Books, Mechanixsburg, PA, 1999.

Allen, Thomas B., and Polmar, Norman, "Invasion Most Costly," U.S. Naval Institute Proceedings, August, 1994.

Armed Forces Radio Video, "Bataan Death March," sixty-minute length.

American Defenders of Bataan and Corregidor, Inc, "The QUAN." Warren, Indiana, multiple issues.

AP, Hiroshima, Japan, "The Star," newspaper, 7 August 1999, "Hiroshima recalls deadly bombing," (would have used the bomb against the United States)

Armstrong, Raymond Paul, *SAN HYAKU GO (305)*, ACO Publishing, Eugene, OR 1992.

Arthur, Anthony, *DELIVERANCE AT LOS BANOS*, St Martins Press, New York, 1985.

Asahi Shimbun Staff, *THE PACIFIC RIVALS*, Weatherhill/Asahi, Nerw York & Tokyo, 1972.

Ashton, Captain Paul L., *BATAAN DIARY*, 1984, Library of Congress ID #85-192945.

Ashton, Captain Paul L., *AND SOMEBODY GIVES A DAMN!*, Ashton Publications, Santa Barbara, CA. 1993.

Ashton, Captain Paul L, conversation during Ex-POWs Annual Convention, Santa Barbara, CA 1996.

Asor, Gerald, *CRISIS IN THE PACIFIC*, Penquin Books, New York, 1995.

Associated Press release from Tokyo, "Details Given of Japan Quest for Atomic Bomb," 30 August 1997.

Associated Press release from Hiroshima, "First Word on Bombing: Tales of City of the Dead," 6 Aug 95.

Associated Press, Oxnard Star, Eric Talmadge, "Hiroshima: 50 Years Later," 6 August 1995.

Associated Press release from Tokyo, "Japanese Court Rules History of Atrocities Be Told," 30 August 97.

Associated Press release from Tokyo, "Japanese Leader Offers Apology," 15 August 1995.

Bacque, James, *OTHER LOSSES*, General Paperbacks, Toronto, 1991.

Baedekers's, *JAPAN*, Prentice Hall, Inc., Englewood Cliffs, NJ.

HARM

Bagnasco, Erminio, *SUBMARINES OF WORLD WAR TWO*, Arms and Armour Press, Lionel Leventhal Limited, London, 1977.

Bain, David Howard, *SITTING IN DARKNESS, AMERICANS IN THE PHILIPPINES*, Houghton Mifflin Company, Boston, 1984.

Baker, Lillian, author, (310) 329-2619, 5237 Chanera Ave, Gardena, CA 90249-4042.

Baker, Russell, "A Rewriting of War History, " The New York Times, 6 August 1995.

Barnow, Ben, crew member USS FLOUNDER when she sunk U-538, telcon 21 October 1997.

Bataan Veterans Organization, *FORTY-NINE DAYS IN HELL*, American Ex-Prisoners of War, Inc., Bellevue, Washington.

Beach, Edward Latime, *HISTORY OF THE U.S. NAVY*, Holt Publishing, New York, 1986.

Beach, Edward L., *SUBMARINE*, The New American Library, New York, NY 1946.

Beach, Edward L., *DUST ON THE SEA*, Holt, Rinehart a Winston, New York, 1972.

Beckstrom, Maja, Staff Writer, Oxnard Star, "Questions on the Landscape, " 5 August 1995.

Belote, James H. and William M., *CORREGIDOR, THE SAGA OF A FORTRESS*, Harper and Row, New York, 1967.

Bergamini, David, *JAPAN'S IMPERIAL CONSPIRACY*, Morrow, New York, 1971.

Bergerud, Eric, *TOUCHED WITH FIRE*, Penguin Books, New York, 1996.

Berry, Glenneth B., ex-POW, 1687 S. Wheeling Circle, Aurora, CO, 80012, (303) 750-9463. 14th Heavy Bomber Squadron, numerous letters and telephone conversations.

Berry, Glenneth B., ex-POW, speaker at Rangeview High School video, May 1995.

Blair, Clay Jr., *SILENT VICTORY, THE U.S. SUBMARINE WAR AGAINST JAPAN*, J.B. Lippincott Company, Philladelphia and New York, 1975.

Blair, Joan and Clay Jr., *RETURN FROM THE RIVER KWAI*, Simon and Schuster, New York, 1979.

Bloomfield, Gary L., "You Will All Die, By Order of the Emperor," VFW Magazine, September 1995, Kansas City, KS.

Boisclaire, Yvonne, *IN THE SHADOW OF THE RISING SUN*, Clearwood Publishers, Bella Vista, CA, 1997.

Bolen, Jeannie, *G-2 CONNECTION*, as told by G. T. Saldana, Saldana, Redlands, CA 1987.

Boyd, Carl, *HITLER'S JAPANESE CONFIDANT*, University of Kansas Press, 1993.

Boyington, Colonel Gregory "Pappy," USMC, *BAA BAA BLACK SHEEP*, G.P. Putnam's Sons, New York, 1958.

Bramley, Clarence, 21st Pursuit squadron, Bataan Death March, 1506 W. 247th Street, Harbor City, CA 90710, (310) 326-1313.

Breuer, William B., *RETAKING THE PHILIPPINES, AMERICA'S RETURN*, Saint Martin's Press, New York, 1968.

Breuer, William B., *THE GREAT RAID ON CABANATUAN*, John Wiley & Sons, Inc., Singapore, 1994.

Breuer, William B., *MACARTHUR'S UNDERCOVER WAR*, John Wiley & Sons, Inc., New York, 1995.

Breuer, William B., *DEVIL BOATS*, Presidio Press, Novato, CA, 1987.

Brooks, Lester, *BEHIND JAPAN'S SURRENDER*, McGraw-Hill Book Company, New York, 1968.

Brown, Josepth Rust, *WE STOLE TO LIVE*, Missourian Litho & Printing Co., Cape Girardeau, MS, 1982.

Buchner, Edward, Associated Press, "The Star," 28 May 2000.

Buell, Thomas, B., *THE QUIET WARRIOR*, Naval Institute Press, Annapolis, MD, 1974.

Bumgardner, John R., MD, *PARADE OF THE DEAD*, McFarland & Co., Inc., Jefferson, NC, 1995.

Butow, Robert J. C., *TOJO AND THE COMING OF THE WAR*, Stanford University Press, Stanford, 1961.

HARM

Bye, William, Wbye@aol.com, nephew of Captain Ernest Bye, Bataan Death March Survivor.

Byrd, Martha, *A WORLD IN FLAME*, Smithmarki Publishers, Inc., New york, 1969.

Casey, Robert J., *BATTLE BELOW*, The Bobbs-Merrill Company, Indianapolis, 1945

Cavendish, Marshall, *WAR DIARY 1939-1945*, Chartwell Books, Inc., Seccaucus, NJ, 1995.

Cervone, John P., "Remembering the Bataan Death March," Military History Magazine, Leesburg, VA, December 1999 Issue.

Chang, Iris, *THE RAPE OF NANKING*, Penguin Putnam Inc., New York, 1997.

Clark, Hugh V., *LAST STOP NAGASAKI*, George Allen & Unwin, London & Sidney, 1984.

Clarke, Robin, *THE SILENT WEAPONS*, David McKay Company, Inc., New York, 1968.

Coffee, Thomas M., *IMPERIAL TRAGEDY*, The World Publishing Company, New York, 1970.

Colan, Captain Vincent J., USNR Retired, "Admiral Kimmel, The Pearl Harbor Scapegoat," Military Magazine, December 1998.

Cole, Captain Bernard D., USN Ret, "The Real Sand Pebbles," "Military History Magazine, USNI, Leesburg, VA February 2000 issue.

Committee for the Compilation of Materials on Damage Caused by the Atomic Bombs . . . , *HIROSHIMA AND NAGASAKI*, Basic Books, Inc., New York, 1981.

Conlin, Captain Cater B., "USS HOUSTON (CA-30) – Pride of the Asiatic Fleet," Shipmate Magazine, Annapolis, Md, March 1996.

Conner, Claudde C., *NOTHING FRIENDLY IN THE VICINITY,*

Conway Maritime Press Ltd., *CONWAY'S ALL THE WORLDS FIGHTING SHIPS 1922-1946*, Mayflower Books, New York, 1980.

Cook, Alvin, *JAPAN, THE FINAL AGONY*, Ballantine Books, New York, 1970.

Costello, Johm, *THE PACIFIC WAR*, Rawson, Wade Publishers, Inc., New York, 1981.

Cox, Gordon C., "P.O.W. Ships," QUAN, #48-5, April 1994.

Craig, William, *THE FALL OF JAPAN*, The Dial Press, New York, 1967.

Cutler, Thomas J., *THE BATTLE OF LEYTE*, Pocket Books, New York, 1994. Savas Publishing Company, Masonn City, IA, 1999.

Darsey, Bernardo J., "Hellfire on Corregidor," Sunday Times Magazine, 9 April 1967, Manila, PI.

Davenport, RADM Roy M., USN (Ret), *CLEAN SWEEP*, Vantage Press, New York, 1986.

Davis, Kenneth S., *EXPERIENCE OF WAR*, Doubleday & Company, Inc., Garden City, NY, 1965.

Daws, Gavan, *PRISONERS OF THE JAPANESE OF WWII IN THE PACIFIC*, Willliam Morrow and Co., New York, 1994.

Daws, Gavan, "Forgotten Infamy," People Magazine, 21 August 1995, pg 84, New York.

Dempster, Prue, *JAPAN ADVANCES*, Methuen & Company, Ltd, London, 1967.

Dietrick, William S., *IN THE SHADOW OF THE RISING SUN*, Pennsylvania State University Press, University Park, PA, 1991.

Doherty, George, 511th Parachute Infantry, "The 11th Airborne Occupies Japan," Millitary Magazine, Vol XII, No. 3, Sacramento, CA.

Dorsey, CDR D.R., CEC, USNR, "South from Cavite," CEC Bulletin, parts 1-5, 1951.

Dower, John, W., *WAR WITHOUT MERCY*, Pantheon Books, New York, 1986.

Dreher, Alfred B., log of his time on board the TAMAHHOKU MARU and TOTTORIE MARU as a POW, 3700 Harbel Drive, Bremerton, WA 98310-4728.

Dunninigan, James F. and Nofi,, Albert A., *VICTORY AT SEA, WORLD WAR II IN THE PACIFIC*, William Morrow and Co., New York, 1995.

HARM

Dull, Paul S., *A BATTLE HISTORY OF THE IMPERIAL JAPA-NESE NAVY (1941-1945)*, Naval Institute Press, Annapolis, 1978.

Duus, Masayo, *TOKYO ROSE, ORPHAN OF THE PACIFIC*, Kodansha International, Ltd., Tokyo, 1979.

Elson, Robert T., *PRELUDE TO WAR: WORLD WAR II*, Time-Life Books, Alexandria, 1976.

Emplos, Sheldon, ex-POW and Bataan Death March survivor, interview upon the occasion of receiving his Purple Heart, 12 July 1997.

Endicott, William P., "The Great Silver Odyssey," "World War II Magazine," July 2000.

Eneriz, Manuel A., Star Free Press ltrs, 1995 through 1999.

Eneriz, Mannuel A., numerous personal interviews, 1995 through 2000.

EX-POW Bulletin, "Japanese Order Posted in POW Camps 1944," submitted by AXPOW Department of the Commonwealth of Virginia, Vol 52, August 1995, No. 8.

Falk, Richard A., Kolko, Gabriel, and Lifton, Robert J., *CRIMES OF WAR*, Random House, NY, 1971.

Falk, Stanley L., *BATAAN: THE MARCH OF DEATH*, W.W. Norton & Co., New York, 1962.

Feinsilber, Mike, "Reasons for Nagasaki Bombing Less Clear-cut than Hiroshima," Associated Press, 9 August 1995.

Feis, Herbert, *JAPAN SUBDUED*, The Atomic Bomb and the End of the War in the Pacific, Princeton University Press, Princeton, NJ, 1961.

Fentiman, Sandra, *THE WORLD AT WAR, 50 YEARS LATER*, Turner Publishing, Paducah, KT, 1997.

Ferguson, John (Jack), wife lived in Luzon during the Death March, interviews, 1119 Barbara St, St #2, Redondo Beach, CA 90277.

Ferrell, Robert H., *OFF THE RECORD*, Harper and Row, New York, 1980.

Feuer, A. B., "USS GROWLER's War Against Japan," World War II Magazine, Leesburg,, VA February 1998.

Fisher, Edward, President of the Bataan Death March Association, 1942 Desert Circle #3, Walnut Creek, CA 94598.

Fitzsimons, Bernard, *WEAPONS AND WARFARE*, Phoebus Publishing Company, London, 1967.

Flanagan, LTGEN E.M., *THE LOS BANOS RAID*, Presidio Press, Novato, CA, 1986.

Flanagan, LTGEN E.M., *CORREGIDOR, THE ROCK FORCE ASSAULT*, Presidio Press, Novato, CA 1995.

Fodor's *JAPAN GUIDEBOOK*, Fodor's Travel Publications, New York and London, 1991.

Forty, George, *A PHOTO HISTORY OF TANKS IN THE TWO WORLD WARS*, Blandford Press and Dorset Poole, New York, 1984.

Frances, Charles A, POW on the CANADIAN INVENTOR, QUAN Magazine Issue #53, March 1999.

Frank, Richard B., *DOWNFALL*, Random House, New York, 1999.

Freeman, Otis W., *GEOGRAPHY OF THE PACIFIC*, John Wiley & Sons, Inc., New York, 1951.

Friedman, George and Leband, Meredith, *THE COMING WAR WITH JAPAN*, Saint Martin's Press, New York, 1991.

Fry, SSGT, Attn: SACC-PA, 1213 Jefferson Davis Highway, Arlington, VA 20202,, DOD 50th Anniversary of WWII.

Gailey, Harry A., *THE WAR IN THE PACIFIC*, Presidio Press, Novato, CA, 1995.

Gautier, SGT James Donovan, Jr., *I CAME BACK FROM BATAAN*, EMERALD HOUSE Group, Inc, Blue Ridge Publishing, Greenville, SC 1997.

Germinsky, Bob, POFC, USNR, "Mighty Mo, USS MISSOURI," Military Magazine,, Vol XII, No. 3, Sacramento, CA.

Giles, RADM Donald T, Jr., *CAPTIVE OF THE RISING SUN*, Naval Institute Press,, Annapolis, 1994.

Gluck, Jay and Suni and Garret, *JAPAN INSIDE OUT*, Personally Oriented, Ltd., Ashiya, Japan, 1964.

Goldstein, Donald M., Dillon, Katherine V., and Wenger, J. Michael. *RAIN OF RUIN*, Brassey's, Washington, 1995.

HARM

Goldstein, Donald M. and Dillon, Kathrine V., *THE PEARL HARBOR PAPERS*, Brassey's, Washington, 1993.

Goldstein, Donald M and Wenger, J. Michael, *THE WAY IT WAS, PEARL HARBOR*, Brassey's, Washington, 1991.

Goebbell, John J., *THE LAST LIEUTENANT*, St Martin's Paperbacks, New York, 1995.

Goodenough, Simon, *WAR MAPS*, St. Martin's Press, New York, 1982.

Grady, Frank J. and Dickson, Rebecca, *SURVIVING THE DAY*, Naval Institute Press, Annapolis, 1997.

Grashio, Samuel C. and Norling, Bernard, *RETURN TO FREEDOM*, University Press, Spokane, 1982.

Graef, Calvin, MSGT, USA, "Transcription of Tapes, survived Arisan Maru sinking.

Grattan, C. Hartley, *THE SOUTHWEST PACIFIC SINCE 1900*, Unniversity of Michigan, Ann Arbor, 1963.

Gunnison, Royal Arch, *SO SORRY, NO PEACE*, The Viking Press, New York, 1944.

Hane, Mikiso, *MODERN JAPAN, A HISTORICAL SURVEY*, Westview Press, Inc., Boulder, CO, 1992.

Harper, Peter and Peplow, Evelyn, *PHILIPPINE HANDBOOK* Moon Publications, Chico, CA 1991.

Harris, Robert and Paxman, Jeremy, *A HIGHER FORM OF KILLING*, Hill and Wang, The Noonday Press, New York, 1982.

Harris, Sheldon H., *FACTORIES OF DEATH, JAPANESE BIOLOGICAL WARFARE, 1932-45 AND THE AMERICAN COVERUP*, Rutledge, London and New York, 1994.

Henshall, Philip, *VENGEANCE, HITLER'S NUCLEAR WEAPON FACT OR FICTION*, Alan Sutton Publishing Limited, Phoenix Mill, 1995.

Hersey, John, *HIROSHIMA*, New York:Alferd A. Knopf, 1969.

Hewlett, Thomas H., MD COL, USA, "Di Ju Bunshyo-Nightmare-Revisited," The Japanese Story, AXPOW Packet #10, Ex-POWs of America.

Hibbs, Ralph Emerson, MD, *TELL MACARTHUR TO WAIT*, A Heathstone Book, Carlton Press, Inc., New York, 1988.

History Channel, "Secrets of World War II," confirming US submarines sinking Japanese cargo including parts for jet aircraft and atomic bombs, 6/14/99.

History Channel, "Deadly Crossing," the sinking of RAYOKU MARU and KACHIDOKI MARU, 6/13/99.

Holmes, W.J., *DOUBLE-EDGED SECRETS, US INTELLIGENCE PACIFIC WWII*, Naval Institute Press, Annapolis, 1979.

Holmes, W.J. *UNDERSEA VICTORY, THE INFLUENCE OF SUBMARINE OPERATIONS*, Doubleday & Company, New York, 1966.

Holmes, W. J., *THE TIDE TURNS*, Zebra Books, Kensington Publishing Corp., New York, 1966.

Honan, William H., *VISIONS OF INFAMY*, Saint Martin's Press, New York, 1991.

Hashimoto, Mochitsura, *SUNK*, Avon Publications, Inc., New York, 1954.

Houser, VADM W.D., "While MacArthur Slept," Naval History Magazine, October 1997, Annapolis.

Hoyt, Edwin P., *JAPAN'S WAR, THE GREAT PACIFIC CONFLICT*, McGraw-Hill Book Company, New York, 1986.

Hoyt, Edwin P., *THE LONELY SHIPS, THE LIFE AND DEATH OF THE US ASIATIC FLEET*, David McKay Company, Inc., New York, 1976.

Hoyt, Edwin P., *SUBMARINES AT WAR*, Stein and Day Publishers, New York, 1983.

Hoyt, Edwin P., *CLOSING THE CIRCLE*, Van Nostrand Reinhold Co., New York, 1982.

Huff, Dorothy A. (Riffen), a POW as a young girls at Los Banos, telcon (805) 498-3391.

Icenhower, RADM Joseph B., *SUBMARINES IN COMBAT*, Franklin Watts, Inc., New York, 1964.

Idlett, George D., "Sukoshi Matte," Ex-POW Bulletin, Vol 52, No.8.

HARM

Ienaga, Saburo, *THE PACIFIC WAR 1931-1945*, Pantheon Books, New York, 1978.

Ito, Masanori, *THE END OF THE IMPERIAL NAVY*, MacFadden-Bartell Book, New York, 1965.

Jacobs, Eugene B., COL, MC, USA, "Three Decades Later: Residuals of Japanese Prisoners of war," Forum on Medicine, Vol 1, No. 6, September 1978.

Jane's *FIGHTING SHIPS 1950-1951*, Arco Publishing, New York, 1951.

Jane's *FIGHTING SHIPS OF WORLD WAR II*, Cresent Books, New York, 1994.

Jane's *ENCYCLOPEDIA OF AVIATION*, Cresent Books, New York, 1989.

Jentschura, Hansgeorg, Jung, Dieter and Mickel, Peter, *WARSHIPS OF THE IMPERIAL JAPANESE NAVY 1860-1945*, Naval Institute Press, Annapolis, 1970.

Joint Army-Navy Assessment Committee, NAVEXOS P-468, *JAPANESE NAVAL AND MERCHANT SHIPPING LOSSES DURING WORLD WAR II BY ALL CAUSES*, U.S. Governemnt Printing Office, Washington, DC, February 1947.

Karig, Captain Walter, USNR; Manson, Lcdr Frank A., USN, Harris, Lcdr Russel L., USNR, *BATTLE REPORT, VICTORY IN THE PACIFIC*, Rinehart and Company, Inc., New York, 1949.

Kase, Toshikaze, *JOURNEY TO THE MISSOURI*, Yale University Press, New Haven, CT, 1950.

Kato, Masuo, *THE LOST WAR*, Alfred A. Knoph, New York, 1946.

Kawasaki, Ichiro, *JAPAN UNMASKED*, Charles E. Tuttle Co, Rutland, VT and Tokyo, 1969.

Keating, Bern, *THE MOSQUITO FLEET*, G. P. Putnam's Sons Company, New York, 1963.

Keats, John, *THEY FOUGHT ALONE*, J.B. Lippincott Company, Philalphia & New York, 1963.

Kerr, E. Bartlett, *FLAMES OVER TOKYO, 1944-1945*, Donald I. Fine, New York, 1991.

Kerr, E. Bartlett, *SURRENDER AND SURVIVAL*, William Morrow & Co. Inc., New York, 1985.

Kerr, George M., *FORMOSA BETRAYED*, Houghton Mifflin Company, Boston, 1965.

King, Fleet Admiral Ernest J., USN, *FLEET ADMIRAL KING*, W.W. Norton & Co, New York, 1952.

Kizirian, Ted, Fresno, California, 1982 with undated UPI report reprinted on July 1996 issue of the WWII Submarine Veterans Newsletter.

Kleen, Bill, "From Cornfields to Killing Fields," Military History Magazine, August 1997 issue.

Knox, Donald, *DEATH MARCH, THE SURVIVORS OF BATAAN*, Harcourt Brace Jovanovich Publishers,, New York.

Kodama, Yoshio, *I WAS DEFEATED*, An Asian Publication, Japan, 1951.

Kolb, Richard K., "World War II Didn't End in 1945," "VFW Magazine," Kansas City, Mo, December 1995.

Kvalheim, Val, "Lisbon Maru Survivors Meet," "Polaris Magazine," Waterloo, SC, December 1998.

La Fortte, Robert S., Marcello, Ronald E., Himmel, Richard L., *WITH ONLY THE WILL TO LIVE*, Scholarly Resources Books, Wilmington, DE, 1994.

Lanigan, Richard, *KANGAROO EXPRESS*, RJL Express Publications, Laurel, FL 1998.

Landreth, William, numerous telcons.

Lawton, Manny, *SOME SURVIVED*, Algonquin Books of Chapel Hill, Chapel Hill, 1984.

Layton, RADM Edwin T., *AND I WAS THERE*, William Morrow and Company, New York, 1985.

Leary, William M., *WE SHALLL RETURN*, University Press of Kentucky, 1988.

Leckie, Robert, *STRONG MEN ARMED*, Bonanaza Books, New York, 1962.

Lewis, Claude, "The Day That Ended The War," Philadelphia Inquirer, 6 August 1995.

Light, Jeanne A., "WWII Prisoner Remembers Three and a Half Year Capture," Press Release, Department of the Navy, NAVFAC, WESTDIV, Pearl Harbor, HI, 96860-7300, 27 August 1986.

Lipe, Frances Worthington, "Food Rations of the Japanese Prisoners of War, WWII During Combat and captivity," The Japanese Story.

Lockwood, VADM Charles A., *SINK 'EM ALL*, E.P. Dutton & Company, New York, 1951.

Lomax, Eric, *THE RAILWAY MAN*, W. W. Norton & Company, New York, 1995.

Long, Gavin, *MACARTHUR, HIS LIFE AND BATTLES*, Combined Publishing, PA, 1969.

Lowder, Hughston, E., *THE SILENT SERVICE*, Silent Service Books, Baltimore, 1987.

Lowe, Karl H., "American Polar Bears, Defense of Vladivostok," "Military History Magazine," Leesburg, VA, October 1997.

Lundstrom, John B., *THE FIRST SOUTH PACIFIC CAMPAIGN*, Naval Institute Press, Annapolis, 1976.

Lynn, Robert A., "Marutas, Japan's Auschwitz, " "VFW Magazine," Kansas City, MO, September 1995.

Machi, Mario, *UNDER THE RISING SUN*, Wolfenden, Miranda, CA, 1994.

M.E.H., Editorial about USS BATFISH (SS-310), "World war II, Leesburg, VA January 1997.

Mallonee II, Richard C., *THE NAKED FLAGPOLE, BATTLE FOR BATAAN*, Presidei Press, San Rafael, CA 1980.

Manchester, William, *GOODBYE DARKNESS*, Little, Brown and Company, Boston, 1979.

Manchester, William Raymond, *AMERICAN CAESAR, DOUGLAS MACARTHUR*, Little & Brown, Boston, 1978.

Mann, David, "Command Clash on Bataan," "Military Magazine," Sacramento, February 1999.

Manning, Paul, *HIROHITO, THE WAR YEARS*, Dodd, Mead and Company, New Yoork, 1986.

Mansfield, John G. Jr., *CRUISERS FOR BREAKFAST*, Media Center Publishing, Tacoma, WA 1997.

Marshall, Chester W., and Thompson, Warren, *FINAL ASSAULT*, Combat Diaries of B-29 Air Crews over Japan, Specialty Press Publishers, North Branch, MN, 1995.

Martin, Adrian R., *BROTHERS FROM BATAAN*, Sunflower University Press, Manhattan, KS, 1992.

Martin, Ralph G., *THE GI WAR 1941-1945*, Avon Books, New York, 1967.

Mason, Herbert M. Jr., "Wartime Amnesia in Japan, " "VFW Magazine," Kansas City, KS, Sept 1995.

Masinick, J. Bud, Sec/Treas Michigan Chapter, US Submarine Veterans, ltr dtd 4 November 1997.

Matson, Eva Jane, *HEROES OF BATAAN, CORREGIDOR AND NORTHERN LUZON*, Yucca Tree Press, Las Cruces, NM 1989.

McCarthy, John C., "Pearl Harbor Epilogue," Naval Affairs, Vol #74, No. 9, Alexandria, VA.

McCullough, David, *THE PATH BETWEEN THE SEAS*, Simon and Schusterm New York, 1977.

McKay, David, "1st Black POW Downplays Ordeal," Detroit Free Press, November, 1995. Member of SALMON Crew alongside USS CANOPUS.

Mellnik, Stephen M., *PHILIPPINE WAR DIARY 1939-1945*, Van Nostrand Reinhold, New York, 1981.

Messer, Dr. Eugene, 2020 Ivanhoe, Oxnard, CA 93030, medical advice.

Michel, John J. A. , *MR. MICHEL'S WAR*, Presideo Press, Novato, CA 1998.

Michno, Gregory, letter dated 5 June 1999, list of hellships.

Middleton, Drew, *SUBMARINE, THE ULTIMATE NAVAL WEAPON*, Playboy Press , Chicago, 1976.

Miller, COL Ernest B., *BATAAN UNCENSORED*, Military Historical Society of Minnesita, 1991.

Miller, Nathan, *WAR AT SEA*, Scribner, New York, 1995.

Moody, Samuel B. and Maury Allen, *REPRIEVE FROM HELL*, Germany and Orlando, 1961.

Mooney, John, "Memories of the Day of Infamy," "Naval Affairs Magazine," December 1995, Vol 74, No. 12, Alexandria, VA.

Morison, Samuel Eloit, *THE LIBERATION OF THE PHILIPPINES, LUZON, MINDANAO, THE VISAYAS, 1944-1945*, Little, Brown and Company, Boston, 1975.

Mosley, Leonard, *HIROHITO, EMPREROR OF JAPAN*, Prentice-Hall, Inc., New Jersey, 1966.

Mulligan, Timothy P., *NEITHER SHARKS NOR WOLVES*, Naval Institute Press, Annapolis, 1999.

Nagal, Takashi, *THE BELLS OF NAGASAKI*, Kodansha Internation, Tokyo and New York, 1949.

"National Geographic Magazine," Vol. 188, No. 2, August 1995, "Hiroshima," page 78.

National Historical Center, "LTJG George Bush, USNR," http://www.history.navy.mil, 3 March 1998; and "U.S. Navy and Marine Corps Casualties inn World War II."

National Imagery and Mapping Agency, *FLEET GUIDE, PUB 941*, US Government, Washington, 1997.

Naval Analysis Division, *THE CAMPAIGNS OF THE PACIFIC WAR*, US Government Printing Office, Washington, DC, 1946.

Nelson, Glen Harold, *COMPANY 194TH TANK BATTALION*, self-published, Saint Paul, MN, 1998.

New York Times News Service, "Japanese Leader offers Apology," Oxnard Star Newspaper, 6 Aug 1995.

Noell, MAJ Livingston P., USAA, "Don't Forget How They Starved Us:The Japanese Story," Packet #10, Ex-POWs of America.

O'Kane, Richard H., *CLEAR THE BRIDGE*, Presidio Press, Novato, CA 1977.

Orita, Zenji, *I-BOAT CAPTAIN*, Major Books, Canoga Park, CA, 1976.

Owens, William A., *EYE DEEP IN HELL, A MEMOIR of the LIBERATION of the PHILIPPINES, 1944-45*, Southern Methodist University Press, 1989.

Pacific War Research Society, *THE DAY MAN LOST*, Hiroshima, 6 August 1945, Kodansha International Ltd., Ottawa, 1972.

Padfield, Peter, *WAR BENEATH THE SEA*, John Wiley & Sons, New York, 1995.

Paillo, Mark P., *THE JAPANESE MERCHANT MARINE IN WORLD WAR II*, Naval Institute Press, Annapolis, 1993.

Pearson, Emmett F., LCDR, MC, USN, "Morbidity and Morality in Santo Tomas Internment Camp, The Japanese Story," Packet #10, Ex-POWs of America.

Peart, Cecil J., "Forty-nine Days of Hell," American Ex-Prisoners of War, Inc.

Petak, Joseph A., *NEVER PLAN TOMORROW, BATTLING BASTARDS OF BATAAN*, Aquataur, Fullerton, CA, 1991.

Phillips,, RADM Neil, USN, Ret, "Slow Boat to China Station," Naval History Magazine, USNI, Leesburg, February 2000.

Potter, E. B., *THE GREAT SEA WAR*, the Story of naval action in WWII, Prentice-Hall, Englewood Cliffs, 1960.

Prados, John, *COMBINED FLEET DECODED*, the secret history of American intelligence and the Japanese navy in WWII, Random House, New York, 1995.

Prange, Gordon, W., *DEC. 7 1941*, McGraw-Hill Book Company, New York, 1988.

Prange, Gordon W., *AT DAWN WE SLEPT*, McGraw-Hill Book Company, New York, 1981.

Price, Willard, *JAPAN'S ISLANDS OF MYSTERY*, The John Day Company, New York, 1944

Prising, Robin, *MANILA, GOODBYE*, Houghton Mifflin Company, Boston, 1975.

Proweleit, Alvin C., MD, "To All Who Should Be Concerned With Our Ex-POWs," "American Ex-POW," Packet #10.

HARM

Provost Marshall General, "Report on American Prisoners of War Interned by the Japanese in the Philippines," 19 November 1945..

Querubin, Francisco A., "Fall of the Fortress (Bataan)," Variety, Manila, Philippiine Islands, 9 April 1967.

Raley, Dana L., Commander, Southern Area Submarine Veterans, crew member USS NARWHAL. Telcons and letters, November 1997.

Reamer, Everett D., POW on TOTORI MARU, QUAN #51-1, July 1996.

Reed, Emil P., MD, "Experiences of a Medical Officer in a Japanese Prison," Texas State Journal of Medicine, Vol 42, January 1947.

Reid, Daniel P., *TAIWAN*, Prentice-Hall–HAAAP–Lansdowne, APA Productions, Ltd, Singapore, 1984.

Reid, Major Pat & Michael, Maurice, *PRISONER OF WAR*, Beaufort Books Publishers, New York, 1984.

Riesenberg, Felix, *THE PACIFIC OCEAN*, Whittlesey House, Armed Forces Edition, New York, 1940.

Riley, Bob; crewmember, USS REDFIN.

Roscoe, Theodore, UNITED STATES SUBMARINE OPERATIONS IN WWII, U.S. Naval Institute, Annapolis, 1949.

Roscoe, Theordore, *PIG BOATs*, Naval Institute Press, Annapolis, 1958.

Rudd, W.B., "Rescue at Sea," – USS QUEENFISH," "Ex-POW Bulletin," Vol 53, #3, March 1996, Arlington, Texas.

Rutherford, Ward, *FALL OF THE PHILIPPINES*, Ballantine Books, Inc., New York, 1971.

Ryan, Michael. "Submarine Warfare in the Pacific," "Polaris Magazine," February 2000.

Saldana, G.T., G-2 CONNECTION, PEARL HARBOR, GUAM, BATAAN & CORREGIDOR, self published, 1987.

Sasgen, Peter T., *RED SCORPION*, Naval Institute Press, Annapolis, 1995.

Schloat, Don T, Army Medical Corps, POW on Bataan Death March, 59326 Yellow Brick Road, Valley Center, CA 92082,(619) 749-8356.

Schloat, Don T., *FREEDOM! BATAAN-POW-PVT*, self published, Valley Center, CA, 1995.

Schratz, Paul R., Capt, USN , SUBMARINE COMMAND, a story of WWII and Korea, University Press of Krentucky, 1988.

Schwartz, J.W., Cdr, CEC, USN, 7 March 1958 ltr to Helen Fairbanks, Historian for Bureau of Yards and Docks.

Schwartz, Otto C., "The Atomic Bomb, A Moral Weapon?" "Ex-POW Bulletin, Vol. 52, #8.

Schwartz, Otto C., "The Fleet That Did Not Exist," U.S. Cruiser Sailors Association Magazine, Vol 6, #1, Rehoboth, MA, winter, 1997.

Seabury, Lawrence G., "Harry Truman," Military Magazine, December 1995.

Seth, Ronald, *SECRET SERVANTS; A HISTORY OF JAPANESE ESPIONAGE*, Straus Farrar, NY 1957.

Skates, John Ray, *THE INVASION OF JAPAN*, University of South Carolina Press, 1994.

Simmons, Charles, WWII crew member USS ANGLER (SS-240) letters and rescue of Panay Island..

Simpson, Sam, "A Reply to 'Courtmartial At Sea,'" Polaris Magazine, Walterboro, SC December 1998.

Sixsmith, E.K.G., *EISENHOWER, HIS LIFE AND CAMPAIGNS*, Combined Publishing, Pennsylvania, 1973.

Smedley, Agnes, *BATTLE HYMN OF CHINA*, Alfred A. Knoff, New York, 1943.

Smith, E.E., *THE UNITED STATES NAVY IN WORLD WAR II*, William Morrow and Company, New York, 1966.

Smith, Norval Giles, "Before the Gates of Hell," Ex-POW Bulletin, October 1998.

Sommers, Stan, "P.O.W. Chaplains, " The Japanese Story, American Ex-POW, Packet #10.

HARM

Sommerfield, Eugene,

Spector, Leonard S., *THE UNDECLARED BOMB*, Ballenger Publishing Co., Cambridge, 1988.

Spector, Ronald H., *EAGLE AGAINST THE SUN*, The Free Press, New York, 1985.

Spurr, Russell, *A GLORIOUS WAY TO DIE*, New Market Press, New York, 1981.

St. John, Bob, "Former POW Recalls Life As a Guinea Pig," Ex-POW Bulletin, March 1998 Issue.

Stanford, Peter, "World War is Over – What Did Victory Mean?" "Sea Victory Magazine," Issue #75, Autum 1995.

Stanton, Shelby L., *ORDER OF BATTLE U.S. ARMY WORLD WAR II*, Presidio Press, Novato, CA, 1984.

Steele, Arvil L., "Mitsushima, Japan, POW Camp," "Ex-POW Bulletin, Vol 54, #1, Arlington, TX, January 1997.

Steinberg, David Joel, *THE PHILIPPINES, A SINGULAR AND PLURAL PLACE*, Westview Press, Boulder, 1982.

Steinberg,, Rafael, *RETURN TO THE PHILIPPINES*, Time-Life Books, Alexandria, VA, 1979

Stephan, John J., *HAWAII, UNDER THE RISING SUN*, Japan's plans for conquest after Pearl Harbor, University of Hawaii Press, Honolulu, 1984.

Stevens, Russell, "V-J Day Should Be Left Alone, For Now," Navy Times, 18 September, 1995 issue.

Stevenson, William, *A MAN CALLED INTREPID*, Harcourt Brace Jovanovich, New York, 1976.

Stewart, Sidney, *GIVE US THIS DAY*, W.W. Norton & Company, New York, 1957.

Swedberg, Claire, *IN ENEMY HANDS*, Stackpole Books, Mechanisburg, PA, 1997.

Takaki, Ronald, *HIROSHIMA*, Little, Brown and Company, Boston, 1995.

Talmadge, Eric, Associated Press, "Hiroshima: Fifty Years Later, " Oxnard Star Free Press, 6 August 1995.

Tanake, Yuki, *HIDDEN HORRORS*, Japanese war crimes in World War II, Westview Press, Boulder, 1996.

Taylor, Lawrence, *A TRIAL OF GENERALS*, Icarus Press, South Bend, Indiana, 1981.

Teikoku, *COMPLETE ATLAS OF JAPAN*, Teikoku-Shoin Co, Ltd, Tokyo.

Tenney, Lester I., *MY HITCH IN HELL, THE BATAAN DEATH MARCH*, Brassey's, Washington, DC, 1995.

Tice, Leon, "Soldier's Will to Live Pulled Him Through Death March . . . ," Santa Barbara News-Press, 12 August 1995.

Thorpe, Brigadier General Elliott R., *EAST WIND, RAIN*, Gambit Incorporated, Boston, 1969.

Tillman, Joe Rutledge, former POW, 9509 Coolbrook, San Antonio, TX 78250, (210) 684-7550.

Time-Life Books, *WOLF PACKS*, Time-Life Books, Inc, Alexandria, 1989.

Time-Life Books, *THE AFTERMATH: ASIA*, Alexandria, 1983.

Tokyo (AP) 20 July 1995, Suzuki, Tatsusaburo, nuclear physicist in Japan during the war.

Toland, John, *THE RISING SUN*, Volumes I & II, Random House, New York, 1970.

Toland, John, *BUT NOT IN SHAME*, Random House, New York, 1961.

Tolischhus, Otto D., *THROUGH JAPANESE EYES*, Reynal & Hitchcock, New York, 1945.

Tolischus, Otto D., *TOKYO RECORD*, Reynal & Hitchcock, New York, 1943.-

Tolley, Kemp, RADM, USN (Ret), *CRUISE OF THE LANIKAI* Admmiral Nimitz Foundation, Fredricksburg, TX, 1995.

Trewarta, Glenn T, *JAPAN A GEOGRAPHY*, University of Wisconsin Press, Madison, WI 1965.

Trewartha, Glenn Thomas, *JAPAN, A PHYSICAL, CULTURAL, & REGIONAL GEOGRAPHY*, The University of Wisconsin Press, Madison, 1945.

HARM

Trumbull, Robert, *TIN ROOFS & PALM TREES*, University of Washington Press, Seattle, 1977.

Underbrink, Robert L., *DESTINATION CORREGIDOR*, U.S. Naval Institute, Annapolis, 1971.

Valentine, Douglas, *THE HOTEL TACLOBAN*, Lawrence Hill & Company, Publishers, Inc., Westport, Connecticut, 1984.

Van Der Vat, Dan, *STEALTH AT SEA*, Houghton Mifflin Company, Boston, 1995.

Vesilind, Priit J., "The last Dive," National Geographic Vol. 196, #4, October 1999, Washiington, DC.

"Veteran's Journal," San Diego County Edition, October 1999, San Diego, CA

Vick, Kenneth, POW #1737, 21st Pursuit Squadron, 4530 Irving Drive, North Hollywood, CA 91602, (818) 761-5986.

Video Visits, "The Philippines," International Video Network, London.

Villarin, Mariano, *WE REMEMBER BATAAN AND CORREGIDOR*, the story of the American and Filipiino on Bataan and Corregidor and their Captivity, Gateway Press, Baltimore, 1990.

Vreeland, Nena, *AREA HANDBOOK FOR THE PHILIPPINES*, Library of Congress DS655.V73, Washington, DC, 1976.

Wade, Nicholas, *A WORLD BEYOND HEALING*, W. W. Norton & Company, New York, NY, 1987.

Wainwright, GEN Jonathan M., *GENERAL WAINWRIGHT'S STORY*, Doubleday and Company, Garden City, NJ, 1946.

Waldron, Ben D., Burneson, Emily, *CORREGIDOR, FROM PARADISE TO HELL*, Pine Hill Press, Freeman, SD, 1988.

Walker, Mark, *NAZI SCIENCE*, Plenum Press, New York and London, 1995.

Warren, Robert H., CAPT, USN (Ret), "USS BATAAN (CVL-29)," U.S. Navy Cruiser – Sailors Organization, Rehoboth, MA 1997 summer edition.

Waterford, Van, *PRISONERS OF THE JAPANESE IN WORLD WAR II*, McFarland & Company, Inc. Publishers, Jefferson, NC 1994.

Weigel, Ed and Norma; former fighter pilot over Japan and USS MISSOURI. His brother Dan lost on Arisan Maru. 161 No F Street, Oxnard, CA 93939-5805.

Weinberg. Gerhard L., *A WORLD AT ARMS*, Cambridge University Press, New York, 1994.

Weintraub, Stanley, *LONG DAY'S JOURNEY INTO WAR, DECEMBER 7, 1941*, Truman Talley Books, Dutton, New York, 1991.

Wenglare, Julius W., MSGT USAF (Ret), "Z Minus Two," "Military Magazine, Vol X!!, #3, Sacramento.

Westar Entertainment, "SLEEP MY SONS," video tape, Shawnee Brittan Film, 1996.

Wheeler, Keith, *THE PACIFIC IS MY BEAT*, E.P Dutton and Company, Inc., New York, 1943.

Wheeler, Keith, *THE FALL OF JAPAN*, Time-Life Books, Alexandria, VA 1983.

Wheeler, Keith, *WAR UNDER THE PACIFIC*, Time-Life Books, Alexandria, 1980.

Whitman, John W., *BATAAN OUR LAST DITCH*, Hippocrene Books, New York, 1990.

Whitman, John W., "Delaying Action in the Philippines, " "WWII Magazine, November 1998 Issue.

Whitmore, Robert L., *I CAME BACK FROM BATAAN*, Emerald House Group, Inc., Blue Ridge Publishing, Greenville, SC, 1997.

Whitney, Dave, "Japan's Atomic Bomb, Too," Military Magazine, Volume XII, #3, Sacramento.

Will, George F., "The Atom as a Possibility," Washington Post, 6 August 1995.

Wilcox, Robert K., *JAPAN'S SECRET WAR*, Japan's race against time to build its own atomic bomb, William Morrow and Company, Inc., New York, 1995.

HARM

Wilkenson, Eugene, USS HOUSTON survivor, telcon, 14 August 1995; "Fierce Naval Battle, Prison Camps Recalled," Santa Barbara News-Press, 12 August 1995.

Willmott, H.P., *EMPIRES IN THE BALANCE*, Allied and Japanese Pacific Strategies to April 1942, Naval Institute Press, Annapolis, 1982.

Winchester, Simon, *THE PACIFIC*, Arrow Books, 1992.

Winslow, W.G., *THE FLEET THE GODS FORGOT*, Naval Institute Press, Annapolis, 1982.

Womack, Tom, "Sword of the Rising Sun," WWII Magazine, Leesburg, VA February 1998.

Wrynn, V.Dennis, "Massaacre at Palawan," "WWII Magazine, Leesburg,, VA, November 1997 issue.

Wyden, Peter, *DAY ONE, BEFORE HIROSHIMA AND AFTER*, Simon and Schuster, NY, 1984.

Yoshihashi, Takehiko, *CONSPIRACY AT MUKDEN*, Yale University Press, New Haven, 1963.

Young, Donald J., *THE BATTLE OF BATAAN*, McFarland & Company, Inc., Jefferson, NC 1992.

Young, Eunice F., COL USANC, "Angels of Bataan," heroic nurses of Bataan and Corregidor, "The Japanese Story," Ex-POWs Packet #10.

Young, Mansfield, Ex-POW and Death March survivor, numerous interviews 1995-2000.

Zedric, Lance, *SILENT WARRIORS OF WORLD WAR II*, Zee61.aol.Com, 232 W. Chestnut #18, Canton, IL, 61520; Pathfinder Publishing of California, Ventura, CA, 1995.

Zedric, Lance Q., "Operation Downfall: the Final Invasion," VFW Magazine, Kansas City, KS, September 1995 issue.

Zich, Arthur, *THE RISING SUN*, Time-Life Books, Alexandria, VA, 1977.

ENDNOTES

1 National Archives and numerous of following references including Time-Life Books. Initally taken by Japanese photographer for propaganda purposes during second day of the Bataan Death March.

2 Boyd, Carl, *Hitler's Japanese Confidant*, University of Kansas Press, Lawrence, KS, 1993.

3 Naval Analysis Division, *The Campaigns of the Pacific War*, US Government Printing Office, Washington, DC, 1946.

4 Stephan, John J., *Hawaii, Under the Rising Sun: Japan's Plans for Conquest After Pearl Harbor*, University of Hawaii Press, Honolulu, 1984.

5 Manchester, William Raymond, *American Caesar, Douglas MacArthur 1880-1964*, Little Brown Company, Boston, 1978.

6 Hoyt, Edwin P., *Japan's War, the Great Pacific Conflict*, McGraw-Hill Book Company, New York, 1986.

7 Hoyt, ibid.

8 Hoyt, ibid.

9 Manchester, ibid.

10 Hoyt, ibid.

11 Hoyt, ibid.

12 Hoyt, ibid.

13 Blair, ibid.

14 Blair, Clay Jr, *Silent Victory*, Bantam Books, Toronto, 1975.

15 Manchester, ibid.

16 Manchester, ibid.

17 Cole, Captain Bernard D., USN, Retired, "The Real Sand Pebbles," Naval History Magazine, Leesburg, February 2000.

18 Blair, ibid; Phillips, RADM Neil, USN, Retired, "Slow Boat to China Station," Naval History Magazine, Leesburg, February, 2000.

19 Winslow, W.G., *The Fleet the Gods Forgot*, Naval Institute Press, Annapolis, 1982.

20 Blair, ibid.

21 Davis, Kenneth S., *Experience of War*, Doubleday & Company, Inc., Garden City, NY, 1965.

22 Stephan, John J., *Hawaii, Under the Rising Sun: Japan's Plans for Conquest After Pearl Harbor*, University of Hawaii Press, Honolulu, 1984.

23 Scuri, Max, former commercial fisherman in San Pedro, interview, Port Hueneme, CA, summer 1996.

24 Winslow, ibid.

25 Hoyt, ibid.

26 Mendenhall, ibid.

27 Hoyt, ibid.

28 History Channel, "Pearl Harbor," broadcast 29 April 2000.

29 Manchester, ibid.

30 Manchester, ibid.

31 Villarin, Mariano, *We Remember Bataan and Corregidor*, Gateway Press, Baltimore, 1990.

32 Manchester, ibid.

33 Holmes, W.J., *Double-Edged Secrets, US Intelligence Pacific WWII*, Naval Institute Press, Annapolis, 1979.

34 Blair, Mendenhall, ibid and Rutherford, Ward, *Fall of the Philippines*, Ballantine Books, New York,1971.

35 Prados, John, *Combined Fleet Decoded*, Random House, New York, 1995.

36 Prados, ibid.

37 Toland, John, *The Rising Sun, Volume I*, Random House, New York, 1970.

38 Mallonee II, Richard C., *The Naked Flagpole, Battle for Bataan*, Presidio Press, San Rafael, CA, 1980.

39 Underbrink, Robert L., *Destination Corregidor*, Naval Institute Press, Annapollis, 1971; Winslow, ibid.

41 Schloat, Don T., *Freedom! Bataan-POW-Pvt*, self published, Valley Center, CA, 1995.

42 Machi, Marion, *Under the Rising Sun*, Wolfenden, Miranda, CA, 1994.

43 Eneriz, Manuel; numerous verbal discussions

44 Lowe, Karl H., "American Polar Bears, Defense of Vladiivostok," Military History Magazine, October 1997.

45 Whitman, John W., *Bataan, Our Last Ditch*, Hippocrene Books, New York, 1990.

46 Young, Mansfield, numerous interviews.

47 Miller, Col Ernest B., *Bataan Uncensored*, Military Historical Society of Minnesota, 1991.

48 Whitman, ibid

49 Miller, ibid.

50 Forty, George, *A Photo History of Tanks in Two World Wars*, Blandford Press and Dorset Poole, New York, 1984.

51 Miller, ibid.

52 Miller, ibid.

53 Mansfield, ibid.

54 Breuer, William B., *MacArthur's Undercover War*, John Wiley and Sons, Inc., New York, 1995.

55 Grashio, ibid.

56 Miller, ibid.

57 Cote,

58 Blair, ibid.

59 Waldron, Ben D. and Burneson, Emily, Corregidor, From Paradise to Hell, Pine hill Press, Freeman, South Dakota, 1988.

60 Eneriz, ibid.

61 Grashio, Samuel C., & Norling, Bernard, *Return to Freedom*, University Press, Spokane, WA, 1982.

62 Vick, Kenneth, POW #1737 interview; Bye, William, nephew of POW Captain Bye, telcons.

63 Breuer, ibid.

64 Young, ibid.

65 Miller, ibid.

66 Grady, Frank J. & Dickson, Rebecca, *Surviving the Day*, Naval Institute Press, Annapolis, MD 1997.

67 Grashio and Grady, ibid.

68 Blair, Clay, Jr., *Silent Victory*, Bantam Books, Toronto, Canada, 1975; and Toland, John, *The Rising Sun, Vol I*, Random House, New York, 1970.

69 Toland, John, *The Rising Sun, Vol I*, Random House, New York, 1970.

70 Grady, ibid.

71 Toland, ibid.

72 Miller, ibid.

73 Young, ibid.

74 Toland, ibid.

75 Blair, ibid.

76 Berry, Col Glenneth B., 14th Heavy Bomber Squadron, ex-POW, telcon interview and letter.

77 Miller, ibid.

78 Blair, ibid.

79 Knox, Donald, *Death March, the Survivors of Bataan*, Harcourt Brace Jovanvich Publishers, New York.

80 Young, ibid.

81 Grashio, ibid.

82 Toland, ibid.

83 Berry, ibid.

84 Grady, ibid.

85 Berry, ibid.

86 Whitman, ibid.

87 Hibbs, Ralph Emerson, MD, *Tell MacArthur To Wait*, a Heathstone Book, Carlton Press, Inc., New York, 1988.

88 Eneriz, ibid.

89 Breuer, ibid.

90 Cole, ibid.

91 Miller, ibid.

92 Mallonee, ibid.

93 Blair, ibid.

94 Cavendish, Marshall, *War Diary 1939-1956*, Chartwell Books Inc., Secaucas, NJ, 1995.

95 Eneriz, Manuel, numerous interviews.

96 Winslow & Villarin, ibid.

97 Beach, Edward L., *Submarine*, The New York Library, New York, 1946.

98 Miller, David

99 Spector, Leonard S., *The Undeclared Bomb*, Bellinger Publishing Co., Cambridge, MA, 1988.

100 Nelson, Glen Harold, *COMPANY 194TH TANK BATTALION*, self-published, St. Paul, MN, 1998.

101 Waldron, Ben D. & Burneson, Emily, *Corregidor, From Paradise to Hell*, Pine Hill Press, Freeman, SD 1988.

102 Cavendish, ibid.

103 Eneriz, ibid.

104 Toland, ibid.

105 Keats, John, *They Fought Alone*, J.B. Lippincott Company, Philadelphia and New York, 1963.

106 Blair, ibid.

107 Blair, ibid.

108 Dorsey, CDR D.R., CEC, USNR, "South from Cavite," CEC Bulletin Parts 1-5, 1951.

109 Dorsey, ibid.

110 Dorsey, ibid.

111 Dorsey, ibid.

112 Miller, ibid.

113 Miller, ibid.

114 Miller, ibid.

115 Miller, ibid.

116 Miller, ibid.

117 Miller, ibid.

118 Waldron, ibid.

119 Grady, ibid.

HARM

120 Miller, ibid.
121 Grasio, ibid.
122 Miller, ibid.
123 Underbrink, ibid.
124 Berry, ibid.
125 Whitman, ibid.
126 Whitman, ibid.
127 Lanigan, Richard, *Kangaroo Express*, Lanigan Press, 1997.
128 Blair, Clair, *Silent Victory*, USNI, Annapolis, 1975.
129 Hibbs, ibid.
130 Hibbs, ibid.
131 Whitman, ibid.
132 Machi, Mario, *Under the Rising Sun*, Wolfenden Publishing, Miranda, CA 1994.
133 Whitman, ibid.
134 Whitman, ibid.
135 Villarine, Mariano, *We Remember Bataan and Corregidor*, Gateway Press, Baltimore, 1990.
136 Villarin, ibid.
137 Young, ibid.
138 Schloat, ibid.
139 Schloat, ibid.
140 Vicks, ibid.
141 Schloat, ibid.
142 Knox, ibid.
143 Young, ibid.
144 Knox, ibid.
145 Miller, ibid.
146 Knox, ibid.
147 Mallonee, ibid.
148 Underbrink, Robert L., *Destination Corregidor*, US Naval Institute, Annaoplis, 1971.
149 Winslow, ibid.
150 Whitman, ibid.
151 Miller, ibid.

152 Whitman and Young, ibid.

153 Whitman, ibid.

154 Whitman, ibid.

155 Machi, ibid.

156 Whitman, ibid.

157 Keats, John, *They Fought Alone*, J.B. Lippincott Co, Philadelphia, 1963.

158 Whitman, ibid.

159 Breuer, ibid.

160 Whitman, ibid.

161 Young, ibid.

162 Eneriz, ibid.

163 Machi, ibid.

164 Eneriz, ibid.

165 Whitman, ibid.

166 Mendenhall, RADM Corwin, USN, Ret, *Submarine Diary, the Silent Stalking of Japan*, Naval Institute Press, Annapolis, 1991.

167 A highly secret code communications group.

168 Blair, ibid.

170 Whitman, ibid.

171 Whitman, ibid.

172 Whitman, ibid.

173 Whitman, ibid.

174 Grashio, ibid.

175 Whitman, ibid.

176 Whitman, ibid.

177 Whitman, ibid.

178 Smurthewaite, David, *The Pacific War Atlas 1941-1945*, CIS-Cardigan Street Publishers, London, 1995.

179 Whitman, ibid.

180 Whitman, ibid.

181 Grashio, ibid.

182 Whitman, ibid.

HARM

183 Whitman, ibid.
184 Young, ibid.
185 Whitman, ibid.
186 Whitman, ibid.
187 Eneriz, ibid.
188 Knox, ibid.
189 Whitman, ibid.
190 Blair, ibid.
191 Prados, John, *Combined Fleet Decoded*, Ransom House, New York, 1995; Roscoe, Theodore , *United States Submarine Operations in WWII*, Naval Institute Press, Annapolis, 1949.
192 Dorsey and Roscoe, ibids.
193 Prados and Blair, ibids.
194 Blair, ibid.
195 Mallonee, ibid.
196 Mallo'nee, ibid.
197 Knox, ibid.
198 Young, ibid.
199 Knox, ibid.
200 Grashio, ibid.
201 Young, ibid.
202 Grashio, ibid.
203 Grashio, ibid.
204 Winslow, ibid.
205 Hibbs, ibid.
206 Pacific War Research Society, *The Day Man Lost, Hiroshima, 6 August 1945*, Kodansha International Ltd, Ottawa, 1972.
207 Blair, ibid.
208 Knox, ibid.
209 Knox, ibid.
210 Grashio, ibid.
211 Grashio, ibid.
212 Whitman and Mallonee, ibids.
213 Knox, ibid.
214 Mallonee, ibid.

ROBERT K. HARMUTH

215 Whitman, ibid.
216 Whitman, ibid.
217 Mallonee, ibid.
218 Provost Marshall General, "Report on American Prisoners of War Interned by the Japanese in the Philippines," 19 November 1945.
219 Falk, ibid.
220 Mallonee, ibid.
221 Falk and Toland, ibid.
222 Hoyt, ibid.
223 Hoyt, ibid.
224 Mansfield Young and Falk, ibid.
225 Falk and Knox, ibid.
226 Breuer, ibid.
227 Knox, ibid.
228 Messer, ibid.
229 Hibbs, ibid. Explanation by Dr. Eugene Messer, Capt, MC, USN (Ret)
230 Lawton, ibid.
231 Hibbs, ibid.
232 Hibbs, ibid.
233 Hibbs, ibid.
234 Eneriz, ibid.
235 Schloat, Don T., Army Medical Corps and POW on Bataan Death March, telcon.
236 Eneriz and Grashio, ibid.
237 Grady, ibid.
238 Young, ibid.
239 Young, ibid.
240 Young, ibid.
241 Grashio, ibid.
242 Young, ibid.
243 Hibbs, ibid.
244 Hibbs, ibid.
245 Mallonee, ibid.

HARM

246 Falk, Ibid.

247 Toland, ibid. Note: Recall Falk relates all the generals rode from Orani to O'Donnell. General Weaver was asked to walk the distance – he did.

248 Toland, ibid.

249 Toland, ibid.

250 Toland, ibid.

251 Knox, ibid.

252 Berry, iibid.

253 Cavendish, Marshall, *War Diary 1939-1945*, Chartwell Books, Inc., Secaucus, NJ 1995.

254 Ashton, Captain Paul L., And Somebody Gives A Damn, Ashton Publications, Santa Barbara, CA 1993.

255 Cavandish, ibid.

256 Young, ibid.

257 Stewart. Sidney, *Give Us This Day*, W.W. Norton & Company, New York, 1957.

258 Villarin, ibid.

259 Madero, Sergeant Mel, 194th Tank Battalion.

260 Knox, ibid.

261 Stewart, ibid.

262 Toland, ibid.

263 Breuer, William B., *MaCarthur's Undercover War*, John Wiley & Sons, Inc, New York, 1995.

264 Toland, ibid.

265 Eneriz, ibid.

266 Armstrong, Raymond Paul, *SanN Hyaku Go (305)*, ACO Publishing, Eugene, OR, 1981.

267 Vick, Kenneth, PO #1737, 21st Pursuit Squadron.

268 Breuer, ibid.

269 Breuer, ibid.

270 Prowleit, Alvin C., MD, "To All Who Should Be Concerned With Our Ex-POWs," "American Ex-POW, " Packet #10.

271 Messer, Captain Eugene, USN, Retired; A fever known today as Southwest Asia hemmorhagic fever.

272 Messer, ibid.
273 Tolanad, ibid.
274 Villarin, ibid.
275 Eneriz and Young, ibids.
276 Knox, ibid.
277 House Document #393, 78th Congress.
278 Eneriz, ibid.
279 Eneriz, ibid.
280 Lawton, Manny, *Some Survived*, Algonquin Books, Chapel Hill, 19984.
281 Underbrink, ibid.
282 Knox, ibid.
283 Eneriz, ibid.
284 Stewart, ibid.
285 Eneriz, ibid.
286 Villarin, ibid.
287 Stewart, ibid.
288 Lawton, ibid
289 Eneriz, ibid.
290 Toland, ibid.
291 Fisher, Edward, ltr, President of the Bataan Death March Association.
292 Bain, David Howard, *Sitting in Darkness, Americans in the Philippines*, Houghton Mifflin Company, Boston, 1984.
293 Lawton, ibid.
294 Creighton, ibid.
295 Breuer, ibid.
296 Winslow, ibid.
297 Belote, James H. and William M., *Corregidor, The Saga of a Fortress*, Harper and Row, New York, 1967.
298 Provost Marshall General, "Report on American Prisoners of War Interned by the Japanese in the Philippines," 19 November 1945.
299 Vick, ibid.
300 Breuer, ibid.

HARM

301 Breuer, William B., *The Great Raid On Cabanautuan*, John Wiley & Sons, Singapore, 1994.

302 Petak, Joseph A., *Never Plan Tomorrow*, Aquataur, Fullerton, CA 1991.

303 Waldron, Ben D. and Burnson, Emily, *Corregidor, From Paradise To Hell*, Pine Hill Press, Freeman, SD 1988.

304 Breuer, ibid.

305 Petak, ibid.

306 Wainwright, General Jonathan M., *General Wainwright's Story*, Doubleday and Company, Garden City, NJ, 1946.

307 Mellnik, Stephen M., *Philippine War Diary 1939-1945*, Van Nostrand Reinhold, New York, 1981.

308 Mellnick, ibid.

309 Mellnick, ibid.

310 Mellnick, ibid.

311 Waldron, ibid.

312 Grashio, Mellnick, and Messer, ibids.

313 Wainwright, ibid.

314 Wainwright, ibid.

315 Grashio and Mellnik, ibid.

316 Mellnik, ibid.

317 Eneriz, ibid.

318 Waldron, ibid.

319 Grady, Frank J. and Dickson, Rebecca, *Surviving The Day*, Naval institute Press, Annapolis, 1997.

320 Hibbs, ibid.

321 Hibbs, ibid.

322 Ashton, ibid.

323 Lajom, Virginia, former resident on Luzon whose mother witnessed the march, was my guide through the countryside, interpreter, and impressionist.

324 Eneriz, ibid.

325 Ashton, Captain Paul L., *And Somebody Gives A Dam!*, Ashton Publications, Santa Barbara, CA 1993.

326 Eneriz, ibid.

327 Ashton and Eneriz, ibids.

328 Waldron, ibid.

329 Ashton and Eneriz, ibids.

330 Eneriz, ibid.

331 Eneriz, ibid.

332 Young, telephone conservation 15 September 99.

333 Grashio, ibid.

334 Young, ibid.

335 Grashio, ibid.

336 Breuer, ibid.

337 Waldron, ibid.

338 Waldron, ibid.

339 Waldron, ibid.

340 Waldron, ibid.

341 Kerr, E. Barlett, *Surrender And Survival*

342 Hoyt, ibid.

343 Breuer, ibid.

344 Grashio, ibid.

345 Lawton, ibid.

346 Breuer, ibid.

347 Breuer, ibid.

348 Ienaga, Saburo, <u>Pacific War, 1931-1945</u>, 1978.

349 Ienaga, ibid.

350 LaVo, Carl, <u>Back from the Deep</u>, USNI Press, Annapolis, MD 1994.

351 Roscoe and LaVo, ibids.

352 Alden, LaVo, and Roscoe, ibids.

353 Schwartz, CDR J. W. CEC, USN, 7 March 1958 ltr to Helen Fairbanks, Hisorian for Bureau of Yards and Docks.

354 Schwartz, ibid.

355 Wilkerson, Eugene, USS HOUSTON survivor, telcon 14 August 1995 and "Fierce Naval Battle, Prison Camps Recalled," Santa Barbara News-Press, 12 August 1995.

356 Young, COL Eunice F, USANC, "Angels of Bataan, Heroic Nurses of Bataan and Corregidor," The Japanese Story, Packet #10, American Ex-Prisoners of War.

357 Colonel Young, ibid.

358 Provost Marshall, ibid.

359 Albertson, Norman, GRENADIER crewmember, personal interviews.

360 Roscoe, ibid.

361 Albertson, ibid.

362 Kerr, E. Bartlett, Surrender and Survival, William Morrow and Company, New York, 1985.

363 Albertson, ibid.

364 Albertson, ibid.

365 Blair, Joan and Clay, Jr., Return from the River Kwai, Simon and Shuster, New York, 1979; and Winslow, ibid.

366 Simpson, Sam, crewmember of PERCH, " A Reply to Courtmartial at Sea," Polaris Magazine, December 1998.

367 Albertson, ibid.

368 Various sources at the CBC Museum Archives, Port Hueneme, California including CDR D.R. Dorsey, "South from Cavite," CEC Bulletin pages 1-5, 1951. Light, Jeane A., "WWII Prisoner Remembers Three and a Half Years Capture," Press Release, US Navy, NAVFAC, WESTDIV, Pearl Harbor, 27 August 1986; Schwartz, J.W., CDR, CEC, USN, 7 March 1958 ltr to Helen Fairbanks, Historian for Bureau of Yards and Docks.

369 Blair, ibid.

370 Blair, ibid.

371 Blair and Roscoe, ibid.

372 Cunnally, Bud, ETC(SS), USN, Ret, "USS CREVALLE's Secret Mission to Negros Island," American Submariner, National Submarine Review #6, November-December 1999.

373 Boyington, Gregory, Baa Baa Black Sheep, Putnam Books, NY, 1958.

374 Boyington, ibid.

375 Provost Marshall, ibid.

376 Landreth, William, telephone conversations 1997.

377 Breuer, ibid.

378 Parillo, Mark P, The Japanese Merchant Marine In World War II, Naval Institute Press, Annapolis, 1993.

379 Weigel, Donna and Ed, WWII USAA fighter pilot with a brother lost on Arisan Maru. Telcon 31 May 1999 and ltr dtd 2 June 1999.

380 Lawton, ibid.

381 Young, ibid.

382 Raley, Dana L., Commander Southern Area Submarine Veterans and crewmember on NARWHAL, telephone conversations and letters November, 1997.

383 Lawton, ibid.

384 Lawton, ibid.

385 Weigel, Donna and Ed, letter dated 31 May 1999 quoting Calvin Graef who was one of only nine survivors of the sinking. Sailing List #87 of Arisan Maru. Ed Weigel was a P-38 pilot in the 49th Fighter Group.

386 Ulio, ibid, statement of investigation re: statements by Lt Binder, USN and Pfc Hughes; survivors.

387 Weigel, ibid.

388 Winslow, ibid.

389 Winslow, ibid.

390 Winslow and others

391 Eneriz, ibid.

392 Winslow, ibid.

393 Eneriz, ibid.

394 Martin, ibid.

395 Eneriz, ibid.

396 Winslow, ibid.

397 Kerr, ibid.

398 Kerr, ibid.

399 Kerr, ibid.

400 Raley, Dana L., former crewmember on NARWHAL and ex-POW. Telephone converstaions and letters in November 1997.

401 QUAN #49-1, June 1994.

402 Blair, Clau Jr., *Silent Victory*, J.B. Lippincott Co., Philadelphia and New York, 1975.

403 Lawton, ibid and discussions with Bataan ex-POWs.

HARM

404 Ito, Masanori, *The End Of The Imperial Japanese Navy*, MacFadden-Bartell Book, New York, 1965.

405 Peart, Cecil J., "Forty-nine Days of Hell," American Ex-POWs of War, Inc.

406 Peart, ibid.

407 Marin, ibid.

408 Lawton, ibid.

409 Bataan Veterans, ibid.

410 Bataan Veterans, ibid.

411 Bataan Veterans, ibid.

412 Bataan Veterans, ibid.

413 Bataan Veterans, ibid.

414 Lawton, ibid.

415 Bataan Veterans, ibid.

416 Lawton, ibid.

417 Alden, and Michno, ibid, NAVEXOS P-468, *Japanese Naval And Merchant Shipping Losses During World War II By All Causes*, Government printing Office, Washington, DC, 1947.

418 Alden and Michno, ibid.

419 Waterford, Van, *Prisoners of the Japanese in World War II*, McFarland & Company, Inc, Jefferson, NC, 1994.

420 Alden and NAVEXOS, ibid.

421 Blair, Lowder, and NAVEXOS, ibid.

422 Kerr, ibid.

423 Ulio, J.A., Major General, Adjutant General of the Army, ltr dated 18 June 1945 to Mr. William Weigel.

424 Ulio, ibid; Statement of investigation.

425 Holmes, W. J., *Undersea Victory*, Doubleday & Company, New York, 1966; and Calvin Graef, one of the survivors; Martin, Adrian R., *Brothers from Bataan*, POWs, 1942-1945, Sunflower University Press, Manhattan, KS, 1992. QUAN #49-5, April 1995.

426 Michno, ibid, Waterford, ibid, and NAVEXOS, ibid.

427 Weigel, Donna J. letter June 1999.

428 American Defenders of Bataan and Corregidor, Inc., "The QUAN," Volume #54, June/July 1999; Michno, ibid.

429 Albertson, Norm, survivor of *USS GRENADIER*, conversation; Icenhower, Joseph R., RADM, USN Ret, *Submarines in Combat*, Franklin Watts, Inc., New York, 1964.

430 LA Examiner Newspaper, 18 April 1943 issue; Blair, ibid; NAVEXOS, ibid.

431 Parillo, ibid, page 34.

432 Blair, QUAN #54, and NAVEXOS, ibid.

433 Martin, Adrian, Kerr, Waterford ibid.

434 Breuer, ibid and NAVEXOS, ibid.

435 Alden, ibid.

436 Blair, ibid and Martin, ibid.

437 Michno, ibid.

438 Alden, ibid.

439 Frances, Charles A, a POW on board, QUAN #53.

430Alden, Blair, Martin, and Morison, ibid.

441 Michno, ibid.

442 Michno, ibid.

443 Michno, ibid.

444 Alden, ibid, Michno, ibid, and NAVEXOS, ibid.

445 Alden, ibid and NAVEXOS, ibid.

446 Alden, ibid and Michno, ibid.

447 Michno, ibid.

448 Michno, ibid.

449 Waterford, ibid.

450 Alden and Waterford, ibid, QUAN #50-2, August 1995.

451 Michno, ibid

452 Michno ltr June 1999.

453 NAVEXOS, ibid.

454 Alden, ibid, Michno, ibid, and NAVEXOS, ibid.

455 Michno, ibid.

456 Breuer, ibid.

457 Weigel, ibid.

458 Alden, ibid.

HARM

459 Michno, ibid.

460 Alden, Michno, and NAVEXOS, ibid.

461 Alden, Michno, NAVEXOS, Waterford, ibid.

462 NAVEXOS and Waterford, ibid.

463 Alden, ibid and Michno, ibid.

464 Michno, ibid.

465 Michno, ibid.

466 NAVEXOS and QUAN #54.

467 NAVEXOS, Weigel, re: Dr. Julian Goodman; Martin, ibids, QUAN #49-5, April 1995.

468 Alden, Michno, NAVEXOS, Waterford, ibid.

469 Michno, ibid.

470 Cox, Gordon C., "P.O.W. Ships," Quan #48-5 April, 1994.

471 Alden, NAVEXOS, and Michno, ibid.

472 Michno, ibid.

473 Aldem, ibid and Michno letter June 1999.

474 Alden, NAVEXOS, ibid.

475 Michno and NAVEXOS, ibid.

476 Alden, Michno, NAVEXOS, ibid.

477 Michno, ibid.

478 Alden, Michno, and NAVEXOS, ibid.

479 Alden, Michno, and NAVEXOS, ibid

480 Michno, ibid.

481 Michno, ibid.

482 Alden, NAVEXOS, Waterford, ibid.

483 Michno, ibid.

484 Alden, Blair, NAVEXOS, ibid; QUAN #47-4, January 1993.

485 Michno, ibid.

486 Michno, ibid.

487 Parillo, Mark P., *The Japanese Merchant Marine in World WAR II*, Naval Institute Press, Annapolis, 1993.

488 Alden, Blair, and Michno, ibid..

489 Alden, ibid and Michno, ibid.

490 Alden, Michno, and NAVEXOS, ibid .

491 Alden, Michno, and NAVEXOS, ibid.

492 Michno, NAVEXOS, ibid.

493 Waterford, ibid.

494 Alden, Michno, NAVEXOS, ibid.

495 Alden, Michno, and NAVEXOS, ibid.

496 Alden, Michno, and NAVEXOS, ibid.

497 Michno, ibid.

498 Alden and Michno, ibid.

499 Alden, Michno, and NAVEXOS, ibid.

500 Waterford, ibid.

501 Alden, NAVEXOS, and Waterford, ibid.

502 Alden and Michno, ibid.

503 Weigel, ibid re: LCDR John Jaegu, USN (ret) and CWO Cletus Jaegu, USN (ret), NAVEXOS, ibid. QUAN ##50-2, August 1995.

504 Waterford, ibid.

505 Alden and NAVEXOS, ibid.

506 Kvalheim, Val, "Lison Maru Survivors Meet," Polaris Magazine, December 1998 issue.

507 Michno, ibid.

508 Michno, ibid.

509 Alden and Blair, ibid.

510 Alden and Michno, ibid.

511 Michno and Waterford, ibid.

512 Manny Eneriz conversation.

513 Hewlett, COL Thomas H, MD, "Di Ju Bunshyo-Nightmare-Revisited," the Japanese Story, Packet #10; Eneriz, Manuel, Kerr and Waterford, ibid.

514 Waterford, ibid.

515 Michno, ibid.

516 Sommers, Stan, "POW Chaplains," The Japanese Story, Packet #10.

517 Michno, ibid.

518 Michno and NAVEXOS, ibid; Parillo, page 60.

519 Michno, ibid.

HARM

520 Lockwood, ADM Charles, *Sink 'Em All*, E.P. Dutton & Company, Inc., New York, 1951, pg 35.

521 Alden and NAVEXOS, ibid.

522 Alden, Waterford, ibid, QUAN #49-5, April 1995.

523 Lanigan, Richard, *Kangaroo Express*, RJL Express Publications, Laurel, FL, 1998, page 136.

524 Michno, and NAVEXOS, ibid,

525 Alden and Michno, ibid.

526 Tanaka, Blair, and NAVEXOS,ibid, page 434.

527 Waterford, ibid.

528 Michno, ibid.

529 Michno and NAVEXOS, ibid.

530 Alden, Blair, Lockwood, and Martin, ibid.

531 Daws, ibid.

532 Kerr, ibid.

533 Remington, Waterford, and Alden, ibid; Jack R. Williamson, QUAD #48-4, February 1994.

534 Waterford, ibid.

535 Murphy, James, *"QUAN Magazine,"* 1430 Fllorette Drive, Santa Maria, CA.

536 Alden, Michno, NAVEXOS, and Waterford, ibid.

537 Weigel, ibid.

538 Breuer, Martin, NAVEXOS, and Waterford, ibid.

539 Michno, ibid.

540 Michno and NAVEXOS, ibid.

541 Alden, Blair, and Holmes, ibid.

542 Blair, ibid.

543 NAVEXOS, ibid.

544 Alden and Michno, ibid.

545 Alden, Michno, and Parillo, ibid.

546 Alden, Michno, and NAVEXOS, ibid.

547 Alden, Michno, and NAVEXOS, ibid.

548 Blair, Clay and Joan, *Return from the River Kwai*, New York, 1979; Waterford, ibid.

549 Alden, NAVEXOS, and Waterford, ibid.

550 Michno, ibid.

551 Michno, ibid.

552 Michno, ibid.

553 Alden and NAVEXOS, ibid.

554 Alden, Michno, and NAVEXOS, ibid .

555 Michno, ibid.

556 Michno, ibid.

557 Regeher, Walter, related the story. Former crew member of *NARWHAL* and a member of the Defenders of Bataan and Corregidor, QUAN #53-4, January 1999.

558 Alden, NAVEXOS and Waterford, ibid.

559 Weigel, ibid re: MAJ Manny Lawton and MSGT George Robinett, survivors; NAVEXOS and Waterford, ibid, QUAN #49-5, April 1995.

560 Spector, Ronald H., *Eagle Against the Sun*, The Free Press, New York, 1985.

561 Alden, ibid.

562 Alden and Blair, ibid.

563 Dreher and NAVEXOS, ibid.

564 Michno, ibid.

565 Michno and Waterford, ibid.

566 Michno, ibid.

567 Michno, ibid.

568 Alden, Michno,and NAVEXOS, ibid.

569 Michno, ibid.

570 Alden, Michno, NAVEXOS, and Waterford, ibid.

571 Alden, Michno and NAVEXOS, ibid.

572 Alden, Michno, NAVEXOS, ibid.

573 Weigel, ibid, QUAN #49-5, April 1995.

574 Alden, NAVEXOS, Lockwood, and Weigel, ibid

575 Alden, Michno, and NAVEXOS, ibid.

576 Michno and NAVEXOS, ibid.

577 Alden, Michno, and NAVEXOS, ibid.

578 Dreher, Alfred B., 3700 Harbel Drive, Bremerton, WA 98310-4728. POW onboard the ship.

579 Alden, Michno, and NAVEXOS, ibid.

580 Alden, Michno, NAVEXOS, and Waterford, ibid.

581 Alden, Michno, and NAVEXOS, ibid.

582 QUAN #49-5 April 1995.

583 Alden, QUAN #54, and NAVEXOS, ibid.

584 Alden, Michno, NAVEXOS, and Waterford, ibid.

585 Alden and Michno, ibid.

586 Alden and NAVEXOS, ibid.

587 Alden and Michno, ibid.

588 Alden and Michno, ibid.

589 Waterford, ibid.

590 Alden, NAVEXOS, and Michno, ibid.

591 Alden, Dreher, and Weigel, ibid, QUAN #51-1 July 1996.

592 Alden and Waterford, ibid.

593 Daws, ibid.

594 Alden and Michno, ibid.

595 Michno, ibid.

596 Alden, Michno and Tanaka, ibid..

597 Weigel, ibid re: LT Samuel Goldbkith, QUAN #49-5, April 1995..

598 Weigel, ibid re: Dr. Julien M. Goodman, MC., Alden and Blair, ibid. QUAN #49-5, April 1995.

599 Waterford, ibid.

600 Waterford, ibid

601 Waterford, ibid.

602 Waterford, ibid.

603 Alden, Blair, Morrison, Lockwood, ibid.

604 Michno, ibid.

605 Michno, ibid.

606 Michno, ibid.

607 Alden,and Michno, ibid.

608 Waterford, ibid.

609 Alden and Michno, ibid.

610 Alden and Michno, ibid.

611 Alden and Michno, ibid.

612 Daws, ibid.
613 Alden, Michno, and Waterford, ibid.
614 Parillo, ibid.
615 Creighton, QUAN #49-5, ibid.
616 Baeder, *Japan*, Prentice Hall, Inc., Englewood Cliffs, New Jersey
617 Daws, Gavan, *Prisoners of the Japanese, POWs of WWII in the Pacific*, William Morrow and Company, New York, 1994.
619 Bergamini, Eric, *Japan's Imperial Conspiracy*, Morrow, New York, 1971 and "LA Examiner."
620 Baeder, ibid.
621 Daws, ibid.
622 Bergamini, ibid.
623 Dempster, Prue, *Japan Advances*, Methuen & Co, Ltd, London, 1967.
624 Eneriz, ibid.
625 Eneriz, ibid.
626 Eneriz, ibid.
627 Leckie, Robert, *Strong Men Armed*, Bonanza Books, New York, 1962.
628 Eneriz and Kerr, ibid.
629 Eneriz, ibid.
630 Eneriz, ibid.
631 Baeder, ibid.
632 Eneriz and Kerr, ibid.
633 Young, ibid.
634 Young, ibid.
635 Young, ibid.
636 Young, ibid.
637 Young, ibid.
638 Young, ibid.
639 Young, ibid.
640 Waterford, Van, *Prisoners Of The Japanese In World War II*, McFarland, Jefferson, NC, 1994.
641 Waterford, Provost Marshall, ibid.

HARM

642 QUAN, November 199 issue.

643 Icenhower, ibid.

644 Hoyt, ibid.

645 Winslow, ibid; Wilcox, Robert K., *Japan's Secret War*, Marlowe & Company, New York, 1995.

646 Spector, ibid.

647 Winslow, ibid.

648 Breuer, ibid.

649 Valentine, Douglas, *The Hotel Tacloban*, Lawrence Hill & Company, Publishers, Inc., Westport, CT, 1984.

650 Breuer, ibid.

651 Breuer, ibid.

652 Valentine, ibid.

653 Breuer, ibid; *NARWHAL* crewmember.

654 Breuer, ibid.

655 Hibbs, ibid.

656 Hibbs, ibid.

657 Hoyt, ibid.

658 Hibbs, ibid.

659 Hibbs, ibid.

660 Breuer, ibid.

661 M.E.H., Editorial about *BATFISH*, "World War II," Leesburg, VA, January 1997.

662 Hoyt, ibid.

663 Hoyt, ibid.

664 multiple sources.

665 Karig, Captain Walter, USNR; Manson, LCDR Frank A., USN; and Harris, LCDR Russell L., USN, *Battle Report, Victory In The Pacific*, Rinehart and Company, Inc., New York and Toronto, 1949.

666 Karig, ibid.

667 Morison, ibid.

668 Morison, ibid.

669 Breuer, ibid.

670 Hibbs, ibid.

671 Hibbs, ibid.

672 Breuer, ibid.

673 OldBill2@aol.com e-mail

674 Owens, William A., *Eye-Deep In Hell, A Memoir Of The Liberation Of The Philippines, 1944-45*, Southern Methodist University Press, 1989.

675 Hull, ibid.

676 Arthur, Anthony, *Deliverance At Los Banos*, St. Martins Press, New York, 1985.

677 Breuer, ibid.

678 Martin, Ralph G., *The GI War 1941-1945*, Avon Books, New York, 1967.

679 Keating, Bern, *The Mosquito Fleet, The History Of The PT Boat In WWII*, G.P Putnam & Sims Company, New York, 1963.

680 Martin, ibid.

681 Kerr, ibid.

682 Bloomfield, Gary L., "You Will All Die, by Order of the Emperor," VFW Magazine, September 1995, Kansas City.

683 Craig, ibid.

684 Hoyt, ibid.

685 Winslow, ibid; Wilcox, Robeert K., *JAPAN's SECRET WAR*, Marlowe & Company, New York, 1995.

686 Spector, ibid.

687 Winslow, ibid.

688 Breuer, ibid.

689 Valentine, Douglas, *THE HOTEL TACLOBAN*, Lawrence Hill & Company, Publishers, Inc., Westport, CT, 1984.

690 Breuer, ibid.

691 Breuer, ibid.

692 Valentine, ibid.

693 Breuer, ibid.

694 Breuer, ibid.

695 Hoyt, ibid.

696 Hibbs, ibid.

697 Hibbs, ibid.

698 Hoyt, ibid.

699 Hibbs, ibid.

700 Breuer, ibid.

701 M.E.H., Editorial about BATFISH, "World War II," Leesburg, VA January 1997.

702 Hoyt, ibid.

703 Hoyt, ibid.

704 multiple sources.

705 Karig, Captain Walter, USNR, Manson, LCDR Frank A.USN,and Harris, LCDR Russel L., *BATTLE REPORT, VICTORY IN THE PACIFIC*, Rinehart and Company, Inc., New York and Toronto, 1949.

706 Karig, iibid.

707 Morison, ibid.

708 Morison, ibid.

709 Hibbs, ibid.

710 Breuer, ibid.

711 Hibbs, ibid.

712 Hibbs, ibid.

713 Breuer, ibid.

714 OldBill2@aol.com email

715 Owens, William A., *Eye-Deep in Hell, a Memoir of the Liberation of the Philippines, 1944-5*, Southern Methodist University Press, 1989.

716 Arthur, Anthony, *Deliverance at Los Banos*, St. Martins Press, New York, 1985.

717 Breuer, ibid.

718 Martin, Ralph G., *The G.I. War 1941-1945*, Avon Books, New York, 1967.

719 Keating, Bern, *The Mosquito Fleet, the History of the PT Boat in WWII*, G.P. Putnam & Sims Company, New York, 1963.

720 Martin, ibid.

721 Kerr, ibid.

722 Craig, William, *The Fall of Japan*, the Dial Press, New York, 1967; Potter, E.B., *The Great sea War*, prentice hall, Englewood Cliffs, 1960.

723 Bloomfield, Gary L., "You Will All Die, by Order of the Emperor," VFW Magazine, September 1995, Kansas City.

724724724724724724463724724 Craig, ibid

725 Hoyt, ibid.

726 Winslow, ibid; Wilcox, Robert K., *Japan's Secret War*, Marlowe & Company, New York, 1995.

727 Spector, ibid.

728 Winslow, ibid.

729 Breuer, ibid.

730 Valentine, Douglas, *The Hotel Tacloban*, Lawrence Hill & Company, Publishers, Inc., Westport, CT, 1984.

731 Breuer, ibid.

732 Breuer, ibid.

733 Valentine, ibid.

734 Breuer, ibid; *NARWHAL* crewmember.

735 Breuer, ibid.

736 Hibbs, ibid.

737 Hibbs, ibid.

738 Hoyt, ibid.

739 Hibbs, ibid.

740 Hibbs, ibid.

741 Breuer, ibid.

742 M.E.H., Editorial about *BATFISH*, "World War II," Leesburg, VA, January 1997.

743 Hoyt, ibid.

744 Hoyt, ibid.

745 multiple sources.

746 Karig, Captain Walter, USNR; Manson, LCDR Frank A., USN; and Harris, LCDR Russell L., USN, *Battle Report, Victory In The Pacific*, Rinehart and Company, Inc., New York and Toronto, 1949.

747 Karig, ibid.

748 Morison, ibid.

749 Morison, ibid.

750 Breuer, ibid.

751 Hibbs, ibid.

752 Hibbs, ibid.

753 Breuer, ibid.

754 <u>OldBill2@aol.com</u> e-mail.

755 Owens, William A., *Eye-Deep In Hell, A Memoir Of The Liberation Of The Philippines, 1944-45*, Southern Methodist University Press, 1989.

756 Hull, ibid.

757 Arthur, Anthony, *Deliverance At Los Banos*, St. Martins Press, New York, 1985.

758 Breuer, ibid.

759 Martin, Ralph G., *The GI War 1941-1945*, Avon Books, New York, 1967.

760 Keating, Bern, *The Mosquito Fleet, The History Of The PT Boat In WWII*, G.P Putnam & Sims Company, New York, 1963.

761 Martin, ibid.

762 Kerr, ibid.

763 Bloomfield, Gary L., "You Will All Die, by Order of the Emperor," VFW Magazine, September 1995, Kansas City.

764 Craig, ibid.

765 Hoyt, ibid

766 Falk, Richard A., Kolko, Gabriel, Lifton, Robert J., *Crimes Of War*, Random House, New York, 1971

767 Wyden, Peter, *Day One Before Hiroshima and After*, Warner Books, 1984.

768 Manchester, ibid.

769 Pacific War Research Society, *The Day Man Lost*, Hiroshima, 6 August 1945, Kodansha International Ltd., Ottawa, 1972.

770 Committee for the Compilation of materials on Damage Caused by the Atomic Bombs, *Hiroshima and Nagasaki*, Basic Books, Inc., New York, 1981.

771 Committee, ibid.

772 Karig, ibid.

773 Craig, ibid,

774 Young, ibid.

775 Karig, ibid.

776 Weintraub, Stanley, *Long Day's Journey Into War, December 7, 1941*, Truman Tailey Books, Dutton, New York, 1991.

777 Craig, ibid.

778 Karig, ibid.

779 Committee, ibid.

780 Wyden, ibid.

781 Hoyt, ibid.

782 Committee, ibid.

783 Nagaii, Takashi, *The Bells of Nagasaki*, Kodansha Internation, Tokyo and new York, 1949.

784 Craig, ibid.

785 Nageii, ibid.

786 Craig, ibid.

787 Committee, ibid.

788 Committee, ibid.

789 Toland, ibid.

790 Summerfield conversations 1996.

791 Craig, ibid.

792 Craig, ibid.

793 Dorr, Robert F., "Torsk Earned a Place in History," "Navy Times" 22 May 2000.

794 Wyden, ibid.

795 Craig, ibid.

796 Craig, ibid.

797 Schartz, ibid.

798 Craig, ibid.

799 Eneriz, ibid.

800 Eneriz in LA Times article, 8 August 1997.
801 Eneriz, ibid.
802 Eneriz, ibid.
803 Eneriz, ibid.
804 Eneriz, ibid.
805 Eneriz, ibid.
806 Vick, Ken
807 Young, ibid.
808 Young, ibid.
809 Eneriz, ibid.
810 Kerr, ibid.
811 Young, ibid.
812 Wilcox, Robert, *Japan's Secret War*, William Morrow & Company, Inc., New York, 1995.
813 Chang, ibid.
814 Van der Post
815 Bergamini, ibid.
816 McCarthy, John C., "Pearl Harbor Epilogue," Naval Affairs Magazine, Vol 74, #9, Alexandria, VA.
817 Englare, Julius W., MSGT, USAF (Ret), "Z Minus Two," Military Magazine, Vol XII, #3, Sacramento
818 Doherty, George, 511th Parachute Infantry, "The 11th Airborne Occupies Japan," Military Magazine, Vol XII, #3, Sacramento, CA.
819 Craig, ibid.
820 Craig, ibid.
821 Germinsky, Bob, POFC, USNR, "Mighty Mo USS MISSOURI," Military Magazine, Vol XII, #3, Sacramento, CA.
822 Germinsky, ibid.
823 Buell
824 Kerr, George M., *Formosa Betrayed*, Houghton Mifflin Company, Boston, 1965.
825 Zedric, Lance Q., "Operation Downfall: the Final Invasion," VFW Magazine, September 1995, Kanasa City, KS.
826 Zedric, ibid.

827 Young, ibid.

828 Wilcox, Robert K., *Japan's Secret War,*

829 Whitney, ibid.

830 Associated Press, 7-20-95, "Star."

832 Tanake, ibid.

833 Agamalian, George S., ltr to editor, "Ventura Star Newspaper," 6 August 1995, ventura, CA.

834 Swartz, Otto C., "The Atomic Bomb, A Moral Weapon?" Ex-POW Bulletin, Volume 52, #8.

835 Stevens, Russell, "V-J Day Should Be Left Alone, For Now," Navy Times, 18 September 1995.

836 Feinsilber, Mike, Associated Press, 9 August 1995.

837 Wilcox, ibid.

838 Winslow, ibid.

839 Valentine, Douglas, *The Hotel Tacloban,* Lawrence Hill & Company, Publishers, Inc., Westport, CN 1984.

840 Dower

841 Tanake, "Hidden Horrors," who used the data from "Horyo Saishu Ronoku Fuzoku-sho'B," Kykuto Kokusai Gunji Saiben No. 337, February 19, 1948.

842 Tanake, ibid.

843 Whitnet, Dave, "Japan's Atomic Bomb, Too," Military Magazine, Volume XII, #3, Sacramento, CA.

844 Ventura Star Newspaper, Associated Press 30 August 1997.

845 Grant, ibid.

846 Daws, Gavan, "Forgotten Infamy," People Magazine, 21 August 1995, page 85, New York.

847 Daws, ibid.

848 Bloomfield, ibid.

849 New York Times News Service, Tokyo, 26 August 1995.

Printed in the United States
5679

9 780738 852744